Multicultural Teaching

A Handbook of Activities, Information, and Resources

Fourth Edition

Pamela L. Tiedt

University of California, Berkeley

Iris M. Tiedt

Moorhead State University

Allyn and Bacon

Boston • London • Toronto • Sydney • Tokyo • Singapore

Series Editor: Virginia Lanigan
Editorial Assistant: Nicole DePalma
Marketing Manager: Ellen Mann
Production Administrator: Joe Sweeney
Editorial-Production Service: Barbara J. Barg
Cover Administrator: Linda Knowles
Composition Buyer: Linda Cox
Manufacturing Buyer: Megan Cochran

Copyright © 1995, 1990, 1986, 1979 by Allyn & Bacon
A Simon & Schuster Company
Needham Heights, Mass. 02194

Library of Congress Cataloging-in-Publication Data

Tiedt, Pamela L.
    Multicultural teaching : a handbook of activities, information,
and resources / Pamela L. Tiedt, Iris M. Tiedt. — 4th ed.
        p.   cm.
    Includes bibliographical references and index.
    ISBN 0-205-15488-3 (pbk.)
    1. Multicultural education—United States.   2. Cross-cultural
orientation—United States.   3. Teaching.   4. Education, Elementary-
Activity programs.   I. Tiedt, Iris M.   II. Title.
LC1099.3.T54   1994
370.19′6—dc20   94-33077
                                                              CIP

Printed in the United States of America
10 9 8 7 6 5 4 3 2 1   99 98 97 96 95 94

This edition of *Multicultural Teaching* is dedicated to:

Doctors Jeffrey Stern, Marshall Stoller, and Peter Carroll
at the University of California, Medical Center, San Francisco
—PLT

and to friends and colleagues at Moorhead State
University, Moorhead, Minnesota.
—IMT

Contents

5 Enlarging Student Perspectives 119

7 Infusing Multicultural Education into Reading and Language Arts Programs 199

8 Multicultural Education across the Curriculum 229

9   Teaching Multiculturally around the Year   277

10   Reflecting on Multicultural Education   323

Appendix: Developing a Knowledge Base for Multicultural Education   347

Index   423

❖
To the Reader

This fourth edition of *Multicultural Teaching* is dedicated to teachers in K–8 classrooms and to students in teacher education programs who will be our future teachers. Because multicultural education is integral to teaching and learning at all levels, it is essential that all teachers be well prepared to infuse multicultural education throughout the curriculum. We know that the goals of multicultural education will not be achieved unless teachers at every level assume responsibility for designing and carrying out an inclusive curriculum. No matter what the color of our skin or the language of our parents, we share a responsibility for seeing that all children learn how to "get along" with others in this gigantic American multiculture and in the world.

As we have prepared each edition of *Multicultural Teaching*, our text has reflected the shifting perspectives of a controversial study. In 1979, this first comprehensive text to appear on multicultural education aimed at helping teachers recognize the need for multicultural instruction for all students. We critiqued the "melting-pot theory," suggested ways of making students aware of diversity as something to be valued, and encouraged teachers to integrate multicultural objectives throughout the curriculum to include the diverse groups living in the United States. We presented a student-centered approach oriented toward language and literacy, at a level appropriate for K–8 teachers which focused on developing student self-esteem and introducing multicultural concepts through literature.

In 1986, the second edition strengthened the above approaches with increased emphasis on multicultural teaching across the curriculum. Two new chapters suggested integrating instruction in reading, language arts, and social studies classes around themes in the self-contained elementary school classroom and cross-disciplinary planning in the middle school. The expanded bibliography reflected the need to include information about a greater variety of cultural groups.

In the third edition we attempted to clarify many of the key concepts associated with multicultural education, such as culture and race. In support of the growing awareness of the teacher's role in delivering the curriculum, we strengthened our emphasis on the knowledge base required for multicultural education. We also added a final chapter to encourage reflection on and discussion of issues related to multiculturalism.

In the present edition we have expanded our treatment of the controversies within the study of multicultural education. We have also strengthened the foundation for multicultural education in, for example, our definition of multicultural teaching and discussion of the spiraling curriculum that we believe is appropriate for teaching and learning in a multiculture. Our presentation of multicultural teaching has two major components: (1) a multicultural knowledge base and (2) learning activities that provide equity for diverse students. This combination provides the foundation for a fully inclusive multicultural curriculum that teachers can implement in K–8 classrooms.

Consistent across the four editions is the underlying assumption that multicultural understandings are fundamental to the education of all children, not only children from "minority" backgrounds. What we describe is what we consider to be the best education for all learners. The range of diversity to be represented in a multicultural curriculum includes young and old, male and female, the physically able and disabled, as well as those who can be grouped by language, national origin, race, or religious belief.

A second assumption is that all of education is inherently multicultural, since it is delivered by and addressed to individuals who represent varied cultures. Recognizing our individual biases, their sources, and the way in which our cultural background affects our thinking is a crucial step toward multicultural understanding. Multicultural teaching is both exciting and painful for teachers and students, because it invites the honest exchange of views on real issues that have no single "right" answer. However, when emotions and deep-seated beliefs enter the classroom, students become involved. Only when students become actively engaged can learning take place.

A final assumption is that multicultural education is as basic to learning as are literacy and quantitative reasoning. Thus, it is an integral part of the curriculum, not a separate course, a special unit of study in February, or a series of discrete activities added to a prescribed curriculum. A commitment to multicultural teaching presupposes creating a climate in which students can dare to question, to take risks, and to learn from one other. This approach to multicultural education prepares students for a world in which learning is neither limited to information presented within the covers of a textbook nor confined within the school walls.

Multicultural Teaching has been designed as a comprehensive text that can be used in a variety of courses, for example:

Multicultural Education or Foundations of Education

Introduction to Student Teaching or Principles of Teaching

Methods of Teaching Language Arts and Reading

Elementary School Curriculum or School Administration

Methods of Teaching Social Studies or Teaching Ethnic Studies

It is especially suitable for staff development for experienced teachers and administrators who want to become involved in multicultural education. Our text offers a strong language and literacy orientation within a student-centered elementary school approach. We consider it essential that multicultural education extend beyond the social studies curriculum to form an integral component of a totally cross-cultural, age-appropriate curriculum at all levels. We hope that we have been able to share ideas in *Multicultural Teaching* that will encourage you to join in this challenging endeavor.

We want to acknowledge the contributions that specific people have made to the preparation of this fourth edition of *Multicultural Teaching*. Thanks to Renee Bexell, Moorhead State University, who created computer art for the text. Thanks also to those who reviewed the manuscript at various stages: Eugene Kim, California State University, Sacramento; Ava McCall, University of Wisconsin, Oshkosh; and Maureen Gillette, College of Saint Rose, Albany, New York.

We would also like to thank the many friends, colleagues, and family members who have provided skills and support over the past several years. Without their invaluable assistance, this book would never have been completed.

Pamela L. Tiedt
Iris M. Tiedt

Multicultural Teaching

Can't we all get along?

—Rodney King

1

❖

Living in a Multiculture

"Can't we all get along?" asked Rodney King[1] following a race riot in Los Angeles. Involved in a chase and brutally beaten by white police officers, this Black American spoke plaintively after days of chaos resulting from the ensuing initial trial and the acquittal of these officers, which triggered widespread protest and destruction. King's question is one we must address in classrooms across the country. Answering this plea is the focus of this text.

The United States houses a diverse complex of cultures. For that reason, we see what some call the "American culture" as an inclusive *multiculture* encompassing a diverse population related to all of the peoples and nations on the planet. Over the life of this country, there have been persistent conflicts among peoples in getting along together, with resulting negative effects stemming from prejudice and discriminatory attitudes toward specific groups within our developing country. Throughout the nation's history, people living in the United States have had to deal with many controversial issues related to sharing space and power. Yet effective laws assuring the rights of diverse groups needing legal protection have been passed only within the recent past, for example, desegregation of schools (1954), civil rights (1964), bilingual education (1968), and guaranteed equal rights for the disabled (1975). Moreover, racist violence and abuse of human rights continue to appear in all areas of the country today, threatening everyone's chance to live a full life. "Getting along" has never been a simple matter. It clearly demands the concerted efforts of all of us.

Learning to get along with the people of diverse backgrounds, needs, and expectations who make up the American multiculture however, requires commitment. And although getting along is not easy, we must strive to eliminate the inequities that persist in our democratic society. Teachers have a significant role to play in guiding children at all levels to recognize and respect diversity as they interact with other young people in and out of school. Supporting individual self-esteem, achieving empathy for others, and recognizing and providing equity for all people living in the United States is the overall goal of multicultural education, the subject we are exploring in this textbook.

After reading this chapter, you should be able to:
- Explain the need for multicultural education.
- Describe the evolution of thinking about cultural diversity in the United States.

- Write a definition of multicultural education.
- Discuss the role language plays in dealing with cultural diversity.
- Reflect on your own ethnic and cultural identity and your experiences as a member of the American multiculture.

THE CONTEXT FOR EVOLVING MULTICULTURAL THEORY

In this section we will examine (1) the historical developments that preceded the present focus on multicultural education and (2) the contemporary conditions that demand multicultural education. We will look at the historical evolution of thinking in the United States. We also will discuss the changing demography of the American population and of the classroom.

How National Thinking Changed

Of course our thinking has changed enormously since the first settlement of Jamestown in 1607. Historically, we can note the controversy among those first settlers, largely from Europe, that led to the Revolutionary War and the early beginnings of the United States. Historically, too, we can trace the evolution of thinking that led to the freeing of the slaves. In this section, we will address the thinking that has moved us to the present conception of multicultural education that we advocate presenting in the schools today. We will examine the legislation that led to our current position, paying special attention to the use of language in the United States.

Rethinking the Melting-Pot Theory

During the first half of this century, the national aim was to assimilate all emigrants into the American culture as quickly as possible. New people were expected to forget their native languages and to learn to speak and write English, the accepted language of the nation, the language of business and society. Metaphorically, the United States was seen as a huge cauldron, a melting pot, into which all diverse immigrants were dumped until their differences melted and they became much alike.

The term *melting pot* comes from a play by that name written by Israel Zangwill in 1909. The following speech illustrates the prevailing nationalist perception of an ideal American living in a homogeneous culture:

> America is God's Crucible, the great Melting Pot where all the races of Europe are melting and reforming! Here you stand, good folk, think I, when I see them at Ellis Island, here you stand in your fifty hatreds and rivalries, but you won't be long like that, brothers, for these are the fires of God. A fig for your feuds and vendettas! Germans and Frenchmen, Irishmen and Englishmen, Jews and Russians—into the Crucible with you all! God is making the American . . . The real American has not yet arrived. He is only in the Crucible, I tell you—he will be the fusion of all races, the coming superman.[2]

This kind of thinking continued well into the twentieth century, and it still exists as we approach the twenty-first century. But the melting-pot metaphor has become inappropriate as we have come to recognize the presence of cultural diversity as a strength, not a weakness. Therefore, we see this country now not as a melting pot but rather as a tossed salad, with various groups contributing to the national multiculture while maintaining their distinct identity. As a result, individuals can be proud of their ethnic heritage instead of ashamed of their differences. This new stance directly affects the school curriculum and how it is presented.

America is a Tossed Salad!

Language is a crucial aspect of this concern for preserving the heritage of different groups. Pressure to include languages besides English in the school curriculum comes from members of many groups who feel that their language is an essential part of their culture. In addition, others point out the students' right to maintain their own languages and have identified the close tie between valuing one's language and self-esteem. The chart on page 6 summarizes the evolution of thinking about language in the United States during the twentieth century.

Emergence of Multicultural Thinking

Many laws and court decisions paved the way for the current trend toward multicultural education. If we examine legislation and court cases, we see the same evolution of theory and philosophy regarding the rights of the individual that we have already discussed as it relates specifically to language. Contemporary court decisions have in certain instances

EVOLUTION OF THINKING ABOUT LANGUAGE IN THE UNITED STATES

Prior to 1914
Many community schools existed to teach a specific language, such as German. Saturday classes were common.

1918
World War I brought about reactions against Germany and a resurgence of patriotic feeling; use of "English only" in schools legislated in many states.

1945
World War II led to realization of need for knowledge of foreign languages; teaching of foreign languages in schools encouraged.

1953
UNESCO published a monograph advocating use of the mother tongue to teach students; not widely accepted in the United States.

1958
Russian launching of Sputnik frightened U.S. leaders who turned to schools. National Defense Education Act (NDEA) passed to help U.S. schools keep up with Russian education. Aid given to promote key subject areas including teaching of foreign languages.

1963
Dade County, Florida, initiated bilingual program for Spanish-speaking Cuban children coming to Miami. Interest spread to other states.

1965
Elementary and Secondary Education Act (ESEA): Funds granted to schools to upgrade education in many areas including English instruction (modern grammar, linguistics).

1968
Bilingual Education Act: Title VII of ESEA promoted bilingual programs in schools.

1971
Massachusetts Bilingual Education Act: Massachusetts was first state to pass law mandating bilingual education for non-English-speaking (NES) children. Other states followed.

1973
Bilingual Education Reform Act: Updated 1968 law; mandated language instruction as well as study of history and culture in bilingual programs.

1974
U.S. Supreme Court Decision: *Lau* v. *Nichols*—NES students have a legal right to bilingual instruction as part of "equal educational opportunity." Aspira Consent Decree class action suit on behalf of Puerto Rican children resulted in New York City Board of Education agreeing to provide instruction in students' native languages.

1981
Senator S. I. Hayakawa first introduced a Constitutional Amendment to declare English the official language of the United States. (Defeated)

1984
California voters passed bill to publish ballots and other election material only in English.

1984–85
Illinois, Indiana, Kentucky, Nebraska, and Virginia passed resolutions declaring English as their official state language.

overthrown earlier legislation related, for example, to human rights and equality of educational opportunity. Today there is a strong push toward multicultural approaches to teaching at all levels.

What are the issues involved? Legal actions affecting the education of minorities, persons of varied cultural backgrounds, and the economically disadvantaged are all relevant. The chronology of such events might rightly begin with the benchmark case of *Brown* v. *Topeka Board of Education.* In 1954 this Supreme Court decision stated that segregated schools are unequal. State laws providing separate schools for black and white students were declared unconstitutional.

Following this decision came legislation establishing the U.S. Commission on Civil Rights in 1957. This independent, bipartisan agency was charged to "investigate complaints alleging denial of the right to vote by reason of race, color, religion, sex, or national origin, or by reason of fraudulent practices."

The commission published *A Better Chance to Learn: Bilingual-Bicultural Education,* a report designed for educators as a "means for equalizing educational opportunity for language minority students." This overview, published in 1975, summarizes efforts to help students in school who speak languages other than English. This agency sees language and culture as basic considerations in providing equal rights.

In 1968 the Bilingual Education Act (BEA) was passed as Title VII of the Elementary and Secondary Education Act. The intent of this law was clarified by President Lyndon B. Johnson:

> This bill authorizes a new effort to prevent dropouts; new programs for handicapped children; new planning help for rural schools. It also contains a special provision establishing bilingual education programs for children whose first language is not English. Thousands of children of Latin descent, young Indians, and others will get a better start—a better chance—in school . . .

Efforts to enforce such legislation also appeared. The Office of Civil Rights Guidelines, for example, indicated that affirmative efforts to give special training to non–English-speaking (NES) students were required as a condition to receiving federal aid to public schools in 1970. The text read:

> Where inability to speak and understand the English language excludes national origin minority group children from effective participation in the education program offered by a school district, the district must take affirmative steps to rectify the language deficiency in order to open its instructional program to these students.

A related issue is the treatment of women in the United States. In 1972, Title IX, an amendment to the Civil Rights Act, stated, "No person in the United States shall, on the basis of sex, be excluded from participation in, be denied the benefits of, or be subjected to discrimination under any education program or activity receiving federal financial assistance."

The most significant case related to multicultural/bilingual education, however, is *Lau* v. *Nichols,* a Supreme Court case that is pressuring all school districts to provide for linguistic and cultural diversity. In 1974 it charged a school district as follows:

> The failure of the San Francisco school system to provide English language instruction to approximately 1,800 students of Chinese ancestry who do not speak English, or to provide

them with other adequate instructional procedures, denies them a meaningful opportunity to participate in the public educational program and thus violates . . . the Civil Rights Act of 1964. . . .

This class-action suit against the San Francisco Unified School District led to a decision that school districts must provide education in languages that meet the needs of students who attend the school. Thus began plans to teach students in their native language, whether it be Yupik or Tagalog, and to provide English as a second language programs specifically designed for each group.

These laws stressed human rights and the need for bilingual education. Out of this thrust came multicultural approaches to teaching that recognized the need for awareness of our culturally diverse society. Teachers in bilingual classrooms are asked to present both linguistic and cultural instruction. Social studies classes must today present multicultural perspectives of sociology and history. Language arts instructors are expected to enrich their classrooms with multicultural literature and language information.

Legislation and court decisions reflect the thinking of our times. It is important to realize, on the other hand, that laws alone do not effect change. What you do in your classroom may, however, serve to break down stereotypes, promote multicultural understanding, and make a crucial difference in the personal development of many individual students. This book is designed to provide activities, information, and resources that will aid you in reaching those goals.

Recap

The development of the United States historically reveals a characteristic openness to change. Although major decisions have typically been controversial, the nation now acknowledges grievous errors made in the past. Over the years we can observe persistent efforts to move the country toward guaranteeing human rights. Concern for the individual remains a basic tenet of our collective philosophy. Such societal thinking is reflected in the schools, directly affecting what and how we teach.

COMPOSITION OF THE AMERICAN MULTICULTURE TODAY

As a result of the mobility within our society, the student mix in most classrooms in elementary schools throughout the United States has changed perceptibly in the past twenty to thirty years. Increasingly, even rural and small-town classrooms in the Midwest more closely reflect the diversity of the total population in the United States. Frequently, the cultural roots of the teacher and the children she or he teaches are very different. Therefore, all teachers must know how to provide an equitable education for students from a wide variety of cultural backgrounds.

Equality for All Americans

Whatever their race, sex, age, national origin, or language, equality of opportunity is a major concern for all members of American society today. Legislation has been passed to provide equal opportunity for education. Efforts have been made to eliminate discriminatory practices in the workplace and to ensure equal pay for equal work. Women and members of minority groups are holding more responsible political positions. Yet we must continue to solve problems daily to ensure that every American can feel equally valued. These changing attitudes have a direct effect on practice in the schools. If all students have a right to equality of education, then textbooks, the concepts presented, and teaching practices must change to reflect that goal.

Teachers need to understand the complexity of our diverse national population and how this diversity has evolved. The history of our pluralistic population begins with the heterogeneous Native American civilizations that flourished here before explorers from Europe encountered them on the North American continent. On the east coast, emigrants in the early years came from various European countries—England, France, Germany, Spain. At the same time, too, exploration was taking place along the west coast as Russian hunters ventured east into the vast territory that is now Alaska and south into California. Cortez and others moved through Mexico into the Southwest and north into California. Following the explorers, some settlers remained to begin farming and developing the land. People continued coming to the New World with many different goals—freedom of religion, the challenge of exploration, and the hope of wealth. In addition, thousands were brought forcibly from Africa as slaves. Twentieth-century immigrants include Vietnamese, Haitians, Ethiopians, and Mexicans. The history of the United States clearly identifies the polyethnic roots of a wide and fascinating variety of peoples, ranging from Scots in Appalachia to Inuits in Alaska, from Polynesians in Hawaii to Portuguese in Boston. Therefore, we find it difficult to identify a single distinctive American culture but rather perceive the people who live in the United States as comprising a giant American *multiculture*.

This multiculture reflects more than our diverse geographic origins, however. We also differ in many other ways that influence how we interact within our democratic society. We have learned to recognize distinct gender differences and expectations, for example, in language variation and career development. We differ, too, in age, with all of us moving in turn from young to elderly, changing our perspectives and needs as we mature. Along the way we identify with many different groups based on family, language, national origin, race, and beliefs. In addition, we often group ourselves by choice to support our interests and concerns, belonging to a number of groups at any one time. Belonging to various groups helps to shape our identities and our ways of thinking as we clarify group needs and shared expectations. Multicultural education should assist us in better understanding the roles individuals and groups play within a diverse society.

Individual Differences

All of us are members of a society; yet each one of us remains a unique individual. Beginning with the accident of birth, we are shaped by the knowledge, experience, values, and attitudes that we encounter in the people with whom we live; we are socialized into a particular community, time, and place. However, out of all the diverse factors that influence our attitudes and values, each of us internalizes a unique self-identity from which we operate.

We teachers therefore need to remind ourselves constantly that the students who face us in a classroom are unique individuals. In our efforts to understand and to teach children from the many groups that make up our multiculture, we often seek to make generalizations about learners who are members of a specific culture. Understanding that respect for the family is a characteristic of the Latino culture justifies neither the assumption that all Latinos possess this characteristic nor the corollary that persons from other cultures do not. Likewise, in learning about Black English, we need to be aware that not all African Americans speak Black English; furthermore, many who can speak Black English readily may be bidialectal, easily switching from this highly colloquial form to educated standard English depending on the situation. To take another example, the "Dick and Jane" readers reflect a fantasy of a time that never truly existed, or at least not for everyone, when the idealized American family consisted of a father who went off to work every day; a mother who stayed at home and baked cookies; two children, one boy and one girl; plus a family dog. Now we recognize the range of "families" that children experience, from those affected by divorce and remarriage to those formed by single parents, adoption, and multiple generations. Teachers must plan carefully to accommodate individual characteristics, permitting children to remain different. We must consciously work to avoid stereotyped thinking about members of any one particular ethnic group; for example, the expectation that all Asian American children are academically talented, mathematical whizzes. Such stereotyped expectations may exert undue pressure on children and be damaging to a young learner's self-esteem. We will discuss how teachers can deal with such individual differences in more detail in Chapter 3.

Accepting Diversity

Never has the need for multicultural education been more clearly evident. Desecration of Jewish cemeteries, ridicule of the mentally retarded, and sexual harassment are not only occurrences of the past. Fear and ignorance still lead individuals or groups to perform demeaning acts against other human beings in the United States. As noted in the introductory paragraphs of this section, almost all of us are children of immigrants from other lands. Beginning in their very early years, young people, who will become our country's adult citizens, need to learn broad concepts of cultural difference and respect for the diversity of our population. This diversity is derived from gender, age, national origin, language background, sexual orientation, religious beliefs, politics, the work world, physical and mental abilities, and individual experiences. All of us can identify and take pride in our ethnic and cultural backgrounds. We can recognize and accept both the differences and the universal human needs we share as we strive to promote appreciation and empathy for the diverse people that live in this complex multiculture.

Clearly, cultural diversity is not new in the United States. It has always been a distinctive characteristic of the American multiculture, and it is increasing rather than diminishing. In 1992 a total of 32 million Americans spoke a language other than English at home; that is one in seven people. This number represents a 34 percent increase between 1980 and 1990. The number of Chinese speakers doubled during that period, while approximately 17 million Americans spoke Spanish in their homes in 1993.[3]

Another indicator of the changing mix in our multiculture is the ethnic composition of persons entering the work force in the United States in 1988 compared with that projected for the year 2000. The following chart shows that the percentage of white American workers, especially males, entering the work force will slowly decrease, while the percentage of American men and women of color will increase so that each of the latter will represent approximately one-fifth of the people entering the work force in 2000:

PERSONS ENTERING THE WORK FORCE

	1988	*Projected for 2000*
Native-born white males	41%	9%
Native-born white females	33%	28%
Native-born males of color	10%	21%
Native-born females of color	9%	21%
Immigrant males	4%	12%
Immigrant females	3%	9%[4]

Native-born white males represented 42 percent of the total work force in 1990. This percentage is projected to diminish slowly to 36 percent by 2010. During the same period the numbers of Asians and Hispanics will increase from 3 percent and 8 percent to 6 percent and 12 percent respectively. These figures regarding the work force give us an indication of the projected demography of the U.S. population. It is estimated that people of color will soon represent approximately one-third of the country's population.[5] Although the number of African Americans will remain fairly constant at 12 percent, the number of immigrants will slowly grow. As can be readily understood, such statistics may be seen as a threat to the native-born Anglo population, which has been accustomed to being the dominant culture in the United States. Studies that lead toward empathy for all groups involved can help them accept the reality of such changes and reconceptualize their impact. Education can help people come to perceive those changes as challenges rather than threats.

Americans must also be prepared to live in a more closely interactive, interdependent world society. No longer is ethnocentrism viable. We must all learn to collaborate in a global, international setting that brings diverse peoples to the negotiating tables. The cultural diversity of the world population is even more pronounced than that of the United States. Of the more than 5 billion people on this planet, only one in six will be of Caucasian origins in the twenty-first century. Thus, persons with "white" skins may often find themselves in the minority on international committees and at business planning meetings. More than ever, to interact within the global village, all Americans must be educated multiculturally.

Recap

In general, national thinking, exemplified by legislation and judicial decision, has evolved over the years toward greater insight and humane practices that accept all of our citizens as having equal worth. Educators value self-esteem—the bottom line for all students—and political leaders are trying to provide equity for all people in the United States. Yet pockets of ignorance continue to exist, and deep-seated prejudices surface unexpectedly from even the highly educated. We need to continue to learn how best to accommodate our diverse population and how to "get along" in this country.

DEFINING MULTICULTURAL EDUCATION TODAY

Many writers refer to multicultural education without clearly defining it. [6] As Stephen May (1993) states, "The problem is, it seems, that no one knows exactly what multicultural education is."[7] For this reason, we believe it is essential to address the meaning and purpose of multicultural education as presented in this text.

Multicultural education has been a source of controversy and confusion. Defined geographically, it has led to studies of other countries and the concept of the earth as a global village. Focus on ethnic studies has brought an awareness of literature and folklore specific to groups that speak the same language or share a religious belief. Concern for the needs of all people has expanded to include newly recognized groups, for example, the disabled, homosexuals, and the elderly. Multicultural education must include these themes and many others.

The concepts that define multicultural education have evolved over a period of time. Rooted in the thinking of the 1950s and 1960s with its focus on civil rights, the term *multicultural education* appeared in the early 1970s with an emphasis on human relations. It continued to develop in the 1980s and 1990s. In this section we begin by first defining *culture* and related terms. We then examine current theory and practice.

Exploring Relevant Terms

As we strive to define multicultural education and multicultural teaching, we focus first on defining the root word *culture* and other related terms: *class, ethnic group, identity group,* and *race*. We also review current accepted terminology for groups of people that will be appropriate to use as we discuss the issues. From that base, we move to the broader concepts inherent in multiculturalism.

Culture connotes a complex integrated system of belief and behavior that may be both rational and nonrational. Culture is a totality of values, beliefs, and behaviors common to a large group of people. A culture may include shared language and folklore, ideas and thinking patterns, and communication styles—the "truths" accepted by members of the group. Members of a culture "speak the same language," so they understand the allusions and humor, and they have similar expectations of life.

Each of us is born into a culture. Our beliefs derive from these ethnic and family backgrounds, but they continue to be shaped by all of our experiences after birth. For the most part, family attitudes, language, and other behaviors are internalized without question. It is only when we encounter other cultures that we begin to observe differences, to wonder, and to ask questions.

Each of us can map the influences that have shaped our individual thinking—our families, the kids we went to school with, the various places we have lived in or traveled to, the person we married or lived with, the people with whom we have worked. Your individual cultural map reflects the culture of your family, but it is not identical to the map of any other member of the family. As we map cultural influences, we must consider the many groups to which we have belonged and the many people with whom we have interacted. Each of us can create a cultural map similar to that completed here for Carlita:

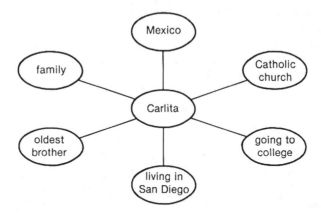

Notice that Carlita, a twenty-year-old college student in San Diego, California, is greatly influenced by her family, some of whom still live in Mexico. She acknowledges the influence particularly of her oldest brother, who serves as head of the family now that her father is dead. Carlita adheres to the tenets of the Catholic church as she has been taught since birth. However, education is causing her to question some basic assumptions of both family and church. She is moving ahead with career plans. We could predict that her individual culture will continue to change as she encounters other career-oriented women and moves up the career ladder in her profession.

As members of a cultural group, we interact with the larger society, and we become aware of different ways of behaving, different expectations; we may gradually change our thinking individually or collectively. Within a culture, subcultures may evolve as groups of people change enough to be identifiable as such.

An example of a large, complex cultural group is those individuals around the world who believe in Judaism. Two geographically-based divisions of this belief developed— Yiddish-speaking Ashkenazi Jews and Ladino-speaking Sephardic Jews. Jews can also trace their ethnic roots to specific nations. Within the largely Ashkenazi Jewish community in the United States we can identify Reform, Conservative, and Orthodox groups within the Jewish culture.

Used in this anthropological sense that is appropriate for multicultural education, *culture* has no social standing. All cultures are distinctive and have identifiable differences, but they are equally acceptable. We need to be aware, however, of other connotations that have been associated with the word *culture*. This term has been attached to a number of categories of activities or knowledge, for example, "pop culture" or the "culture of poverty." Such loosely construed use of this term is confusing. A literary or elitist use assumes that wealthier, better-educated persons have more "culture" than do poor, uneducated people. This definition equates culture with knowledge of the arts and literature. Operating from the anthropological viewpoint, we would not say, "He is a very cultured man." In this text we acknowledge that all people have a culture, and we judge all cultures as being equally valid and having equal worth. All of us are acculturated or socialized to live appropriately within a particular culture from birth. Much of our learning is the result of socialization or cultural conditioning.

Class, on the other hand, does connote status in the society. Social class is closely associated with socioeconomic status (SES). We sometimes think of the United States as a "classless" society because these strata are not clearly defined, and it is possible for persons to move from one class to another. Yet there are distinctions based on wealth, education, and the kind of work one does. These distinctions may be revealed through aesthetic tastes, linguistic characteristics, and privilege as well as opportunity. Interesting studies have been made of different groupings, for example, those who drink Pouilly Fuissé, attend the symphony, and read *The New Yorker,* and those who drink Miller Lite, attend the local football games, and read *People* magazine. There is an ever-widening gap between the upper middle class and those who live in poverty. As teachers, we need to be aware of class-based, stereotyped expectations and attitudes toward children, for example, that poor children who come to school in less attractive clothing are not as bright as well-dressed, more advantaged children and thus cannot learn more advanced thinking skills.

Ethnicity is an umbrella term that has been used to include varied groupings based on national or linguistic backgrounds as well as religion, class, and regional identification. The origin of this term is the Greek *ethnos,* which means *nation.* This term is often used inaccurately to refer to members of all minority groups within the society. The term *ethnocentrism* refers to the centrality of dominance of the national group identity that may limit an individual's perspective. Ethnic studies may focus on national origins, but they have also often included Black Studies programs. *Ethnography* is the study of groups; this term is used to describe a kind of qualitative research that observes group interaction and effects.

The use of the word *ethnic* needs to be clarified. An example of a large ethnic group in the United States is Mexican Americans, who share a complex culture. This group is often subsumed within the category Hispanic, although not all Mexicans originated from Hispanic roots, speaking the language of Spain. See the discussion under the heading *Group names.*

Identity groups are people who share interests, concerns, or roles and "speak the language" common to that group. Members may share attitudes and needs and work toward a cause. They may share special skills and behaviors that bring them together for learning or performance events. Identity groups may be based on vocational or professional roles. We all belong to many identity groups. A culture is a more broadly encompassing identity group. (Note, however, that an identity group is not a culture as we have identified it above.) The "Women's Movement" grew out of the needs of an identity group. The disabled are now speaking as a group to achieve equity and to fight discrimination. Identity groups do effect change.

Race is another term that has been inappropriately used and needs to be defined technically. Race is not synonymous with nationality, a language spoken, or a culture. It is incorrect, therefore, to speak of the Jewish race, the English-speaking race, or the Negro race. For many years it was the practice to identify three races: European (white), African (black), and Asian (yellow). As scientific information about blood types grew, a number of major races have been identified. Sometimes called geographical races, they constitute nine groups:

1. African (Negroid)—Collection of related persons living south of the Sahara. Black Americans are mostly of this origin.
2. American Indian (Amerindian or American Mongoloid)—Related to the Asian geographical race; only group in the Western Hemisphere for many years.
3. Asian (Mongoloid)—Persons in continental Asia except for those in South Asia and the Middle East; includes Japan, Taiwan, the Philippines, and Indonesia.
4. Australian (Australian aborigine or Australoid)—A group of people in Australia.
5. European (Caucasoid)—Located in Europe, the Middle East, and north of the Sahara; includes persons living on other continents.
6. Indian—Persons in South Asia from the Himalayas to the Indian Ocean.
7. Melanesian (Melanesian-Papuan)—Dark-skinned persons living in New Britain, New Guinea, and the Solomon Islands.
8. Micronesian—Dark-skinned persons living on islands in the Pacific: Carolines, Gilberts, Marianas, and Marshalls.
9. Polynesian—Many persons living in the Pacific Islands such as Hawaii, Easter Island, and the Ellice Islands.

Group names have changed periodically. As changes have been made, there has been controversy about which terms are acceptable. More militant members of ethnic groups have at times preferred one term while less militant members of the same group use another. Such terms as *Chicano, Mexican American,* and *Hispanic,* for example, are widely used today, and each has its own rationale.

Teachers must be aware of changing terminology. We demonstrate our awareness of how thinking has changed by our own use of appropriate terms. The once widely accepted term *culturally disadvantaged,* for example, is no longer acceptable because many people are aware of its loaded implications. We recognize that all groups have cultures that are unique and at the same time have much in common. *Disadvantaged* is an evaluative term that assumes a standard against which all cultures are judged and has led to the assumption that minority groups do not have a culture of their own. Following is a brief discussion of terminology that may need clarification.

Asian Americans. The more specific terms *Chinese Americans* or *Japanese Americans* are acceptable, too. The use of *Oriental* has fallen into disrepute because it connotes stereotyped views, for example, "the inscrutable Oriental."

Black Americans. Many Blacks accept the term *Negro,* which is the Spanish word for black. Others who wish to stress their African origins prefer *African American.* In general, *Black American* or *African American* is acceptable. Certainly, such derogatory terms as *colored, darky, nigger,* and so on are not acceptable.

Latinos. The term *Chicano* was adopted by Mexican American leaders who wished to stress that they are developing a unique culture in this country. The term *Mexican Ameri-*

can is preferred by some groups. At times there have been references to the *brown movement*, but the term was not generally accepted. More widely used is the group label *Hispanic*, a term that includes all persons who use Spanish as a native language. This term has been questioned because it includes many groups that differ greatly, for example, people who came from Spain (Hispania), those from Mexico, Puerto Rico, Cuba, and immigrants from the many Spanish-speaking Latin American countries. Also, it focuses more on the colonization by Spain and less on the Native American heritage. *Latino* is gaining acceptance because of its clear reference to common language roots.

Minority Group.   "Minority" is a term that is being questioned when used in the sense of "minority group." Frequently, speakers equate "minority" with "subordinate" or "oppressed." They refer to persons who have been underrepresented or discriminated against, for example, African Americans or Pacific Islanders, as "minorities." Identifying membership in "minority groups" is a typical aspect of hiring practices intended to achieve more equitable representation. However, as the percentage of such groups of people changes across the country, general use of the label "minority" may become inappropriate. In some neighborhoods, Asian Americans outnumber other groups. In California, for example, Caucasians are rapidly losing their numerical advantage. At historically black colleges, the African American is hardly a minority person. Teachers should be aware of the potential misuse of this term and should use it with care. This term is often replaced with "people of color."

Native Americans.   The terms *Indian* and *Native American* are used. The only problem with using *Native American* is that it is nonspecific, including many Indian tribes as well as a number of Eskimo groups. If possible, it is preferable to designate a specific group, such as Hopi or Aleut.

People of Color.   The term "people of color" has come into common usage in the 1990s, usually referring to African Americans, Native Americans, and Hispanics. Care must be taken not to confuse this term with *colored people* or *coloreds,* demeaning terms associated with slavery. Referring to people of color is also confusing because in reality we are all "people of color." We prefer to use the names of specific groups wherever possible.

Capitalization of terms can be a problem. Frequently people express confusion about how to handle the capitalization of ethnic terms, particularly those that include the word *black*. There clearly is a need for some logical consistency. It is also important to respect the wishes of the persons involved. Taking these points into consideration, we have decided on the following practices.

Since many Blacks prefer to substitute that term for Negroes, we capitalize both Negroes and/or Blacks as names for a distinct group. The singular forms would also then be capitalized as proper nouns, Negro and Black.

The term *Black American* is analogous to *Irish American* and *Jewish American* and is capitalized in similar fashion. Black is not capitalized, however, when used as an ordinary adjective as in black car, black man, and black child. The word *chicano* would follow the same pattern, as in Chicanos and chicano child.

Recap

As teachers we need to be as informed as possible in order to take a stance regarding specific issues related to multicultural education. We need to be certain that we are using such words as *culture* and *race* correctly as we lead discussion with young learners. Although not everyone agrees on terminology and some persons are offended by what they term "political correctness," we believe that language does make a difference. Try always to use skill and sensitivity in your choice of words.

Current Theory and Informed Practice

All people in the United States need multicultural education to assist them in operating effectively in a democracy made up of a diverse population. For the most part, educators agree on defining the general parameters of multicultural education, as follows:

> An education that is multicultural is comprehensive and fundamental to all educational endeavors. Given an understanding of the nature of human differences and the realization that individuals approach concepts from their own perspectives, advocates of education that is multicultural are consistent in their belief that respect for diversity and individual difference is the concept's central ingredient.[8]

However, among educators there remain differences in interpretations of theory and how theory should inform practice. In 1986, Sleeter and Grant identified five discreet theoretical approaches to multicultural education: assimilation, human relations, focused group studies, integrated studies within the total curriculum, and social reconstructionism.[9]

In this text, we acknowledge the positive contributions of these theoretical approaches as we develop our definition of multicultural education. We also would add a sixth, that is, the influence of global and international studies.

Assimilation

Assimilation theory, which dominated the thinking of the early United States, assumes that all persons living in the United States should be acculturated to become *Americans*. According to this view, everyone should be culturally similar as in the "melting-pot" metaphor we discussed previously. This theory lies behind the contemporary "English only" movement and is inherent in many of the questions related to immigration. The problem is that those who espouse assimilation may equate *difference* with *deficiency*. This stance can scarcely be termed multicultural, but it is a viewpoint that still appears in newspapers, and is clearly lodged in the minds of many Americans who were educated to perceive assimilation and the melting-pot concept positively.

One aspect of assimilation theory that we continue to support, however, relates to programs teaching English as a second language. While we believe that children should always be encouraged to use their native oral language as a way of learning and communicating and that there is value in knowing more than one language in today's world, we nevertheless encourage students to learn English as a means for entering the mainstream culture and preparing for a future career. It would be unrealistic for any teacher to pretend that learning English is not a desirable goal for all children in American schools today.

Human Relations and Ethnic Studies

The concern for human rights that characterized the civil rights movement of the 1960s led directly into the human relations movement in education with its emphasis on valuing the individual, nurturing individual self-esteem, and helping everyone succeed. In 1972, for example, the American Association of Colleges for Teacher Education (AACTE), defined multicultural education as follows:

> ... education which values cultural pluralism. Multicultural education rejects the view that schools should seek to melt away cultural differences or the view that schools should merely tolerate cultural pluralism. Instead, multicultural education affirms that schools should be oriented toward the cultural enrichment of all children and youth through programs rooted in the presentation and extension of cultural alternatives. Multicultural education recognizes cultural diversity as a fact of life in American society, and it affirms that this cultural diversity is a valuable resource that should be preserved and extended. It affirms that major education institutions should strive to preserve and enhance cultural pluralism. Multicultural education programs for teachers are more than special courses or special learning experiences grafted onto the standard program. The commitment to cultural pluralism must permeate all areas of the educational experience provided for prospective teachers.[10]

At the same time, many states began incorporating elements of this widely accepted statement into teacher education requirements. In 1972, for example, Minnesota adopted a human relations requirement for the licensure of teachers, including courses in such areas as cultural pluralism, interpersonal communication, and ethnic studies. Anyone wishing to teach in the state today must meet that requirement.[11]

Note that part of this "human relations" requirement even then was—and still is—focused on studies of ethnic groups. Many universities created Black Studies or Mexican American programs at that time. Following this period into the 1980s, James Banks and others wrote books advocating ethnic studies and presenting methods for teaching ethnic studies, particularly at high school and university levels. Such focused ethnic studies courses emphasized pride in one's heritage, which is still an important goal of multicultural education. These programs also stressed interpersonal communication skills. Human relations programs remain an important tool for teaching how to get along in a culturally diverse society.

Integrated Multicultural Education

The broader term *multicultural education* was not widely used in educational literature until the late 1970s. It appeared for the first time in *Education Index* in 1978. In 1977, however, the National Council of Accreditation of Teacher Education rewrote its standards to include one on multicultural education. The first edition of this text, *Multicultural Teaching*, which appeared in 1979, was the first comprehensive textbook to address multicultural education in the schools. In 1980, AACTE published *Multicultural Education: An Annotated Bibliography of Selected Resources* "to stimulate discussion, study, and experimentation of multicultural education among educators." [12]

Because the K–12 curriculum often lags behind, however, it was not until 1988 that Minnesota's Board of Education adopted a ruling directing all school districts to develop and deliver a curriculum plan that emphasized: (1) the cultural diversity of the United States and the contributions made by diverse ethnic groups to the country's development, (2) the historical and contemporary contributions of both women and men to society, and (3) the historical and contemporary contributions to society by disabled (at that time termed handicapped) persons. The curriculum that is now being implemented is expected to be gender-fair and sensitive to the needs of the disabled.

Concern for the needs of all people now extends to include newly recognized groups and their concerns, for example, the elderly, homosexuals, working women, people with AIDS, and disabled persons. Efforts to teach multicultural concepts and processes as an integral aspect of every subject area reach into all levels of education, including the preschool years. Multicultural education covers broad, inclusive themes touching on human relations, morality, values, and ethics; and it draws heavily on the study of pedagogy, for example, in its recognition of differing learning styles and individualization of instruction.

Global and International Education

Defined more broadly, thus, multicultural education connects the study of other countries, the concept of the world as a global village, and recognition of the need for everyone on this planet to collaborate to ensure clean air and preserve our resources. Focus on international studies brings an awareness of the shared concerns of nations around the world. It leads to a greater understanding of other people and the universal issues human beings face. Such studies engage us in reading the literature and becoming familiar with the folklore of specific groups around the world that may speak the same language or share a religious belief, thus helping to broaden studies across the total curriculum in the United States.

Activism

Active efforts to bring about a change in thinking and behavior have always been integral to our society—from the behavior of the eighteenth-century revolutionaries to contemporary efforts to challenge established views on such issues as abortion and the right to control one's own death. Activism is perhaps the newest approach to multicultural education. We all have a responsibility to speak out against injustice, discrimination, and prejudice and to work to assure that human rights are upheld for all. Individual involvement in this social reconstructivism will vary, but increasingly, educated Americans are intervening when unthinking individuals tell stories that insult certain ethnic groups or use insensitive language. Others join groups that work actively to achieve and maintain civil rights for specific groups. It is important to take a stance and to make our viewpoints known. Teachers have a special responsibility to manage classroom procedures and to plan the multicultural curriculum.

A Contemporary Definition for Multicultural Education

Any definition of multicultural education must recognize all of the above influences and clearly demonstrate awareness of the changing thinking that has taken place in the United States. Such a definition must also include respect for the diversity that characterizes our American multiculture, and it must touch every individual. Multicultural education is justified on the following grounds: *Morality*—equality of all human beings; *Demography*—needs of a diverse student body; *Civics*—an educated citizenry required by a democracy; *Enhancement*—multiple cultural viewpoints that enrich knowledge; and *Politics*—empowerment for all students.[13]

To achieve these ends, we must design a multicultural curriculum that draws on a sound knowledge base. We must plan multicultural teaching that considers the needs of every student. This is a complex task. In this book, we define multicultural education as a process that:

- Guides students to identify their individual ethnic identities.
- Promotes a positive feeling of self-esteem in every learner.
- Clarifies personal and social responsibility for each member of our democratic society.
- Generates empathy among diverse learners.
- Utilizes teaching strategies that provide equity for all learners.
- Engages students in reflecting on broad multicultural themes and world concerns.

Defined thus, multicultural education is fundamental to all learning. It is an integral aspect of the discussions about fair behavior on the playground that might concern primary grade children. It underlies the dialogue of middle school youngsters as they respond to Maniac Magee's efforts to get along in a hostile society.[14] Multicultural education belongs in science, history, mathematics, language arts, and the fine arts. To be effective, multicultural education must be infused throughout any well-designed curriculum. It requires the efforts of committed teachers at all levels of education.

Recap

Defining multicultural education is a task that requires knowledge of such basic terms as *culture* and *race*. It also demands a review of past positions, for example assimilation theory, and current theories, such as internationalization of education, that are influencing the development of multicultural education. A review of this knowledge base leads us to define a broadly inclusive approach to multicultural education that encompasses self-esteem, empathy, and equity for all learners.

PREPARING TO TEACH IN A MULTICULTURE

Everyone in the United States needs multicultural education, and we recognize that such learning must begin during the early years. If schools are to promote multicultural understanding, they need to begin by educating teachers. Both preservice and inservice education are necessary to prepare teachers to present multicultural concepts to P–12 students. Ideally, multicultural concepts will be interwoven throughout courses and experiences in a teacher education program. Multicultural education will appear in foundation courses, psychology and assessment coursework, and courses focusing on methods and materials of teaching. Field experiences should engage future teachers in volunteer work with both children and adults from diverse cultures, as well as student teaching at appropriate levels.

In the same way, multicultural concepts should thread through the total P–12 curriculum. Students should be constantly reminded of the achievements of diverse members of our population, and they need continuing opportunities to extend their thinking abilities beyond the two-dimensional stereotypes exemplified by "good-bad" or "right-wrong" distinctions.

In this section, we will identify the outcomes expected from a multicultural program. We will also summarize the assumptions that underlie the presentation of multicultural education in this text.

DESIRED OUTCOMES FOR EVERY STUDENT

Today we know that effective education is based on outcomes and their assessment. Just what are we trying to achieve with students during the time they spend in our classrooms? Multicultural education should lead to the achievement of specific learning outcomes for children and young people in our schools. The outcomes we specify for multicultural teaching are often interpersonal; they are both cognitive and affective objectives. These outcomes will be integrated into the list of expected achievements for any course or program.

If our multicultural curriculum is effectively taught, students will be able to:
- Identify a strong sense of their own self-esteem and express the need and right of all other persons to similar feelings of self-esteem.
- Describe their own individual cultures, recognizing the influences that have shaped their thinking and behavior.
- Identify racial, ethnic, and religious groups represented in our pluralistic society (e.g., African Americans, persons from Italian backgrounds, Jews).
- Discuss the history of emigration to the United States after its discovery and the changing thinking about immigrants that evolved over the years.
- List identity groups to which each person belongs based on age, sex, or physical condition.
- List special interest groups to which each person belongs by choice (e.g., lawyers, feminists, swimmers, Republicans).
- Identify needs and concerns universal to people of all cultures (e.g., love, family, and health) and compare interesting cultural variations (e.g., food preparation, naming practices, or dance).
- Read and discuss literature by and about members of diverse cultures.
- Share folklore from different cultures, noting the common subjects and motifs that occur in folk literature.
- Discuss special gender-related concerns (e.g., sexual abuse, job discrimination based on sex, or the socialization of children).
- Discuss age-related concerns (e.g., rights of children, problems of the adolescent, or caring for the elderly).
- Discuss the needs of persons with disabilities (e.g., mainstreaming in school, parking facilities, special equipment).
- Identify examples of stereotyped thinking and prejudice in real life and in literature, and discuss the negative effects of such thinking.
- Inquire multiculturally as they engage in broad thematic studies related to any field (e.g., science, history, or health).

- Demonstrate knowledge of such related topics as slavery, the United Nations, the history of the English language, or desegregation.
- Participate in community and school affairs as informed, empathetic young citizens who know and care about other people and recognize the enriching effect of having many cultures represented in our population.
- Continue to learn about cultural diversity as part of lifelong learning.

Such outcomes can be assessed through students' speaking or writing performances as well as observed in their body language or behavior. Students should discuss a list of expected outcomes for any study they undertake before the work begins. The outcomes listed above can be adapted for inclusion in the outcomes for a particular unit of study in any subject area, as we will discuss in the chapters that follow.

Basic Assumptions Underlying This Text

Based on our study of multicultural education over a period of time, we offer the following twelve basic assumptions or beliefs in support of a strong multicultural education program in P–8 classes throughout the United States. These assumptions undergird everything we present in the chapters that follow.

This We Believe . . .

1. In the United States we live in a multiculture, a society comprised of many diverse cultures. All of living, including schooling, involves contact between different cultures and is therefore multicultural. No one culture can be considered more American than any other.

2. The United States is gradually modifying its expressed goal of assimilation, or making everyone alike (the melting-pot metaphor), in favor of recognizing and appreciating the diversity in our society (the "tossed salad," or mosaic, metaphor). Educators play a role in disseminating this knowledge and acting on its implications.

3. Multicultural education is too complex and pervasive a topic to be encompassed in a single course for teacher educators. All of education must reflect multicultural awareness, and curricula in the K–8 classrooms must therefore be designed to teach content about our multiculture and to provide equity for all learners in all subject areas.

4. We should not pretend or even aim to be creating teaching materials that are bias-free. Instead, we should guide students to recognize the biases from which they and all people operate.

5. We need to clarify our use of such terms as culture, ethnicity, and race. We also need to be aware of accepted labels for groups of people within our population, speaking out against insensitive usage whenever appropriate.

6. Although every child grows up within a given culture, he or she is shaped over the years by other influences, such as education and personal interactions with other people. Education can guide students to become more aware and appreciative of their individual culture and heritage. Children also can learn to become open to the cultural ideas shared by others so as to avoid ethnocentrism.

7. All children enter school with a store of prior knowledge, closely aligned with their individual cultural backgrounds, on which we can build.

8. Education can guide all students to become more aware and appreciative of the many cultures that have contributed to what is now the United States. Because of our history, we cannot identify a single "American" culture; rather, together we comprise a giant multiculture composed of a diverse national population, a characteristic that makes our country unique. Diversity should be viewed as a strength, not as disunity.

9. Teachers need to be aware of their own cultural backgrounds and biases. And they must recognize how these biases might influence their expectations of students and how they interact with others. Open dialogue with students will acknowledge these cultural influences as common to us all. Teachers and students can learn together about different ideas and ways of thinking.

10. Multicultural teaching is exciting because it is grounded in reality. Through active, constructivist learning strategies, students can become directly involved in their learning. At the same time, teachers may find such multicultural approaches more difficult because dialogue may include controversy and emotion. Open discussion may lead to expressions of anger or hostility, pain, and guilt. Since such discussions do not usually lead to identification of "right answers," the resulting ambiguity may cause students to feel unsettled.

11. Multicultural education, global studies, and internationalization of the curriculum are interrelated in their focus on human concerns. Thus, a study of universal needs suggests topics that overlap, so that the three are not completely separate areas to be added to the school curriculum.

12. Multicultural education deals with values and attitudes as well as knowledge. We can guide students to be aware of their own thinking and that of others. We guide them to make choices based on expressed reasoning, problem solving, and decision making. Changes in values and attitudes and the development of empathy take time, so that assessing such changes quickly is not possible.

Multicultural education is for all of us. Just as we help preschoolers learn to play fair and to respect the toys of others, we continue to help students learn to value the opinions of others and to acknowledge human rights. We all need many opportunities to celebrate the diversity of which we are an essential part.

These broad assumptions are developed in more detail in the chapters that follow. They will shape curriculum development and help us select outcomes as we teach any subject at any level. They will guide our selection of instructional and assessment strategies. They underscore the criteria for choosing literature and other materials to use in classrooms or to purchase for school libraries.

An Overview of This Text

We begin to apply these assumptions as we discuss multicultural teaching in Chapter 2, "Teaching for Diversity." In that chapter we present the model on which this multicultural program is based, beginning with **Esteem**, which leads to the development of **Empathy** and moves to **Equity** with multicultural issues and concerns.

In Chapter 3, "Building on Student Strengths," we address students as individuals, focusing on how a student-centered classroom can accommodate individual differences. Learning styles and the development of self-esteem for each student are integral to successful learning. Considered the foundation for equitable learning, esteem is promoted through successful experiences in living long before a child enters school. The teacher's role therefore includes repairing damaged self-concepts. This discussion involves attitudes and processes that permeate the total curriculum and require far more than a single, packaged program applied as a Band-Aid.

Chapter 4, "Making All Students Feel Included" discusses the development from positive feelings for self to recognition of the rights of others for self-esteem also. Although diversity is accepted and appreciated, the teacher also should emphasize the commonalities that we all share, for example, the need for food and love.

Chapter 5, "Engaging Student Perspectives" deals with concerns of the larger community. It demonstrates how teachers can guide young learners to appreciate other people in the classroom and in the local community. It moves beyond the United States to engage students in such global issues as saving the planet.

Chapter 6, "Exploring Language and Linguistic Diversity," guides teachers to celebrate language diversity in the classroom, abandoning an "English only" approach as children become aware of how interesting other languages can be. Support for learning English as a second language is also addressed in this chapter.

In Chapter 7, "Infusing Multicultural Concepts into Reading and Language Arts Programs," we begin moving across the curriculum to discover how readily multicultural concepts can be included in language and literacy activities. Special attention is given to the selection and use of multicultural literature throughout the curriculum.

This approach continues into other subject areas in Chapter 8, "Multicultural Education across the Curriculum." Special attention is given here to art, music, physical education and health, mathematics, science, and social studies. A fully developed unit on China and Chinese Americans is included in this chapter.

Chapter 9, "The Multicultural Calendar," provides an invaluable resource for teachers. Included are calendars for each month, which teachers can replicate, as well as detailed information for special dates and events. Far more than a "heroes, heroines, and holidays" approach, however, the calendar activities included throughout this resource chapter suggest the development of broad themes over a period of time. These activities are meant to enhance the total curriculum presented throughout the school year.

Chapter 10, "Reflecting on Multicultural Teaching," provides an overview summary of relevant issues and concerns. Of special interest are the discussion of the pros and cons of controversial issues related to multicultural education and the suggestions for further study. A fitting end for this text is the self-assessment chart, which students should find useful in thinking about what they have learned.

Following the ten chapters is the Appendix "Developing a Knowledge Base for Multicultural Education," an extensive listing of resources for the teacher. Focusing chiefly on books for the young reader, this section also includes lists of addresses that students and teachers can write to for additional information, for example about specific countries.

Throughout this text, we have attempted to include information about various groups that live in the United States. Special features have been included on the following groups:

Some groups are featured in more than one place, so the reader should refer to the index for full coverage. We have tried to include information related to a variety of different cultures, but we could not give full attention to every group represented in the United States. The task of additional exploration and collection of data remains to be undertaken by you and the students you teach.

REFLECTIONS

This introductory chapter summarizes the evolution of multiculturalism in the United States and the changing ways of thinking that impact directly on the schools. It is important that we teachers recognize our own ethnicity as a way of addressing the needs of our students. We can begin with our own stories and then reach out to take in the stories of the students with whom we work. In this book we define multicultural education broadly as imparting a strong knowledge base about the diverse people that populate the United States. Another major concern is providing an education that is equitable for all students. The basic assumptions that underlie this presentation must surely lead to a student-centered multicultural education for students at all levels.

We believe that ways of thinking are shaped by education—in the home, in the school, and in the larger societal context. Through education we can broaden our awareness of other people, their needs, their hopes and dreams. We can learn to collaborate at all levels within the United States and in a world setting. Educators need to lead the way in breaking down the stereotyped thinking that traditionally leads to dissension and war. A humane approach to education threaded throughout the total curriculum and presented over twelve or more years may eventually lead to a truly democratic society. The intent of this book is to suggest ways of delivering this message to students in all elementary classrooms, beginning in the earliest years. Unless future teachers of children in the United States truly believe in multicultural education and accept responsibility for teaching that provides equity for all learners, the changes that are badly needed will not occur.

APPLICATIONS

In this part of each chapter, we present ideas and activities designed to challenge your thinking and to lead you toward greater understanding of the issues involved in multicultural education. We recommend working in cooperative learning groups (CLGs) to explore these kinds of activities. Often findings in one CLG can be shared with the larger group.

1. Purchase a large three-ringed notebook in which to begin your Reflective Teaching Portfolio (RTP). This portfolio will summarize multicultural education and its impact on you as an individual, a teacher. To begin your portfolio, mark dividers to begin organizing the record of your progress toward becoming a multiculturally competent teacher. Include dividers for LEARNING LOG, INFORMATION, TEACHING IDEAS, and RESOURCES. Later, you may need to add other dividers. As the first entry in your portfolio, write several sentences about each of the twelve assumptions listed at the end of Chapter 1. These comments will provide a benchmark, summarizing your present position regarding multicultural education. Date this sheet and place it in your LEARNING LOG.

2. In addition to this notebook, you will need to begin a larger resource file (perhaps a heavy cardboard apple box with a lid) in which you can collect printed materials, including books, pictures, charts, and realia (artifacts representing different cultures). Purchase a packet of manila folders in which to store such resources as clippings, pictures, and booklists. Your portfolio can be stored at the front of your resource file. Include a pack of 4" × 6" cards on which to record information about pertinent books you read.

3. Many foreign-born parents want their children to be bilingual. They want their children to remember their origins. A Korean parent in Chicago stated, "What I intend to say to my children is 'You're never going to be Americans . . . Even though you live here 100 years or 200 years, you're still Korean.'" Discuss this issue in your CLG. As a teacher, what would you want to say to this father? Have someone from your group summarize your responses for the whole class.

4. Visit your local library to explore its multicultural offerings. Check the catalog to see what is listed under "Multicultural Education." Talk to the children's librarian to find out what resources are available in this field. Also peruse the audiovisual catalog to see if you can borrow films, videotapes, and other media from your library.

Referring to the extensive listing of books that begins on page 347, select an ethnic group that interests you and scan through the titles to note several that you might like to read. When you finish reading a book, bring the book to your CLG to share the contents and the strengths of this piece of literature with your colleagues. Each member of the group can then make a card for the book you presented.

5. In 1993, the Association for Supervision and Curriculum Development passed a resolution focusing on equalizing educational opportunities, stating in part: "The widening gap between rich and poor results in disenfranchisement. This exclusion creates lifelong negative consequences for children, their families, and our global society. The gap is manifest in demonstrable differences in health care, school settings, access to information, learning environments, student expectations, and ultimately, in the academic, economic, and social success of students." How can teachers deal with this concept, sometimes called the "culture of poverty"? Write your ideas in your LEARNING LOG. Think about what you need to learn in order to help students who may need support. Will they all come from homes on a low socioeconomic level?

Endnotes

1. Quoted widely in newspapers and on television, 1992.
2. Israel Zangwill. *The Melting Pot* (play), 1909.
3. Associated Press, 1993.
4. Bureau of the Census. *Statistical Abstracts of the United States*. U.S. Government, 1991.
5. Ibid.
6. Ricardo Garcia. *Education for Pluralism: Global Roots Stew*. Phi Delta Kappa, 1981, p. 15.
7. Stephen A. May. "Redeeming Multicultural Education." *Language Arts* 70, 5: 364–72, September, 1993.
8. Carley H. Dodd. *Dynamics of Intercultural Communication*. Brown, 1987.
9. Christine Sleeter and Carl Grant. *Making Choices for Multicultural Education: Five Approaches to Race, Class and Gender*. Merrill, 1988.
10. AACTE Newsletter, 1972.
11. Minnesota Commissioner of Education. Ruling, 1988.
12. *An Annotated Bibliography*. American Association of Colleges of Teacher Education, 1972.
13. L. Border and N. Chism. *Teaching for Diversity*. Jossey-Bass, 1992, p. 1.
14. Jerry Spinelli. *Maniac Magee*. Viking, 1992.

Exploring Further

The following books should be available in your library as reference resources for you to continue expanding your knowledge base.

James A. Banks and Cherry A. Banks, eds. *Multicultural Education: Issues and Perspectives*. Allyn and Bacon, 1993.

Laura Border and Nancy V. Chism. *Teaching for Diversity*. Jossey-Bass, 1992.

Children's Defense Fund. *The State of America's Children*. The Children's Defense Fund, 1991.

Antonia Darder. *Culture and Power in the Classroom: A Critical Foundation for Bicultural Education*. Bergin and Garvey, 1991.

Mary E. Dilworth. *Diversity in Teacher Education: New Expectations*. Jossey-Bass, 1992.

Carl A. Grant. *Research & Multicultural Education*. Falmar, 1993.

Carl A. Grant, ed. *Toward Education That Is Multicultural: Proceedings from the First Annual Meeting of the National Association of Multicultural Education*. Silver Burdett, 1992.

Jonathan Kozol. *Savage Inequalities: Children in America's Schools*. Crown, 1991.

Merri V. Lindgren, ed. *The Multicolored Mirror: Cultural Substance in Literature for Children and Young Adults*. Highsmith Press, 1991.

National Council for Social Studies. *Curriculum Guidelines for Multicultural Education*. 1991.

Theresa Perry and James Fraser, eds. *Teaching in the Multicultural Classroom*. Routledge, 1993.

Christine Sleeter, ed. *Empowerment through Multicultural Education*. State University of New York, 1991.

Kenneth M. Zeichner. *Educating Teachers for Cultural Diversity*. National Center for Research on Teacher Learning, 1993.

I touch the future.
I teach.

—Christa McAuliffe

2
❖
Teaching for Diversity

As John Dewey wrote in 1902, "Education enables individuals to come into full possession of all their powers."[1] The aim of all good teaching should be to assist each student in reaching his or her fullest potential. Therefore, this text emphasizes not only the need to provide multicultural understandings for all students at all levels but also how to teach so as to accommodate individual difference or diversity. To achieve this two-pronged goal, the teacher must plan with both the curriculum and the student in mind. A multicultural curriculum must be carefully designed, based on an identified body of knowledge that can be infused throughout the total elementary school curriculum. The multicultural curriculum must then be effectively presented through what we call "multicultural teaching," that is, instruction that aims to provide equitable opportunities for all students addressing cultural diversity in its full complexity. Carried to its ultimate end, multicultural teaching enables each student to reach his or her greatest potential. Thus, multicultural teaching can be described succinctly as "the best teaching for all students."

Effective multicultural education, then, will exemplify the same quality indicators as those of any outstanding school program. It is the program that parents with the greatest command of resources would choose for their children. A carefully designed, student-centered multicultural program both challenges and helps learners to succeed. And through achievement they gain self-esteem. The key elements of such a program are (1) a broad multicultural knowledge base infused throughout the total curriculum, (2) the teacher's planning and delivery strategies, and (3) the students' responsible involvement and success in meaningful learning. Above all, the curriculum is presented in a climate of acceptance, respect, and caring that guarantees successful learning experiences for all. In this chapter we will discuss these aspects of multicultural education.

To support multicultural teaching, we present a lesson model designed to involve students in practicing critical and reflective thinking skills as they deal with multicultural content. We also describe interactive teaching methods recommended for work in any content area and suggest applications specific to multicultural education.

After reading this chapter, you should be able to:

- Demonstrate learning and teaching processes that support the development of self-esteem.
- Plan learning activities that offer equal opportunities for all children to learn.

- Design a yearlong multicultural study that includes information about the diverse peoples living in the United States.
- Identify values and attitudes that are part of both the "hidden" and the explicit curriculum.
- Demonstrate teaching strategies that support the concepts of equity, break down stereotypes, and express value for diversity.
- Design lessons that lead students to reflect on and to respond critically to what they observe, hear, or read about multicultural concepts and issues.

The purpose of this chapter is to address teaching and learning processes that will enable us to present multicultural education most effectively. We will consider the diverse needs of students as well as the content to be presented.

IDENTIFYING A KNOWLEDGE BASE FOR INSTRUCTION: THE MULTICULTURAL CURRICULUM

In this section we will determine the content that needs to be presented in a multicultural curriculum. We begin by identifying the outcomes expected from implementing such a program. After the content to be taught is established, we will consider the needs of diverse student learners, including those who are at risk. We recognize that students have different learning styles and abilities, which are influenced by culturally diverse backgrounds. Such thinking may cause us to reflect further on the content to be taught, particularly regarding when to introduce concepts and how to present them most effectively within a spiraling curriculum. Studying the content to be learned and the students who will be involved sets the stage for a discussion of teaching and the processes that promise to be most effective.

Outcomes for Multicultural Education

Before we select specific concepts to be taught, we need to identify the student learning outcomes we expect to achieve. As a result of studying the proposed curriculum, we might expect students to be able to do the following:

1. Identify their own cultural roots.
2. Define and use pertinent terminology appropriately.
3. Express concepts about people that are accurate and free of stereotypes and bias.
4. Role-play and empathize with the perspectives of different groups.
5. Respect and appreciate cultural diversity as a characteristic of the population of the United States and of the world.
6. Interact positively with diverse individuals regardless of race, gender, and/or abilities.
7. Study instructional materials that reflect all cultural groups.
8. Identify multicultural concepts in all subject learning.
9. Apply evaluation and assessment measures that are equitable for diverse persons.
10. Assess their own experiences with cultural diversity.

Our scope and sequence for multicultural education begins with the outcomes we expect students to achieve. Outcomes assessment, then, will continually remind us and the students themselves of the intent of the program and, referred to periodically, will enable us to assess their progress toward the established objectives. Even preschool children can begin working toward these goals.

What are we trying to achieve? What should students be able to do? How will their thinking be affected? As we design a multicultural education curriculum, involving all faculty members in identifying competencies for the multicultural program will ensure that each person assumes responsibility for its success. Objectives must be both affective and cognitive, and they must not only apply across the total curriculum but also permeate deeply into our actual teaching practices. Objectives will be written in active terms to engage students in, for example:

acting out	describing	reciting
analyzing	explaining	retelling
applying	identifying	solving
comparing	listing	stating
deciding	observing	visualizing
defining	recalling	writing

The overall goal of the multicultural program has been expressed in the definition of multicultural education offered in Chapter 1. We want to increase students' self-esteem, enhance their understanding and appreciation of others in our society, and deepen their concern for the needs of all people in the United States and the world. We also want to provide equitable opportunities for all students to learn. The objectives we write may first focus on the subject area we are teaching, but they also will include those that lead directly to multicultural outcomes. The end result will be better instruction in all areas of the curriculum.

As pointed out above, therefore, all teachers in a school should be involved in the planning process; those who are engaged from the beginning will be committed to carrying out the program they plan together. We need to consider these factors for each curriculum area—reading, oral and written language, mathematics, social studies, science, and so on. Many of the objectives we propose for multicultural education are the same ones we would write for good teaching in general. Again, multicultural education equals the best teaching for all students.

It is not difficult to incorporate multicultural objectives, both affective and cognitive, and to reflect sound theory and practice in the list of aims for any class. In teaching science, for example, a teacher might include the following objectives for a study of animals:

Students will
- Keep a learning log summarizing what they learn each day (reinforces learning; individualized).
- Identify stereotypes that we associate with specific animals (introduces concept in nonthreatening context).
- Compile information to support or disprove one specific stereotype (the scientific method).
- Discuss stereotyped thinking in general (transfer of knowledge).
- Recognize the need to support generalizations with scientific facts (inquiry method; thinking skills).

Objectives that promote self-esteem and the appreciation of others can be inserted into the list of behaviors expected for every instructional area. Consider how these objectives could fit into a reading lesson or a social studies unit.

Students will

- List their own personal strengths.
- Identify areas in which they need to grow.

Students will

- Express positive feelings for other students.
- Work cooperatively in group situations to help each other.

Students will

- Learn facts about their family origins.
- Identify the many groups to which they belong.
- List ethnic groups in the community.

Students will

- Describe the contributions made by diverse groups to our pluralistic society.
- Define such terms as *racism* and *sexism*.
- Discuss the importance of understanding among the peoples of the world in order to achieve world peace.

It is unlikely that any one of the objectives presented in this section will be fully achieved in one lesson; thus we need to think in terms of how each concept can be introduced and reinforced at different levels over a period of time. In short, we need to begin defining a spiraling curriculum that will grow with the students.

The Spiraling Multicultural Curriculum

A spiraling curriculum moves upward from the bottom line of self-esteem for every child in wide, unpredictable swings. The curriculum is built concept by concept over a period of time, as depicted. Note that concepts will appear and reappear throughout the elementary and middle school curriculum; obviously, it is impossible to present the total curriculum in this simple, graphic display. The less complex ideas absorbed by six-year-olds will be built on as they progress through the upper grades. Each concept will be expanded and extended according to the learners' abilities. The spiraling curriculum reaches up and out so that students remain proud of themselves and their families while learning to respect the rights of others.

Eubanks points out the "acute need . . . to assure that educational programs reflect the best knowledge available on education that is multicultural, and that this knowledge be ingrained throughout our educational programs" at all levels.[2] Multicultural education is best woven into the total curriculum in an elementary school. To have the greatest effect, it must be presented in every primary, elementary, or middle school classroom, whether self-contained, team-taught, or departmentalized. Requiring careful planning and evaluation, developmental programs also must involve committed teachers and adminis-

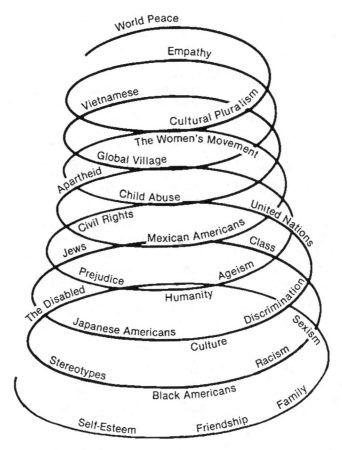

A Spiraling Curriculum for Multicultural Education

trators at all levels to specify outcomes and select activities and materials for instruction together.

The knowledge base selected for multicultural education may duplicate some aspects of the knowledge base recommended for teaching and learning in other subject areas. The knowledge base will be the same, however, whether the program is designed or delivered in a single classroom or is part of a schoolwide effort. In addition, the knowledge base we identify should be sufficiently broad to cover K–8 levels in a well-articulated, districtwide program. We begin with identifying a knowledge base that will be shared by all participating teachers.

As already stated, we perceive multicultural education as a thread running through the total curriculum; not a single syllabus for a class taught in seventh grade or one unit of study presented in grades 3 and 6. Infusing multicultural concepts throughout the P–8 curriculum is admittedly more difficult than teaching a single class, but we feel that this spiraling approach is infinitely more meaningful. Moreover, curriculum consists of more than overt messages given in lectures and textbooks. It also includes the "hidden," or covert, curriculum that is seldom recognized and almost never assessed. Consider what students learn in these classrooms:

> Motherly Mrs. McIntyre loves children and loves to teach first-grade reading. She always brags to the principal about the wonderful readers in her Great Books group and has one of them read aloud when he visits the classroom. (How do the less able students feel? What knowledge and attitudes are they internalizing?)

> Jim Melville loves to teach fourth-grade language arts. He reads aloud to his students and brings in piles of books from the library. He tells students that he always picks out books about boys because he knows boys hate stories about girls but girls enjoy the adventure stories about boys. (How might this practice affect the self-esteem of girls in this classroom? What message are the boys and girls absorbing?)

> Eighth-grade history teacher Donna Fosdick has regular celebrations to remember the events of Pearl Harbor Day, Martin Luther King's birthday, and Cinco de Mayo. She comments that she can't afford more time from the curriculum for these extra observances. (Is there more to understanding other cultures than just observing these few holidays? What do students learn from hearing this attitude expressed? What are they failing to learn?)

In offering an inclusive educational program that serves the needs of all students, we must avoid what some have referred to as a "tourist curriculum." Specifically, we want teachers to avoid the following pitfalls:

Trivializing. Don't organize activities only around holidays or only around food, and don't involve parents only for holiday or cooking activities.

Tokenism. Don't display one black doll amidst many white dolls or one multicultural book among many others; avoid any kind of minimal display in the classroom.

Disconnecting cultural diversity from daily classroom life. Avoid reading multicultural books only for special occasions or teaching one unit related to cultural diversity and never addressing the topic again, for example, by featuring African Americans only during Black History Month in February or talking about Native Americans only in relationship to our November Thanksgiving celebration. (See Chapter 9 for additional ideas along this line.)

Stereotyping. Don't present people of color always in the context of past history or always as poor and uneducated.

Misrepresenting American ethnic groups. Avoid using only books about Mexico, Japan, or African countries to teach about contemporary cultural groups in the United States. We may be confusing Mexican Americans with Mexicans.[3]

We need to think of a curriculum as transcending the many disciplines that we teach. A curriculum that achieves cultural literacy in its broadest sense demands far more than learning a conglomeration of facts; it must encompass full comprehension and changes in thinking revealed through clearly demonstrated understanding and empathy for others.

Recap

The multicultural curriculum begins with a study of self as students become aware of their own cultural backgrounds, their beliefs and attitudes, their eating habits, and other ways of behaving. Building from a sense of their own self-worth, students can then begin to compare and contrast their cultural identities with those of others in the classroom. Thus, guided by a knowledgeable teacher, they begin to discover that diversity is fascinating, not threatening. The curriculum presented, both overt and hidden, leads students toward an understanding of others that may enable them to share the world in peace.

Multicultural education in the schools is designed for students. It begins rightfully with each student's concept of self and expands in ever-widening circles in the direction of understanding others. In other words, it leads students to move from egocentrism to involvement and consideration for others. Eventually, multicultural education engages students in the larger issues and problems of the world, as depicted in this diagram.

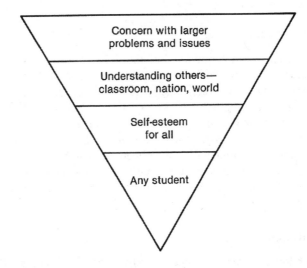

FOCUSING ON THE STUDENT LEARNER

Multicultural education must be student-centered. In learning to teach for diversity, we need to perceive students as individuals, being careful to avoid generalizations that lead to stereotyped thinking. Jalongo cautions the teacher as follows:

1. Be aware that multiculturalism must begin with adults.
2. Know your students and their cultural backgrounds.
3. Expect conflict and model conflict resolution.
4. Use literature to enrich children's learning and understandings about cultural pluralism.[4]

The learning of multicultural concepts and attitudes must be carefully articulated from the beginning levels in the home and in preschools through the elementary and middle school years and on into high school. According to the spiraling curriculum we have just described, knowledge increases with maturity, building incrementally to achieve the final goal: an educated adult who is fully prepared to live in a multiculture. Attention to critical transition points is crucial in achieving steady growth toward this goal.

Our intent in developing multicultural education during these early years is to have an impact on student thinking. We want learning to take place that will result in changing behaviors. Therefore, it is important that we consider the students in our classrooms in terms of their physical and psychological needs as well as the values and culture they bring to the classroom from their prior knowledge and experience. This awareness will help us to deliver our carefully designed curriculum effectively.

Student-centered instruction recognizes student learning as the ultimate aim of education. We want students to be self-motivated learners, to inquire and to discover, and also to question established practices or assumptions. At the same time, students need to be aware of the responsibilities that are directly related to choice and decision making.

Early Childhood Years

During the 1980s and continuing into the 1990s, efforts such as Head Start have made a demonstrable difference in the education of our youngest children. We must plan carefully to "ensure that young children experience transitional continuity in programming" as they move from preschool into kindergarten and the primary grades.[5] This collaborative effort involves parents and community agencies working closely with the schools to maintain continuity as children progress from level to level.

Successful learning builds self-esteem. Research supports the importance of making sure that children develop an "I can" attitude during these formative years. The Shipman study, described below, demonstrates the effect that schooling can have when transition is not planned skillfully.

The Shipman Study

Young children approach life eagerly, positively, no matter what their backgrounds. Self-confidently they reach out to learn. They work hard, for example, to master the complexities of language and to figure out how to function in their social environment—family, neighborhood, and school. What happens in school has a significant effect on the development of this natural potential to learn. Teacher expectations directly influence children's performance, and this effect can be adverse.

A six-year study of children from low-income homes by Virginia Shipman and others investigated "how home and school work together to influence the child's development."[6] After surveying more than 1,000 children from 1969 to 1975, the researchers made the following findings:

1. "Disadvantaged" and middle-class children enter school with the same average level of self-esteem.
2. Children from low-income homes enter school with as broad a range of abilities as any other group.

3. Low-income homes contain the same range of positive and negative influences on learning as do middle-class homes.
4. After three years of schooling, children from low-income homes experience a significant drop in self-esteem compared with their middle-class peers.
5. Although there is a loss of self-confidence, children from low-income homes still feel positive at this stage rather than negative about their ability to take care of themselves.

By clarifying the characteristics of children from low-income homes, the Shipman study may serve to dispel some stereotyped thinking. Her findings should help teachers rid themselves of the misconceptions that low socioeconomic status automatically means little value for learning; the findings should equally underscore the need for viewing each child as an individual. The implications of this study also support the need for teacher expectations to remain high for children from low-income homes. Shipman notes, "It gets down to what happens in the classroom between the teacher and the child—how much encouragement that child is given, how much stimulation and warmth." Teachers who have low expectations of students may have an adverse effect on children's performance.[7]

Teacher expectations based on income level or cultural background are not the only factors affecting student performance. Teachers need to consider the advantages the English-speaking child has on entering most U.S. schools compared with the non-English proficient (NEP) child.

English-speaking child

1. Language used is familiar.
2. Teaching materials are presented in English, and the child learns to read English.
3. Child's self esteem is supported by experiences in school.
4. He or she graduates from high school and may enter college.

Non–English-speaking child

1. Language used is strange.
2. Child is expected to use materials presented in English; child may be illiterate in his or her native language.
3. Child feels unhappy, is unsuccessful in school, and cannot wait to go home.
4. He or she drops out of school as soon as possible.[8]

While such research findings are valuable, they tend to polarize characteristics in a way that may support stereotypes. We need to be aware, for example, that NEP students from higher socioeconomic backgrounds or high-prestige groups may perform very well. However, we do need to be aware of the differences in these children's school experience. The role of the teachers should be to minimize the ways in which NEP students feel at a disadvantage, for language is closely allied with the students' self-concept. (The activities in Chapter 3 support the development of positive self-concepts.)

Children who have experienced failure and frustration may perceive themselves as having limited ability or little chance of success and may not even try a task before saying, "I can't." They have internalized a negative perception of themselves, and this attitude will influence their whole approach to life. These children need to be revitalized and reassured. That task is not easy, even working with a young child of four or five; it becomes increasingly difficult as the child grows older.

The Widening Gap between Teachers and Students

In *Educating Teachers for Cultural Diversity*, Kenneth Zeichner addresses another key issue in teacher education: Teachers are becoming increasingly different from the students they teach. Furthermore, the number of teachers of color entering the teaching field is much too small to overcome the discrepancy between the teacher's cultural background and that of the culturally diverse group of students in most classrooms.[9] It is essential, therefore, that teachers acquire the appropriate attitudes, knowledge, and dispositions needed to work effectively with students who come from varied cultural backgrounds. This cultural diversity includes social class as well as ethnic variation and language difference. It is important to recognize, too, that not only will teacher and student be different but also that students will differ from one another. A commitment to multicultural education requires teachers to plan an inclusionary classroom in which children respect each other.

This may be a special challenge to those of us who come from middle-class families of European origins and speak standard English. Can white monolingual teachers, members of the so-called dominant group, rise to the challenge of reaching out to ethnic and language-minority students? Can we prepare ourselves to work with children of color, or children whose parents were born in a different country and may still be preparing to be naturalized? Can we bridge the gap? We can, if we believe that we can and if we are committed to teaching for diversity. All of us can begin by reflecting on our personal experiences, perhaps concerning the marginalization of women or experiences with poverty. If we are to be effective teachers, we must make a concerted effort to understand the differences and also the commonalities between our experiences and those of our students, whoever they are.

Students At Risk

Many children are at risk of not succeeding in the schools today. We recognize that "school people did not create or cause most of the problems that confront young people today, nor can they solve the problems by themselves."[10] On the other hand, educators have a responsibility to try to alleviate the conditions that place some students at risk and to help them overcome obstacles that impede their success in school. The following proposed "Bill of Rights for Children: An Education Charter for the Decade of the Child" was drafted by Thomas Sobol, commissioner of education in New York state.

All children have the right to:
- A healthy, secure, nurturing infancy and early childhood;
- A free, sound, basic education;
- An education appropriate for their needs;
- An education which respects each student's culture, race, socioeconomic background, and home language;
- Schools and educational programs which are effective;
- Educational programs which prepare them for jobs, for college, for family life, and for citizenship in a democracy;
- The resources needed to secure their educational rights;
- Education in school buildings which are clean, safe, and in good repair;

- Pursuance of their education without fear;
- An education which involves responsibilities as well as rights.[11]

The nation is finally realizing the economic as well as the human importance of saving students "at risk"—those students who will drop out of school as soon as possible. Since these students form a kind of identity group and many of them also tend to be members of minority groups, it seems appropriate to address this problem in a book on multicultural education. For too long we have failed to solve the problem of reaching these students by intervening in the early years and providing models with whom they can identify. For example, our teaching has been inappropriate, failing to recognize that "at-risk students need to learn higher order thinking skills such as problem solving, not just basic skills that may keep them dependent thinkers all their lives"[12] Multicultural approaches to education may act as a bridge to these students, reaching them through selected literature with which they can find a common bond and providing equitable opportunities for successful learning experiences beginning in the primary grades. We must recognize that failing to support at-risk students today may have serious economic consequences for all of us in the next century.

Phi Delta Kappa, an educational honor society, sponsored extensive research into at-risk students, young people who most need the benefits of multicultural teaching. Begun in 1988, the study is based on reports from almost 22,000 elementary, middle school, and high school students, including about 30 percent African American, Latino, Native American, and Asian students. Researchers identified thirty-four indicators of risk, which they grouped into the following five categories or factors:

Personal pain (drugs, abuse, suspension, suicide)
Academic failure (low grades, failure, absences, low self-esteem)
Family tragedy (parent illness or death, health problems)
Family socioeconomic situation (low income, negativism, lack of education)
Family instability (moving, divorce)

Researchers addressed four major questions and obtained findings that have significance for teachers at all levels.

1. Who is at risk? Only one in five students interviewed had no risk factors; one in four had three or more risk factors evident. Older students were more at risk than younger ones; African Americans more at risk than whites; Latinos more at risk than Asians; and boys more at risk than girls.

2. What factors put them at risk? "Most of the risk factors are beyond the sphere of influence of the school." If one risk factor is present, usually there are others. More than half of students who were retained came from broken homes. One-third of them had low grades, and 17 percent had fathers who had not graduated from high school.

3. What are schools doing to help these students? Nearly one-fourth of the 9,700 teachers interviewed say they spend more than 50 percent of their time with at-risk students. Strategies used by more than 75 percent of teachers include individualized scheduling, conferences with parents, extra time on basic skills, emphasis on thinking skills, notification of parents, and federally funded remedial programs. The following practices were judged to be at least 75 percent effective: special teachers, smaller classes, special education, individualized scheduling, conferences with parents, extra time on basic skills, peer tutoring, vocational courses (in high school), special study skills, emphasis on coping skills, emphasis on thinking skills, notification of parents, funded programs, and teacher aides. A significant finding was that "teachers and principals provide students who are at-risk with more instructional efforts than students who are not at-risk, and teachers are committed to and are concerned with helping students who have special problems, whatever those problems might be."

4. How effective are the schools' efforts? Although teachers and principals considered their efforts only 71 percent to 75 percent productive, principals reported that their schools had a great deal of influence over students' reading comprehension, math, writing, and listening skills; daily attendance; general behavior and attitude toward school; completion of homework; attention in class; and higher-order thinking skills.[13]

From the findings of this study, we can see that assessment of students' backgrounds and abilities is essential in planning instruction designed specifically for students who are at risk. Teachers must recognize that, according to this study, these students may come from stimulus-poor homes and read very little. They often have not mastered learning skills and may have a low school achievement record. However, we need to consider the strengths and weaknesses of each student as we plan individually for their growth. Simply offering more drill work or lecturing will not solve their learning problems.

On the other hand, the study states that teachers can do only so much; "the energy for learning comes from the student, and the responsibility for learning must be assumed by the student." Teachers can help children learn to assume this responsibility early in their schooling. In summary, "understanding students, caring about them as individuals, nurturing the development of responsibility in them, and then emphasizing academic skills" holds some promise of helping at-risk students. These efforts must begin early in the student's schooling and continue throughout the later school years.

Yale professor James Comer, author of *Beyond Black and White*, supports these recommendations, noting: "Black children need somebody to care about them, first of all. They need somebody who wants them to learn, who believes they can learn, and who gives them the kind of experiences that enable them to learn. That's what all children need."[14] Comer has summarized what we envision as "teaching multiculturally."

Success for All—A Support Program for Literacy Learning

Success for All, developed by the Center for Research on Elementary and Middle Schools (CREMS), addresses teaching reading skills more effectively during the early years. Led by Robert Slavin, the research team attempts to provide support for children during the crucial preschool and primary-grade years when the "die for failure is cast" for many children. Support is provided for children at risk through the use of certified teachers who serve as reading tutors. A tutor spends twenty minutes a day working one-on-one with a child during nonreading class time. Performance assessment is ongoing, so that support is given only when help is indicated.

"Working one-on-one is a uniquely different situation from group teaching," reports Slavin. "There are no problems with student motivation; no management problems—you put your arm around a child and teach that child what he or she needs to know."[15] As Frank Smith phrases it, "You respond to what the child is trying to do."[16]

Success for All focuses on storytelling. Children listen to the teacher read an interesting book, for example the fine translation of *The Crane Wife* by Katherine Paterson or John Steptoe's beautifully illustrated African tale, *Mufaro's Beautiful Daughters*. The children talk about the story, retelling especially interesting parts. Discussion includes questions and speculation about possible answers, thus stimulating thinking abilities. The children also act out activities, playing roles and providing dialogue that fits the performance. The teacher may have cards on which paragraphs from the story are printed so that children can rearrange the cards in the correct sequence. As they handle the cards, children are rethinking and rereading the story. Thus, the story is told and retold in many ways without exhausting the children's interest. Throughout these activities, teachers are expanding children's language and immersing them in words used in context. Gradually, children move into more structured literacy activities, with greater emphasis on reading literature and responding in writing.

Recap

Research findings support our conviction that effective multicultural teaching is student-centered rather than teacher-dominated. The teacher does not abdicate his or her position but rather plans quality learning activities that engage students in active, hands-on experiences and builds on success to develop students' self-esteem. The teacher models appreciation for diversity by building on students' prior knowledge and setting clear, realistic expectations for each student's abilities. Learning experiences are designed to promote student interaction and to generate inquiry and thinking through both talking and writing. The total effort aims at achieving broad cultural literacy for all. Such approaches benefit all students, but they are especially recommended for those who may be at risk.

DELIVERING THE CURRICULUM: TEACHING FOR DIVERSITY

As stated previously, multicultural teaching provides the best teaching for each individual learner. Emphasizing learning processes, it attempts to allow every child to learn and to reach his or her highest potential. Multicultural education begins with clearly defined outcomes, reflecting a carefully designed curriculum. Achieving these outcomes, however, requires the selection of the best strategies—the delivery system—to enable all children to learn. Finally, the assessment of student achievement is an integral aspect of teaching. This section focuses on just how we can bring about multicultural education.

The Teacher's Role

Ernest Boyer states: "I'm convinced the time has come to . . . focus on the leadership of the principal, the renewal of the teachers, and above all, the dignity and potential of every student."[17] Any multicultural program should plan for the effective presentation of the curriculum. We need to make certain that teachers and administrators are well informed and that their knowledge is accurate and up-to-date, but a well-planned delivery system is also crucial if learning is to take place. Teachers need to know how to use the best teaching strategies—questioning, cooperative learning, engaging students in active, hands-on learning activities. They need to select methods and materials that will involve students in thinking about real issues that affect their daily lives.

Since the teacher is the key to the success or failure of any program, what you do in your own classroom every day is of primary importance. From the moment students enter the classroom, they begin learning. The climate of the room, the way you treat students, the language you speak—all serve as models for student behavior. Fair evaluation, recognition of individual needs, and a clear sense of liking students as you work with them will demonstrate attitudes you want to teach. Your role is to select the best teaching methods, to choose the materials you will use wisely, and to communicate to parents. Good teaching is student-centered.

Teachers who respect students select their teaching methods accordingly. For example, good teachers do not need to use sarcasm, they recognize that such a negative approach is unproductive. Respect for students is best demonstrated by accepting of their idiosyncrasies and recognizing their needs as growing young people. Teachers should also have reasonable expectations of students and understand how to encourage their participation in school activities.

Evaluating student performance is a particularly sensitive aspect of teaching. As you consider "putting grades on report cards," you should be aware that students see you as "putting grades on them," which can be very threatening, indeed. As you plan for evaluation, keep the following alternative methods in mind:

1. *Grading.* Don't put grades on everything a student does. Have many short writing and speaking activities that are not graded but shared with other students, or perhaps placed in a class collection that students can read at their leisure.

2. *Writing (in all subject areas).* Never grade the first draft of a student's writing. Periodically have students revise a selection that will be published in some way (on the bulletin board, in a class book, in the newspaper). Tell the students that you will put a grade on this work after they have revised it to their satisfaction. (See Chapter 7.)

3. *Establishing criteria.* Always make clear your criteria for grades you give. What does a student have to do to receive an A, B, or C? Talk with students about the characteristics of outstanding work, average work, and poor work as you give a specific assignment, and show them examples.

4. *Self-evaluation.* As far as possible, have students check their own work. Provide answer sheets so that they can discover mistakes immediately. Stress the need to read items over again to find and correct errors. If you eliminate yourself from this kind of "grading," you cease to be the ogre who has all the "right" answers.

5. *Individual conferences.* Have a short conference, or conversation, with each student once a week, if possible. Five minutes of individual attention does a lot for children who need support. Use this opportunity to examine children's writing or to talk about the library book they are currently reading. Focus on supporting the students' efforts, not correcting errors, at this time.

6. *Send a commendation to parents.* Several times during the year, send a letter to each parent commending at least one thing their child has accomplished. Children will be

glad to take a Good Work letter home. Make an effort to write this letter in the language of the home, even if you have to prepare translations into several different languages. (Ask for help, as needed.)

7. *Accentuate the positive!* Focus on what students accomplish, not what they fail to achieve or the mistakes they make. Compare:
Wow, you spelled thirteen words out of fifteen correctly!
Too bad, you missed two words out of fifteen today.

Choose instructional techniques that allow for individual differences and ones that add a spark of excitement to classroom activities. Reject dull, fill-in-the-blank workbooks or dittoed sheets in favor of activities that engage students in really listening, speaking, reading, writing, and thinking—active involvement that results in learning across the curriculum. Read journals and attend current workshops to discover innovative strategies to make teaching more effective and fun.

You do not have to be bilingual to introduce concepts about various languages and dialects in your classroom. It is important that students become aware, for example, of the wide variety of languages that people throughout the United States use daily. Even though you may have a bilingual program in your school, it probably deals with only one of those languages. It is important for children and teachers to recognize that English is not the only language spoken in the United States.

If you are monolingual, you can bring in speakers of other languages to broaden student perspectives. Not only will visitors introduce different languages, they also can share ideas and values from other cultures. You can facilitate this kind of interaction, explore the resources of your community, and plan learning experiences designed to teach children about the multilingual/multicultural nature of our population. If you are fluent in a second language, or even if you know a little about another language, you can share your knowledge. Naturally, we do not expect children to become bilingual through brief exposure to phrases in several languages, but learning to say *hasta luego!* (Spanish—so long!), *nee hao (Chinese—hello),* or *Gesundheit!* (German—to your good health!) opens doors to new knowledge that can be fascinating to young language learners and exposes them to multicultural perspectives.

Sharing stories from different cultures also offers a way of expanding student horizons. Folklore from Russia (discover the wicked Baba Yaga), Native American Indians (laugh over the antics of Coyote the Trickster), black Africa (look for Anansi the Spider), or lore from the American West (Pecos Bill and Paul Bunyan) can be enjoyed equally by students and teachers.

According to Zeichner (1993), university students who intend to become teachers today must have the following key characteristics to be effective as teachers of multicultural concepts:

- A clear sense of their own ethnic and cultural identity.
- High expectations for student success.
- The expectation that all students can succeed and that they can help them succeed.
- Commitment to achieving equity for all students.
- The ability to accommodate different learning styles and abilities.

- The ability to bond with students as a result of genuinely caring about young people and their welfare.
- A strong multicultural knowledge base that encompasses ethnic studies, gender concerns, and sensitivity to persons with special needs.[18]

Strategies and skills that effective teachers need to be able to use include the following:

- Planning meaningful learning tasks based on the curriculum.
- Engaging students in interactive and collaborative learning tasks.
- Challenging students to develop higher-level thinking skills.
- Providing scaffolding (support) for students to ensure that they can succeed.
- Building on students' prior knowledge.
- Communicating to students the expectation that they can succeed and that you, the teacher, will help them.
- Explaining the culture of the school to students.
- Maintaining students' sense of ethnocultural pride and identity.
- Involving parents in their children's education.[19]

Teaching multiculturally is not the easiest way to teach. It requires a teacher who is committed to the welfare of students, one who is willing to accept a challenge. The rewards lie in seeing students succeed.

Recap

Research shows that good teaching is not teacher-dominated. Effective teachers will plan integrated studies that engage students in, for example, actively reading and writing about the Civil War as they also learn about the plight of Africans brought forcibly to the United States. Students will engage in inquiry as they search for information to share with their study group. Good teachers are enthusiastic about the content to be studied, but they also care about the needs of the learners who are spending considerable time in their classroom. Good teaching is also reflective; teachers think consciously about what is happening in the classroom and how teaching and learning can be improved in an ongoing assessment process.

RECOMMENDED TEACHING STRATEGIES

Methods of instruction are as important as the content listed in the curriculum. As we consider just how to introduce multicultural concepts to students, we need to think not only about what to teach, but also how to engage students in active learning that requires analysis, evaluation, and reflection. The same effective strategies can be used in delivering the multicultural curriculum, whether lessons are closely tied to the social studies program or are taught within the context of an English language arts program that strongly emphasizes literature by and about members of various cultures.

The strategies we select for use in the classroom reflect our view of both students and the learning process. This section presents several recommended teaching strategies that will benefit students in any classroom, no matter what the subject or level of instruction:

Using a sound lesson model   Brainstorming ideas
Reciprocal teaching/cooperative learning   Teaching a thematic unit of study
Using literature as a rich source of ideas

Using a Sound Lesson Model

In planning any lesson it is important to think through the entire process. First of all, what are your objectives for teaching the lesson? What do you want students to be able to do? Remember that objectives can, and should, be both affective and cognitive. The following lesson model begins with stating the expected outcomes.

Next, begin thinking about how you can reach these outcomes. What procedures will you use? What materials—films, books, pictures, records, objects—will help you stimulate student learning? Now determine what students will do in response to the stimulus. Plan an active, hands-on experience—something all students *can* do (realistic expectations). Then decide on the follow-up. What do students do after participating in the learning activity? How do they share the results? Finally, but not to be forgotten, how will you know they have met the objectives you specified? Evaluation techniques will range from acting out to telling to writing, but they involve some sort of performance by the student (not limited to the commonly used paper and pencil test).

By following this model, you will plan a theoretically sound learning experience for children. The acronym SAFE will help you remember to incorporate all four components required to produce an effective lesson that you and your students will enjoy.

      Stimulus   **A**ctivity   **F**ollow-up   **E**valuation

DESIGNING A LESSON: THE SAFE MODEL FORM

Title of lesson: _____

Intended grade levels: _____

Outcome(s): (What will students do?)
1. _____
2. _____
3. _____

Brief description:
_____
_____
_____
_____
_____

Procedures:
STIMULUS (Tell the teacher-reader what to do using specific material.)
ACTIVITY (What will students do? Include suggestions to the teacher.)
FOLLOW-UP (Individual, pairs, small group, large group—suggestions.)
EVALUATION (Criteria for success of lesson based on objective(s).)

A SAMPLE LESSON FOLLOWING THE MODEL

SAFE Lesson 1: A Biographical Sketch

Level of Difficulty: Grades 7–8

Outcomes

Students will do the following:

1. Read a short biographical sketch of a minority author.
2. Analyze the quality of the writing.
3. Identify the features of a biographical sketch.
4. Compose a biographical sketch following a model.
5. Share information about minority authors and their writings.

Procedures

This lesson should be developed over a period of several days. Duplicate copies of the following biographical sketch of Alex Haley.

Introducing Alex Haley.   Alex Palmer Haley is the well-known author of *Roots: The Saga of an American Family*, which was published in 1976 and made into a stirring television miniseries watched by millions of Americans. Born August 11, 1921, in Ithaca, New York, Alex Haley was the son of a professor and a teacher.

Alex Haley served as a journalist in the U.S. Coast Guard. He tells of writing love letters for his fellow seamen who weren't particularly good at writing. He won their admiration and gratitude (and earned considerable money, too) by composing romantic letters to ensure that the men's sweethearts would be waiting when they returned to port.

Haley soon decided that he wanted to concentrate on writing full-time. After struggling for a number of years to earn a living as a writer, he finally succeeded by working with the author of *The Autobiography of Malcolm X*, which appeared in 1965.

But it was *Roots* that brought Haley real acclaim. Recognizing this unique contribution to American literature, the noted writer James Baldwin observed:

> Roots *is a study of continuities, of consequence, of how a people perpetuate themselves, how each generation helps to doom, or helps to liberate, the coming one—the action of love, or the absence of love, in time. It suggests, with great power, how each of us, however unconsciously, can't but be the vehicle of history which has produced us. Well, we can perish in this vehicle, children, or we can move on up the road.*

After twelve years of painstaking genealogical research, Haley collected the life story of seven generations of his family in the United States and several more generations in a village on the Gambia River in West Africa. He presented these authentic facts in a fictionalized story, a form he called "faction"—a delicate combination of fact and fiction which allowed him to flesh out these ancestral characters, and include their thoughts and emotions. The resulting novel touched the lives of millions of readers in a way that a scholarly report would never have achieved. As Haley noted, "When you start talking about family, about lineage and ancestry, you are talking about every person on earth."

Stimulus

Have students read the sketch of Haley's life. Tell students that this form of writing is called a biographical sketch. Ask students to note and then discuss particular words they find interesting. Identify collectively and list on the chalkboard the features of a well-written biographical sketch, for example:

> Tells where and when the person was born
> Makes clear why the person is known
> Uses a quotation about the person's work

Tell students that they are going to write a biographical sketch about any minority (broadly interpreted) writer whose work they have read or want to read. (You may brainstorm a list of recommended authors on the board, such as Laurence Yep, Virginia Hamilton, Isaac B. Singer, Richard Wright, or Richard Rodriguez.) Students may begin with an encyclopedia entry, but they are to use other resources, too. You may wish to specify that they consult at least two sources other than the encyclopedia.

Activity

Take students to the library to locate the encyclopedias, check out books by the author selected, and find other sources of information. Point out *Current Biography* and *Contemporary Authors*. Students should take notes from resources they cannot check out. For homework, they should begin the first draft of the biographical sketch to present in class on the following day.

Follow-up

On the next day review the features of a biographical sketch and make any additions recommended. Then have students work in pairs as they read the first drafts of the sketches and check their writing together against the list of features. The partners should work cooperatively to suggest revisions that will strengthen each paper. You may wish to use another day for students to work in groups of five or six so that a broader audience can respond to second drafts prepared for homework.

Evaluation

The aim is to communicate interesting content using clear, expository prose. Students can evaluate the finished products as Grabs Me! (5 points), So-So (3 points), and Not So Hot (1 point). Students should be permitted to improve their writing to gain more points. Cooperative learning techniques can help all students achieve the top score. Note that this teaching strategy aims to develop self-esteem by facilitating success. All students are learning to collaborate to reach a goal.

Collect the polished biographical sketches in a class book entitled "Authors We Have Known." Students may refer to this book when they are selecting books to read. The collection can be further developed by including book reviews (see page 209). Note that students are learning about contributions made by members of diverse cultures to what we call "American literature." They learn about these authors as people, and as they are introduced to literature, they may be motivated to read based on a classmate's recommendation.

Recap

In planning any lesson it is essential to include a warm-up period that prepares students to succeed at the task they are to undertake. Directions must be clear, and resources must be readily available. Students need adequate time and formative, ongoing evaluation to help them complete the task. Cooperative learning techniques enable students, with guidance, to learn from one another. As students work in pairs and small groups, they have an opportunity to get acquainted and are motivated to help each other succeed. Such understanding and behavior undergird multicultural teaching and are indeed essential components of all effective teaching.

Reciprocal Teaching

Students often find cooperative methods of studying text material an effective way to learn. Even very young children can learn specific skills that increase thinking abilities and reading comprehension through group study. The problem with many collaborative group activities is that they lack clear directions, outcomes and procedures are vague, and it is not certain what students are to learn.

Reciprocal teaching, an interesting group technique developed by A. Palincsar and others[20], engages students in working with an adult to teach each other. In 1987, University of California researcher Ann Brown began a longitudinal study using this method.[21] She studied 300 primary-grade children and also 300 junior high school students who were judged at risk and were poor readers. All students were placed in "reciprocal teaching groups" and given daily comprehension tests. Eighty percent of the students were rated successful at the end of the study, having achieved at least 80 percent accuracy on five succeeding tests.

Reciprocal teaching procedures are worth trying to develop literacy skills and social studies or multicultural content at any level. To begin with, students are grouped in same-age working units of six to eight led by an adult. They read together (or listen to an adult read) a book selected for what it has to teach. For example, middle school students might read Katherine Paterson's *The Great Gilly Hopkins* as a way of gaining insight into the feelings and problems of a young girl who has been buffeted by a hostile world. The aim of having students read this book would be for them to achieve empathy for another person and to recognize common human problems. This book would be read chapter by chapter.

Following the reading of each book or chapter, the adult and student learners take turns leading a discussion about what has been read, thus sharing teaching responsibilities. Note that each student is involved in, and also assumes responsibility for, his or her own learning. At first, the leader models the process by asking questions about the text the group has studied together. Following the discussion, the leader summarizes what has been said. As stated in Ann Brown's research, "Summarization is a comprehension monitoring strategy." The group helps adjust the accuracy of this summary, which then can be recorded on a computer and printed to provide a copy for each member of the group for each daily lesson. Then, students take turns being the leader.

The intent of this exercise is to construct meaning from a text. Fiction and nonfiction work equally well as students study for different purposes. This collaborative study method focuses learning activities on a clear goal. Such collaborative learning activities lend themselves to theme or unit studies as described in the following pages of this chapter.

Using Literature as a Rich Source of Ideas

Literature is a particularly fine resource for the development of a multicultural education curriculum. Literature

- Communicates the universality of human emotions
- Models prosocial behavior
- Makes children proud of their ethnic heritage
- Introduces children to contemporary families both similar to and different from their own
- Reveals to children how it feels to be different
- Enables children to participate in another social era

Reading Literature Aloud to a Class

Reading aloud to students is an outstanding method of ensuring that even less able readers have an opportunity to know good literature. Begin by presenting the book, short story, article, or poetry as writing by another human being with whom students can enter into a transaction. The aim of the transaction is to construct meaning collaboratively. Tell students that all they have are the words before them that an author wrote and their own ideas; encourage them to ask questions about what the author might be saying and also about their responses to these ideas. (Avoid having all the "right" answers that you expect students to know.)

Use reading aloud as a method of engaging students at all levels and in all subject areas with the ideas presented in books. As you read a novel by Lloyd Alexander, a picture book by Byrd Baylor, or the poetry of Langston Hughes, students are learning many things.

1. *What book language sounds like.* Remember that written language is different from speech. More formal, usually representing the standard English dialect, book language is what they will gradually learn to write. It is not the familiar language that they speak with their family and friends. Before they can be expected to produce this written dialect, they need to hear it, to begin acquiring that dialect of English in much the same manner that they earlier acquired the ability to speak English.

2. *Forms that writing can take.* As students listen to language or read it, they also gain knowledge of the forms (genres) through which they can express their ideas. Through listening to novels or short stories, for example, students are developing a "sense of story." They are learning how an author engages characters in dialogue and how character traits are revealed through behavior. They are introduced to such concepts as theme, setting, and plot development. Sharing other forms—a haiku, a song lyric, an editorial, a letter of complaint—helps students learn how to write those forms too.

3. *Grammatical structures.* As students listen to good writing, they hear a variety of sentence structures. They hear sentences composed of varied combinations of clauses, phrases, and strings of words. They are adding to and reinforcing their knowledge of English grammar as they listen to the opening sentences that William Saroyan wrote for *The Human Comedy,* speaking in the third person of the omniscient author:

> The little boy named Ulysses Macauley one day stood over the new gopher hole in the backyard of his house on Santa Clara Avenue in Ithaca, California. The gopher of this hole pushed up fresh moist dirt and peeked out at the boy, who was certainly a stranger but perhaps not an enemy. Before this miracle had been fully enjoyed by the boy, one of the birds of Ithaca flew into the old walnut tree in the backyard and after settling itself on a branch broke into rapture, moving the boy's fascination from the earth to the tree.

4. *Feelings, ideas, content.* A good book presents interesting content, vicarious experiences, and ideas that students can talk and write about. The characters share emotions with which the reader can identify. Students gain insight into the lives of others and begin to understand the concepts of diversity and universality applied to the people with whom they inhabit the earth.

5. *The sound of fluent reading; intonation.* As you read, students hear what fluent reading sounds like. They hear the accents and pauses, the intonation that a good reader uses automatically. They can talk about the meaning that intonation adds to language. They are learning to enjoy reading and talking about good books together.

6. *The joy of reading; what books have to offer.* Less able readers may be hearing a book that they could not read independently, whereas able readers are often motivated to read a book that you have shared. All enjoy the experience of sharing an exciting story, laughing together, or even sharing the vicarious experience of death. The students are developing positive attitudes toward reading through your enthusiastic sharing.

Every piece of literature—every example of writing—that we share through reading aloud teaches students more about language and literature. Your reading aloud, however, offers additional assets as a teaching strategy of which you should be aware. One important advantage is that reading an article, a short story, or a chapter from a book means that *the whole class has a body of shared content to which all can respond immediately.* Your teaching is not hampered by students who have not read the assignment or completed their homework. Nor do you have to locate multiple books. Reading aloud is *efficient and economical.*

Furthermore, reading aloud is *very enjoyable.* A sense of *camaraderie* develops through this shared experience—a *rapport* between you and your students that benefits the total learning program you present.

Choosing multicultural literature that supports instruction in the subject you are teaching adds the opportunity to deal with breaking down stereotypes and enhancing student knowledge of people from diverse cultures. The following are representative of the multicultural fiction and nonfiction you might choose to read aloud and to talk about:

Primary Grades

Ezra Jack Keats, *The Snowy Day*. Viking, 1962.
   A young African American boy experiences snow.
Taro Yashima, *Crow Boy*. Viking, 1955.
   A boy who is different comes to be accepted by other children.
Rosa Guy, *Billy the Great*. Delacorte, 1992.
   Perspective on prejudice; friendship.
Pat Mora, *A Birthday Basket for Tia*. Macmillan, 1992.
   A traditional Mexican celebration for an aunt's ninetieth birthday.

Upper Elementary Grades

Laurence Yep, *Dragonwings*. Harper, 1977.
   An historical novel about the Chinese in California.
Malka Drucker, *Grandma's Latkes*. Harcourt, 1992.
   A grandmother passes on her Jewish family's traditions to Molly.
Gary Soto, *The Skirt*. Delacorte, 1992.
   A picture of a Mexican-American family in California.

Advanced and Gifted

Mary E. Lyons, *Letters from a Slave Girl: The Story of Harriet Jacobs*. Scribner's, 1992.
   Historical fiction told through letters from a woman who became an abolitionist.
Brenda Seabrooke, *The Bridges of Summer*. Cobblehill, 1992.
   Friendship between two girls across racial divisions in South Carolina.

Brainstorming Ideas about a Problem or Topic

Brainstorming is a good way of engaging students in developing ideas related to a theme. Brainstorming is an accepted technique for collectively generating solutions to a problem. Ideas are suggested and listed without evaluation, critical analysis, or even comment. Usually even wild ideas can be expected in the spontaneity that evolves when you suspend judgment. Practical considerations are not important at this point. The process should stimulate creativity. At this stage, the quantity of ideas counts, not their quality. All ideas should be expressed, not screened out by any individual. Generating a quantity of ideas will increase the likelihood of finding outstanding ones. Encourage piggybacking (building on the ideas of other group members) whenever appropriate to pool creativity. Students should be free to build on ideas or to make interesting combinations of various suggestions. Focus on a single problem or issue. Don't skip around or try to brainstorm a complex, multiple problem. Establish a congenial, relaxed, cooperative climate, and make sure that all members, no matter how shy and reluctant to contribute, get their ideas heard. Record *all* ideas, writing them on the chalkboard or on large sheets of paper. After numerous ideas are generated, follow these procedures:

1. Review the list of ideas, selecting the top five to discuss further in terms of practicality. Have small groups discuss each one in detail. Have each group present the pros and cons of that idea for consideration.

2. Vote on the top two or three ideas to try. Place them in order of priority according to your purpose or need.

3. Begin implementing the ideas in order.

Multicultural topics lend themselves to such brainstorming techniques. Invite students to suggest alternative solutions or ideas about questions such as the following:

- How can we help students who are having trouble getting along in school?
- Why should we be concerned about what is happening in Israel or Somalia?
- How have African Americans contributed to the development of the United States?
- What would be appropriate behavior if someone called you an insulting name?
- What might you do if you witnessed such an incident?

Brainstorming helps students share ideas and structure their thoughts. Such exercises help groups reach consensus. Here are some variations on this approach to brainstorming: clustering (illustrated in the next section), mapping (see page 239), and the Venn diagram (see page 241). Such brainstorming techniques facilitate expression through speaking or writing. All can be used with groups or individually before students begin to write or plan a speech.

Teaching a Thematic Unit of Study

Focusing units of study on broad themes provides perhaps the best way of integrating factual knowledge with the understandings that we want to promote. You might develop such a study by beginning with the following:

A novel (*The Sign of the Beaver*; *Sounder*)
A current event (conflict in Bosnia; Native American rights)
A broad topic (aging, poverty, patterns, death, play)
A cultural group (the Acadians, Hawaiians)
A picture book (*Katie-Bo, An Adoption Story*; *Don't You Know There's a War On?*)
A biography (*Nelson Mandela*; *César Chávez*)

We can begin a unit of study by clustering ideas around the topic to be studied. The example presented here is based on reading a book, Lois Lowry's *Number the Stars* (Houghton Mifflin, 1989). This historical novel won the Newbery Award for excellent writing in children's literature. As the teacher reads this novel aloud, students begin constructing a web of ideas about life in Copenhagen in 1943, the Nazi soldiers who fill the town, and the Danish Jews they are persecuting. They continue adding to the large network of ideas daily as they read together. When the book is completed, the collection of ideas might look something like that on the opposite page.

Notice how the ideas develop in clusters of related concepts or categories. In this case reading the novel and clustering the ideas presented by the author will lead to a broader study of Jewish beliefs, the wholesale persecution of Jews during World War II by the Nazis, and the life of Jews in the United States today. Reading this novel will motivate students to become involved with the characters and the action described. They will want to know why the German soldiers behaved as they did and why the Jews in particular were

threatened. They can depict scenes on a large floor map as they follow events in the story. To provide accuracy, small groups can research the history and geography related to this novel. Through this study, students should gain insight into the plight of the Jewish people during the Holocaust, the historical significance of World War II, and the role that the United States played in that war. This study is an excellent example of how to align an international focus with ethnic studies in the United States.

Students may also be stimulated to read other fiction and nonfiction about Jewish people and the horrors they have experienced as they have tried to survive. For example, they might like to read *The Diary of Anne Frank* or *Letters from Rifka* by Karen Hesse (Holt, 1992).

Recap

Methods of instruction are crucial to the success of any learning experience. The way in which students are engaged in learning influences their involvement and level of interest. Collaborative methods of learning, including reciprocal teaching, provide support for students at all levels. Reading literature provides an inexhaustible source of ideas and information. The integration of learning activities around a theme helps students make connections. Brainstorming engages students in collaborative thinking. These interactive strategies are useful instructional techniques that can be used with any content matter and at all grade levels.

REFLECTIONS

Teaching for multicultural understanding requires a well-planned curriculum based on clearly stated outcomes. The teacher's role in delivering this curriculum is to guide student inquiries and to serve as a facilitator and resource person. The student learner also plays an active part in initiating avenues of inquiry together with a group of fellow researchers. We must select the best methodologies and resources as we develop an integrated humanistic study to further multicultural understanding.

As we teach for diversity, we employ the best of thinking based on educational research, for example: (1) teaching is not "telling." The learner must be actively engaged in inquiring and constructing his or her own meaning, if learning is to take place; (2) cultural literacy is more than learning lists. It is accumulated over a period of years and must be acquired within a context that enables students to integrate knowledge with understanding. Broad humanistic studies will lead students to encounter factual information and to give it meaning by fitting each piece into the big picture; (3) all students come to school with a vast store of knowledge. The five-year-old brings a wealth of information based on his or her individual culture and experiences during the long period of rapid learning since birth. We need to recognize this prior knowledge as we introduce new concepts, helping the student become aware of how the new knowledge relates to what is already known; and (4) teacher attitudes and expectations concerning how students can or will perform affect children's achievement in school. A sound multicultural education program depends on careful planning across grade levels and across subject areas. The quality indicators of an effective program include the following:

- Content that makes interdisciplinary and multicultural connections.
- Teachers who recognize the need for multicultural education, who are involved in the planning, and who are willing to learn with their students.
- Students who are self-motivated learners concerned about their own rights as well as the rights of others.

When we successfully bring these three components together, we will have an outstanding multicultural education program. All children will learn.

APPLICATIONS

Try the following activities as you prepare to introduce multicultural education at the primary, elementary, or middle school level.

1. As we discussed, it is important to address multicultural concepts at an early age. Work with a group of students who are especially interested in the preschool or primary-grade child to develop a file of multicultural education resources for young children. Include an annotated list of books, lesson plans, and other activities that you might use with young learners. Begin by exploring the university library for such titles as the following:

Mary Lee Allen. *Helping Children by Strengthening Families: A Look at Family.* Washington, D.C.: Children's Defense Fund, 1991.

Elizabeth Grugeon and Peter Woods. *Educating All: Multicultural Perspectives in the Primary School.* Routledge, 1990. Interesting British viewpoint; focuses on racism.

Patricia G. Ramsey. *Teaching and Learning in a Diverse World: Multicultural Education for Young Children.* Teachers College Press, 1987.

Edwina B. Vold. *Multicultural Education in Early Childhood Classrooms.* National Education Association, 1992.

Compile a list of books that you might use with young children. Note the strengths of each one in terms of multicultural education, for example:

Ann Whitford Paul. *Eight Hands Round: A Patchwork Alphabet.* Harper Collins, 1991. Each letter is associated with something characteristic of life in the early years of our country: anvil, buggy, churn, storm, tobacco. Each is connected to a familiar quilt pattern. A number of multicultural concepts are introduced in context, for example, the Underground Railroad, as well as the sense of history and community that quilts exemplify. Children can make a Friendship Quilt as a class project.

Phil Mendez. *The Black Snowman.* Scholastic, 1989. An unusual interweaving of fantasy and realism that emerges from the tradition of African storytelling; a magic kente empowers the storyteller whose story deals with a young African American's feelings. Students can improvise a colorful kente to throw around their shoulders as they take the storyteller's role.

Maria C. Brusca. *On the Pampas.* Holt, 1991. A little girl spends a wonderful summer on her grandparents' ranch in Argentina. Offers an opportunity to get out the world map, also to compare similarities and differences.

2. Begin a resource file in which to place the materials you collect related to multicultural studies. This file will complement your card file record of books you have read. Use a large cardboard carton that will hold standard file folders. Make folders for topics such as the following: Mexico and Mexican Americans, China and Chinese Americans, Our Community, or Africa. Continue to add folders as you learn more about this broad subject. Watch for informative articles, news items, and pictures related to topics that you will talk about in your classroom. Begin sending for free travel posters and other materials that will increase your multicultural knowledge base as you grow professionally. Enlarge the posters presented at the beginning of each chapter of this text. Include items that will help students understand the concepts you want to teach.

3. Select a topic, book, or group that you would like to study. Plan a unit of study following the procedures described at the end of this chapter. As this project grows, you may need a whole box to hold this unit and the realia (musical instruments, maps, toys, statues) you collect.

Endnotes

1. John Dewey. *The Child and the Curriculum*. University of Chicago Press, 1902.
2. Eugene E. Eubanks, president, American Association of Colleges of Teacher Education. Speech, February, 1989.
3. Mary Jalongo in Edwina B. Vold. *Multicultural Education in Early Childhood Classrooms*. National Education Association, 1992, pp. 56–62.
4. Ibid.
5. Association for Supervision and Curriculum Development. *1993 Resolutions*, The Assn., 1993, p. 1.
6. Virginia Shipman et al. *Young Children and Their First School Experiences*. Educational Testing Service, 1976.
7. Ibid.
8. Ibid.
9. Kenneth Zeichner. *Educating Teachers for Cultural Diversity*. University of Michigan, National Center for Research on Teacher Learning, 1993.
10. Jack Frymier. *Growing Up Is Risky Business, and Schools Are Not to Blame*, Phi Delta Kappa, 1992. Copies of this final report may be obtained for $.50 each from Phi Delta Kappa, Box 789, Bloomington, IN 47402–0789.
11. Thomas Sobol, commissioner of education, New York State Department of Education. Undated.
12. Louise Derman-Sparks. *Anti-Bias Curriculum: Tools for Empowering Young Children*. National Association for the Education of Young Children, 1989.
13. James Frymier, ibid.
14. James Comer. "Dr. James Comer's Plan for Ensuring the Future." *Black Issues*. 10, 6:46, May 20, 1993.
15. Robert Slavin. Wisconsin Center for Education Research. *WCER Highlights* Vol. 3, No. 1, Fall, 1990, pp. 1–2.
16. Frank Smith. *Understanding Reading*. Holt, 1973.
17. Ernest Boyer. "On the High School Curriculum: A Conversation with Ernest Boyer." *Educational Leadership, 46*, 1 (September 1988): 4–9.
18. Zeichner, p. 23.
19. Ibid.
20. Ann Brown and Annemarie Palincsar. "Interactive Teaching to Promote Independent Learning from Text." *The Reading Teacher,* 39:770–77, 1986.
21. Wisconsin Center for Education Research. *WCER Highlights,* Vol. 3, No 1, Fall, 1990, pp. 7–8.
22. Mary Jalongo, ibid., pp. 62–63.

Exploring Further

Laura A. B. Border and Nancy Van Note Chism. *Teaching for Diversity*. New Directions for Teaching and Learning Series. Jossey-Bass, 1992.

Charles S. Claxton and Patricia H. Murrell. *Learning Styles: Implications for Improving Educational Practices*. Association for the Study of Higher Education, 1987.

Leslie W. Crawford. *Language and Literacy Learning in Multicultural Classrooms*. Allyn and Bacon, 1993.

Ricardo L. Garcia. *Teaching in a Pluralistic Society: Concepts, Models, Strategies*. Harper, 1991.

Lynn Paine. *Orientation towards diversity: What do prospective teachers bring?* U.S. Dept. of Education, Office of Education Research and Improvement, 1990.

Theresa Perry and James Fraser, eds. *Freedom's Plow: Teaching in the Multicultural Classroom*. Routledge, 1993.

Chris Stevenson and Judy F. Carr, eds. *Integrated Studies in the Middle Grades: "Dancing through Walls."* Teachers College, 1993.

Iris M. Tiedt et al. *Teaching Thinking in K–12 Classrooms*. Allyn and Bacon, 1989.

Kenneth Zeichner. *Educating teachers for cultural diversity*. University of Michigan, National Center for Research on Teacher Learning, 1993.

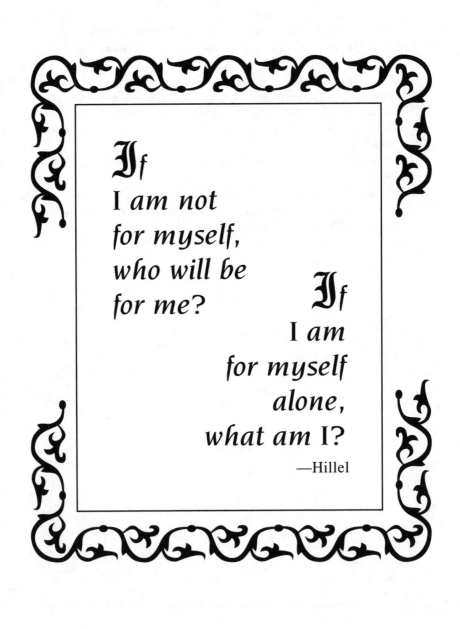

If
I am not
for myself,
who will be
for me?

If
I am
for myself
alone,
what am I?

—Hillel

3
❖

Building on Student Strengths

This chapter focuses on the need for self-knowledge. When we reflect on ourselves, our strengths and weaknesses, and all the factors that have contributed to our personality, life experience, and beliefs, we learn how to see others for who they are and to appreciate how they are both similar to and different from ourselves. These differences then become more a subject of interest and less a direct threat to us.

In each of the following chapters, we adopt a particular lens through which to view the process of multicultural learning. For this chapter, the lens is the individual.

Examining multicultural learning from the perspective of the individual means looking at students as "active" learners, able to construct their own identity, instead of seeing them as passive receptacles of the messages of their family, community, and culture. When we bring the students' culture into the classroom, it is more than just a topic of historical interest. We want to encourage students to become thoughtful possessors of a tradition, rather than prisoners of a cultural straitjacket. As each group interprets the old messages in new ways, students can learn that they, too, are a part of the continuing development and redefinition of their cultural heritage.

How do you, the teacher, help develop active student learners? Because learning takes place as students build on prior knowledge and make connections to new information and experience, you can provide rich environments of activity and discussion, where students reflect on the relationships and patterns they discover. Because students are eager to teach and learn from other students, you want to structure multiple opportunities for students to test their ideas against others through talk and small group work. And because students learn, not by smoothly and steadily accumulating knowledge, but by taking small steps and giant leaps, often in unexpected directions, you can't know how much your students are capable of unless you listen to them carefully. All students, no matter what their ethnicity, language, or family background, have the potential to succeed in school.

After reading this chapter you should be able to:

- Understand what factors affect student identity.
- Plan for and monitor learning experiences that challenge all students.
- Better appreciate the need for equity between the sexes in the classroom.

WHO WE ARE

As students learn about themselves, they prepare to learn about each other. They are engaged in the developmental tasks of developing empathy and learning to see the world from another's point of view; they begin to separate who they are from who others may be. Teachers can help to bridge the transition from home to school by making the school environment less foreign. Encourage students to bring important parts of themselves to school to share with others.

Special Recognition

In a large class, inevitably some students receive more attention (positive or negative) than others. Keep a copy of your class list handy and glance at it often, especially during transitions between activities. Check to see that you have some contact with each student in the class every day—a quick compliment or even a friendly, personal smile. Through recognizing each student as an individual, you provide an opening for further discussion. Also, you may see that someone needs help or reassurance.

Listen to the students. Is someone more quiet than usual? Or is someone talking more than normal? Often these are signals that something is troubling the student. You can take the student aside later for a private chat or offer a special reward or activity that can serve as positive attention.

Tell students what you like about their work. Too often, most of the feedback students receive on their efforts is negative. We tend to see the errors students make rather than their successes. Remember to acknowledge what students have accomplished. Be sincere and be specific.

Special Days

Students' birthdays offer an opportunity to recognize students as individuals. On your class calendar, list the birthdays that will occur each month. Let the birthday student do something special that day, for example:

- Wear a special hat.
- Choose a game for everyone to play.
- Teach the class a poem.
- Distribute papers or books for the teacher.
- Use a favorite color on the bulletin board.

Another way of recognizing a student is to have the rest of the class brainstorm what they like about that person. These comments can be written down and collected in a book for the student to take home. The students can also make up a song about that person and sing it, perhaps to the tune of "Happy Birthday."

Ask students how birthdays are celebrated in their families. Do they have any special customs or ceremonies? Suggest that there are many different ways to honor people on their special day.

Although most students enjoy being the center of attention for a day, many may also be shy or embarrassed by the publicity. Monitor your birthday activities to make sure that the student feels like an important part of the class and not singled out for uncomfortable attention.

The "Me" Collage

Have students clip from magazines and prepare a collage that reveals facts about their lives. Talk about the things they might include, for example:

- Birthplace—picture, part of a map
- Baby pictures
- Things they like—food, sports
- Their family—people, pets
- Where they have lived or traveled

Words as well as pictures can be included to help tell others in the classroom more about themselves. Clippings are pasted on a large piece of colored construction paper or cardboard. A frame can be attached after the collage is completed.

Have students write a brief biographical description that can be attached to the collage or read aloud to the class. Feature a different student's collage every week.

These collages make interesting displays for Open House when parents visit the school. Record each student's presentation of the biographical sketch that accompanies his or her collage. Play the tape continuously as parents visit the classroom. Post an order of the presentations on the board so people can tell when their child will be heard.

Why We Are Different

Read the following story about French poet Jean Cocteau to the students. Follow up with a discussion about diversity and conformity.

There's Nobody Like You!

The French poet Jean Cocteau found out early in life why diversity is better than uniformity.

As a young man, M. Cocteau was designing a stage set which required a tree as background. He spent night after night in the theater basement cutting out individual leaves for his creation.

Then a wealthy friend, whose father owned a factory, approached him with another idea.

"Give me the design of that leaf," he said, "and in three days you will have thousands of them here."

After his friend's return, they pasted the multitude of identical leaves onto the branches.

The result, M. Cocteau recalled, was "the most boring package of flat, uninteresting forms one can see."

At last he understood why each leaf of a tree and each man in the world are different from any other.

—*Christopher News Notes,* no. 187, May 1971

Everyone Has Fears

Introduce the subject of being afraid by reading a book such as *There's a Nightmare in My Closet* by Mercer Mayer (Dial, 1987). Then ask the students to write a sentence or two about something of which they are really afraid. You participate, too. With no names attached, each paper is folded up tight and put in a box. You might say:

Now that you have your fear written on paper, I want you to fold it up tight and put it in this box. (Collect everyone's fears.) Here we have everybody's fears collected in a box. Sometimes the things we're afraid of are only fearsome because we can't talk about them. We keep them hidden inside us. Today we're going to bring some of these fears out in the sunshine where we can look at them. I'm going to ask somebody to pick up one of these fears and read it out loud. If the one that's drawn is yours, you don't have to tell anyone because your name isn't on the paper.

Discuss the fear that is drawn from the box: "How many of you have been afraid of the dark when you go to bed? What did you do about it?" Repeat this activity as long as the group is interested. Then set the box aside for further discussion at irregular intervals.

Another sensitive presentation of a common concern is *Ira Sleeps Over* by Bernard Waber (Houghton Mifflin, 1972). Ira is worried about going to a friend's house to sleep for the first time. His sister tells him that his friend will laugh at him if he sleeps with his teddy bear. Read this book aloud to the class, pausing at each page to have students predict what will happen next and to recommend ways to handle Ira's concerns.

How We Differ

Discuss with students some of the ways in which they differ from one another. They are different sizes, and they wear different clothes. Some of them have straight hair, some curly. They come from different families; some of them have older or younger brothers and sisters, and some do not; their parents have different kinds of jobs. Extend this discussion to explore the multitude of factors that make up individual identity:

We live in different places (house, apartment, farm).
We were born in different places.
We enjoy different recreational activities.
We are good at different skills and activities.

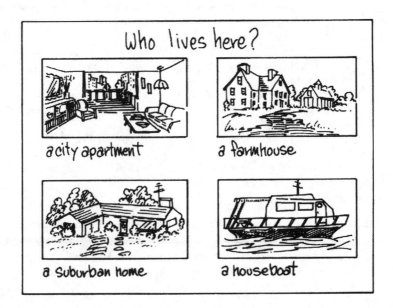

Who lives here?

a city apartment   a farmhouse

a suburban home   a houseboat

Are there advantages to being different from each other? What can we learn from these differences?

Personal Writing

An excellent way to promote writing that supports student self-esteem is to encourage freewriting in a journal. Journals can be spiral-bound notebooks or sheets of composition paper stapled together. Schedule a specific time for writing in student journals, and continue this writing for at least three weeks. The journals should be kept in the classroom so that all students have their journals on hand at the scheduled time. We recommend that you, too, write in a journal, both to demonstrate the value of the activity and to share entries periodically. Journal writing should never be graded or corrected. At times, students may select an entry to share, but the option of privacy must be assured.

At all times, students should feel free to write about something important to them. However, you may want to suggest a topic each day for those who need an idea. Use some of the following topics for journal writing:

- Friends are important.
- I felt sad when . . .
- Some of my favorite things are . . .

Before you embark on this activity, recognize that students may write about painful or intimate topics. Decide in advance how you might handle some unpleasant or upsetting discussions. If you share writing with the class or in small groups, don't force reluctant students to contribute.

Here are some recommended resources to help you introduce journal writing in the classroom:

Nancie Atwell. "Writing and Reading from the Inside Out." In Jane Hansen, Thomas Newkirk, and Donald Graves, eds. *Breaking Ground: Teachers Relate Reading and Writing in the Elementary School*. Heinemann, 1985.

Lucy Calkins and Shelley Harwayne. *Living between the Lines*. Heinemann, 1991.

Toby Fulwiler, ed. *The Journal Book*. Boynton-Cook, 1987.

James Moffett and Betty Wagner. *Student-Centered Language Arts: K–12,* 4th ed. Heinemann, 1991.

Donald Murray. *Write to Learn,* 3rd ed. Holt, Rinehart, and Winston, 1990.

We All Belong to Many Groups

Ask students to list on a sheet of paper all the groups they belong to. After they have had time to write a number of ideas, ask each person to tell one group they belong to; encourage them to share different ideas as much as possible. As new ideas are suggested, have students add to their individual lists. Then ask children to draw pictures of themselves and to list all the groups they belong to. Display these pictures on the wall. They can then be bound in a class book: Room 15, the Class of 1996.

Sue Wong is . . .
a girl
a daughter
a member of the Wong family
a Californian
a San Franciscan
a member of this class
a twelve-year-old
a Chinese American
a U.S. citizen
an acrobat

My Lifeline

Have students draw a series of mountain peaks across a sheet of paper. Tell them that this line represents their life. What are the big peaks in their life? What are the smaller peaks? Have them identify the peaks in their lifetime so far as they write on each mountain.

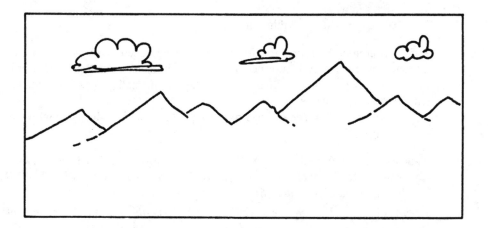

This idea can be extended by describing their usual daily existence across the base of the mountains. A few fantasies can be added on clouds: "Someday I'd like to . . ."

The Color of Me

Cut a number of strips of paper in a variety of colors, for instance, red, yellow, green, blue, purple, orange, brown, gray, black, and white. For a class of thirty, you may need twenty pieces of each color.

Ask the children to close their eyes. Then say, "Imagine that you are looking at a painting of yourself. What color would you be? If you could choose one color, what color would you choose to be you?" Have children come to the table on which the colored strips of paper are spread out to choose the color with which they identify. Divide the class into small groups to talk about the colors selected and what they mean to each person.

Afterward, students can extend their explorations of color by acting out the characteristics of the colors they have chosen. How would the color red walk across the room? What kind of voice does the color blue use? See Chapter 4 for more activities related to this subject.

Writing on Self-Perception

Have each child mount the strip of paper chosen in the preceding activity on a sheet of composition paper. The students can explain why they see themselves as this color by writing a short personal essay beginning with these words: "I think I am _____ because . . ."

This is a very revealing step toward self-awareness and it will provide insight into the child's self-perception. This is not the type of writing to display on the wall, but children may voluntarily share their writing in small groups. Be careful not to make evaluative comments, saying only perhaps, "Thank you for sharing, Bopha."

Metaphors of the Self

After students have explored some of the possibilities of these associations, introduce the idea of metaphor to describe what they have been doing. This kind of reasoning—analogical or metaphorical—is different from the literal, concrete thinking common in classrooms and textbooks. Students need the opportunity to stretch their minds with this alternative reasoning and to experience making unexpected associations, especially because such thinking is often restricted to extra-credit activities or students in high-ability groups.

I Am a . . .

Children can become more aware of themselves by selecting other things with which they identify. In addition to color, have children answer these kinds of questions: What food are you? What kind of car are you? What kind of building are you?

After each person has answered the questions on paper, have the children talk about the questions in small groups in which each person can participate directly. Although the choices are revealing in many ways, usually people are not threatened by this neutral approach. Sometimes this occasions laughter as children share the humor of someone's choice. Like most people, children enjoy talking about themselves. They may contribute such metaphoric ideas as these:

Ali: I think I'm a peanut because I've got a hard shell and you can't see inside.
Juana: I'm a big office building because I'm involved in many activities; there are many different people inside me.
Shanti: I'm a little red sports car, I can't keep still and I like to talk.

What I Like about My Life

Encourage children to talk about what they like about their lives and what they do not like. Ask the following questions:

- Name one thing you think is really great about your life.
- If you could change one thing in your life, what would you change?

Follow this discussion by writing a poem about something important to you—love, music, sister, time, food, flying, whatever. Follow this pattern:

Line 1: 1 word—the subject
Line 2: 2 words—describe the subject
Line 3: 3 words—express a feeling
Line 4: 4 words—describe an action
Line 5: 1 word—refer to the subject

Give Yourself a Present

Another question to stimulate reflection is: "If you could give yourself a present, what would you choose?" This should start a lively discussion. After students have talked about their ideas, ask them to write about the present they would choose. Ask them to describe the present and tell why they selected that particular thing.

Valued Characteristics

Provide a list of characteristics from which students select those they would most like to have. Each student gets a copy to mark individually. Before they mark their papers, discuss the meaning of each item. (See the form below.)

WHAT KIND OF PERSON WOULD YOU LIKE TO BE?

Mark 1 before the word that is most important to you. Mark 2 before the next most important, and so on. The number 14 will mark the quality that is least important to you.

I would like to be

_____ Polite	_____ Loving
_____ Dependable	_____ Creative
_____ Hardworking	_____ Brave
_____ Cheerful	_____ Capable
_____ Neat	_____ Respectful
_____ Helpful to others	_____ Truthful
_____ Smart	_____ Open-minded

After papers are marked (with no names attached), have students tally the results on the board. Students can keep their own papers to do this. Simply tally the number of children who marked 1, 2, or 3 for each item. Then tally the number who marked 12, 13, or 14 for each item. This gives you an indication of the high-valued and low-valued items. Discuss the results: Which items are the most popular and why? Why do students disagree?

NAMING OURSELVES

Names are one of the most salient features of our personhood, representing our individual identity as well as our connection with our family and our heritage. Names also have a great deal of influence on our expectations of others. Studies show that teachers consistently grade students with "normal" names higher than they do children with unusual names. As a teacher, you need to consider how you respond to your students' names. Do you see unusual first names as a sign of creative flair or an expression of cultural pride? Will these names doom the children to peer ridicule and stigmatization? In addition, American last names have historically been short and simple, like Smith and Jones. Immigrants used to change their names on arrival to fit into this pattern. But as appreciation of diversity has increased, people are proud of the distinctive names that reflect their culture of origin.

My Name

Talk about names with the children. Discuss how they feel about their first names, and what names mean.

Have the children make designs based on their first names. Color the name designs for display on the bulletin board. This design makes a good cover for a personal collection of writing.

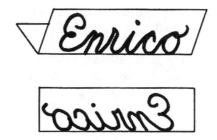 

Choosing Names

Ask children how they got their first names. Are they named after someone, perhaps an aunt or grandfather? Perhaps they have a family name, like Jamison, or an invented name composed of both parents' names, such as Rayella. Ask them to write about one of these topics:

- I like my first name because _____ .
- I wish I could change my first name because _____ .
- If I could choose a name for myself, it would be _____ because
_____ .
- If I had a child, I would name the baby _____ because
_____ .

Chrysanthemum by Kevin Henkes (Greenwillow 1991), a book for primary students, tells the story of a young mouse who loves her unusual name until she starts school. The other students make fun of her, saying her name is too long and not appropriate for a mouse. But one of her teachers helps her learn that her name is as special as she is.

Naming Customs

Talk about different customs of naming children. Children will be interested in knowing about confirmation names in Catholic families or the Jewish practice of naming children after dead relatives. Ask the children to share information from their personal experience. You might read the first few pages of *Roots* (Doubleday, 1976) in which Alex Haley describes the naming of Kunta Kinte.

Names and Stereotypes

In 1991 the most popular names for baby girls were Ashley, Amanda, Jessica, Samantha, and Stephanie. The top names for baby boys were Michael, Christopher, Matthew, Joseph, and Daniel. In the last ten years, however, many African American parents have been giving their children names that reflect an African or Islamic heritage, such as Kenyatta and Imani. More recently, many parents have been giving their children unique or invented names that stand out for their creativity. Are some names better than others? Can you judge people by their names? Young students may not be aware how much they are influenced by social expectations regarding common names and unusual names. Discuss their reactions to different kinds of names. Are some names exclusively for boys, others for girls? Why?

The purpose of raising this issue is to get students to think carefully and critically about their attitudes and prejudices. Talking about these concrete examples and airing assumptions helps students to become more aware of stereotyped beliefs and learn to evaluate their actions.

What People Call You

Observe that some families use pet names or nicknames. In some regions, children are commonly called by both the first and middle names, for example, James Leroy or Nancy Kathryn. Ask students: "What does your mother call you? How about your friends?" Discuss what the children like to be called. Ask them what they would like you to call them in school. Practice pronouncing these names as the children do until you can say them easily. Encourage mutual respect by using the preferred forms yourself, so that all students can learn to use the unfamiliar names.

One Name in Many Languages

Students will be interested, also, to discover that the same name is used in many languages. One illustration is the name John, which can be found in a variety of languages:

Yohanna (Arabic)	Jannis (Greek)	Johan (Norwegian)
Iban (Basque)	Yohanan (Hebrew)	Ivan (Russian)
John (English)	Sean (Irish)	Ian (Scots)
Jean (French)	Shane (Irish)	Juan (Spanish)
Hans (German)	Giovanni (Italian)	Evan (Welsh)
Johannes (German)	Jan (Northern European, Dutch)	

See if the students can discover the equivalent in other languages of such names as Peter, James, David, William, Mary, Rose, and Helen.

Family Names

Whether Greek (Stephanopoulos), Belgian (Van Der Mensbrugghe), Georgian (Shalikashvili), Laotian (Khammoungkhoune), or Indian (Umamaheswaran), American family names are becoming megasyllabic—and people are learning to spell and pronounce names with which they might not have been comfortable a decade ago. Discuss family names (surnames). Why do we need them? Where do they come from? Have children state their surnames as you write them on the chalkboard. Observe the variety of names in the classroom. Some are long and some are short. Some have only one syllable (Wong) and others contain several syllables (Asakura, Rodríguez, Anderson).

Use surnames in classroom learning experiences. Have students line up alphabetically for lunch. Younger students can line up according to the first letter only, while older students can check the second and third letters as needed for more precise order.

Discuss the characteristics of surnames. "Mc" and "Mac" names originated in Ireland and Scotland, for example. Let students make generalizations about the names represented in their classroom, for example:

- We have many Spanish names: Castañeda, Chávez, Feliciano, Vásquez.
- Chinese names are short: Wang, Lee, Ching.
- Many Vietnamese people have the same last name, but aren't related: Nguyen, Ng, Huynh.

Family Names in Different Cultures

Different cultures have different rules for family names, or last names. In English-speaking countries, most children take the last name of the father. Some countries use both the mother's and father's names. In other countries, parents give different forms of the father's first and last names to male and female children.

In Spanish, for example, a person's surname consists of the father's family name followed by the mother's family name.

Teresa	Pérez	Gutiérrez
	(father)	(mother)
Carlos	Chávez	Martínez
	(father)	(mother)

Sometimes the word *y* (and) is inserted between the surnames of the father and mother, for example; Juan López y Benavente. Juan would be called Señor López, however, and his name would be under L in the telephone directory. Likewise, Teresa and Carlos would be listed as follows:

> Pérez Gutiérrez, Teresa
> Chávez Martínez, Carlos

Some women have rejected the patrilineal custom of passing on only the father's name by choosing to maintain their mother's family name or adopting an alternative family name as a personal expression. In addition, as more women keep their names after marriage, children are showing up with many variations on both parents' names, from hyphenated versions to creative combinations. Divorce and "blended" families contribute to these changes in naming. In the classroom, you cannot assume that all members of a family share the same surname.

Origins of Names

Family names are interesting to children when they discover the meanings that lie behind them. They can easily see that those names that have *-son* or *-sen* at the end carry the meaning "son of"; for example, Anderson, Christianson, Petersen, and Williamson. One of the most common names is Johnson, son of John. Endings that mean *son of* in other languages include *-ez* (Spanish), *-tse* (Chinese), *-wicz* (Polish), and *-ov* (Russian and other Slavic languages).

> Rodríguez (or Rodrígues) = son of Rodrigo (Roger)
> Ivanov = son of Ivan (John)

Many last names are associated with a person's line of work; for instance, Carpenter, Farmer, Baker, Miller, and Smith (blacksmith). Characteristics of a person often led to the use of other names, such as Young, Black, Long, White, and Little.

Surnames can also represent a painful history. Africans brought to the United States as slaves were taken away from their families and their names. Slaves had no last name of their own; instead, they were given their owner's family name. When we talk about surnames indicating pride in one's heritage, it is also important to recognize that African American surnames often preserve the memory of slavery. Leaders such as Sojourner Truth (once Isabella van Wagener) and Malcolm X (once Malcolm Little) chose to cast off these humiliating reminders.

For names of foreign origin, use a dictionary for that language. Set out on a discovery trip in which all can participate as they help each other find the origins of their family names.

Study of Names

If students become especially interested in names, you might want to begin a more extensive study of American names. Look for the following books that provide information about the meanings of common names and their origins:

Eloise Lambert and Mario Pei. *Our Names: Where They Came from and What They Mean.* Lothrop, 1960.

C. M. Mathews. *How Surnames Began.* Lutterworth Press, 1967.

Charles Panati. *Browser's Book of Beginnings.* Houghton Mifflin, 1984.

Milton Meltzer. *A Book about Names.* Crowell, 1985.

Young students will appreciate the following book:

Mary Lee and Richard Lee, *Last Names First—and Some First Names Too.* Westminster Press, 1985.

WHERE WE COME FROM

As students begin to bring significant parts of themselves, their home, and their family into the school setting, they discover that school is not just for learning about other people and other places, unfamiliar and unconnected facts and skills. Teachers model active learning when they show students how to connect themselves with what they are learning.

A Family Tree

Students can ask their families about family history and write the information on a chart, such as the diagram on p. 70. They can interview their parents and any other relatives to assemble as much information as possible. Younger children can construct a family tree using the information they collect.

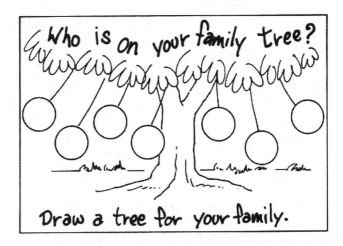

When introducing this kind of activity, be aware that parents may be offended by this potential invasion of privacy. Therefore, it is important to discuss the project in the class-room first so that children have a clear sense of your intent, namely, developing *pride in the family,* the importance of remembering our ancestors, our *roots.* You might, for example, tell the group something of your own origins.

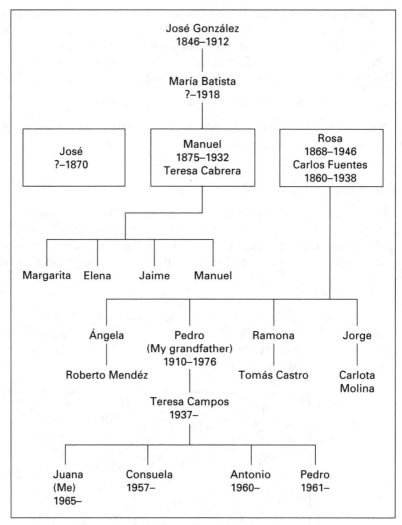

The Family Tree of Juana Fuentes

What Is Genealogy?

Introduce the big word *genealogy* (notice the spelling), which means the study of lineage, family history. Many people trace their family history as a matter of pride. Today there are societies focusing on such study.

An interesting book for upper elementary and junior high students is *Who Do You Think You Are? Digging for Your Family Roots* by Suzanne Hilton (Westminster Press, 1976).

Younger students will enjoy *Rosy Cole Discovers America!* by Sheila Greenwald (Little, Brown, 1992) in which Rosy, disappointed in her ordinary immigrant ancestors, invents a royal past for herself.

Families Differ

Discuss the topic: What is a typical family? Students will probably arrive at the stereo-typed perception of a family as a mother, father, and two children. They may even feel that the boy is the older of the two children.

Is this what families are really like? How many families represented in the classroom consist of two parents and two children? What other arrangements do the children know about? List them on the chalkboard.

Father   Mother   One Child
Father   Mother   More than Two Children
Mother   One Child
Grandmother   Three Children
Father   Two Children
Father   Mother   One Child   Grandfather

The point of this discussion is to show children that families differ. It also opens up an opportunity for students to talk about their own families, something about which they may have felt uncomfortable. It helps to know that other parents have been divorced or that someone else's parent has died.

Related topics that can be discussed without evaluation include the following:

• Some mothers work and some do not.
• Sometimes relatives live together.
• Some children have a mother, a father, a stepmother, and a stepfather.
• Some children have half-brothers and half-sisters.
• What constitutes a family?
• Some children are adopted.

Special Families

Most discussions of families presume the existence of a mother and a father, even when only one parent lives at home. However, there are children whose family consists of two Moms or two Dads. These children go to school like any other children. In addition, students may know of such families in the community. Classroom discussion of families headed by same-sex partners requires considerable sensitivity, yet open and careful discus-sion can allow children to feel more comfortable without exposing them to public humili-ation and thoughtless ridicule by other children.

In your discussion, you can help students move from the stereotype of the nuclear family to the concept that a family can be built in many different ways and is held together by bonds of love and responsibility. Homophobia, fear of or discrimination against people because of their homosexual orientation, is based on an intolerance for differences, just like prejudices such as racism and anti-Semitism. And just as with these other prejudices, the fear of differences correlates closely with labeling others inferior or disgusting, and making them a target for violence.

A book such as Christina Salat's *Living in Secret* (Bantam, 1993), written for inter-mediate students, is useful for raising these issues in class. It presents the story of a girl who has to lie about her life with her mother and her mother's "girlfriend" and the effects that this concealment has on her.

Books about Different Family Arrangements

Children's books are helpful in exposing children to different family arrangements. It is helpful for all children to have a broadened perspective of this institution as it is rapidly changing in our society. Here are a few titles that you might want for your library:

Primary Grades

Karen Hess. *Lavender.* Holt, 1993. Codie's aunt is having a baby, and Codie wonders if her aunt will still have time for her.

David Kherdian. *A Song for Uncle Harry.* Illustrated by Nonny Hogrogian. Philomel, 1989. Set in the 1930s, this story describes the special relationship between Pete and Uncle Harry.

Anne Herbert Scott. *Sam.* Illustrated by Symeon Shimin. Philomel, 1992. Reissue of an old favorite. Sam's family don't seem to want him around. Finally they realize he needs a job of his own.

Camille Yarbrough. *Cornrows.* Illustrated by Carole Byard. Coward, 1979. As the girls have their hair braided into cornrows, Grammaw and Mama entertain them with stories of their African origins.

Paul Zindel. *I Love My Mother.* Harper and Row, 1975. Mother and boy.

Joan Lexau. *Me Day.* Dial, 1971. Young black boy visits with divorced father.

Lucille Clifton. *Everett Anderson's Nine Months Long.* Holt, 1987. Everett's mother has remarried and is going to have a baby. Look for other stories about Everett, an African American boy.

Upper Elementary Grades

Brenda Wilkinson. *Ludell.* Harper and Row, 1975. Grandmother and fifth-grade girl; unwed mother does not live with them.

Zilpha K. Snyder. *The Witches of Worm.* Atheneum, 1972. Twelve-year-old girl and divorced mother.

Rose Blue. *A Month of Sundays.* Watts, 1972. Boy and divorced mother.

Charlotte Anker. *Last Night I Saw Andromeda.* Walck, 1975. Eleven-year-old girl and mother; father visits.

Melrose Cooper. *Life Riddles.* Holt, 1993. With Daddy gone and the family on welfare, mother tries to keep the family together.

Candy Dawson Boyd. *Chevrolet Saturdays.* Macmillan, 1993. Joey, a fifth grader, can't accept his mother's remarriage, but his family understands him.

Marc Talbert. *The Purple Heart.* HarperCollins, 1992. Luke's picture of his dad as a war hero doesn't match the man who comes home.

Patricia MacLachlan. *Journey.* Delacorte, 1991. Journey's mother leaves him when he is eleven. He has to learn to accept her for what she is.

Susan Beth Pfeffer. *Make Believe*. Holt, 1993. Carrie and Jill's friendship is affected by Jill's parents' divorce.

Harriet Langsam Sobol. *We Don't Look Like Our Mom and Dad*. Coward, 1984. This is the story, in photographs, of two Korean boys adopted by an American couple. The boys learn to develop pride in being both Korean and American.

When you read such stories as part of your regular time for reading aloud to the class, you help students feel comfortable knowing that there are other young people like themselves; and you provide a safe environment for discussing potentially difficult topics.

Food as Cultural Identity

One area where ethnic diversity has been much appreciated is food. Food habits and the preparation of traditional dishes are central to the identity of a culture, and they linger long after other cultural characteristics are lost. Because sharing food is such a positive experience, food is also a subject that breaks down barriers between members of different cultures.

Teachers can present food from different cultures as a yearlong theme, in a special unit, or as a follow-up activity to another unit (such as a study of haiku poetry). The following concepts can be developed from studying food in other cultures:

- People of all groups have a contribution to make.
- People are more alike than they are different.
- Differences in customs and attitudes can be an asset to society.
- Prejudice and stereotyping are usually based on lack of information.
- Understanding others will enrich our own lives.

Favorite Foods

Start a discussion about foods and different customs by asking students what they eat for breakfast. Write some of the different responses on the board. Why does this variety exist? Some students may have invented unique breakfast menus, whereas others eat foods that are representative of a particular culture. What do they consider a "typical" American breakfast? Is that what they eat? Would they like to eat a "different" kind of breakfast? Why or why not?

Use this discussion to talk about eating habits as an example of a custom, based on a culture. Students can begin to see themselves as inheritors of a cultural tradition, and other students as representatives of different cultural traditions. You also can point out examples of cross-cultural borrowing, as students suggest foods they like that have come from other cultures.

Students will be curious to find out what the other students in the class eat everyday and what the differences and similarities are. Have students keep a log of what and when they eat in one day, including snacks; then share this list with the class. What do they notice? Does everybody eat exactly the same foods at the same time? Why not? Discuss influences on variation such as individual taste, family customs, cultural background, and examples set by other people.

Snacks—A Universal Food

Everybody loves snacks. Have students prepare and conduct a survey to find out which snacks are most popular. Brainstorm as a class what questions to ask (What do you eat? How many? Where? Favorite?) and whom to ask (other classes, friends, family). Ask students to write their predictions for the results of the survey. Develop a form to record results and set a deadline for reporting back. When you have assembled a quantity of data, discuss how to organize it in an easy-to-understand way. Finally, when you have analyzed the data and compared your predictions against the conclusions, write a report for the school newspaper or make copies for the school.

You can develop a unit on nutrition based on this information. In presenting the food groups and nutritional needs, focus on the ways different groups meet the same dietary requirements. Not everybody eats dairy products, for example. Many Asians, Africans, East Europeans, and people from those backgrounds cannot tolerate the lactose in milk, cheese, and ice cream. Also, many food charts do not include the diversity of foods that children actually eat, from tortillas to rice porridge.

Food around the World

Using a map of the world, find out what people eat in other countries. Every country and culture has some version of bread, rice, potato, or other starch. In what countries do people eat rice? Where do they eat noodles? Is the bread that people in India eat similar to or different from the bread that people eat in your community? Students' exposure to different national or regional cuisines and food customs may vary, but they can all share what they know about their family's cooking. If possible, invite parents or others from the neighborhood to the class to demonstrate how to prepare some traditional foods. The following books will help you plan this study:

Patricia C. Marden and Suzanne I. Barchers. *Cooking Up World History: Multicultural Recipes and Resources.* Teacher Ideas Press, 1994. The book surveys cookery in more than twenty countries and regions, providing recipes and information to help students make the connection between culture, food, and history.

Milton Meltzer. *The Amazing Potato.* HarperCollins, 1992. This book for young people tells the incredible history of the potato, weaving in stories of the Incas, European conquerors, wars, and immigrants.

Jack Weatherford. *Native Roots: How the Indians Enriched America.* Fawcett, 1991. An eye-opening account for adults of the vital role of Indian civilizations in the making of the United States.

Raymond Sokolov. *Why We Eat What We Eat: How the Encounter between the New World and the Old Changed the Way Everyone on the Planet Eats.* Summit, 1991. Essays and references on food provide a humorous exploration of the post-Columbus migration of ingredients and ideas from the New World to the Old and back again.

These following two books are from a series introducing children to the food of different cultures.

Alphonse Bisignano. *Cooking the Italian Way.* Lerner, 1982.

Danuta Zamojska-Hutchins. *Cooking the Polish Way.* Lerner, 1984.

Class Recipe Book

Collect recipes to be duplicated and made into a collection for each student to take home. Students can bring in recipes for their favorite foods or a special dish from their family or culture. Each student can explain his or her recipe and talk about the preparation and ingredients. If possible, invite a parent or a member of the family to come to the class and show everyone how to make one of these dishes. (You might even ask students to bring in samples of their favorite foods.)

Class work with recipes leads naturally to a study of measurement (weight, mass) and the mathematics of conversion. Students can practice measuring with different instruments and multiplying quantities for larger groups. Students may also want to investigate the scientific questions of cooking; for example, how food changes from raw to cooked.

International Foods

When we borrow a food from another country, we often borrow the name for it, too. See how many foods the students can name that come from different countries. What countries are these from?

sauerkraut	spaghetti	enchiladas	macaroni
tortillas	quiche	wontons	croissant

The Origin of "American" Foods

Students can investigate the origin of such typically American foods as pizza, hot dogs, and hamburgers. Where do noodles come from? (The Italians got them from China.) What common foods come from the New World (and hence were unknown in Europe before Columbus)? (Tomato, potato, chocolate.) Do students know that the tomato used to be considered poisonous when raw?

Another area for students to research is the variety of regional names for food items. One popular sandwich is called a hoagy, grinder, submarine, poor boy, or Dagwood, depending on where you live. Where does the word *sandwich* come from?

Food Prejudices

People in most cultures have strong ideas about which foods are considered acceptable for eating and which are not. For example, many people in the United States turn up their noses at foods that are delicacies in other countries, such as snails and frog's legs. Likewise, people in other countries think the American custom of eating corn on the cob is disgusting because to them, that food is fit only for pigs. Sometimes, just altering the name can change people's willingness to try new foods. People who would never eat squid may try *calamari* (Italian for squid).

Children are notoriously reluctant to try new foods. Have students investigate their own food prejudices. Select several unusual foods (you can find imported canned foods at most supermarkets). Tell the students the name of each food or show them the labels. Ask them to write a short description/reaction to the idea of eating the food. Then have them taste each food while blindfolded and write down their impressions without identifying the food.

Afterwards, discuss the difference in reactions. Would they have ordered any of the foods in a restaurant or tried them at home? Did they react more positively when they didn't know what they were tasting? What difference does being able to see the food make? Are they more likely now to try something new? Why or why not?

FOCUS ON WOMEN: THE 51 PERCENT MINORITY

How does the term "minority" relate to women? Despite their numbers, women earn 69 percent as much as men with the same education and are disproportionately concentrated in jobs at the low end of the ladder both in earning power and prestige. These statistics are evidence of the historical pattern of overt and subtle discrimination that defines a minority group. When does this discrimination begin? Many of us would claim that schools provide an equal environment for boys and girls. Certainly Title IX, which outlawed sex discrimination in education in 1972, has had a tremendous impact on opportunities for girls, especially in sports. But, even in elementary school, girls are underserved and underrepresented. From textbook phrasing such as "the pioneers and their wives," implying that only men were the pioneers, to a curriculum that has focused on the deeds of "great men," schooling has ignored the needs of girls. We now have increasing evidence of the often unconscious ways teachers discriminate against girls in their classrooms. The behaviors that are praised in girls—compliance, selflessness, silence—tend to make them less adept competitors in the work force. Meanwhile, the qualities needed to thrive in American life—strength, courage, independence—are promoted among the boys. Despite current awareness of gender issues, today's children seem to be as locked into these sex-role stereotypes as were the children of earlier decades.

How can we reduce sexism and promote gender equity in our classrooms? A gender-fair curriculum, claims Gretchen Wilbur, quoted in the AAUW report *How Schools Short-change Girls* (p. 64) would:

1. Acknowledge and affirm variation among students.
2. Be inclusive of all students.
3. Present accurate information.
4. Affirm differences in values.
5. Represent multiple perspectives.
6. Be integrated, weaving in males and females.

Research shows that one teacher can make a difference for students. In your selection of materials, in your discussions, in your responses to students, you can communicate the message that both boys and girls should speak up, that all students need to learn how to work together, and that girls are just as capable in math and science as boys.

What Do Students Know?

When beginning a unit focusing on women and equity, assign a brief exercise to check what students know about the contributions of women. Ask students to write down, without discussing their answers with anyone, the names of ten famous women, not including actresses, entertainers, or musicians.

After allowing time for students to complete their list, discuss what they learned from the exercise. Is this a difficult task? Could everyone think of ten names? Write on the board some of the names that students suggested. What do students notice about these names—are they repeated many times? What are these women famous for? What gaps in students' knowledge of women's accomplishments show up in this exercise? Use this discussion to plan further study as students themselves identify areas they need to explore.

Sex-Role Stereotypes

Ask students to make individual lists of characteristics of men and women. After each has had time to write a number of items, ask each one to contribute something to add to a class compilation of these characteristics. The list may include items like this:

Men	*Women*
Don't cry	Cook meals for family
Play sports	Wear makeup
Support the family	Giggle a lot
Fix things around the house	Do the grocery shopping

Discuss the items on the list to find out if all men or all women do these things. Do women do some of the things on the men's list and do men do some of the things on the women's list? Have students respond from their personal experience. Afterward, have students rewrite each item as a sentence with an adverb such as *usually, frequently, always, never, sometimes, rarely, etc.,* for example:

- Men often play sports.
- Women usually cook meals for the family.

Role Reversals

In the primary classroom, you can talk with students about mommies and daddies, boys and girls, using dolls, tools, and cooking equipment for role-play activities. While children generally hold rigid sex-role stereotypes at this age, listen to their comments about appropriate roles for males and females and suggest alternative options. Ask questions to help them reflect on what they are saying: Can mommies use tools? Do daddies know how to cook?

Sexual Harassment

Because we tend to associate the problem with adults, we may neglect the issue of sexual harassment among young people. Although we as teachers may not want to acknowledge the presence of sexual behavior and talk in the elementary school, part of making the classroom fair for boys and girls is raising everyone's awareness of behaviors that we consider unacceptable.

Begin a discussion of this sort by defining sexual harassment: unwelcomed sexual behavior or talk. This may include activities such as calling girls or boys sexual names, public humiliation of girls or boys by referring to their body parts, and touching or grabbing others in inappropriate places. Ask if anyone has noticed this kind of behavior. How would they feel if it happened to them? What could they do about it? Brainstorm suggestions to resolve such incidents if they occur in the future. Establish the students' right to complain to someone in authority if this happens to them or if they see someone else involved.

Many students are confused about how to approach other students, particularly of the opposite sex. Talk with them about positive strategies to get to know another person. Develop a list of approaches students recommend if someone wants to become friends with them. This kind of discussion in a safe environment, with the teacher as mediator, may defuse some of the tension surrounding friendships between boys and girls at this stage.

Doctors and Other "Wise Men"

Students have absorbed many rigid ideas about men and women and the stereotypical occupations for each. Assess their awareness of one common stereotype by asking them to draw a picture of a doctor. After they have completed their drawings, talk about the similarities and differences among the drawings. What conclusion can they reach about the image of a doctor? (Talk about characteristics of race, sex, dress, age, etc.) Now ask them to describe their own doctor. Do the pictures they drew match the doctors they know, or do the pictures represent a generalized idea, a stereotype? Where do students think this idea comes from if not from their experience? Can they think of other ways they might be influenced?

Feature books in the classroom that subvert these sex-typed expectations. In *The Straight Line Wonder,* well-known Australian teacher and writer Mem Fox tells the story of a boy who wants to become a ballet dancer, despite the misgivings of his family. Another of her books, *The Secret World of Leo Lipinski,* presents a male character who escapes the conventional career his family has planned for him in order to become an artist. Andrea Davis Pinkney's *Alvin Ailey,* illustrated by Brian Pinkney (Hyperion, 1993), is a colorful biography of an African American man who became a dancer and choreographer, eventually leading his own dance company and revolutionizing modern dance by incorporating African American music.

Take Our Daughters to Work Day

On April 28, 1993, many companies participated in a program sponsored by the Ms. Foundation to introduce girls aged nine to fifteen to opportunities for women in the workplace. In your classroom, support these efforts to build girls' self-esteem by planning to expose them to a greater variety of careers. Contact companies associated with your school and invite women who hold different positions to speak to the class. Survey parents and friends for suggestions of women who have interesting jobs. Feature photographs, news articles, and biographies of diverse women with a variety of careers. Use students' stereotypes as starting points for discussion. They probably know that girls can be secretaries, but do they know that girls can be financial planners? Extend their awareness of the possibilities. Is baseball only for boys? Pose questions that connect careers with early education and training. What skills do you need to be a maintenance supervisor?

Influential Women: Past and Present

Women have been left out of most accounts of history. They are rarely seen as developers of ideas, initiators of events, or inventors of technology.

The National Women's Hall of Fame, located in Seneca Falls, New York, conducted a survey of more than three hundred historians and scholars to determine who were considered the most influential American women of the twentieth century. The following are the top ten names. How many of these women are familiar to students?

1. Eleanor Roosevelt
2. Jane Addams
3. Rosa Parks
4. Margaret Sanger
5. Margaret Mead

6. Charlotte Perkins Gilman
7. Betty Friedan
8. Barbara Jordan
9. Helen Keller
10. Alice Paul

Use this list as a starting point for a discussion of women's achievements. Groups of students can research each woman's life and accomplishments to determine why she was voted into the Women's Hall of Fame.

This list includes two African American women but there are no Asian, Latina, or Native American women. Challenge students to develop their own list: Who do they think belongs in the Women's Hall of Fame?

Offer students biographies that illustrate the range of women's roles, from politics to science to sports. The following are exceptionally well written:

Russell Freedman. *Eleanor Roosevelt: A Life of Discovery.* Clarion, 1993. Shows how Roosevelt overcame lack of support from her family, who considered her an ugly duckling, and her own shyness to create a new role as First Lady. She established herself as an individual, not just a politician's wife, and continued to make significant contributions after her husband's death.

Patricia McKissack. *Sojourner Truth: Ain't I a Woman?* Scholastic, 1992. A biography for intermediate students presents the life of the extraordinary woman who was born Isabella van Wagener in 1797 and died in 1883. Although she couldn't read or write, she became an eloquent speaker for the abolition of slavery.

Women in Folklore

Positive models and stories of successful women can help us persevere, overcoming obstacles and others' lack of faith. Folktales, a traditional source of community wisdom, often reflect stereotypical roles for men and women. However, alternative models do exist. Present tales of strong women to counteract popular folklore images, such as Cinderella and Sleeping Beauty, of passive women who need a man to rescue them.

Robert San Souci. *Cut from the Same Cloth: American Women of Myth, Legend and Tall Tale.* Illustrated by Brian Pinkney. Philomel, 1993. Less well known tales of strong and determined women, including African and Native American traditions.

Ethel Johnston Phelps. *The Maid of the North: Feminist Folk Tales from around the World.* Holt, 1981. Stories with interesting and clever heroines; a good resource for storytelling.

Suzanne I. Barchers. *Wise Women: Folk and Fairy Tales from around the World.* Teacher Ideas Press, 1990. Collection of stories and teaching ideas.

Aaron Shepard. *Savitri: A Tale of Ancient India.* Whitman, 1992. A strong-woman story from the Mahabharata.

Featuring Women Artists

Show students that art is not the sole property of dead, white, European males. The following books will broaden students' ideas about art and may inspire some to follow in the footsteps of these famous women.

Leslie Sills. *Visions: Stories about Women Artists.* Whitman, 1993. This collection features Mary Cassatt, Leonora Carrington, Betye Saar, and Mary Frank. Although they came from different backgrounds and lived at different times, they all had to overcome similar obstacles to pursue their careers as artists.

Leslie Sills. *Inspirations: Stories about Women Artists.* Whitman, 1989. An introduction to four diverse women artists (Georgia O'Keeffe, Frida Kahlo, Alice Neel, Faith Ringgold) with brief biographies and generous color reproductions of their works.

Peggy Roalf. *Self-Portraits.* Hyperion, 1993.

Peggy Roalf. *Children.* Hyperion, 1993. These books show how different artists have treated the same theme. The artists selected include women and men of diverse backgrounds. *Self-Portraits* features Frida Kahlo on the cover; *Children* features Mary Cassatt.

Robyn Montana Turner. *Faith Ringgold.* Little, Brown, 1993. (From the series *Portraits of Women Artists for Children.* Other books in the series include *Rosa Bonheur, Georgia O'Keeffe, Mary Cassatt,* and *Frida Kahlo.*) From her childhood in Harlem in the 1930s to her current stature as a recognized artist, this detailed biography follows Faith Ringgold's life and development as an artist, setting it in the context of the African American experience of the time. This artist is particularly interesting because she is alive today; she uses African and African American materials, content, and techniques; and she has turned her story quilt paintings into children's books such as *Tar Beach.*

Countering Sex Stereotypes in Children's Literature

Frequently you will encounter examples of stereotyped thinking and behavior in books that you use with students in the classroom. Over 75 percent of the characters in children's books are male. In addition, the male characters tend to take action, while the female characters stand on the sidelines. Stereotypes weaken the value of these books because they result in cardboard characters and predictable plots. However, you cannot eliminate all examples of stereotyping. Instead, help students practice critical thinking skills by identifying stereotypes and evaluating sexism in the books they read. (For more information about stereotypes, see Chapter 4.) An example of such stereotyping is *Sylvester and the Magic Pebble* by William Steig (Simon and Schuster, 1969). Although the characters are drawn as donkeys, they conform to stereotyped sex roles. The mother donkey wears an apron and acts "helpless," the father donkey sits smoking his pipe and reading the newspaper while his wife sweeps under his feet.

When you discuss stories with students, ask them to consider the following questions. Could the male characters be changed to female? The female characters changed to male? How would these changes affect the story? Students can choose to rewrite a familiar story with the characters' genders reversed. An alternative is to retell the story from another character's point of view.

Positive Models in Books for Children

We know that books transmit values to children, particularly when the messages are subtle. As much as possible, choose books that portray males and females in nonstereotyped roles and in multicultural settings. Share with students old favorites such as *Madeline* by Ludwig Bemelmans and *Pippi Longstocking* by Astrid Lindgren. Here are some more recent books that you will enjoy.

Especially for the primary grades

Jay Williams. *Petronella*. Parents, 1974. This king's daughter does not want to play the passive princess.

Camille Yarbrough. *The Shimmershine Queens*. Putnam, 1989. Self-esteem and achievement counter the negative images of sexism and racism that face black girls.

For older students

Patricia Wrede. *Dealing with Dragons*. Harcourt, Brace, Jovanovich, 1990. Princess Cimorene is not going to wait around for someone to rescue her. Look for more books about Cimorene's adventures.

Jerry Spinelli. *There's a Girl in my Hammerlock*. Simon and Schuster, 1991. Maisie faces opposition from her family and friends when she chooses wrestling.

Carol Ann Duffy. *I Wouldn't Thank You for a Valentine: Poems for Young Feminists*. Illustrated by Trisha Rafferty. Holt, 1994. Woman poets from many cultures and backgrounds tell of ways in which women are phenomenal.

Tryntje Van Ness Seymour. *The Gift of Changing Woman*. Holt, 1993. When an Apache girl comes of age, there is a special ceremony to teach her the story of creation and her place in the world.

Sex-Typed Play

Even children's toys and games perpetuate ideas of sex-role stereotypes. Ask students to list examples of boys' toys and girls' toys. What kinds of toys are considered suitable for boys? For girls? Might girls want to play with games that are supposed to be for boys? Or boys play with girls' games? What would happen? (Who has the most interesting, inventive games?) This discussion should result in increased options for boys' and girls' play and decreased negative response to behavior that does not fit sex-role stereotypes.

Students can also investigate use of sex-role stereotypes in the marketing of toys and games. Look at television commercials, packaging, and names. Can you tell whether they are directed at boys or girls? Why would manufacturers choose to do this? If students study examples of stereotyping, they may want to write letters to the companies, explaining their investigation and their findings. They can also make recommendations for changes.

Sources of Information for Teaching about Women and Gender Equity

Myself and Women Heroes in My World; Women at Work, Home and School; Women as Members of Groups; and *Women as Members of Communities*. These integrated social studies/language arts elementary curriculum units (1985) are available from

National Women's History Project, 7738 Bell Road, Windsor, CA 95492–8518. They include both famous (Harriet Tubman) and not-so-famous (Dolores Huerta) women of the past and the present.

Carol Burgoa and Barbara Tomin. *Multicultural Women's History Curriculum Unit.* Available from NWHP (see address above). A variety of cross-curricular activities for intermediate grades cover five women of different ethnic backgrounds and time periods: Mary Shadd Cary, abolitionist; Tye Leung Schulze, immigration officer at Angel Island (CA); Frances Willard, leader of the WCTU; Felisa Rincon de Gautier, former mayor of San Juan, Puerto Rico; and Ada Deer, Native American rights activist.

National Women's History Project. *Women's History Resources.* Updated regularly. This book contains state and national lists of information, people, and publishers as well as annotated lists of resources for Native American, Asian, Hispanic, and African American women.

Edward T. James and Janet Wilson James, eds. *Notable American Women 1607–1950.* 3 vols. Short biographies of 1,359 women who influenced their time and society, including many from diverse ethnic backgrounds about whom little is known.

Barbara Sicherman and Carol Hurd Green. *Notable American Women: The Modern Period.* A companion to the earlier work includes 442 biographies of historically significant women who died between 1951 and 1975.

Edith Blicksilver. *The Ethnic American Woman: Problems, Protests, Lifestyle.* The voices of women, both historical and contemporary, representing twenty-five different ethnic groups.

REFLECTIONS

Students need to reflect on who they are and what forces have influenced them. As teachers, we offer them that opportunity by bringing their own background into the classroom. We offer books and activities that help them recognize themselves. We value what they have to bring to the classroom instead of making them over in one image. We model learning as a process of integrating and connecting who we are with what we know.

APPLICATIONS

1. In your learning journal, write a response to the Hillel quote that opens this chapter. Many approaches to cross-cultural learning have focused on learning about "the other." In what ways might learning about yourself strengthen your learning about others? In your experience, what has helped you to understand people from other groups?

2. Reflect on your learning experiences, formal and informal, in school and out, as a child and as an adult. What modes of learning have been most effective for you—oral or written explanation, trial and error, direct observation, guided practice, sink or swim? What has made learning difficult for you? How would you characterize your own learning style? Discuss this with others in your cooperative learning group and compare learning experiences. Are there significant differences between learning as a child and learning as an adult? What can you use from your own learning history to make you a better teacher?

3. How do you plan to organize your classroom and your
equity for both sexes? Plan a unit on sex-role stereotyping. What mate..
will you use? How will you assess student learning?

4. Where do *you* come from? What in your family history has brought you
point in your life, has made you what you are today? Draw up a chart of your famn.,
history. Are there relatives who have had a particular influence on you, through family
stories or by example? What different cultural, linguistic, and historical forces have resulted in your presence here today?

Exploring Further

The AAUW Report. *How Schools Shortchange Girls.* AAUW and NEA, 1992.

Mary Field Belenky, Blythe McVicker Clinchy, Nancy Rule Goldberger, and Jill Mattuck Tarule.
Women's Ways of Knowing: The Development of Self, Voice and Mind. Basic Books, 1986.

Michele Borba. *Esteem Builders: A K–8 Self-Esteem Curriculum for Improving Student Achievement, Behavior, and School Climate.* Jalmar Press, 1989.

Lyn Mikel Brown and Carol Gilligan. *Meeting at the Crossroads.* Ballantine, 1993.

Jack Canfield and Harold Wells. *100 Ways to Enhance Self-Concept in the Classroom.* 2nd edition.
Allyn and Bacon, 1994.

California State Department of Education. *Beyond Language: Social and Cultural Factors in
Schooling Language Minority Students.* 1986.

Courtney Cazden and Hugh Mehan. "The Social Context of Teaching." In Maynard Reynolds, ed.
Knowledge Base for the Beginning Teacher. Pergamon, 1989.

Louise Derman-Sparks. *Anti-Bias Curriculum: Tools for Empowering Young Children.* National
Association for the Education of Young Children, 1990.

Carol Gilligan. *In a Different Voice: Psychological Theory and Women's Development.* Harvard
University Press, 1982.

Kevin Leman. *Bringing Up Kids without Tearing Them Down.* Delacorte Press. 1993.

Anne Macdonald. *Feminine Ingenuity: How Women Inventors Changed America.* Ballantine, 1992.

Ana Consuelo Matiella. *Positively Different: Creating a Bias-Free Environment for Young Children.*
ETR Associates, 1991.

Patricia Ramsey. *Teaching and Learning in a Diverse World: Multicultural Education for Younger
Children.* Teachers College Press, 1987.

Myra and David Sadker. *Failing at Fairness: How America's Schools Cheat Girls.* Macmillan,
1994.

Robert Slavin, Nancy Karweit, and Barbara Wasik. *Preventing Early School Failure: Research on
Effective Strategies.* Allyn and Bacon, 1994.

Peter Smagorinsky. *Expression: Multiple Intelligences in the English Class.* National Council of
Teachers of English TRIP booklet, 1991.

Barbara Thomson. *Words Can Hurt You: Beginning a Program of Anti-Bias Education.* Addison-
Wesley, 1993.

Diane Williams. *Self-Esteem.* Teacher-Created Materials, 1990.

Let us put our minds together and see what life can make for our children.

Tatanka Iotanko
Sitting Bull, Lakota Sioux, 1877

4
❖
Making All Students Feel Included

All children come to school as members of specific cultural groups. Along with their native language, they learned a particular way of being in the world; they were socialized into their culture. And they come to school carrying their parents' hopes for the future.

In this chapter we consider multicultural learning through the lens of culture. The Brazilian educator Paulo Freire defines culture as anything that humans make. This broad definition serves to distinguish things cultural from things natural. Culture is what we elaborate on the basic biological framework that we are given. Less effort is required to focus on its visible, concrete aspects: food, shelter, music, clothing, art. However, on a deeper level, culture is invisible. We may be unaware of how our culture shapes our interpretation of the world, our perception of reality, our sense of what is normal. But the omnipresence of culture is expressed in the remark, "That's just the ways things are done around here."

From family and community members, children unconsciously absorb standards of behavior, attitudes towards authority, patterns of speaking, and spiritual values. But when they enter school, they are exposed to another set of values and expectations, called "school culture." In school, for example, students are expected to work independently and often competitively. They are called on to show off in front of others or to expose their imperfect reading. Rewards are given for speed and uniformity. How can we provide a bridge between students' home culture and the school? How can we keep students from feeling excluded? Today's multicultural classroom requires teaching that incorporates and responds to the many cultural influences affecting students' ability to learn.

The process of becoming a culturally responsive teacher has three facets. First, you have to learn about your own cultural background. Because so much of one's culture is taken for granted, this process entails making the unseen visible. Otherwise, you may unconsciously assume that the way you live is the only way to live (provincialism) or that your own cultural system is superior to others (ethnocentrism). Instead of glossing over the differences in the way people think and act, we want to draw conscious attention to them. The more we understand why we make the judgments we do, the more we will be able to accept how other people can reach different conclusions. The second facet of culturally responsive teaching involves learning about your students. Your students may, for example, know a language that you don't, practice a religious philosophy that is considerably older than your own, have made life-or-death choices that you hope never to face. A little humility, some admitted ignorance, and a willingness to learn more about others will help you cope with potentially overwhelming differences in culture. The third facet of culturally responsive teaching requires you to share your own culture, your customs and beliefs, with the students. By doing so, you model respect for others and demonstrate how culture is important in everyone's life. This reciprocity makes it easier for students to inquire and explore: what does it mean when someone . . . ? A culturally responsive teacher can be a valuable translator and guide for students, helping them bridge the gap between the familiar and the unknown.

After reading this chapter, you should be able to:
- Provide a welcoming environment in the classroom for all students.
- Develop a positive classroom climate.
- Plan lessons that expose stereotyping and prejudice.
- Introduce students to aspects of Native American history and culture.

GETTING ACQUAINTED

The first step in learning to work well together is getting to know one another. In today's schools, the students may not all come from the same community, so they may not be aware of backgrounds or experiences that they share with other students. In addition, a teacher who comes from a background different from that of the students must make an extra effort to get to know the students' community. Teachers can create unity among diverse students by helping students get to know one another, breaking down barriers of ignorance and suspicion, and providing the shared experience that creates group cohesiveness. The goal is to build an atmosphere of trust in the classroom. In order to learn, students need to feel comfortable taking risks and exposing themselves to the possibility of failure.

Welcoming the Child

Make a welcome message as clear as possible by displaying the word on a bulletin board. (If you have Spanish-speaking children in the classroom, use the word *bienvenido.)* Find out how to say *welcome* in other languages. Teach students several different ways to say *welcome.*

New Student Orientation

Challenge a group of older students to organize a "Welcome Wagon" that would assume responsibility for personally welcoming newcomers to the school. Students of all levels could be part of this team effort. Encourage students to brainstorm possibilities for making students feel at home in their new surroundings. They might ask themselves, "What would make me feel good about coming to a new school?" Here are some ideas.

- Introduce the student to several children who live near him or her.
- Meet the child at the principal's office to express a welcome and to introduce him or her to the classroom teacher.
- Give the newcomer a small gift, such as a welcome card made by students or a flower to pin on (if everyone knows this symbol, they can be encouraged to smile their own welcome or to say hello).
- Assign a buddy in the class to help the newcomer with classroom routines.

Ten Things about Me

An activity for the beginning of the year is to ask each student to write ten things about himself or herself. Students can list anything, for example:

> *Alice Hafoka*
> I get up at 5:30 each morning to deliver papers.
> I live next to Julio and Uriel.
> My favorite food is groundnut stew.

Introducing

Students can exchange the lists they wrote in the previous activity. Working in small groups, each person then introduces the student whose paper he or she received. The student introducing Alice might say:

> I'd like you to meet Alice Hafoka. She gets up at 5:30 every morning and makes breakfast for her brothers and sisters. I'm impressed—my mother won't let me cook anything on the stove. Her favorite food is groundnut stew. That's an African dish. Groundnuts are also called peanuts.

A Class Directory

Type a list of the students' names to give to the children in your room. You may include their addresses, birthdays, or other information that might interest the children as they become acquainted. They will be highly motivated to read this directory even though names of students and streets may be difficult.

Have students introduce themselves according to this listing. They may simply say, "I am Takasoto Watanabe. I live on Fairglen Avenue." Or they might add other information, such as what they like to do on Saturdays or where they were born. Ask the students what they would like to know about each other and what each is willing to share.

Perception of Others

A group that has been together for a period of time will benefit from sharing their perceptions of each other. Prepare a chart on which students record information. Give each child a copy of this chart, which he or she completes for everyone in the group.

Going around the circle, each person then tells the items he or she has written in the columns for a person. Naturally they will differ, but the items selected and the reasons given provide interesting insights that add to each person's understanding of other people.

	Color	Food	Car	Building
Miho				
Ajay				
Shawna				
Jesus				
Troy				
Shahid				

If you are working with a small group of students, include your own name on the chart. The students will be interested in how you perceive them, and their perceptions of you will be enlightening.

Origins and Differences

Because students are curious about one another, prepare a chart to describe the class. Use a map to show where students were born and where their families come from. Mark locations with pins and name tags. Connect the pins to the classroom location with yarn. Which students have come the farthest? How many students were born outside the United States? How many were born in a different state? Where have students traveled? Have any of them visited other countries?

What languages do the students speak? If you include the languages their parents speak, how many languages are represented in the classroom? Consider ways to use these differences as assets. Have students teach others a few words in another language. Ask students to tell the class about life in a different region. Was the weather different? Did they play different games? Ask newcomers what they found particularly different or hard to get used to in their new environment.

Children's Lore

Engage students in the study of children's folklore: riddle games, jump-rope rhymes, numbering chants, etc. Children who come from different regions or different ethnolinguistic backgrounds can compare their versions. Are the same rhymes used by children from different parts of the United States? The class can make a collection of the stories and verses that they collect. They may be surprised to learn that adult scholars study children's folklore.

For a description of the origins of this field, see Iona and Peter Opie, *The Lore and Language of Schoolchildren*. This work reports an extensive study of children in Britain. Students can compare the folklore that they collected with the British versions.

An American collection is *A Rocket in My Pocket: The Rhymes and Chants of Young Americans* by Carl Withers, which includes over four hundred verses.

BUILDING A COMMUNITY

Shared experiences through the year help bring students together. Remind students of past events and activities and help them reflect on the process of learning as it takes place. Students need guidance to find out how much they are alike underneath superficial differences.

Managing Conflict

What do people argue or fight about? Ask students to suggest areas where children and parents might disagree. Is it ever possible that both sides could be right? Does the biggest (or oldest or strongest) person always win?

Develop an analogy with a baseball game. Have students describe an argument and a baseball game. Write the characteristics on the board. Then ask students: "How is an argument like a baseball game?" Possible answers include the following:

- You make points off each other.
- One side wins.
- People get more and more involved.

Then ask them: "How is an argument different from a baseball game?" Possible answers include the following:

- You're not always on the same side.
- There's no umpire to make sure you fight fair.
- Both sides aren't evenly matched.

Although students may take time to warm up, they will enjoy this challenge as long as you reinforce the idea that there are no right or wrong answers.

Sharing Problems

After discussing situations that can lead to conflict, students may want to write their own examples of problems. These can be used for a finish-the-story activity (other students write an ending), creative drama (students act out the situation for the class to watch and comment on), or role-play (students take on the roles involved and develop them out of their own experience).

Playing a Part

Through role-play, students can experience potential sources of conflict and ways to reach an agreement in a nonthreatening way. Have the class generate a list of topics or situations. Even the shyest students will participate and contribute when they lose themselves in acting out the part of another person. The following are some guidelines to setting up a successful role-play.

1. Use props such as hats or masks to help students assume their roles.
2. Set a time limit. Keep role-plays short at first.
3. Assign students to partners or groups so that they don't always work with friends.

4. Give them an explicit, detailed situation or explanation to get started. Or have them draw the plot elements (who? what? where?) out of a box.

5. Start with focused sessions before you try open-ended, more complex situations.

6. Consider the best arrangement of the classroom and decide in advance where to place students.

7. Encourage all communication and praise originality.

Sample Topics for Role-Play

Role-play offers students a chance to think about and identify with the point of view of another person. Here are some topics that will stimulate heated discussion and involvement.

- Would you tell on a friend if you saw her break something but she told the teacher she didn't do it?
- All the other kids get a larger allowance than you do. Could you convince your parents to raise it?
- If you're at a friend's house and you forget the time and you get home really late, what would your parents (mother, father, guardian) say?
- Your parents only allow you to watch television at certain hours but you want to watch a particular program outside that time. Could you persuade them to change the rules, even if it is a school night?
- What if you borrow your friend's bike and then someone steals it? What should you say or do?
- All the other kids are calling the new student names. Would you join in? What would you do?
- The teacher asked each student to bring $4 for the class picnic. Your mother says she can't afford it but you're too embarrassed to tell the teacher. What should you do?

Facing Problems

Read books aloud occasionally about students who have problems. Talk about the characters and their problems with the group. You might use some of the following books:

Primary Grades

Joseph Kraus. *Leo, the Late Bloomer.* Windmill, 1971. A little tiger is slow about doing things, but he finally "blooms."

Cindy Wheeler. *Marmalade's Nap.* Knopf, 1983. A cat tries to find a quiet place to snooze.

John Steptoe. *Stevie.* Harper and Row, 1969. A young black boy resents having Stevie in his home but misses him when he is gone.

Charlotte Zolotow. *A Father Like That.* Harper and Row, 1971. A story of a small boy without a father.

Taro Yashima. *Crow Boy.* Viking, 1955. A young Japanese boy feels rejected at school until an understanding teacher helps.

Brinton Turkel. *The Adventures of Obadiah.* Viking, 1972. A young Quaker boy living in colonial Nantucket faces the problem of lying; see other books about Obadiah.

Diane Stanley. *The Conversation Club*. Macmillan, 1983. Peter Fieldmouse is welcomed to a new neighborhood.

Kevin Henkes. *Owen*. Greenwillow, 1993. The question of whether a tattered security blanket should go to school creates a family crisis for a young mouse.

Upper Elementary Grades

Maia Wojciechowska. *Shadow of a Bull*. Atheneum, 1964. The son of a great Spanish bullfighter fears being a coward.

Yoshiko Uchida. *Journey to Topaz; A Story of the Japanese-American Evacuation*. Scribner's, 1971. Yuki and her family were interned in Utah during World War II.

Virginia Sorenson. *Plain Girl*. Harcourt Brace Jovanovich, 1955. An Amish girl learns to think for herself.

Emily C. Neville. *Berries Goodman*. Harper and Row, 1965. Two city boys learn the meaning of prejudice, in this case, against Jews.

Jean Little. *Kate*. Harper and Row, 1971. In this sequel to *Look through My Window,* Kate learns to value her Jewish heritage.

Joseph Krumgold. *And Now Miguel*. Crowell, 1953. This is a moving story of New Mexican sheepherders and Miguel's problems of growing up.

Janet Lunn. *The Root Cellar*. Scribner's, 1983. An unhappy orphan discovers an exciting fantasy world.

Friendship

What is a friend? Why do we need friends? Read poems to students from the collection *I Like You, If You Like Me: Poems of Friendship* edited by Myra Cohn Livingston. These capsules of the special emotion called friendship can serve as springboards for discussion of this topic, which is so important to children. Provide opportunities for students to reflect on what friendship means to them by writing a story, creating a poem, or drawing a picture. "Publish" their efforts in a class book called *Friendship Is . . .* This book can be shared with other classes. Older students can read their stories or poetry to primary-grade students.

What Are Friends For?

How does it come about that friends can make us feel better about ourselves? Discuss the qualities of friendship with students to start them thinking about similarities and differences. Do we expect our friends to be just like ourselves? Why or why not? How are our relationships with our friends different from our relations with our brothers and sisters? Explore the dimensions of friendship through books that talk about how far we should go for the sake of a friend, or books honoring friendships that cross boundaries such as race, sex, or age.

Patricia Polacco. *Chicken Sunday.* Philomel, 1992. Two African American boys and a friend (the author as a girl) try to earn enough money to buy the boy's grandmother an Easter hat from a Jewish shopkeeper.

Lucille Clifton. *Everett Anderson's Friend*. Holt, 1976. Everett is disappointed in his new neighbor because she's a girl. But it turns out all right when he finds she can run and play ball.

Kevin Henkes. *Julius, the Baby of the World*. Greenwillow, 1990. An older sister finally acknowledges that her baby brother is someone special.

Marcia Savin. *The Moon Bridge*. Scholastic, 1992. The friendship of two fifth-grade girls survives the hatred and prejudice of World War II, even when Mitzi Fujimoto, a Japanese American, is sent to an internment camp.

Paulsen, Gary. *The Night the White Deer Died*. Delacorte, 1978. Explores the friendship between fifteen-year-old Janet, one of the few Anglos in her New Mexico community, and Billy Honcho, an old Pueblo Indian.

Mildred Taylor. *The Friendship*. Bantam, 1989. Two friends are divided by racial prejudice.

Dirlie Herlihy. *Ludie's Song*. Puffin, 1990. In Georgia in the 1950s, Marty goes against community prejudice by making friends with a black family.

Jean Little. *Different Dragons*. Viking, 1986. This story by a Canadian writer features a boy who has a secret fear. When he makes friends with a neighborhood girl, he learns that everyone has different dragons to overcome.

Bruce Coville. *Jeremy Thatcher, Dragon Hatcher*. Harcourt Brace Jovanovich, 1991. At first, Jeremy is embarrassed that Mary Lou is the only one who understands what he is going through.

Jerry Spinelli. *Maniac Magee*. Scholastic, 1990. An extraordinary boy brings racially divided communities together.

Yoshiko Uchida. *The Bracelet*. Philomel, 1993. Before Japanese American Emi and her family are taken to the relocation center, her friend Laurie gives her a bracelet as a symbol of their friendship.

Kevin Henkes. *Words of Stone*. Greenwillow, 1992. Two motherless children, Blaze and Joselle, find comfort in each other.

Further Resources for Teaching about Friendship

From the Heart: Books and Activities about Friends by Jan Irving and Robin Currie (Teacher Ideas Press, 1993) includes literature-based programs and units, games, and speaking and writing activities for friendship-related themes in the primary grades. Books featured include *The Wednesday Surprise, Chester's Way, Frog and Toad Are Friends, Jessica, Won't Somebody Play with Me?,* and *Henry and Mudge*.

Cooperation

Talk about ways we depend on other people. What would we do without people in the helping professions—firefighters, police, nurses, doctors? Bring an article from the newspaper about people helping one another to share with the class.

Students also help each other. Discuss the importance of assisting other people in school or at home. Have students answer the following questions:

- How do you help your family?
- How do your family and neighbors help each other?
- How does a friend help you?
- How can students help each other at school?

Differences in answers may reveal some of the cultural diversity in what is considered *acceptable* helping behavior. Sometimes, "helping" someone can get you into trouble, like helping with the answers on a test. Students can discuss these differences and develop a list of acceptable helping behaviors for the classroom.

Using the information on the list, prepare a chart for the classroom so that all students understand the rules and new students will be able to fit in easily.

Family Roles

All students have jobs that they do as part of their family, ranging from taking care of younger brothers and sisters to working in the family business. Help them learn to see these responsibilities as examples of how important a part they play in the survival of their family. In families, everyone depends on one another.

Muriel Stanek. *I Speak English for My Mom*. Whitman, 1989. Lupe has to help her mother who doesn't speak English.

Eve Bunting. *The Wednesday Surprise*. Clarion, 1989. A young girl secretly teaches her grandmother to read.

Diane Hoyt-Goldsmith. *Arctic Hunter*. Holiday, 1992. The photographs in this book show how much is expected of each family member, including 10-year-old Reggie, when they go to their fishing camp each spring.

Ruth Yaffe Radin. *All Joseph Wanted*. Macmillan, 1991. Joseph loves his mother, but her illiteracy is hard on him. Finally, Joseph convinces his mother to go to an adult literacy class.

Learning from Others

Students in school sometimes feel terribly ignorant because there's so much for them to learn. However, they don't realize the wealth of knowledge and skills they already possess. Brainstorm a list of what the students in the classroom know how to do. All of them speak at least one language, for example. Some may play different sports, ride a bicycle, or play an instrument. Help students think of what to include to show how smart they all are together. Make sure that everyone has at least one item listed.

Develop a chart of the skills and abilities of the students, with a list of student names and a place to sign up for peer tutoring if anyone wants to learn something about that subject. A good student who wants help with English (or math or science) can ask someone who is good at that subject for assistance. Or a student may be interested in another student's hobby, like bird watching or stamp collecting. Provide a short period (perhaps after lunch) for the groups to get together and set up trial meetings. After several weeks, check to see if students are still meeting. At this point, students may have questions about different ways to explain ideas and teach other people. The class can discuss the experience and suggest effective ways of peer tutoring.

Cooperative Learning

Many teachers are implementing plans for small-group learning that are cooperatively rather than competitively based. In cooperative learning, students are assigned to teams containing heterogeneous skills and ability levels. All the members of the team get credit for the work done by the team, but their grade is based on improvement, not a curve. Each student is responsible for knowing all the information prepared or studied by other team members.

A cooperative classroom is not just a place where students work collaboratively and share materials but a structure in which students are rewarded as a group for collective behavior. Developing student interaction skills requires careful, ongoing feedback from the teacher. You can enlist your students' help in finding ways to work together effectively without giving in to domination by the few, unequal workloads, or pressure to conform.

In cooperative learning, students will learn to appreciate the different skills of others and the value of these skills. Because they are assigned to work with students they may not know, they will learn about people from different backgrounds. They will learn how to depend on others, learn from others, stand up for themselves, and handle disagreements. The following books provide examples and support for building a cooperative learning environment in your classroom.

Eliot Aronson, *Jigsaw Classroom*. Sage, 1987.

Shlomo Sharan et al., eds. *Cooperation in Education*. Brigham Young University Press, 1980.

Susan Ellis and Susan Whalen. *Cooperative Learning: Getting Started*. Scholastic, 1990.

David Johnson and Roger Johnson. *Learning Together and Alone: Cooperative, Competitive, and Individualistic Learning*. 3rd edition. Allyn and Bacon, 1991.

Robert Slavin. *Using Student Team Learning*. Johns Hopkins University, 1989.

Death and Grieving

Well-written literature can help children learn how to manage the emotional and practical aspects of loss. Reading about other children who have gone through similar experiences, from the upheaval of moving to the loss of a loved one, will provide models of coping strategies, language to organize and process their experience, and a safe setting in which to express their emotions. Select stories that demonstrate the variety of approaches people have used to confront these problems.

Paul Goble. *Beyond the Ridge*. Aladdin, 1993. This picture book shows an old woman confronting death according to the beliefs of the Plains Indians. For her, dying is like climbing up a difficult slope toward a high ridge. Beyond the ridge, she can see the Spirit World. Death may seem like an end but it is not.

Rylant, Cynthia. *Missing May*. Orchard, 1992. In this extraordinarily sensitive novel, winner of the Newbery Award, twelve-year-old Summer grieves for her Aunt May, who took her in when no one else in the family wanted her.

Lucille Clifton. *Everett Anderson's Goodbye.* Holt, 1983. In one of a series of picture books that show the warm family life of Everett Anderson, a young African American boy, his father dies.

Tomie de Paola. *Nana Upstairs and Nana Downstairs.* Puffin 1973. Tommy loves to visit his grandmother (who is "Nana Downstairs") and his great-grandmother ("Nana Upstairs"). When Nana Upstairs dies, he seeks reassurance from his family.

Judith Viorst. *The Tenth Good Thing about Barney.* Aladdin, 1975. Grieving for his cat, Barney, a young boy is encouraged to think of ten good things about him.

Mavis Jukes. *I'll See You in My Dreams.* Knopf, 1993. A young girl finds an outlet for her grief over her dying uncle by dreaming of writing a message in the sky.

BREAKING DOWN PREJUDICE AND STEREOTYPES

Students bring unquestioned stereotypes and expectations to the classroom that they have picked up from their own family, the media, and their experiences outside of school. In order to work together, students have to learn how to bring these out into the open and examine them through discussion. Students already know about bias and fair and unfair approaches to life. Teachers can help them see how to generalize from their individual experiences with prejudice to a positive approach to diversity.

Establishing a Baseline

Stereotypes are often based on lack of information. Before beginning a unit of study, take time to find out what students know or think they know about the subject. Brainstorm ideas, phrases, sentences, and feelings with the class and keep a record of what the students produce. This simple preassessment can be used to design exercises or activities based on student misconceptions or ignorance. It can also serve to test what students have learned by the end of the unit. You can use the same brainstorming technique and compare the two lists, or you can present the first list as a question-and-answer or true-false exercise to show change.

Stereotypes of Animals

Many people have developed rigid ideas about many animals, and children learn this when quite young. Have students verbalize these stereotypes by describing the following animals in one or two words: mouse, fox, deer. Where do these ideas come from? Have they ever seen one of these animals? If a student has had a mouse as a pet, he or she may give specific examples to contradict the general statements made by others.

Focus on one animal, such as the wolf. Have students describe this animal. Record what they say in writing or on a cassette. Then read a story that portrays a sympathetic picture of the wolf, such as *The Friendly Wolf* by Dorothy and Paul Goble, *Mowgli and His Brothers* by Rudyard Kipling, or *Julie and the Wolves* by Jean Craighead George.

After completing the story, ask students to comment on what wolves are like. Record this session also. Play the first recording for the class. Has there been a change of opinion? Why?

Recent studies of wolf behavior in the wild have demonstrated that the wolf's reputation for being a "rapacious killer" is unfounded. In fact, wolves seem to possess many of the qualities associated with dogs, including sociability, lack of aggression, and family loyalty. Yet the negative image from "Little Red Riding Hood" remains. Challenge this picture by having students rewrite the story from the wolf's point of view. All we know is Little Red Riding Hood's side. What if she were wrong? What might have happened, according to the wolf? Or students could write the grandmother's experience. What really happened to her? Discuss several different solutions offered, stressing the idea that there is not one "correct" answer.

Color Associations

Talk about the associations we have with colors. Ask: "What do you think of when you think *red*?" List the ideas on the board, for instance fire, anger, burning, blood.

Then discuss how children feel about red. They may, for example, conclude that red is not a good color but that it is exciting or signals danger.

Follow this discussion by thinking about our use of the word *red* in expressions in our language. List the ideas:

- To get red with anger
- Blood red, as red as blood
- To blush red with embarrassment

Group Exploration of Color

Have the class break into groups of five or six and ask each group to explore one specific color. They can collect ideas related to things associated with the color, kinds of feelings associated with the color, and expressions using this color. The object of this exploration is to demonstrate that we have developed stereotyped ideas about color. What do we mean when we say, for example, "I am blue"?

- Blue is sad. (I am blue.)
- Yellow means cowardice. (I am yellow.)
- Green means young or unskilled. (I am green.)

Ask students to consider how these stereotyped ideas might have developed. If there are students in the class from different backgrounds, they may have very different associations with these colors. Discuss how such stereotypes can vary from culture to culture.

If *White* Means Good, Then *Black* Means . . .

Children quickly learn to make the association that *white* = good and *black* = evil, and to transfer this association to people. The many references in our society that represent black as evil or bad serve to reinforce this association. To help students become more aware of how their attitudes are conditioned, discuss expressions that include black. List examples given by students. How many of them are positive, how many negative?

blackmail	black eye	blackhead	black market
black flag	black lie	black-hearted	black mark
black rage	black mood	black magic	black humor
blackball	blackout	black sheep	in the black
Black Death	in black and white	blacken	black depression

What does *black* mean in each of these expressions? What does *black* mean when we are talking about a person's skin color? Does the word *black* used in the expressions Black Power and "Black is beautiful" have any connection with the expressions listed? These are important questions for students to discuss in order to eliminate the stereotype that black is negative.

Point out that despite the overwhelming number of negative associations, we can still find some affirmative meanings for the color *black*. Consider the circumstances in which wearing black signals respect, for example, at funerals, for ministers, for formal occasions.

Defining *Stereotype*

Now that students have seen for themselves examples of stereotypes and how they color our thinking, you can talk about the term itself and what it means. Do they know *stereo* from *stereophonic?* Or *stereoscopic?* They probably associate *stereo* with two (speakers, pictures) but actually it refers to the three-dimensional quality obtained by using two speakers for sound or two pictures for vision. How is this related to *stereotype?* Have students look up the word, preferably in different dictionaries, and compare definitions. Can they see the connection between *stereo* and *stereotype?* (A stereotype reduces the complex, multidimensional nature of human beings, or other things, to a single statement, image, or attitude.)

After completing a unit on stereotypes, have students write their own definitions of *stereotype*. Collect these in a book and discuss.

Images of Native Americans

Students are surrounded by negative and inaccurate images of Native Americans or Indians. Many materials used in schools reinforce these and are demeaning to Indians. You may have Native American students in your class who find it convenient to "pass" as Hispanic or Anglo since they often have Spanish or French last names.

Talk about the ideas students have about Native Americans. Brainstorm a list on the board or on a chart of all the information students can think of. They will probably reflect the common stereotypes of Native Americans as savages, fighters, or primitives. They may mention rain dances or tom-tom drums. Many may think the Native Americans had no language other than grunts or gestures.

Use this list to investigate the reality and rich variation of Native American life. Look at the Native American groups that used to live in your area. What happened to them? What were they like? Research the present situation for Native Americans. Check the stereotypes against the facts. How would students feel if someone used these stereotypes about them? Would they be insulted?

Discuss the stereotypes that students had. Do they still think these are true? Talk about where they got their stereotyped information and compare it to their current study. Why do most people still hold the same old inaccurate, insulting ideas?

Use this technique to deal with stereotypes about any group represented in the classroom. The best way to handle omnipresent stereotyping is to confront it directly, identify it as stereotyping, present facts that contradict the stereotypes, and model recognition and acceptance of diversity.

Evaluating Books for Children

How can you evaluate literature for use in the classroom? We need to examine books in terms of (1) realistic portrayals of members of ethnic groups, (2) inclusion of a fair representation of persons that make up our society, and (3) an honest attempt to break down existing stereotypes and prejudices.

You can design your own checklist especially to fit your own purposes. You can also guide students in developing a checklist and in applying this instrument. A simple checklist might look something like this:

Book Title _____

Author _____ Publisher _____ Year ____

Illustrator _____ Pages _____

Positive images: Negative images:

Story	*Art*		*Story*	*Art*	
		women			women
		men			men
		aged persons			aged persons
		ethnic groups (list below)			ethnic groups (list below)

This checklist notes only what is present. The lack of checkmarks means, therefore, that there was nothing offensive, but that neither was there a positive effort to combat stereotypes.

Comparing Evaluations of Books

Students can compare their evaluation of specific books with evaluations that have been published. The Council on Interracial Books for Children, for example, has published *Human Values in Children's Books,* which analyzes contemporary books. Older students could easily read this report and discuss the evaluation. Here are two sample evaluations, one for *Ludell,* a book ranked outstanding, and the second for *Three Fools and a Horse,* a book that was severely criticized.

Ludell

Brenda Wilkinson. Harper and Row, 1975. Grades 5 and up.

In this sensitive and powerful novel, the positive and the negative sides of growing up in a rural southern Black community are revealed through the eyes of fifth-grader Ludell. The place is Waycross, Georgia, in the 1950s where Ludell Wilson lives with her grandmother ("Mama"). Next door is the Johnson crew: Mrs. Johnson, sixteen-year-old Mattie and her child, Ruthie Mae (Ludell's best friend), Willie, Hawk and Cathy.

Ludell's keen perceptions expose the harsh underside of life in Waycross—the poverty, the selfishness and unconcern of her teachers in the segregated school she attends, the constant reminders that both Mama and Mrs. Johnson work as maids in white people's homes. Whenever racism and oppression are manifest, it is commented upon and clearly defined.

Each experience, whether humorous or tragic, contributes to Ludell's growing awareness of herself and of others. The reader can sense that one day her aspirations will lead her to seek a life outside of Waycross and to exercise more control over her destiny.

Author Wilkinson effectively captures the subtle nuances of Black southern dialect and draws readers inside the Black experience. In addition she provides a truly positive role model for young Black readers. Ludell has a keen sense of who she is, shares with those less fortunate than herself and is shown overcoming adversities in her life.

	ART	WORDS		ART	WORDS			ART	WORDS	N.A.
anti-Racist		✓	non-Racist			Racist	omission			
							Commission			
anti-Sexist			non-Sexist		✓	Sexist				
anti-Elitist		✓	non-Elitist			Elitist				
anti-Materialist			non-Materialist		✓	Materialist				
anti-Individualist		✓	non-Individualist			Individualist				
anti-Ageist			non-Ageist		✓	Ageist				
anti-Conformist			non-Conformist		✓	Conformist				
anti-Escapist		✓	non-Escapist			Escapist				
Builds positive image of females/minorities		✓	Builds negative image of females/minorities				Excellent	Good	Fair	Poor
						Literary quality		✓		
Inspires action vs. oppression			Culturally authentic		✓	Art quality				

Source: Adapted from *Human Values in Children's Books.* Council on Interracial Books for Children, Inc., 1841 Broadway, New York, NY.

Three Fools and a Horse

Betty Baker. Illustrated by Glen Rounds. Macmillan. Grades 3 and up.

The Foolish People were an imaginary group invented by the Apaches as an object of humor. *Three Fools and a Horse* chronicles the misadventures of three of the Foolish People of Two Dog Mountain—Little Fool, Fat Fool and Fool About. The trio decide they must have one of the horses of the "flat land men" (Plains Indians) in order to be "big men, the biggest men of the Foolish People." Little Fool challenges one of the flat land men to a horse race (Little Fool has no horse). Surprisingly, he wins the race and the horse. Unexpected consequences follow from the Fools' attempt to ride horseback.

Native American folk stories should be told by Native Americans, not appropriated from "folklore and anthropology magazines" and then vulgarized by whites. Ms. Baker has no business writing about the Foolish People if their stories are going to be, as they have been in this book, "combined, slightly changed and much elaborated. . . ." The Apache's Foolish People stories are entertaining in their own context, and their misrepresentation here is unethical and racist. Both the Fools (portrayed as ugly and self-seeking) and the Plains Indians (equally ugly and ridiculous) are maligned. The flat land people are differentiated in looks from the Fools only by the addition of leggings, braids, feathers and hook noses.

Though the author claims these stories taught moral lessons to Apache children her book strongly reinforces the "heap dumb Injun" stereotype.

	ART	WORDS		ART	WORDS			ART	WORDS	N.A.
anti-Racist			non-Racist			Racist	omission			
							Commission	✓	✓	
anti-Sexist			non-Sexist			Sexist				✓
anti-Elitist			non-Elitist	✓	✓	Elitist				
anti-Materialist			non-Materialist	✓	✓	Materialist				
anti-Individualist			non-Individualist	✓	✓	Individualist				
anti-Ageist			non-Ageist			Ageist				✓
anti-Conformist			non-Conformist	✓	✓	Conformist				
anti-Escapist			non-Escapist	✓	✓	Escapist				
Builds positive image of females/ minorities			Builds negative image of females/ minorities	✓	✓			Excellent	Good	Fair	Poor
							Literary quality		✓		
Inspires action vs. oppression			Culturally authentic				Art quality		✓		

Source: Adapted from *Human Values in Children's Books.* Council on Interracial Books for Children, Inc., 1841 Broadway, New York, NY.

Types of Stereotypes

Discuss the categories listed in the preceding evaluation. Ask students to think of an example of each of the types: Racist, Sexist, Elitist, Materialist, Individualist, Ageist, Conformist, Escapist. Can students define these terms? Why would we want to rate books along these lines? What do these terms have in common? Have students bring in their own books and talk about the presence or absence of these features. Discuss with the class what "N.A." means (not applicable—used on the preceding checklist).

The Quilt: A Metaphor for American Life

We need a new way to talk about the differences that exist in the classroom and in society, to replace the image of the "melting pot." The "melting-pot" metaphor implied that the diversity brought to this country by immigrants vanished as they were transformed into "Americans." But as we become more aware of the importance of preserving these differences, as well as of the value of our diverse history and heritage, we move away from the old assimilationist metaphor toward the idea of American society as a mosaic or a quilt.

The image of a quilt of many cultures and many histories provides a positive way in which to think about our country. The stitches of a quilt may come from many people, all contributing their skills to create a beautiful and useful object. The makers of quilts were traditionally anonymous, ordinary people who assembled scraps of cloth, each with a story attached, into striking new patterns. In the patchwork squares of American society today, the small scraps are preserved, yet also changed, by their placement next to cloth scraps from different sources. We see our familiar discards in new ways as the tiny squares and triangles are transformed; the basic pattern is repeated, yet no section is identical to any other.

The following books illustrate some of the power of the quilt metaphor to represent our lives and our history.

Faith Ringgold. *Tar Beach*. Crown, 1991. In this children's picture book based on an African American artist's famed story quilt painting, fabric pieces frame memories of summer evenings on a rooftop in Brooklyn.

Eleanor Coerr. *The Josefina Story Quilt*. Harper, 1989. When Faith's family sets out for California in 1850, she insists they bring her old hen, Josefina. To everyone's surprise, Josefina redeems herself by saving them from robbers. Faith sews a quilt to commemorate Josefina and the good times and bad times of the trip.

Deborah Hopkinson. *Sweet Clara and the Freedom Quilt*. Illustrated by James Ransome. Knopf, 1993. As a slave, young Clara is not allowed to read or write, so she carefully stitches into a quilt the information she needs for her escape north.

Patricia Polacco. *The Keeping Quilt*. Simon and Schuster, 1988. Polacco traces her family's Russian Jewish heritage through a quilt made from relatives' clothing and passed down through generations to celebrate births, marriages, and deaths. In each shape she can see the stories she's been told of her family.

Ann Whitford Paul. *Eight Hands Round: A Patchwork Alphabet*. Illustrated by Jeanette Winter. HarperCollins, 1991. This ABC book explains the origin of the interesting names for patchwork quilt patterns (Flying Geese, Rocky Road to Kansas), shows the different designs, and tells the story of the people behind the quilts.

Valerie Flournoy. *The Patchwork Quilt*. Illustrated by Jerry Pinkney. Dial, 1985. When Tanya's grandmother gets too sick to work on her quilt and tell stories about the family history, Tanya decides to help her finish it.

After reading these books, students who are motivated to make their own quilt can each contribute a square for a thematic quilt that represents their different heritages, significant events in their life, or their heroes. Or they can cut out shapes from magazines or wrapping paper to assemble in a patchwork pattern. These shapes can be glued to poster board and mounted on the wall.

Disability

Nearly 10 percent of all American adults are severely disabled, according to a 1992 survey. Approximately twice that number report some disability. Despite the frequent association of the terms "disabled" and "handicapped" with wheelchairs, people in wheelchairs make up only one part of the disabled population. More numerous are those with less visible disabilities: people who cannot walk a short distance, lift light objects, read normal print, or hear normal sound levels. When talking about diversity, be sure to include the children in your classroom who have invisible disabilities due to chronic illnesses, those whose mother or father uses a wheelchair because of multiple sclerosis, and those with family members or friends with cerebral palsy or Down's syndrome. There will be few families in the community who have not been touched by disability in some form, whether temporary or permanent, visible or invisible.

Although people are familiar with blue handicapped parking signs, the term "handicapped" has negative connotations, signaling inferior, less-than-human status. "Disabled" is preferred, but most disabled people would like to be treated as ordinary individuals who happen to lack a specific physical capability, not as people deprived of all their ability to function. Introduce models of disabled people to overcome student ignorance and embarrassment and to provide an opportunity to respond to student curiosity. Note that deaf people are not considered disabled. Rather, they belong to a different linguistic and cultural community. See Chapter 6 for a discussion of American Sign Language under language issues.

Barbara Dugan. *Loop the Loop.* Greenwillow, 1992. Mrs. Simpson, who travels in a wheelchair and performs tricks, befriends lonely young Anne.

Michelle Edwards. *Alef-Bet: A Hebrew Alphabet Book.* Lothrop, Lee and Shepard, 1992. While the focus of this ABC book is on the Hebrew language, the illustrations feature warm and lively family scenes with three children, the oldest in a wheelchair with spina bifida.

Nancy Hope Wilson. *Bringing Nettie Back.* Macmillan, 1992. Eleven-year-old Raz and Nettie are best friends until Nettie has a stroke and suffers brain damage. Raz has to accept that Nettie will never be the same.

Sally H. Alexander. *Mom's Best Friend.* Photographs by George Ancona. Macmillan, 1992. This is the author's second book about a mother who is blind. The book focuses on the extensive training of guide dogs for the blind and the period of adjustment required for both to work well together.

Jill Krementz. *How It Feels to Live with a Physical Disability.* Simon and Schuster, 1992. This is a good source for information about a particular disability, if you have a disabled child in the classroom. It includes photographs of twelve children, representing common disabilities, who tell their own stories.

Reference work

Joan Brest Friedberg, June B. Mullins, and Adelaide Weir Sukiennik. *Portraying Persons with Disabilities: an Annotated Bibliography of Non-Fiction for Children and Teenagers,* 2nd edition. Bowker, 1992.

FOCUS ON NATIVE AMERICANS: THE INVISIBLE MINORITY

When white explorers and settlers encountered the native population in North America, they tended to see the Indians as simple primitives, a view which justified paternalistic treatment and genocide. This was succeeded by the Noble Savage, a romanticized image of a lost tradition. Such stereotypes of Native Americans fix them in the past, making it difficult for young Native Americans to develop a cultural identity suitable for the twentieth century.

Indians haven't been absent from the school curriculum as much as they have been reduced to cardboard figures, all wearing headdresses and saying "How." Young Native American students may cope by hiding behind apparent Latino or Black ancestry rather than risking humiliation and embarrassment. Life outside the reservation brings economic opportunities but cultural starvation. Teachers can help support young Native Americans in their search for identity and a place in the world. Teachers can also make sure that all students learn more about Indian life, historical and modern.

Planning Your Study

When initiating a unit on Native Americans, you have to consider carefully what you want the students to learn. Here are two possible strategies:

1. An in-depth presentation on local groups. For this study, you will want information on the history of the Native Americans in your area, the present conditions of Native Americans, and the problems they face today.
2. An overview of the diversity of Native Americans. The goal of this unit would be to expand student awareness of Native American history, culture, and present life through examples that are representative of different regions.

Starting Out

Before beginning a study of Indians in the United States, use some means of assessing student information and attitudes. This will provide an interesting and instructive comparison at the end of the study. Try some of these ideas:

• Have each student draw a picture of an Indian engaged in some activity.
• Ask students to complete this sentence at least three times: An Indian . . .
• Ask students to list as many Indian tribes as they can.

Put these sheets away until the study is completed. After the study you might have the students repeat the same activities. Then compare the results.

Native American Tribes

Draw a large outline map of the United States on which to locate the various groups of Indian tribes. They can be grouped as follows according to similar modes of living:

Eastern Woodland Area Algonquin, Delaware, Iroquois, Massachuset, Mohawk, Mohegan, Narraganset, Onandaga, Penobscot, Powhatan, Tuscarora, Passamaquoddy, Pawtuket, Tippecanoe, Wampanoag, Wyandot

Great Lakes Woodland Area Chippewa/Ojibwa, Huron, Illinois, Kickapoo, Miami, Oneida, Ottawa, Potawatomi, Sauk and Fox, Seneca, Shawnee, Winnebago

Southeastern Area Catawba, Cherokee, Creek, Lumbi, Natchez, Seminole, Yuchi

North Central Plains Area Arapaho, Axikara, Assiniboin, Blackfeet, Cheyenne, Cree, Crow, Gros Ventre, Mandan, Pawnee, Shoshone, Sioux/Dakota

South Central Plains Area Caddo, Chickasaw, Choctaw, Comanche, Iowa, Kaw/Kansa, Kiowa, Omaha, Osage, Ponca, Quapaw

Southwest Area Apache, Hopi, Maricopa, Navajo, Papago, Pima, Pueblo, Zuñi

California Area Chumash, Hoopa, Maidu, Mission, Modoc, Mohave, Mono, Pit River, Pomo, Tule River, Wailaki, Yahi, Yokuts, Yuma, Yurok

Northwestern Plateau Area Bannock, Cayuse, Coeur D'Alene, Colville, Flathead, Kalispel, Klamath, Kootenai, Nez Percé, Paiute, Puyallup, Spokane, Ute, Walla-walla, Wasco, Washoe, Yakima, Nisqually

Northwest Pacific Coast Area Aleuts, Eskimo, Haida, Lummi, Makah, Muckleshoot, Nootka, Quinault, Salish, Shoalwater, Snohomish, Suquamish, Tlingit

Native American Reservations

The following chart shows states with Indian reservations, the Indian population of those states, and the names of the tribes or nations.

FEDERAL INDIAN RESERVATIONS AND TRUST LANDS

State	No. of Reser.	No. of persons	Major tribes and/or nations
Alabama	1	16,504	Poarch Creek
Alaska	1	85,698	Aleut, Eskimo, Athabascan
Arkansas	1	—	unknown
Arizona	23	203, 527	Navajo, Apache, Papago, Hopi, Yavapai, Pima
California	96	242,164	Hoopa, Paiute, Yurok, Karok, Mission Bands
Colorado	2	27,776	Ute
Connecticut	1	6,654	Mashantucket Pequot
Florida	4	36,335	Seminole, Miccosukee
Idaho	4	13,780	Shoshone, Bannock, Nez Percé
Iowa	1	7,349	Sac and Fox
Kansas	4	21,965	Potawatomi, Kickapoo, Iowa
Louisiana	3	18,541	Chitimacha, Coushatta, Tunica-Biloxi
Maine	3	5,998	Passamaquoddy, Penobscot, Maliseet
Massachusetts	1	—	Wampanoag

State	No of Reser.	No. of persons	Major tribes and/or nations
Michigan	8	55,638	Chippewa, Potawatomi, Ottawa
Minnesota	14	49,909	Chippewa, Sioux
Mississippi	1	8,825	Choctaw
Missouri	1	—	unknown
Montana	7	47,679	Blackfeet, Crow, Sioux, Assiniboine, Cheyenne
Nebraska	3	12,410	Omaha, Winnebago, Santee Sioux
Nevada	19	19,637	Paiute, Shoshone, Washoe
New Mexico	25	134,355	Zuni, Apache, Navajo
New York	8	62,651	Seneca, Mohawk, Onondaga, Oneida
North Carolina	1	80,155	Cherokee
North Dakota	3	25,917	Sioux, Chippewa, Mandan, Arikara, Hidatsa
Oklahoma	1	252,420	Cherokee, Creek, Choctaw, Chickasaw, Osage, Cheyenne, Arapahoe, Kiowa, Comanche
Oregon	7	38,496	Warm Springs, Wasco, Paiute, Umatilla, Siletz
Rhode Island	1	4,071	Narragansett
South Dakota	9	50,573	Sioux
Texas	3	65,877	Alabama-Coushatta, Tiwa, Kickapoo
Utah	4	24,283	Ute, Goshute, Southern Paiute
Washington	27	81,483	Yakima, Lummi, Quinault
Wisconsin	11	39,387	Chippewa, Oneida, Winnebago
Wyoming	1	9,479	Shoshone, Arapahoe

Source: Bureau of Indian Affairs, U.S. Dept. of the Interior (data as of 1990).

Which states have the most reservations? Which have the largest Indian populations? How many states do not have Indian reservations?

English Words from Native American Languages

Words borrowed into English show how much the first settlers owed the Native Americans they encountered. Most words come from the Algonquin languages, spoken along the East Coast. Can students guess the English equivalent? Develop a chart to show the relationship.

chitmunk	(chipmunk)	paccan	(pecan)
aroughcoun	(raccoon)	pasimenan	(persimmon)
squnk	(skunk)	msickquatash	(succotash)
ochek	(woodchuck)	askootasquash	(squash)
musquash	(muskrat)	wikawam	(wigwam)
moos	(moose)	tamahak	(tomahawk)
aposoun	(opossum)	mohkussin	(moccasin)
pawcohiccora	(hickory)		

Other Gifts from the Native Americans

Students will be interested in learning of the many things we gained from the Native Americans. They knew the best trails and ways of traveling across the country by canoe and by snowshoe. They invented hammocks. The Native Americans were the first, too, to grow and use tobacco and rubber. They introduced white settlers to the following foods that we use today:

corn	tomatoes	chicle (for chewing gum)	grits
potatoes	vanilla	beans	hominy
chilies	avocados	chocolate	popcorn
pineapples	peanuts	maple sugar	succotash
squash	cranberries	artichokes	

Have several students prepare an illustrated chart of these foods. You may experiment with preparing hominy or grits, dishes that are easy to make in the classroom.

Of course, Native American contributions were not limited to food supplies. The following books suggest areas that students can explore further:

Jack Weatherford. *Native Roots: How the Indians Enriched America.* Fawcett, 1991. This book argues that wherever you look at American life, you will find Indian origins below the surface. Parts of the U.S. Constitution are based on the Iroquois Confederacy.

Jack Weatherford. *Indian Givers: How the Indians of the Americas Transformed the World.* Fawcett, 1989. Many gifts to world civilization come from Native Americans, from the superior cotton of the Sea Islands to plants with medical applications such as quinine and coca.

Native American Place Names

Many state names, such as Massachusetts, originated in Native American languages. Names of many rivers, such as the Ohio and Mississippi, and cities, such as Pontiac, Michigan, and Chicago, Illinois, also originated from Native American languages.

Look for evidence of specific tribes. For example, there are many Abenaki place names in Maine, Vermont, and New Hampshire.

Androscoggin	place where fish are cured
Connecticut	the long river
Katahdin	the principal mountain
Kennebec	long water without rapids
Merrimack	at the deep place
Nashua	between streams

For more information on where names come from, see *Indian Place Names of New England* by John C. Huden (Museum of the American Indian, New York: Heye Foundation, 1962).

Prepare a map on which to locate Native American names. Include a chart to explain what the names mean and where they come from.

The "New World" in 1492

What did the world of the Native Americans look like when the European explorers arrived, beginning with Columbus in 1492? Students may be surprised to learn that there were no horses (dogs and turkeys were the only domestic animals). It is impossible to know how many people lived on the North American continent at the time, but there were more than a few complex cultures, based in different regions, and trading with others.

Dennis Fradin's historical biography *Hiawatha: Messenger of Peace* (McElderry, 1993) provides much background information about the Iroquois. Although Hiawatha lived five hundred years ago, she made significant contributions to American history. As a leader in her tribe, she helped set up the Iroquois Confederacy, the most politically complex group in 1492. Iroquois customs and beliefs eventually influenced the development of the U.S. Constitution. Also see volumes on the Iroquois and the Mohawk in the Chelsea House series *Indians of North America* for historical data.

For more information on Native American life in 1492, see the following books:

Jean Fritz, Jamake Highwater, Margaret Mahy, Patricia and Fredrick McKissack, and Katherine Paterson. *The World in 1492*. Holt, 1992. Provides a detailed description of each part of the world—Africa, Asia, Europe, Australia, the Americas—and how the people there lived at that time.

Michael Dorris. *Morning Girl*. Hyperion, 1992. An extraordinary novel, told in alternating chapters by a Taino brother and sister, depicting their life and everyday concerns on an island in the Bahamas. The story ends with the arrival of strangers dressed in unusual clothing. What will life be like for this Taino family after their encounter with Columbus?

What Happened to the Native Americans after 1492?

After setting the stage with a picture of the Native Americans before the European conquest, continue the story and explore how the Native Americans were affected by it. Several books deal with specific tribes in specific regions.

Florida

Eva Costabel. *The Early People of Florida*. Atheneum, 1993. Presents the history of tribal groups such as Calusa and Tequesta present in 1492. First the Spanish and the French fought over their lands, then the British came.

Colorado

Albert Marrin. *Cowboys, Indians, and Gunfighters: The Story of the Cattle Kingdom*. Atheneum, 1993. Outlines the destruction of the Plains Indians' way of life, from 1521 when the first cattle arrived from Hispaniola to the killing off of the buffalo.

Plains

Paul Goble. *Death of the Iron Horse*. Aladdin, 1993. This picture book tells the true story of the Cheyenne's struggle to preserve their way of life after soldiers and settlers invade their territory with the steam locomotive.

North Dakota

Russell Freedman. *An Indian Winter*. Paintings and drawings by Karl Bodmer. Holiday House, 1992. Journal of a German prince and scenes painted by a Swiss artist who spent a winter with the Mandans in 1833–34 in today's North Dakota. Afterwards, the Mandan and Hidatsa were devastated by smallpox and their traditional way of life vanished. The detail of this text and pictures bring to life the vanished customs of the people.

General

Simon Ortiz. *The People Shall Continue*. Children's Book Press, 1988. Overview of Native American history from a Native American perspective.

Native American Life Today

Bring your historical account of Native American life up to the present. Students may be surprised to realize there are modern Native American children like themselves, not just characters out of history. Young Native Americans face many of the same issues concerning growing up that all children face. In addition, they may struggle to learn more about their heritage and the history of their people. They may wonder why people are prejudiced against them or their people. And they face the question of how to maintain their culture in a hostile world. Look for a variety of children's books to show students what it feels like to face these concerns.

Sandra Markle. *The Fledglings*. Bantam, 1992. Fourteen-year-old Kate and her Cherokee grandfather fight to save eagles from poachers. An orphan, she discovers a relative and a way of life she never knew when she lives with him for a summer in the Blue Ridge Mountains in North Carolina.

Russ Kendall. *Eskimo Boy: Life in an Inupiaq Village*. Scholastic, 1992. Children will be fascinated by the photographs of seven-year-old Norman, who lives in a remote village off the northwest coast of Alaska. He is learning both about his Inupiaq heritage and how to find his way in the modern world. Like most young children, he hates to go to the dentist, a visit that for Norman means a long airplane trip to Nome.

Peggy Thompson. *Song of the Wild Violets*. The Book Publishing Co. Life on a Chippewa reservation is hard in the 1940s, but wild violets help a young girl rekindle her parents' pride in their heritage.

Ted Wood with Wanbli Numpa Afraid of Hawk. *A Boy Becomes a Man at Wounded Knee*. Walker, 1992. Photographs tell the story of eight-year-old Wanbli, who joins his father and uncles for a five-day trek commemorating the massacre of the Lakotas one hundred years ago.

Paulsen, Gary. *The Night the White Deer Died*. Delacorte, 1978. Fifteen-year-old Janet, one of the few Anglos in her New Mexico community, learns about prejudice from Billy Honcho, an old Pueblo Indian.

Jean Craighead George. *Water Sky*. Harper, 1987. Lincoln Noah Stonewright goes from Boston to Barrow, Alaska, to stay with an Eskimo family and learn what happened to his uncle, who had wanted to stop the Eskimo whaling there.

Ron Hirschi. *Seya's Song*. Illustrated by Constance Bergum. Sasquatch Books, 1992. A S'Klallam grandmother and grandfather pass on their language and stories to a young girl. The story includes many S'Klallam words, such as *Seya* (grandmother), to help preserve heritage and culture, as the language is no longer spoken by many. It also incorporates information on the life and customs of the S'Klallam people, who live in Washington and British Columbia.

Normee Ekoomiak. *Arctic Memories*. Holt, 1990. A picture book of an Inuit childhood in Quebec illustrates a way of life that is almost extinct. Text in Inuktitut and English.

Tryntje Van Seymour Ness. *The Gift of Changing Woman*. Holt, 1993. When an Apache girl comes of age, she goes through a special ceremony to teach her the story of creation and her place in the world. The book includes pictures painted by Apache artists and words of the Apache people.

Joseph Bruchac. *Dawn Land*. Fulcrum, 1993. This saga illuminates the centuries-old value system of the Abenaki.

Native American Folklore

Folklore from the various Native American tribes is an excellent source for storytelling activities. Older students can learn one of these tales to present to students in the primary grades. All of these stories adapt well to other modes of oral presentation, such as reader's theater. In addition, when you read one of the teaching stories to the class, students can respond to the moral by drawing a picture of what it means to them.

When selecting folktales for use with students, consider carefully the image presented of the people in the group. Many writers have written versions of Native American tales without respect for their authentic cultural background. Contrast these with books by writers such as Paul Goble and Gerald McDermott, who are scrupulous in citing the sources of their stories and in presenting appropriate cultural context in their illustrations. Also look for books by Native American authors, which have become more available as individuals and tribal organizations promote culturally sensitive materials. A booklist is available from Oyate, 2702 Mathews Street, Berkeley, CA 94702.

Paul Goble. *The Girl Who Loved Wild Horses*. Aladdin, 1993. She loves taking care of her tribe's horses so much that she decides to become one herself in order to run free.

Retold by Tony Hillerman. *The Boy Who Made Dragonfly*. University of New Mexico Press, 1986. Retelling of a Zuni myth about how a young boy and his sister gain the wisdom to become the leaders of their people.

Gerald McDermott. *Raven: A Trickster Tale from the Pacific Northwest*. Harcourt Brace Jovanovich, 1993. How the raven steals the sun from the Sky Chief so that the people can have light.

Paul Goble. *Crow Chief*. Orchard, 1992. A combination of several Plains Indian tales explains why crows are black.

Shonto Begay. *Ma'ii and Cousin Horned Toad*. Scholastic, 1992. This Navajo teaching tale includes text in Navajo. Coyote is hungry but is too lazy to get his own food.

Retold by Jonathan London with Lanny Pinola. *Fire Race*. Illustrated by Sylvia Long. Chronicle Books, 1993. The tale of what happens when Coyote steals fire from yellow jackets.

Leanne Hinton. (trans.). *Ishi's Tale of Lizard*. Farrar Straus Giroux, 1992. Recent translation of a Yahi tale. Ishi, the sole survivor of the Yahi people, emerged from hiding in 1911.

Natalia Belting. *Moon Was Tired of Walking on Air*. Houghton Mifflin, 1992. Creation myths from Native groups of South America.

When studying Native American folklore with students, encourage them to look for patterns. Can they find several examples of a "trickster" tale? Compare some trickster tales in other cultures. Are there several versions of one tale? How do the versions differ? In folklore, stories are transmitted orally, so several different written versions may all be authentic. What values do these stories teach?

Other teaching stories can be found in the collection:

Michael Caduto and Joseph Bruchac. *Keepers of the Animals: Native American Stories and Wildlife Activities for Children.* Fulcrum, 1991. A teacher's guide was published in 1992. Look for Bruchac reading and telling Abenaki stories on audiocassette.

Students Write Their Own Tales

Encourage students to bring in examples of tales from their own family. Are there favorite stories in their family? (Stories to make them go to bed, scary stories, stories of what will happen if they don't behave properly.) Point out common themes and lessons. Students can write or tell their tales, collect them in a book or record them on tape to share with others. See Chapter 5 for more information on a folklore unit.

Making Navajo Fry Bread

Create a learning center at which children can take turns making a semiauthentic version of fry bread. (Teacher supervision is necessary for this activity.)

Directions
Fill the electric skillet half full of oil. Turn on high to heat.
Measure into bowl:

4 c. flour	1 tsp. salt
3 tsp. baking powder	1½ c. water

Gradually add the water as you stir.

Knead the dough until it does not stick to your hands. Add a little more flour as needed. Divide the dough into small balls. Then flatten them until thin and make a hole in the center like a doughnut. Slide into hot oil. Fry on each side until light brown. Remove and drain on layer of paper towels. Eat while warm.

Sports from the Native Americans

Many of the sports we know today originated in games the Native Americans first played. They played shinny, a game with a puck that was played on ice, similar to ice hockey. Native American children played such games as hide and seek, follow-the-leader, crack-the-whip, prisoner's base, and blindman's bluff. They also had games not unlike hop-scotch, marbles, and jack straws.

For more information about Native American sports and how to play them, look for *Sports & Games the Indians Gave Us* by Alex Whitney (McKay, 1977). This author shows children how to make gaming equipment for use in the games described. Stick dice are easy to make, for example. Use a stick about one-half inch wide and four inches long. With a knife round off the ends of the stick. Paint one side red and paint a multicolor design on the other side. With the red side counting as one point and the design as two, see who can get twenty points first.

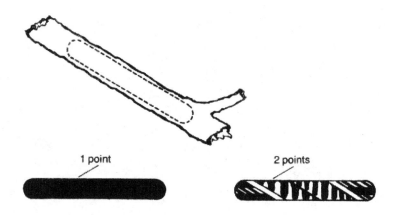

1 point

2 points

A Weaving Center

Weaving is an art that has been practiced by many cultures. You may wish to construct one or two large looms on which students can create a decorative piece of cloth cooperatively. Students can create miniature looms on which they can work individually. Directions given are for the large loom, but small looms can be made in similar fashion.

Obtain two lightweight logs about five feet long. Cut off any branches, but leave the rough ends sticking out. Suspend one log from the ceiling to simulate the limb of a tree. The second log is then suspended from the first by rough rope as shown on the next page.

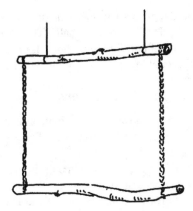

If suspending the log from the ceiling is not possible in your classroom, fasten four logs together with rope to form a loom frame, as shown here:

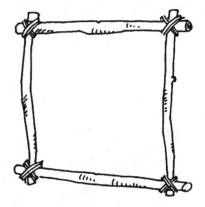

Thread the loom with heavy rug yarn choosing natural colors as much as possible rather than the bright, artificial colors. Using black or beige, loop the yarn around the log to keep it from sliding, thus:

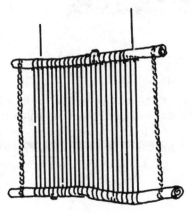

Students can make wooden shuttles of flat pieces of wood. They can alternate colors to form stripes of varied widths.

Native American Masks

Begin a study of masks by showing the excellent film, *The Loon's Necklace* (Britannica Films, 11 minutes), a legend told by the artful filming of authentic masks from a museum.

Students can create their own masks from heavy cardboard. Folding the cardboard in half makes it fit the child's face more closely. A piece of elastic holds it securely in place.

The shape of the mask and the way the eyes are developed serve to suggest the person or animal. It is not necessary, however, to be overly realistic. Masks can then be used to tell folktales, perhaps the pourquoi tales the children have written.

A good resource for making masks is *Creative Masks for Stage and School* by Joan Peters and Anna Sutcliffe (Plays, Inc., 1975).

Native American Poetry

Share these poems with the children in your room. Because they are short, you might print one or two on posters for display in the classroom.

Song of Failure

A wolf
I considered myself,
But the owls are hooting
and the night
I fear.
    —*Teton Sioux*

Spring Song

As my eyes search the prairie,
I feel the summer in the spring.
    —*Chippewa*

Glyph

Truly buzzards
Around my sky are circling!
For my soul festers,
And an odor of corruption
Betrays me to disaster.
Meanness, betrayal and spite
Come flockwise,
To make me aware
Of sickness and death within me.
My sky is full of the dreadful sound
Of the wings of unsuccesses.
    —*Washoe-Paiute*

May I Walk

On the trail marked with pollen may I walk,
With grasshoppers about my feet may I walk,
With dew about my feet may I walk,
With beauty may I walk,
With beauty before me, may I walk,
With beauty behind me, may I walk,
With beauty above me, may I walk,
With beauty under me, may I walk,
With beauty all around me, may I walk,
In old age wandering on a trail of beauty, lively, may I walk,
In old age wandering on a trail of beauty, living again, may I walk,
It is finished in beauty.
    —*Navajo*

Reading poetry written by people from another culture is an excellent way of learning about shared values and cultural differences. Feature examples from the following excellent collections.

Hettie Jones. *The Trees Stand Shining: Poetry of the North American Indians*. Illustrated by Robert Andrew Parker. Dial, 1993. These oral tradition poems are really folk chants and songs, preserved for generations and only written down and translated in the nineteenth century. Each is short, identified by tribe, and grouped by similar topic.

Joseph Bruchac and Jonathan London. *Thirteen Moons on Turtle's Back: A Native American Year of Moons*. Illustrated by Thomas Locker. Philomel, 1992. Each page presents a poem about the moon, representing traditions from a different tribe, from Pomo to Cree to Abenaki. These poems transmit respect for the power and wisdom of the natural world.

Joseph Bruchac, ed. *New Voices from the Longhouse: An Anthology of Contemporary Iroquois Writing*. Greenfield Review Press, 1989. Poems and short prose represent thirty contemporary adult writers. The book includes photographs, brief biographies of the poets, and a map of Iroquois settlements.

Arlene Hirschfelder and Beverly Singer, eds. *Rising Voices: Writings of Young Native Americans.* Scribner's, 1992. Poems and short prose by middle and high school students represent a variety of tribes and regions. The poems were chosen to reflect concerns about identity, education, and harsh realities.

After reading some of these examples, students can choose to write poems based on similar themes of nature or identity. Students can also write poems as a response to the unit on Native Americans, to show their reactions to what they have learned.

A Mural of Native American Life

After students have gained information through reading and discussing topics related to Native American life, have them plan a large mural to which each one can contribute. The space of the mural might be considered similar to the map of the United States. Roughly, then, space could be allocated to activities associated with the Plains Indians, those of the Southwest, the Pacific Northwest, and so on. Sketch this plan on the chalkboard.

Bring in books with pictures that suggest scenes to be included. Crayons can be used for the figures, and the background can be painted in with pale brown tempera or light green, as appropriate.

When the mural is completed, display it in the school hall or a room where all can see it.

An All-School Assembly

Plan a school assembly to share the results of your study. Let students discuss various ways they can present an informative and entertaining program. Consider some of the following activities:

- An introduction (the purpose of your study and some of the things you learned).
- Presentation of the mural with an explanation of the many Native American tribes in what is now the United States.
- Reader's theater presentation of Native American folklore, which might include music.
- Demonstration of Native American sports, dances, and so on.
- Creative dramatization of a Native American story.
- An invitation to visit your room to see the things you have made.

Sources of Information

Beverly Slapin and Doris Seale, eds. *Through Indian Eyes: The Native Experience in Books for Children.* New Society Publishers, 1992. Includes guidelines for evaluating treatment of Native Americans in curriculum materials.

Oyate, 2702 Mathews Street, Berkeley, CA 94702. A Native American organization working to ensure that Native American lives and histories are portrayed honestly.

Collect pictures for display in the classroom. The following are good sources:

Society for Visual Education, 1345 Diversey Parkway, Chicago, IL 60614.

Arizona Highways, 2039 W. Lewis, Phoenix, AZ 85009.

Sources of recordings:

Folkways/Scholastic Records, 50 W. 44th St., New York, NY 10036. Music Division, Library of Congress, Washington, D.C. 20540.

A variety of information can be obtained from these sources:

The American Indian Museum of Natural History, Central Park West and 79th Street, New York, NY 10024.

Bureau of Indian Affairs, Department of Interior, Washington, D.C. 20242. Ask for their list of penpals.

Museum of the American Indian, Broadway at 155th St., New York, NY 10032.

Also refer to sources listed in the Appendix.

REFLECTIONS

Students are individuals, and they bring their cultural backgrounds with them to school. Because culture is usually invisible, it is often difficult to recognize its effects. As teachers, you cannot resolve all the social issues that beset children's lives, but you can make a difference through effective teaching. Student-centered teaching involves students in a partnership, as everyone brings something to the classroom.

APPLICATIONS

1. How influential is our language in creating and maintaining stereotypes and prejudices? Pick a group that you belong to, for example:

student	athlete
parent	blonde
male	bespectacled
female	musician

What phrases or descriptions are associated with the group you selected? Do they carry positive or negative connotations? How do they make you feel when somebody uses them? What effect might these words have on children's ideas about you? Discuss your results in small groups. Would you want to change some of the language used?

2. Begin to collect a picture file. Look for pictures of men, women, boys, and girls who represent a variety of ethnic and racial backgrounds and who are engaged in both common and unusual activities. Mount them on cardboard with a plastic overlay for protection, then group them according to subject or possible use. Is it easy to find pictorial representations of all groups in our society (or in the world), in all occupations? Which groups are rarely depicted? What impression do students receive who seldom see pictures of people like themselves or their family? Write two lesson plans using your picture file.

3. Using the evaluation form given in the chapter (or one of your own), select ten children's books (fiction and nonfiction) to evaluate for race, age, sex, or other stereotypes. Decide how you would use each book to promote awareness and acceptance of diversity. What would you do with such books as *Huckleberry Finn* or *Little House in the Big Woods*, which some have condemned for their racism? How could you use each book to discuss the destructiveness of stereotyping? Develop two lesson plans about books that present subtle or overt stereotyped images and thinking. Select two books that have been criticized for racism or sexism and develop a lesson plan that uses each book to teach critical thinking.

Exploring Further

Deborah Byrnes. *"Teacher, They Called Me a _____!" Prejudice and Discrimination in the Classroom.* Anti-Defamation League of B'nai B'rith, 1988. (823 United Nations Plaza, New York, NY 10017.)

Interracial Books for Children Bulletin. The Council on Interracial Books for Children.

E. Pepitone, ed. *Children in Cooperation and Competition.* Heath, 1980.

Christine Sleeter and Carl Grant. *Making Choices for Multicultural Education: Five Approaches to Race, Class and Gender.* Merrill, 1988.

John Ogbu. "Understanding Cultural Diversity and Learning." *Educational Researcher* 21:8, November, 1992.

Courtney Cazden and Hugh Mehan. "Principles from Sociology and Anthropology: Context, Code, Classroom, and Culture." In Maynard Reynolds, ed. *Knowledge Base for the Beginning Teacher.* AACTE/Pergamon, 1989.

Susan Florio-Ruane. "Social Organization of Classes and Schools." In Maynard Reynolds, ed. *Knowledge Base for the Beginning Teacher.* AACTE/Pergamon, 1989.

Margaret Wang and AnneMarie Palincsar. "Teaching Students to Assume an Active Role in Their Learning." In Maynard Reynolds, ed. *Knowledge Base for the Beginning Teacher.* AACTE/Pergamon, 1989.

Ronald Waterbury. "Culture, Society, and the Interdisciplinary Teaching of World Studies: An Anthropological Perspective." *The Social Studies,* March/April 1993.

Violet Harris, ed. *Teaching Multicultural Literature in Grades K–8.* Christopher/Gordon, 1993.

Evelyn Wolfson. *From Abenaki to Zuni: A Dictionary of Native American Tribes.* Walker, 1988.

Alvin Josephy, ed. *America in 1492.* Knopf, 1992.

Peter Nabakov, ed. *Native American Testimony: A Chronicle of Indian-White Relations from Prophecy to the Present, 1492–1992.* Viking, 1991.

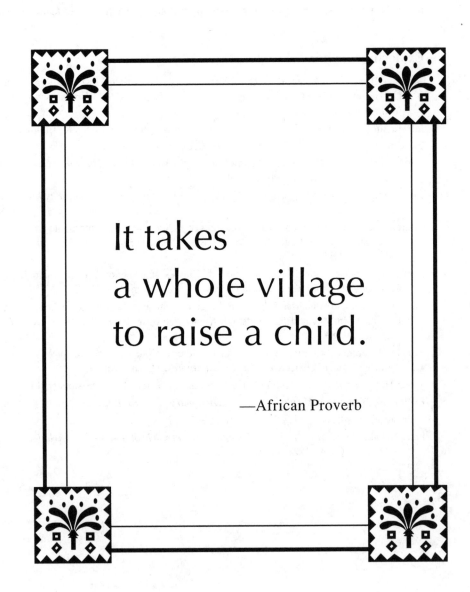

It takes
a whole village
to raise a child.

—African Proverb

5

❖

Enlarging Student Perspectives

One of our primary tasks as teachers is to prepare students to live in the wider world. Because we cannot know exactly what they will face, we try to give them the adaptability and self-confidence to make their way under any circumstances. Because we are all part of a community, we cannot separate the interests of some people from the interests of the rest, the success of some students from the success of all. Every one of us has a stake in the task of educating our children for the future. We have to define our community to include people who might otherwise have been left outside.

The lens through which we view multicultural education in this chapter is that of power. Although discussion of power may conflict with the American ideology of democracy, equal opportunity, and achievement through individual effort, we can see the effects of the unequal allocation of social resources in our students and the schools. When students walk through the door on the first day of school, experienced teachers can sort them into groups: those who have absorbed the belief that the world belongs to them and those who have learned that the world is not set up for people like them. Early experiences of privilege or marginalization based on skin color, language, or culture, are powerful forces in the maintenance of the social status quo.

Multicultural education is often equated with support services for "minority" students. But the term "minority" is misleading because it focuses attention on the relative size of a group rather than its lack of access to power. Consider societies such as South Africa in which the apartheid system enabled the white minority to maintain control. "Historically disadvantaged" may be a more accurate term, reflecting long-standing policies of social, economic, and legal exclusion. For example, women are still struggling to achieve parity with men in many spheres. However, multicultural education must include any group whose members have been denied access to the full human rights enjoyed by others. In this chapter, we open students' eyes to the full range of the human community, including such diverse groups as disabled people and the elderly.

By 2050, half of all Americans will probably be non-white. Our definitions will have to change: who is an "American," who has control over increasingly scarce resources, whose history is studied in books, whose culture is represented in school. These shifts are reflected in the problems facing teachers today. Schools are institutions that preserve and transmit fixed knowledge, yet teachers are expected to prepare students for the future. How will this affect your teaching and your relations with students?

After reading this chapter, you should be able to:
- Direct students' attention to problems and issues in their community.
- Increase students' understanding of the diversity of cultures in the United States.
- Develop students' skills for living in a larger world.
- Incorporate information about the history and accomplishments of African Americans into the curriculum.

EXPLORING YOUR COMMUNITY

Most students today live in urban settings. They are familiar with violence, poverty, and the increasing breakdown of traditional social support systems. Focus attention on the nature of their community and the factors that influence its condition. Show students that school can be a place to talk about what is most important in their lives. At the same time, expect them to learn how to analyze and think critically about their circumstances.

The Neighborhood

Explore the concept of a neighborhood with your students. Does the area where your school is located have a name? Do all students live in the same neighborhood? Talk about the neighborhood. What are the most significant spots to students? (Church, school, park, ice cream store, etc.) Bring a city map and have the students mark where they live. You can show students that a word such as *neighborhood* is a *concept,* an idea in people's minds, rather than a physical object, so that there may be more than one definition of the neighborhood.

Have students write a description of their neighborhood. How do they feel about it? What are some of the people and places in it? What sights, sounds, smells do they think of?

For another writing activity have students complete these sentences.

My favorite place in the neighborhood is _____ .
I like it because _____ .
The most important thing that ever happened to me in the neighborhood was

_____ .

When I think of my neighborhood, I think of _____ .

Students' responses to these prompts can be collected into an illustrated book entitled *Thoughts about Our Neighborhood.*

Neighborhood People

What's a neighbor? Do students know their neighbors? Discuss what neighbors can do for you. Some students' neighbors may take care of them after school; others may organize a local baseball team. How do neighbors help each other?

Have students draw a picture of a neighbor who has done something special for them—helped them when they were sick, given them a present, etc.—and have them tell the class about this person. What makes this neighbor a special person for them?

Students may be interested in knowing that neighbor comes from the Old English words *nēah* (near) *gebūr* (dweller).

A Neighborhood Map

Talk about maps with students. What are different kinds of maps? What goes into a map? What can maps be used for? In discussions about the neighborhood, students have talked about places and people of importance to them. Now each student can propose a list of elements to be included on a map of the neighborhood.

Construct a class map on a large sheet of butcher paper. Depending on the level of the students, you may decide to represent only one or two main streets, an interpretation of a larger area (not to scale), or a standard grid map with scale and/or cardinal directions. Students will enjoy developing symbols to use on the map (explained in the *key*) and illustrating or landscaping the map as much as they choose. A more elaborate project would be to create a relief map or three-dimensional model from clay, plaster, or similar material. Such a project will give students a different perspective of the place where all of them live.

A Place to Live

One issue that has become critical in many neighborhoods is the homeless. Perhaps as many as seven million Americans were homeless at some point in the late 1980s. Students may be aware of this problem through family and friends, or through the growing presence of people on the streets in their neighborhood. Talk with students about the importance of having a place to live. All people, all living things need shelter.

A good introduction to the concept of shelter for primary-grade students is Mary Ann Hoberman's *A House Is a House for Me,* illustrated by Betty Fraser (Viking, 1978). This pattern book lists shelters for many animals in rhyme. The final line is "the earth is a house for us all."

Another book, *Houses and Homes* by Ann Morris (Lothrop, Lee, and Shepard, 1992), offers a global approach, with photographs of people and their homes from around the world.

Enlist students in some form of action, to express their concerns about homelessness, such as writing to organizations that support better services, especially for homeless children. Share books such as Judith Berck's *No Place to Be: Voices of Homeless Children* (Houghton Mifflin, 1991), which includes quotations, photographs, and statistics about the causes and conditions of homelessness. Other books you can read with the class include the following:

Stephanie Tolan. *Sophie and the Sidewalk Man.* Four Winds, 1992. Sophie is saving money to buy a stuffed animal, but when she sees a homeless man sitting on the sidewalk she decides to give him half of her savings.

Paula Fox. *Monkey Island*. Orchard, 1991. Clay's mother has disappeared, leaving him in a welfare hotel. He takes to the streets, where he makes friends; but they're attacked, and Clay ends up in the hospital with pneumonia.

A Community Guidebook

What kinds of things do students know about their community? How would they describe it to visitors? What do they think visitors might want to know about it?

Talk about the different elements that make up the community, such as people, services, places, history, and customs. Who might arrive in the community and need information? Have any students recently moved into the area? What did they have to find out? Talk about different types of visitors (including new arrivals), their reasons for coming, and the kind of information they would require. For example, if a family with young children moved into the area, they would want to know about schools, playgrounds, inexpensive family restaurants, and so on.

Decide what to include in your guidebook by determining who could benefit most from it. If there are other guidebooks to your area, examine them to discover what they have and have not included.

Divide students into small groups. Each group can take responsibility for a section of the book. They must decide among themselves how best to present this information (a list, description, story, illustration, etc.). Each student should have the opportunity to contribute something. Include other work done by students related to the community, such as the maps suggested in a previous activity.

When the groups have finished, their efforts can be assembled into a book that everyone will be proud of. You can have it duplicated for the parents, or even consider having it reproduced professionally and distributed by a group such as the local chamber of commerce.

Community History

Each community has its own history, reflecting the contributions of the various groups that comprise it. The history of the development of the community may reflect a mini-history of the state, or it may represent idiosyncratic development. In either case, students can learn a lot about the forces that formed this country by studying the example of their own community.

What is history? Talk about the idea of history. More than just a list of past presidents, history deals with events and their consequences, change, and the influence of the past on the present. Ask students why we would want to study history. Have them brainstorm a list of reasons and objectives for studying local history. What do they want to find out? The students might pose some of the following questions:

- Who was here first?
- What happened to them?
- Why did they come?
- What traces have they left behind?
- What did this area look like then?
- How did people live?

Next, talk about where the students would go to find the information they are seeking. Have students suggest as many different sources as possible. They might mention the following:

- Visit the local library.
- Interview people who have lived there a long time.
- Read old newspapers.
- Review city records (archives)—maybe old maps.

The results of student research can be compiled in a booklet that is organized according to the questions the students asked and the answers they found. This information would also be interesting to the community, so you might look into having it reproduced on a larger scale.

If your students are interested in continuing their study, consult David Weitzman's *My Backyard History Book* (Little, Brown, 1975) as a community history resource. This classic book, written by kids and teachers, is full of practical and creative ways to learn about the past and other people.

A Local Language Survey

Do students know what languages are spoken in their area? Begin with local names. What languages have influenced local names? Ask families. What languages are spoken in the students' families? Do students know people who speak different languages?

Make a map or chart of the area on which to record the information students find. Have them research local history to see what the earliest languages were. Were there any Native American groups living nearby? What language did they speak and what happened to them? What do names of local places mean in these languages? Ask who the first settlers were and what languages they brought with them. Trace the language history down to the present time. Students should be able to discover what the major local language groups are and how long their speakers have been in the area.

Once the major languages are identified, they can become an important resource for further study. Plan lessons around examples from these languages. Bring in people who speak various languages so that students can hear what the languages sound like.

Interviewing

Investigating your community's history can turn into a yearlong project if students decide to find out more information by interviewing people about their past. As students define questions they would like to have answered, they can begin to create a list of people who might know the answers. Brainstorm a list of possible interviewees. Have students tell everyone they know about the project in order to identify more names of people to interview. They might ask the following questions:

- How long have you lived here?
- What was this town like when you first came?
- Where did you live when you were a child about my age?
- What was school like for you at that time?

Discuss what an interview is. What does the interviewer do? What is the interviewee supposed to do? Decide what questions you want to ask. Decide how you will record the information. (Tape recorder, notes on paper?) Prepare an interview schedule.

The most important aspect of this activity is the process that students go through, so the task should be carefully adapted to suit the level of the students. Students will come into contact with a different group of people (older people) and they will learn about people who are similar to and yet different from themselves. Children not only gain information related to social studies through this technique, they also increase language abilities. Both oral and written skills are developed as they conduct the interview, report back to the class, and record the results for a class book.

An English teacher in an Appalachian community developed the study of oral history to such an extent that his students have published several collections of their writings, starting with *The Foxfire Book* in 1972. There are now nine Foxfire books, edited by Eliot Wigginton and published by Doubleday Anchor Books. Wigginton has also published *Sometimes A Shining Moment: The Foxfire Experience* (Doubleday, 1985) and *Foxfire: 25 Years* (Doubleday, 1991). Information about the Foxfire Teacher Networks is available from Foxfire Teacher Outreach, PO Box 541, Mountain City, GA 30562.

A Community Time Line

A time line can help students organize the information they have discovered about their community. Make a list of all the various dates, events, and historical periods that are important to your study of the community. Transfer this list, in chronological order, to a line drawn across several sheets of butcher paper. This can become a class mural as students add to the time line and update it. You can also have students draw or cut out illustrations for significant historical events.

Making a Personal Time Line

As students learn more about the concept of history and the history of their community, they can transfer this understanding to their personal history. Have students draw a time line, beginning with their birth. On it they are to locate four or five dates or periods that are important to them personally, such as the birth of a brother or sister, a new pet, an illness, or moving to a new school. Talk about why these events were important. How did the students feel at the time? How would their life have been different if this event had not happened? Sometimes, knowing that other students have been through the same experience makes it easier to cope with painful memories or consequences.

Talk about the future. How do the students see themselves five years from now? Ten years? Have students write a description of themselves and their life, as they imagine it, five years in the future. Encourage students to be creative, since there is no "right" answer.

Personalizing History

When students compare their own time lines with that of their community, they can begin to see the connections between historical events and what has happened to them. What was happening in the community when they were born? Have them ask their parents, or other relatives what they remember from that time. Students also can look up the front page of the local newspaper for their birthdate to see what people were thinking and talking about. Then they can report to the class on the significant events of the day that was most significant to them.

What has happened in the community and the world since the students were born? Using the time line they developed for their community and researching important inventions and world events, they can construct a list of the most significant happenings of the past ten years, more or less. (Opinions on what to include may vary among the students.) Now have students discuss and write about how these events affected them and their family. How has the world changed since they were born? How is it the same?

CONTRIBUTIONS OF DIFFERENT GROUPS

As we look at the variety of groups in the United States, we can see that the assimilationist model is an illusion. Immigrants from different countries were glad to achieve greater freedom and economic opportunities, but they never lost awareness of their distinct heritage. For many of these groups, schooling has been a double-edged sword. It has provided the necessary access to prestige, knowledge, and skills; yet at the same time it has acted as a mechanism to reduce the uniqueness of local identities and traditional cultures. Today, as we shift our perspective to look at diversity as an asset, schools can welcome many cultures that were not acknowledged before.

Write an "Autobiography"

As students find out more about the history of their community and their origins, they can personalize their study by researching and writing an autobiography of an imagined ancestor. Tell the class to choose a period and decide what their ancestors might have been doing then—arriving in America, pioneering the West, struggling in a city or on a farm. Students will need to read books, both fiction and nonfiction, to supply information on how people lived, as well as the position or treatment of groups in that period. Their autobiographies can take the form of a day in their character's life, several journal entries, or a description of the influences on that person. They can also illustrate their account and read it to the class.

Immigration

Most of the population of the United States arrived here through immigration, but many people whose families have been here several generations don't know what it means to be an immigrant and to struggle for survival. Nearly half the current population of the United States can trace their ancestors back to Ellis Island, the famous threshold of arrival in New York. In the peak years of immigration (from 1900 to 1914), the Ellis Island immigration station processed five thousand people a day. *Ellis Island: Gateway to the New World* by Leonard Fisher (Holiday House, 1986) contains photographs and stories of immigrants.

Now both legal and illegal immigration are topics in the news as people from non-European countries arrive in increasing numbers. Students can explore this topic in terms of family history (When did their ancestors immigrate? How were they treated when they arrived?), as a human issue (How does it feel to leave your country? What factors make people take this risk?), and as a source of social questions (Can we accommodate all people, including families, from different countries?). By reading some of the following books, students can take the first steps toward understanding and empathizing with immigrants of previous generations and of today.

Bette Bao Lord. *In the Year of the Boar and Jackie Robinson.* Harper, 1984. The accomplishments of Jackie Robinson, black baseball star, help Shirley Temple Wong make the adjustment from China to America.

Russell Freedman. *Immigrant Kids.* Dutton, 1980. Photographs and stories of immigrants to New York, from the late nineteenth to the early twentieth century, focus on children's experiences.

Margy Burns Knight. *Who Belongs Here: An American Story.* Illustrated by Anne Sibley O'Brien. Tilbury, 1993. The story of Nany, a Cambodian refugee, who encounters racism and distrust of immigrants in the United States. The book asks who would be left if all the immigrants had to go back to their home country. The book also introduces people working to help immigrants succeed. Although a picture book, the ideas will be provocative for students at all levels.

Karen Hesse. *Letters from Rifka.* Holt, 1992. The journey of a Jewish family from Russia to the United States, told in letters from a young girl, reveals courage and perseverance.

Frances Temple. *Grab Hands and Run.* Orchard, 1993. Twelve-year-old Felipe is a political refugee. His father has disappeared in El Salvador. Only his mother remains to lead the family to a safe haven in Canada.

Susan Kuklin. *How My Family Lives in America.* Bradbury, 1992. This book presents pictures of today's "American" families. Sanu's father comes from Senegal, Eric's family is from Puerto Rico, and April's family comes from Taiwan.

Life in a Relocation Camp

Students can learn what many Japanese American children of their own age went through in this country in the 1940s. Several books describe life in a relocation camp, where large groups of families were imprisoned for several years, and the effect that this period had on children and the Japanese American community.

Ken Mochizuki. *Baseball Saved Us.* Lee & Low, 1993.

Takashima. *A Child in a Prison Camp.* Morrow, 1971.

Jeanne Houston. *Farewell to Manzanar.* Houghton Mifflin, 1973.

Daniel Davis. *Behind Barbed Wire: The Imprisonment of Japanese Americans during World War II.* Dutton, 1982.

Yoshiko Uchida. *Journey to Topaz.* Scribner's, 1971.

Read passages from one of these books to the class. If you have time, read the whole book. Afterwards, discuss the students' reactions to the book. They can discuss how they would feel going to a camp, what the people guarding the camp thought about their prisoners, whether this could happen again today, or what the people thought about the United States when they were released from the camp.

Have students write a letter to a friend, as if they lived in one of the camps, describing their life in the camp, or write a diary entry, telling what they do every day and how they feel.

Intergenerational Relations

A very different kind of grouping in our society is the elderly. An indication of our confusion over how to treat this group is the variety of labels used to identify the group. Ask students if they know anyone who is "older." Perhaps a grandparent or other older relative is living with their family. What do we call these people? Labels that have been used include senior citizen, aged, mature adult, retirees, third agers. Which would students rather be called when they are old?

Relationships with people from another generation provide multiple opportunities for children. They can have a relationship with an adult who has time for them, grandparents and other older adults can tell them stories about the past and their childhood, and they can learn to see the world through the eyes of another person. The following books are useful for starting discussions and enriching a unit on families. They can also motivate students to investigate the treatment of older people in our society. Students may choose to visit a nursing home or to write letters to elderly people who have no family.

Some of the most stirring books in this category are picture books. These books will provoke thought when read aloud at any grade level.

Karen Ackerman. *The Song and Dance Man*. Knopf, 1988. The children are the audience as Grandpa is transformed into the vaudeville performer he once was.

Eve Bunting. *The Wednesday Surprise*. Clarion, 1992. Anna helps her grandmother learn to read.

Judith Caseley. *Dear Annie*. Greenwillow, 1991. Annie has been receiving mail from her grandfather since she was born. At first her mother answers, but as she gets older, she responds on her own. She takes the collection of letters to school for show and tell. As a result, the class decides to begin a pen pal program.

Barbara Cooney. *Miss Rumphius*. Puffin, 1982. Miss Rumphius never forgot her grandfather's message to make the world more beautiful. When she grows old and lives by the sea, she plants a garden for others to enjoy.

Donald Crews. *BigMama's*. Greenwillow, 1991. Young Donald is pleased to find that everything is still the same on his annual summer visit to his grandmother's house.

Arthur Dorros. *Abuela*. Dutton, 1991. Young Rosalba and her grandmother imagine wonderful flying adventures as they travel through New York.

Barbara Dugan. *Loop the Loop*. Greenwillow, 1992. Anne and elderly Mrs. Simpson develop a special relationship and stay friends even when Mrs. Simpson has to go to a nursing home.

Valerie Flournoy. *The Patchwork Quilt*. Dial, 1985. When her grandmother is too ill to quilt, Tanya decides to finish the quilt, that includes scraps from the family's heritage.

Mem Fox. *Wilfred Gordon McDonald Partridge*. Kane/Miller, 1989. Wilfred lives next door to a nursing home. When Miss Nancy loses her memory, he asks the other people where to find it.

Gloria Houston. *My Great-Aunt Arizona*. HarperCollins, 1992. Arizona comes from Appalachia and grows up to become a teacher who influences generations of children.

Jeanne Lee. *Ba-Nam*. Holt, 1987. A young Vietnamese girl visiting her ancestors' graves finds the caretaker helpful.

Bill Martin and John Archambault. *Knots on a Counting Rope*. Bantam, 1987. A grandfather tells a blind boy stories of his heritage and helps him understand how to live in the world.

Carmen Santiago Nodar. *Abuelita's Paradise*. Whitman, 1992. Marita listens to her grandmother's stories of growing up in Puerto Rico, a paradise.

Patricia Polacco. *Mrs. Katz and Tush*. Bantam, 1992. A special friendship develops between Mrs. Katz, an elderly Jewish widow, and Larnel, a young African American.

Books for independent readers

John Chech. *My Grandmother's Journey*. Bradbury, 1991. A Russian grandmother tells of her early life and how she came to the United States.

Eth Clifford. *The Remembering Box*. Houghton Mifflin, 1985. Nine-year-old Joshua learns about his family history from his grandmother when he visits her every Jewish Sabbath. The memories help him cope when she dies.

Kathryn Lasky. *The Night Journey*. Puffin, 1981. At first, thirteen-year-old Rachel finds her visits to her great-grandmother boring. But soon Rachel is caught up in Sashie's tales of the czar's armies, pogroms, and the time the nine-year-old Sashie planned her family's escape.

Patricia MacLachlan. *Journey*. Delacorte, 1991. Journey and Cat are dumped on their grandparents by their mother. In trying to overcome his feelings of abandonment, Journey develops a closer relationship with his grandparents.

Sharon Bell Mathis. *The Hundred Penny Box*. Scholastic, 1975. Michael's 100-year-old great–great-aunt has a special box filled with a penny for each year of her life.

Cynthia Rylant. *Missing May*. Orchard, 1992. Adopted by her elderly aunt and uncle, twelve-year-old Summer struggles to cope with her aunt's death.

Cynthia Rylant. *An Angel for Solomon Singer*. Orchard, 1992. An old man living in a residential hotel dreams of what he can't have, but a friendly waiter in a cafe gives him a kind of home.

Useful for dispelling myths and misconceptions

John Langone. *Growing Older: What Young People Should Know about Aging*. Little, Brown, 1991.

Exploring Regions and Cultures

Throughout our country there are small pockets of people who share a unique culture. Challenge students to discover such groups as the following: Amish, Pennsylvania Dutch, Mennonites, Creoles, Hudderites.

They will discover a variety of interesting ideas, living patterns, and contributions. For example, the Pennsylvania Dutch have developed an attractive and distinctive style of art. They share such folk songs as the following with us:

Johnny Schmoker

Find out how the Amish live by reading Doris Faber's *The Amish* (Doubleday, 1991).

We Are All Americans

Focus attention not only on heroes and heroines, the people whose names are well known, but also on ordinary people of different ethnic groups who make up this country. Prepare a display, for example, based on Walt Whitman's well-known poem, "I Hear America Singing," from the collection *Leaves of Grass*. Use the title of the poem as a caption.

Around the poem display pictures of Americans at work. Include members of different ethnic groups as well as people performing nonstereotyped jobs, such as a woman working on lines for the telephone company or a black father caring for his children.

Varied Religions

Help your students recognize that there are many religions represented in the United States.

Dominant religions in the U.S. and Canada (1991):

Christians	237.3 Million
Nonreligious	25.3 Million
Jews	7.0 Million
Muslims	2.6 Million
Others	5.7 Million

What do students know about these religions? There are also less well-known religious groups, such as Quakers and Mennonites, that have rich traditions of service to the community and support for equality of all peoples. Encourage students to become familiar with varied beliefs. The following books will help:

Malka Drucker. *Shabbat: A Peaceful Island.* Holiday House, 1983.

Kathleen Elgin. *The Mormons, The Church of Jesus Christ of Latter-Day Saints.* McKay, 1969.

Kathleen Elgin. *The Quakers: The Religious Society of Friends.* McKay, 1968.

Larry Kettelkamp. *Religions, East and West.* Morrow, 1972.

Susan G. Purdy. *Jewish Holidays: Facts, Activities, and Crafts.* Lippincott, 1969.

Elizabeth Seeger. *Eastern Religions.* Crowell, 1973.

Invite guests to the classroom—a rabbi, a priest, a Protestant minister (a woman?)—to talk briefly about a specific religion.

Recognizing Contributions of Others

Focus on broad topics that make it possible to observe the contributions of people from many ethnic groups. Consider such subjects as art through the ages, folklore and mythology, foods of the world, and the urban environment. Within such studies students will learn that cultures have their distinctive qualities and contributions. Students will discover the universals of art as well as folklore and mythology. They will also discover such human needs as eating and the problems of living together.

City Life

Urban living is a broad topic that encompasses many subjects of interest to those who live in the city as well as those who live in suburban or rural settings. As the subject of city living is explored, an important element to consider is the multiethnic population. Explore books such as the following about people living in the city:

Rachel Isadora. *City Seen from A to Z.* Greenwillow, 1983.

Martha Munzer and John Vogel, Jr. *New Towns: Building Cities from Scratch.* Knopf, 1974.

Robert A. Liston. *The Ugly Palaces: Housing in America.* Watts, 1974.

Share poems about city living as another way of exploring. A useful collection for younger children is *A Song in Stone: City Poems,* compiled by Lee Bennett Hopkins (Crowell, 1983). A collection for upper elementary and junior high level is *On City Streets,* selected by Nancy Larrick (Bantam, 1969).

Writing City Poems

Children can write city poems, too. Begin with the words, *A city is. . . .* Collectively or individually, children can add phrases like this to form an unrhymed poem:

A city is . . .
> Horns honking—
> Red lights,
> Green Lights—
> Traffic on the go!

A city is . . .
> People walking—
> Down the street,
> Up the street—
> In sun or rain or snow.

Sharing What You Have Learned

A task card such as the following is an effective way to finish a unit of study. Working in small groups, students can present their work to the class and explain what they learned.

MAKE A COLLAGE

Make a collage about a group of people in the United States.

Native Americans	Women
City Dwellers	Black Americans
Aged Men and Women	Children
Workers	Drivers

Clip words and pictures to picture this group. Glue everything on a large piece of cardboard at least 18″ × 24″ in size.

HOW WE LIVE IN A GLOBAL VILLAGE

It has become increasingly obvious that the way we live affects people in other countries and that what they do affects us here. From the clearing of the rain forests in the Amazon, to an oil spill in Alaska, human actions can upset the earth's elaborately balanced ecological system. Political events also spill over national boundaries. The overthrow of Apartheid in South Africa and the dismemberment of the former Soviet Union have consequences for people in many other countries. Your teaching must prepare students to live in a world that is becoming more interdependent. More than ever before, students need to know about their peers in other countries and to understand how people think and live in other parts of the world.

Topic for Thought

Discuss the Chinese proverb found on page 132. Have students notice the progression from *right* to *peace*. Students can discuss the importance of peace and how it can be brought about.

If there is right in the soul,
There will be beauty in the person;
If there is beauty in the person,
There will be harmony in the home;
If there is harmony in the home,
There will be order in the nation;
If there is order in the nation,
There will be peace in the world.

Chinese Proverb

This poetic presentation can also be used as a model for student writing. They can follow this pattern:

If there is _____ ,
There will be _____ .

Two-line free verse poems can be produced like this:

If there is prejudice anywhere,
There will be unhappiness.

Repeating this pattern produces additional verses. The verses could be rhymed, thus:

If there is one friend in your life,
There will be singing.
If there is love in your life,
There will be joy-bells ringing.

The Study of Folklore in the Classroom

In his work *The Uses of Enchantment,* Bruno Bettelheim claimed that we read folktales in order to master the psychological problems of growing up. In addition, E. D. Hirsch argues that all children should be exposed to the classic fairy tales and myths because they are a basis for our culture. Today, teachers cannot assume that children are familiar with the traditional Western fairy tales (folklore). One of our goals, then, is to incorporate these stories into our teaching, so that all children can benefit from this rich base.

In addition, we want students to have access to the multicultural understandings that come from learning about the folklore of other cultures. These stories bring the flavor of a different point of view, a different time into the classroom, and remind us of the value of diversity. Despite similar themes across cultures, no two stories are alike. All stories reflect their passage through many storytellers.

To help you begin the study of folklore with students, consult *Once upon a Folktale: Capturing the Folklore Process with Children* edited by Gloria Blatt (Teachers College Press, 1993).

Incorporating Western Folklore in the Classroom

If you plan to study Western folklore with students, you have to plan ways to introduce the stories to students who are not familiar with them without ignoring the interests of those who know the tales very well. One way to solve this difference in level is to have students work in cooperative learning groups and study familiar stories as a basis for writing their own versions. The examples below can serve as models. Depending on the age level, students can write modernized versions or more sophisticated parodies.

Janet and Allan Ahlberg. *The Jolly Postman, or Other People's Letters.* Little, Brown, 1986. This spirited look into the world of Mother Goose rhymes features the correspondence of familiar names such as the Wicked Witch, Cinderella, and Jack and the Beanstalk. Students who know the stories will enjoy retelling them to the class. Older students will appreciate the level of detail in the samples of letters that are included.

William Brooke. *Untold Tales.* HarperCollins, 1992. These are wacky versions of familiar folktales that will spark student interest in writing their own.

Scieska, Jon. *The Stinky Cheese Man.* 1992. Nine parodies of well-known folk tales are narrated by Jack (of Beanstalk fame).

Scieszka, Jon. *The Frog Prince Continued.* Viking 1991. This version tells what happened after the popular ending "and they lived happily ever after." Students can make up their own endings for traditional tales.

Babette Cole. *Prince Cinders.* Putnam, 1987. This rewrite features a boy in the role of Cinderella. Imagine how the story would be changed.

Ed Young. *Seven Blind Mice.* Philomel, 1992. Noted illustrator's interpretation of a traditional story about the blind men and the elephant.

Folklore in Different Cultures

Feature examples of folktales from different countries and different cultural traditions within the United States. True folktales are anonymous tales that have been passed down through oral tradition. Literary folktales, on the other hand, may draw on folk traditions but show the presence of an author in their more polished language. In selecting examples to use with students, consider whether the story and illustrations are culturally authentic, as opposed to generic or a hodgepodge of mixed features. Finally, the best test is to read the story aloud. The language should flow easily and draw the audience along. A folktale unit can also be organized around themes, such as trickster tales (Anansi, Raven, Coyote), "pourquoi" stories (why or how something happened), or creation stories.

Jeanne Lee. *Toad Is the Uncle of Heaven.* Holt, 1985. In this Vietnamese folktale, the lowly toad uses his wits to allay the wrath of the king of heaven.

Laurence Yep. *The Butterfly Boy*. Illustrated by Jeanne Lee. Farrar Straus Giroux, 1993. A boy thinks he's a butterfly in this southern Chinese folktale. (Most Chinese Americans come from southern China but most Chinese folktale collections are from northern China, a distinction comparable to the difference between the northern and southern United States.)

Virginia Hamilton. *In the Beginning: Creation Stories from around the World*. Illustrated by Barry Moser. Harcourt Brace Jovanovich, 1988. A collection of tales retold by Hamilton, this book is particularly suitable for storytelling. Stories from many different regions are represented, including Australia, Africa, Asia, and America. Information is included on origins and further sources.

Jane Yolen. *Dream Weaver*. Illustrated by Michael Hague. Philomel, 1989. One of many collections of a respected folklorist's stories, reflecting universal themes. Great for reading aloud or learning for storytelling because of the exceptional quality of the language.

Robert San Souci. *The Talking Eggs*. Illustrated by Jerry Pinkney. Dial, 1989. This retelling of a Creole folktale is set in the American South, with African American characters. It is the story of two sisters, one good and one bad. The bad one has to learn that surface appearances are not always a guide to the quality inside.

Sumiko Yagawa. *The Crane Wife*. Translated by Katherine Paterson. Illustrated by Suekichi Akaba. Mulberry, 1987. One of Japan's best-known folktales, this is the story of a peasant who tends a wounded crane. Later, a beautiful woman comes to be his wife and weaves him exquisite cloth. But he loses her when he breaks his promise not to spy on her.

Retold by Jonathan London with Lanny Pinola. *Fire Race: A Karok Coyote Tale about How Fire Came to the People*. Illustrated by Sylvia Long. Chronicle Books, 1993. A Pomo/Miwok storyteller and Karok scholar, with author London's assistance, tell the story of what happens when Coyote steals fire from the yellow jackets.

Retold by Alma Flor Ada. *The Rooster Who Went to His Uncle's Wedding*. Illustrated by Kathleen Kuchera. Putnam, 1993. This is a tale the author first heard as a child in Cuba about a rooster who couldn't get clean.

Diane Goode. *Book of Silly Stories and Songs*. Dutton, 1992. Sixteen favorite nonsense stories from around the world.

Yoko Kawashima Watkins. *Tales from the Bamboo Grove*. Bradbury, 1992. The author's parents kept their Japanese culture alive in Korea by telling these folktales.

Katherine Paterson. *The King's Equal*. Illustrated by Vladimir Vagin. HarperCollins, 1992. This Russian-based literary folktale, illustrated by a noted Russian artist, presents a message of harmony and equality.

Margaret Hodges. *The Golden Deer*. Illustrated by Daniel San Souci. Scribner's, 1992. Tales of the Buddha from India.

Robert San Souci. *Cut from the Same Cloth: American Women of Myth, Legend, and Tall Tale*. Illustrated by Brian Pinkney. Philomel, 1993. Collection of lesser-known tales about larger-than-life women, drawn from diverse ethnic and regional sources.

Charlie Chin. *China's Bravest Girl.* Translated by Wang Xing Chu. Illustrated by Tomie Arai. Children's Book Press, 1993. This bilingual tale recounts the fifth-century legend of a young girl who goes to war when her family has no sons.

Folktale resource for teachers

Jan Irving and Robin Currie. *Straw into Gold: Books and Activities about Folktales.* Teacher Ideas Press, 1993. Intended for use with primary-grade students, this work includes variations, activities, games, and plans for theme-related teaching.

Students Collect Folklore

After discussion of folktales from different cultures, students will be encouraged to research stories from their own culture. Explain that very few folktales are ever written down. Although today folktales are often considered a part of children's literature and of interest only to children, in the past scholars often visited the elders of a cultural group and recorded the tales that they told. Why would anthropologists and folklorists be interested in stories from different, obscure cultures?

Students can act as their own folklorists, to discover and preserve the valuable tales of their heritage. If no one asks to hear these stories or records them, the stories may be lost forever. Brainstorm with students ways to go about initiating this folklore investigation. Whom can they ask? What do they say if people claim they don't know any stories? Plan how to record the stories. Some students may have relatives who can write the stories in their original language. Students can translate the story and preserve both versions. In other cases, students can record the person telling the story and transcribe it later. If necessary, students can write the story down as the teller dictates it to them.

Students can choose one of the stories to present to the class. Students who speak the same language or share the same heritage can work together to develop a presentation that includes information about the culture and history of the tale.

One Tale, Many Lands

Once students have read a variety of folktales, they will begin to notice many versions of the same story. The tale of Cinderella, for example, is found in many cultures. Have students look at different versions and compare them. How is the text different? How do the illustrations differ? What choices have the reteller and illustrator made to emphasize certain points or create different effects? What features define a story as a "Cinderella" story?

Charles Perrault. *Cinderella, or The Little Glass Slipper.* Illustrated by Errol Le Cain. Puffin, 1972. The full-page, elaborate, and fanciful illustrations are humorous and focus on the fable-like quality of this familiar story.

Charles Perrault. *Cinderella.* Retold by Amy Ehrlich and illustrated by Susan Jeffers. Dial, 1985. Again the focus is on the illustrations. The story is told from Cinderella's point of view, with a classic setting of eighteenth-century castles.

Charlotte Huck. *Princess Furball.* Illustrated by Anita Lobel. Greenwillow, 1989. This version of the Cinderella tale features a spunky princess who escapes a difficult situation through her own ingenuity.

Ai-Ling Louie. *Yeh-Shen: A Cinderella Story from China.* Illustrated by Ed Young. Philomel, 1982. One of many versions of the Cinderella story in other cultures.

Living in Other Countries

One of the best ways for students to experience what it is like to live in different countries is to read books about children of their own age who have traveled to a different country or who are growing up in another country. Here are some books you can suggest:

Books about Childhood in Another Country

Egypt: Betsy Byars. *The 18th Emergency.* Viking, 1973.

England: Lucy Boston. *The Children of Green Knowe.* Harcourt Brace Jovanovich, 1955.

England: Mabel Alan. *A Dream of Hunger Moss.* Dodd, 1983.

Greece: William Mayne. *The Glass Ball.* Dutton, 1962.

Netherlands: Meindert DeJong. *The Wheel on the School.* Harper and Row, 1954.

Soviet Union: E. M. Almedingen. *The Crimson Oak.* Coward, 1983.

Spain: Maia Wojciechowska. *Shadow of a Bull.* Atheneum, 1964.

Books about American Children Living in Other Countries

China: Jean Fritz. *Homesick: My Own Story.* Putnam, 1982.

France: Carol Ryrie Brink. *Family Sabbatical.* Viking, 1956.

Italy: Leo Politi. *Little Leo.* Scribner's, 1951.

Lebanon: Belle D. Rugh. *Crystal Mountain.* Houghton Mifflin, 1955.

A Visitor

After reading a book about children in another country, students can pretend to be someone from that country visiting the United States for the first time. What do they think would be their first impressions? What would be strange? What would they like or dislike? What might they not understand? Students can discuss their ideas and then write a brief account of their "visit."

What Others Believe

Invite students to share with the class some of their religious beliefs, if any. Since stereotypes and prejudice are fed by ignorance, open discussion will aid in accepting and understanding different beliefs. Almost every Jewish child has seen a Christmas tree but how many non-Jewish children have seen a *dreidel?* Mormon children are sometimes taunted by those outside their faith because of misconceptions about Mormonism.

An investigation of different religions can focus on the importance of symbols and the universal themes. Is the cross used in any religion besides Christianity? If not, it would be more accurate to say "Christian denominations" instead of "religions." What does the cross represent? Another common symbol is the star. What are some religions that use a star? What does the star mean?

A discussion of such symbols should include examples that students would be familiar with from their daily lives. In talking about the power of an object to represent many different objects, ideas, and feelings, students' suggestions may range from corporate insignia to road signs.

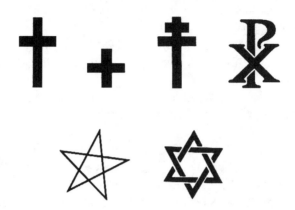

Dealing with Larger Social Issues

As you talk with students about issues such as prejudice, racism, and the homeless, recognize their desire to take some action based on their beliefs. Although these large social questions will not be solved simply, do not discourage students from wanting to be involved. Despite their young age and lack of power in society, students have strong feelings about injustice. In discussing books and topics that raise troublesome questions, guide student responses into productive channels. What can students do? They can publicize problems, write letters, organize people, talk to others, invite people to speak, and publish their efforts. In *It's Our World, Too!* (Little, Brown, 1993), Phillip Hoose describes young activists who have taken a stand on sensitive issues such as sexism, racism, and the homeless and shows the power of people of any age to make a difference.

One topic that concerns young people very much is war, or any violent conflict, and its impact on people. The following books will stimulate discussion of student fears and how these issues affect them:

Elizabeth Laird. *Kiss the Dust.* Dutton, 1992. Tara, thirteen, and her family are Kurds who are forced to flee Iraq during the 1984 war. They face a harsh existence in refugee camps.

Eleanor Coerr. *Sadako.* Illustrated by Ed Young. Putnam, 1993. This is a picture book rewrite of the author's famous earlier book, *Sadako and the Thousand Cranes*, about the fate of a young Japanese girl after the atomic bomb was dropped on Hiroshima at the end of World War II.

Eleanor Coerr. *Mieko and the Fifth Treasure.* Putnam, 1993. Ten-year-old Mieko has to reckon with the physical and psychological aftereffects of the atomic bomb.

Yukio Tsuchiya. *Faithful Elephants: A True Story of Animals, People and War.* Translated by Tomoko Tsuchiya Dykes. Illustrated by Ted Lewin. Houghton Mifflin, 1988. The story of what happened to the elephants in the Tokyo zoo at the end of World War II, when there was no more food. This story has been read aloud in Japan for twenty years to mark the anniversary of the end of the war and as a reminder of the uselessness of war.

Florence Heide. *Sami and the Time of the Troubles*. Clarion, 1992. A picture book about Sami, a ten-year-old Lebanese boy who spends his life in the basement bomb shelter hoping for peace.

Gaye Hicyilmaz. *Against the Storm*. Dell, 1993. This novel for older students is set in contemporary Turkey and focuses on the plight of displaced people and the strategies they use to survive.

Rian Verhoeven and Ruud van der Rol. *Anne Frank*. Viking, 1993. This photographic remembrance of Anne Frank shows her as more than just a passive victim. Use this with other books about the Holocaust and people's response to it.

Ann Turner. *Katie's Trunk*. Macmillan, 1992. This story about the American Revolutionary War is told from the Tory point of view. Katie learns that there are good people on both sides.

Laurie Dolphin. *Neve Shalom/Wahat Al-Salam: Oasis of Peace*. Scholastic, 1993. Describes a unique village near Jerusalem where Israeli Arabs and Jews choose to live and work together. Although the Arab and Jewish families maintain separate cultures, they meet in the bilingual, bicultural school setting.

Making Sense out of Population Figures

How many people live in the world today? Have students guess and write their estimates on the board. Did anyone come close to 5.423 billion? (Source: Bureau of the Census, 1991.) Such a large number has virtually no meaning to most of us unless we can express it in familiar terms. Research some comparative figures. How many people live in your city? How many live in the state? What's the population of the United States?

Have students predict what country has the largest population and what country has the greatest land area. They may be surprised to learn that China has the largest population of any country in the world: over 1.1 billion inhabitants, 21 percent of the world's population. India is second with almost 900 million people; its population expected to reach 1 billion by the end of the decade. The United States is next, with a population of only 250 million, followed by Indonesia, Brazil, and Russia. Russia has the largest land area, over 6.5 million square miles, followed by Canada, China, the United States, and Brazil.

Explore different strategies to represent the relative sizes of the population of the United States and the world. Students can make pie charts or block graphs. Another technique is to choose a small object such as a book, pencil, or apple to represent a fixed number (1,000, for example). How many books would it take to show the population of your city, state, country, or the world? Demonstrations like this help students to understand and visualize large numbers and the relation between thousands, millions, and billions.

Studying Population: Demography

Ask students if they know what a demographer does. Can they figure it out on the basis of the roots *demo* and *graph?* (Think of other words that have these roots in them.) Reward the first student who uses the meanings of the roots to come up with a definition close to "one who measures population and its characteristics."

Challenge students to become *demographers* and find out how fast the population is growing. Has the rate of growth changed over time? Compare the growth rate in this century with the past century. What does this growth rate predict for the next ten years? Twenty years? Some areas are growing at different rates. How will the composition of the world change in the next ten years? Twenty years? What about age? How will the percentage of old and young people change over the next ten years? Why will this change? What effects might this have on all of us?

How do we count population figures? Is it really possible to count everyone living in the country on one day? What factors might affect the accuracy of this figure? Are there specific groups that might be "undercounted" or "overcounted"?

Dance—A Universal Language

Dance is something that is shared and understood around the world. Demonstrate the universality of dance and its themes by showing films of dancing performed by different cultures. Here are a few examples:

African Rhythms. 13 minutes, color. Associated Film, Inc., 1621 Dragon St., Dallas, TX 75207.

The Strollers. 6 minutes, color. The Moiseyev Dance Company in a Russian folk dance.

Dancer's World. 30 minutes. NET. Martha Graham discusses dancing as her students dance the emotions of hope, fear, joy, and love.

Students can learn some simple folk dances to perform.

International Folk Dancing, a book by Betty Casey. Doubleday, 1981. Includes directions and pictures of costumes for students.

Different Rhythms for Movement

Encourage students to move to various rhythms by playing recordings of music from different countries around the world. Representative records available include the following:

Authentic Afro-Rhythms. LP 6060, Kimbo Educational, P. O. Box 246, Deal, NJ 07723. Rhythms from Africa, Cuba, Haiti, Brazil, Trinidad, and Puerto Rico.

Authentic Indian Dances and Folklore. Kimbo Educational. Drumming and storytelling by Michigan Chippewa chiefs who narrate history of dances.

Authentic Music of the American Indians. 3 records. Everest. Chesterfield Music Shops, Inc., 12 Warren St., New York, NY 10007.

The Lark in the Morning. Songs and Dances from the Irish Countryside. Everest.

The REAL Flamenco. Everest.

Folk Music from around the World

Folk songs from other countries offer immediate enjoyment through their patterned verses and easy-to-learn choruses. You will find listings for recorded songs from Mexico, the British Isles, France, and many other countries in the catalogs of Caedmon and Folk-ways.

Kathleen Krull. *Gonna Sing My Head Off!* Knopf, 1992. Folk music accompanied by energetic artwork.

Sports in Other Countries

Sports and games are of universal interest. Offer students the opportunity to learn about different games from other cultures. Students may already be aware of significant sports figures from other countries. In an Olympic year, plan activities related to the widespread interest in these sports and the countries represented.

Arnold Arnold. *The World Book of Children's Games.* World, 1972. Informal games for all ages.

Frederic Grunfield. *Games of the World.* Holt, 1975. Games for all ages, including history and illustrations.

Richard Lyttle. *The Games They Played: Sports in History.* Atheneum, 1982. Includes games from Greek, Roman, Egyptian, Spanish, Eskimo, and Mayan cultures.

The Way to Play: The Illustrated Encyclopedia of the Games of the World. Barton, 1970.

The Olympics: An Educational Opportunity Enrichment Unit. 1750 East Boulder St., Colorado Springs, CO 80909. Curriculum materials for all grade levels, based on the Olympian theme.

David Wallechinsky. *The Complete Book of the Olympics.* Penguin, updated after each Olympiad. History and statistics of the Olympic Games.

Human Needs

Looking at other cultures can help students learn more about themselves and their culture. After you have been studying a particular group of people, or reading tales from several cultures, ask students to list the most basic needs they think are common to all cultures. Focus on the fundamental human needs for love, food, and shelter. Relate these to students' lives. How are these provided for in their lives? How do different groups satisfy them?

Students can brainstorm examples of how different people respond to one need, such as *love.* Then they can write personal responses, completing the sentence "Love is . . ." and illustrate their ideas. As a class, students can prepare a collage for the bulletin board, showing how different needs are met in different cultures, based on their own illustrations or examples they have found.

FOCUS ON AFRICAN AMERICANS: A CASTELIKE MINORITY

When African Americans were slaves, the struggle to learn to read and write despite legal prohibitions was the focus for education. Later, Booker T. Washington and W. E. B. Du Bois debated whether the appropriate education for African Americans would be a vocational track, because those were the jobs Blacks were most likely to get, or a university degree, which might lead to aspirations that were less likely to be fulfilled. Today African Americans still experience the limited access to economic opportunities that sparked the original discussion. By birth, they enter what has been described as a "caste"; their prospects for health, work, and education are circumscribed by their race.

The Supreme Court decision of *Brown* v. *The Board of Education* in 1954 established that separate schools for Blacks were inherently unequal. But inequality persists and school districts try to plan for a more even distribution of Blacks and students of other races. Meanwhile the basic notion of community is being questioned, as some educators propose separate schools for African Americans, or African American boys. How do we respond to this lack of progress? What is required for African American students to receive the "best education any parents could want for their child?" As a teacher, you have to confront these issues which influence your attempts to build community among your students and to share African American history and culture with all students.

Famous Black Americans

Students need to hear about black men and women who have made contributions in areas other than sports and music. Challenge students to match these names with their contribution.

C	Matthew Henson	A. astronomer
A	Benjamin Banneker	B. first person killed in Boston Massacre
D	Charles Drew	(Revolutionary War)
B	Crispus Attucks	C. went to North Pole with Admiral Peary
G	Shirley Chisolm	D. invented blood transfusions
E	Phillis Wheatley	E. poet in colonial America
F	Harriet Tubman	F. led slaves to freedom
		G. first black female in Congress

Once students realize the number of Blacks who have been recognized for their accomplishments, they will want to discover more names and find out more information about these people. Start a chart on the bulletin board where students can write the name of an achiever or someone they admire, and the reason. Students will be motivated to seek out names of historical figures, as well as people they know and respect today. *Profiles of Black Americans,* by Richard Boning (Dexter and Westbrook, 1969), is an excellent source of more information. Also see listing in the Appendix.

Heroes and Holidays

Several holidays provide reminders of African American accomplishments. Kwanzaa, celebrated in December, acknowledges African cultural roots. Feature books about Kwanzaa and about Africa.

Denise Burden-Patmon. *Imani's Gift at Kwanzaa.* Illustrated by Floyd Cooper. Simon and
   Schuster, 1992. Explains the customs of Kwanzaa through the story of Imani, who
   learns to share the spirit of unity by introducing another girl to Kwanzaa.

Andrea Davis Pinkney. *Seven Candles for Kwanzaa*. Illustrated by Brian Pinkney. Dial, 1993. Kids make presents and adults light candles. Kwanzaa is like a family holiday, Thanksgiving and a birthday all in one.

Another special day is Martin Luther King's birthday in January. On this day, provide opportunities to discuss King's work. What have we achieved in civil rights? How far do we still have to go?

Linda Lowrey. *Martin Luther King Day*. Carolrhoda, 1987. The story of Dr. King's work in the context of the black struggle for civil rights. The book is aimed at all children, not just Blacks. Includes statements by others involved in the civil rights movement, which can serve as a basis for discussion.

Myra Cohn Livingston. *Let Freedom Ring: A Ballad of Martin Luther King, Jr.* Illustrated by Samuel Byrd. Holiday House, 1992. Livingston's verse incorporates quotations from King's speeches, reflects his voice.

Jean Marzollo. *Happy Birthday, Martin Luther King*. Illustrated by Brian Pinkney. Scholastic, 1993. A child asks his family why they celebrate King's birthday, and family members share their memories of King's accomplishments.

Another significant African American holiday is Juneteenth, commemorating the day that the slaves in Texas finally learned about the Emancipation Proclamation. This would be a good time to focus on black history, particularly the period of slavery.

African American History

The story of African Americans should be a part of the history that all of us learn. Unfortunately, presentations that focus on African Americans tend to occur in clumps in February and remain rare the rest of the year. Spread discussion of African American history throughout the curriculum with books that make black people more visible and help black students find their lives in history.

Jacob Lawrence. *The Great Migration: An American Story*. HarperCollins, 1993. Paintings by the famous artist Jacob Lawrence, accompanied by explanatory text, show the movement of Blacks from the rural South to the urban North. Lawrence also painted sequences of the lives of Harriet Tubman and Frederick Douglass. The epilogue is a poem by Walter Dean Myers.

Walter Dean Myers. *Now Is Your Time: The African American Struggle for Freedom*. HarperCollins, 1991. The history of African Americans starts in 1619 (before the Mayflower arrived) and continues today. This book is significant in showing African Americans not as victims but taking action on their own behalf.

Faith Ringgold. *Dinner at Aunt Connie's House*. Hyperion, 1993. Another book by distinguished artist Ringgold, based on her African American story quilt/paintings. When the children visit Aunt Connie, her paintings of African American historical figures come to life and the women tell their stories. Voices of Mary McLeod Bethune, Madame Walker, and others will encourage readers to discover more about significant Black women.

Gwen Everett. *John Brown*. Paintings by Jacob Lawrence. Rizzoli, 1993. In this dramatic account, Annie Brown describes how her father led a "liberation army" in Virginia in 1859.

Does Negro Mean Black?

Does it make any difference what a group is called? Most people must think so, since they make such a point of it. What are some of the labels that Blacks have used or have had applied to them? List some on the board, for example:

Black Americans	Negroes
Afro-Americans	African Americans
Blacks	Colored

Can students put these labels in historical order from the oldest to the most recent? Discuss how they made their decisions. What are the relative positive and negative qualities of each label? What does each one focus on? Talk about each label and how it originated. Do students know that *negro* means the color *black* in Spanish? *Colored* is still used in South Africa and Great Britain to refer to the nonwhite population, which in these countries includes people from India. *African* is used to connote pride in African origins, though Blacks have been in this country for so long that they barely resemble their African ancestors.

Which label do students think is the most positive? Which would they prefer to use for themselves? Ask them to suggest alternative labels. Have students vote on their favorite. They can write a brief explanation of why they prefer the one they chose.

Featuring African American Authors and Illustrators for Children

Talk about the authors and illustrators of the children's books you share with students. How many of them are African American? Make sure that students know who these people are. Show them pictures from the book covers and talk about the artists as real people.

African American authors who have written a number of exceptional books for young people include Virginia Hamilton, Mildred Taylor, John Steptoe, and Walter Dean Myers. Investigate books by some more recent authors, for example, Patricia McKissack, Angela Johnson, and Faith Ringgold.

After reading several books by the same author, analyze the author's style. What themes does this author prefer? Does the author use a particular style of language? What is the author's attitude toward his or her characters? Does the author favor a specific genre, or type of book, such as folktale, history, mystery, and so on?

African American illustrators are receiving increasing recognition. Names such as Tom Feelings, Floyd Cooper, Leo and Diane Dillon, and Jerry Pinkney appear on many excellent children's books.

Look for more information about favorite authors and illustrators in the following:

Leslie Sills. *Inspirations: Stories about Women Artists*. Whitman, 1989. Four artists are featured, including Faith Ringgold.

Robyn Montana Turner. *Faith Ringgold*. Little, Brown, 1993. Focuses on her work as an artist but provides background so that readers can understand the sources of her children's books.

Pat Cummings, ed. *Talking with Artists*. Bradbury, 1992. Conversations with fourteen children's artists, including Leo and Diane Dillon, Tom Feelings, Pat Cummings, and Jerry Pinkney. Includes a list of the illustrators' books.

Helen E. Williams. *Books by African-American Authors and Illustrators for Children and Young Adults*. American Library Association, 1991.

Positive Images of Black Families in Literature

Students need to see realistic yet positive images of the lives of people like themselves. Well-written children's books can give students a mirror against which to measure themselves as well as a chance to imagine a better world. The following books acknowledge the problems and conflicts typical of African American children's lives and at the same time offer hope. In addition, the quality of the writing ensures that children from other racial backgrounds will appreciate the stories too.

Jacqueline Woodson. *Maizon at Blue Hill*. Delacorte, 1993. When Maizon is accepted at Blue Hill, an elite, mostly white boarding school, she has to leave behind her grandmother, her best friend, and her familiar neighborhood. She struggles to find her own place despite the barriers at Blue Hill. Look for other stories about Maizon.

Lucille Clifton. *Some of the Days of Everett Anderson*. Illustrated by Evaline Ness. Henry Holt, 1970. The famous black poet has written a series of books about lively Everett, including ones in which his father dies and his mother remarries. Warm picture of family life in an apartment in the city.

Mildred Taylor. *Roll of Thunder, Hear My Cry*. Bantam, 1976. Classic story of a southern black family maintaining its pride and its land despite the humiliations of racial prejudice. A Newbery Award winner, it is especially noteworthy for its acknowledgment of the complexity of black-white relations. Other books by Taylor continue the story of Cassie, based on her father's family.

Faith Ringgold. *Tar Beach*. Crown, 1991. Cassie and BeBe in Brooklyn dream of flying away from the pressures of the world.

Phil Mendez. *The Black Snowman*. Illustrated by Carole Byard. Scholastic, 1989. Jacob learns pride and bravery from a snowman that he builds with his younger brother.

Margaree King Mitchell. *Uncle Jed's Barbershop*. Illustrated by James Ransome. Simon and Schuster, 1993. A black man dreams of owning his own barbershop, not an easy goal in the 1920s.

Robert San Souci. *Sukey and the Mermaid*. Four Winds, 1992. Sukey finds comfort from a mermaid in her escape from her stepfather. Set in the Sea Islands, off the Carolina coast.

Sherley Williams. *Working Cotton*. Harcourt Brace Jovanovich, 1992. The story of an African American girl and her family's work in the cotton fields of central California. A Caldecott Medal book.

Mary Hoffman. *Amazing Grace*. Illustrated by Caroline Binch. Dial, 1991. Grace likes to act out characters from stories she reads. When her school decides to put on a play, she wants to be Peter Pan. The others tell her she can't because she's a girl and because she's black. But her grandmother shows her a black ballerina and tells Grace she can be anyone she wants to be.

Gloria Pinkney. *Back Home*. Illustrated by Jerry Pinkney. Dial, 1992. Eight-year-old Ernestine from the city visits relatives on a farm in North Carolina. She's eager to fit in, but the country ways are different. This story of a black family presents universal themes of home, family, and belonging.

Learning Pride in One's Culture

African American children are surrounded by negative images of their race and culture. They need to have many opportunities to take pride in their history and heritage. Books can reach across time and space to supply what may be lacking in their own community. The following books give students something to hold on to, to help them counterbalance feelings of inferiority. After reading these books, have students share examples of family stories and customs.

Lucille Clifton. *All Us Come Cross the Water*. Illustrated by John Steptoe. Holt, 1973. Ujamaa is confused about his heritage until Old Tweezer tells him that the same boat—slavery—brought everyone here, making everyone brothers.

Anita Rodriquez. *Aunt Martha and the Golden Coin*. Clarkson-Potter, 1993. One of a series of books about Aunt Martha, who tells the children learning stories from her African American heritage. In this one, she has a magic coin which gives her the strength to fend off a burglar. But is the coin really magic, or does Aunt Martha's own strength of mind save her?

Camille Yarbrough. *Cornrows*. Illustrated by Carole Byard. Sandcastle Books, 1991. Mama and Great-Grammaw pass on their African American heritage with pride as they braid cornrows in the children's hair, telling stories of the power and richness of African traditions.

Relations between Black and White

Literature can provide case studies of prejudice and conflict in the relationships between Blacks and Whites. Students from interracial families may feel that they belong in neither camp. Use these examples to stimulate student problem solving. How would they resolve these conflicts? Is it possible to be friends with someone from another race? Are some solutions preferable to others?

Mildred D. Taylor. *The Friendship and the Gold Cadillac*. Bantam, 1989. Two stories of prejudice, one told by Cassie Logan, about a neighbor who thought he had a special relationship with a white man, and another about an African American family from Ohio who travel south to Mississippi and are frightened by the racial hostility they experience.

Dirlie Herlihy. *Ludie's Song*. Puffin, 1990. In Georgia in the 1950s, Marty stands up against community prejudice to maintain her friendship with a black family.

Arnold Adoff. *All the Colors of the Race*. Illustrated by John Steptoe. Lothrop, Lee and Shepard, 1982. "All the colors of the race are in my face," begins the poetic expression of a young girl's experience in an interracial family. (Adoff is married to Virginia Hamilton.) The poems express with poignancy how hard it is to cope with other people's expectations of being one or the other, black or white.

African American Folklore

Some of the richest American folklore comes from the African American tradition. Read examples aloud to students to stimulate their interest in this oral tradition. Have students work in groups to present a tale to the class or for a schoolwide program. Students who may not do as well with written work have a chance to shine as performers. And all students have the opportunity to develop their speaking skills as they concentrate on delivering their dialogue with appropriate emotions.

Oral performance provides a context in which to talk about different ways of speaking. Students can have some of the characters speak formal English and others speak so-called Black English. How will students distinguish these ways of speaking? Because students have had different amounts of experience with formal English, encourage them to share their knowledge as they work in groups to decide how each character will talk.

Virginia Hamilton. *The People Could Fly: American Black Folktales*. Illustrated by Leo and Diane Dillon. Knopf, 1985. A rich, well-written collection.

Ezra Jack Keats. *John Henry*. Knopf, 1987. Picture book version of folk hero.

Patricia McKissack. *The Dark Thirty: Southern Tales of the Supernatural*. Illustrated by Brian Pinkney. Knopf, 1992. Favorite scary stories. Students will probably recognize familiar tales.

Virginia Hamilton. *Drylongso*. Illustrated by Jerry Pinkney. Harcourt Brace Jovanovich, 1992. It is 1975 and Lindy and her family live on a farm suffering from drought. Drylongso, a mysterious boy, appears in a dust storm to tell people how to treat the earth. The character personifies drought, longing for rain and ordinariness. Drylongso has become a word, probably from Gullah, meaning drought, then extended to mean "ordinary."

Robert San Souci. *The Talking Eggs*. Illustrated by Jerry Pinkney. Dial, 1989. This retelling of a Creole folktale is set in the American South with African American characters. It is the story of two sisters, one good and one bad. The bad one has to learn that surface appearances are not always a guide to the quality inside.

Black English in Books

Many contemporary writers attempt to reproduce the sound of Black English in their books. Some just include black slang and others incorporate both vocabulary and grammatical features of Black English. Unfortunately, no written version can accurately portray spoken Black English, just as standard spoken English is very different from written English. However, these books have the advantage of sounding more familiar to speakers of Black English and are sometimes easier to read than standard English. They also are important for introducing other students to Black English, because the context makes the meaning of unfamiliar words and constructions clear.

Read passages from some of the following books to the class and discuss the language used. How do students feel? Does it sound realistic or familiar? Do they understand what the people are saying? Why would someone want to write like that?

Brenda Wilkinson. *Ludell.* Harper and Row, 1975.

Eloise Greenfield. *There She Come Bringing Me That Little Baby Girl.* Lippincott, 1974.

Virginia Hamilton. *Sweet Whispers, Brother Rush.* Philomel, 1982.

John Steptoe. *Train Ride.* Harper and Row, 1971.

Walter Dean Myers. *Fast Sam, Cool Clyde, and Stuff.* Puffin, 1975.

Patricia McKissack. *Mirandy and Brother Wind.* Knopf, 1988.

See Chapter 6 for more information about the structure of Black English.

Poetry by Black Poets

How many students know the names of any black poets? Students may be surprised to learn that there are famous male and female black poets. Share with the class poems such as "Motto" by Langston Hughes and "We Real Cool" by Gwendolyn Brooks. Both of these poems make especially effective use of "street" language.

As you discuss the poems, ask students why the poets chose to use this kind of language. The poems don't read like conventional poetry—can we still call them poems? Are they written to be read silently or aloud? Using these poems as models, students will be motivated to write poems based on their experience, with familiar words and rhythms.

Collections of poetry by African Americans for children include the following:

Joyce Carol Thomas. *Brown Honey in Broomwheat Tea.* Illustrated by Floyd Cooper. HarperCollins, 1993.

Deborah Slier, ed. *Make a Joyful Sound: Poems for Children by African American Poets.* Illustrated by Cornelius Van Wright and Ying-Hwa Hu. Checkerboard, 1991.

Tom Feelings. *Soul Looks Back in Wonder.* Dial, 1993. Feelings illustrated the book, then selected poems by thirteen African American poets, past (Langston Hughes) and present (Maya Angelou), to accompany them. Provides an unblinking look at African American life and issues today.

Wade Hudson, ed. *Pass It On: African-American Poetry for Children.* Illustrated by Floyd Cooper. Scholastic, 1993. Includes information on the poets.

Many contemporary African American poets have written books of poetry for children. Look for collections by Lucille Clifton, June Jordan, and Nikki Giovanni.

Slavery and the Civil War

The history of African Americans in the United States is overshadowed by their involuntary presence as slaves. A common misconception is that the slaves accepted their condition passively until they were freed by Abraham Lincoln. In fact, free Blacks worked unceasingly to abolish slavery, while enslaved Blacks exercised what resistance they could. Correct student misconceptions by telling stories of African American resistance to slavery. When studying the history of the United States up to the Civil War, make sure that the story of slavery is included.

Display a map of the United States to the class. Which were the slave states and which the free states? Have students trace the paths by which slaves could escape to freedom (to the North, frequently later to Canada, and also to the Bahamas, since they were British and, therefore, free). How far would slaves have to travel and how long would it take? What motivated people to risk such a long, difficult journey into unknown territory?

Since they couldn't read maps or directions, one way people found their way North was to follow the North Star. Learn the song "Follow the Drinking Gourd," which commemorates the advice passed among slaves to watch for the Big Dipper and follow the direction it pointed.

Research the history of the Underground Railroad in your area, if possible. Are there any remains or memories of stations where slaves were directed and hidden? Helping slaves escape was illegal and especially dangerous in the South, yet all kinds of people (northerners, southerners, Indians, Quakers, Canadians, British, free Blacks, and other slaves) risked their own lives. Why would people do something for which they could be arrested or killed?

Read biographies and historical accounts to understand the extraordinary people who fought against slavery.

Jeri Ferris. *Go Free or Die: A Story about Harriet Tubman.* Carolrhoda, 1988. Harriet Tubman, an escaped slave, returned to slaveholding territory nineteen times to rescue other slaves, despite a high bounty on her head. She lived long enough to see the end of the Civil War and the results of her efforts.

Jeri Ferris. *Walking the Road to Freedom: A Story of Sojourner Truth.* Carolrhoda, 1988. This northern-born slave became a sought-after speaker against slavery; she pleaded for the rights of Blacks and women.

Virginia Hamilton. *Anthony Burns: The Defeat and Triumph of a Fugitive Slave.* Knopf, 1988. The federal government supported fugitive slaves but was forced to give way to slaveholding interests. Burns became a symbol of this struggle when he escaped to Boston and his return was sought by his owner.

Mary Lyons. *Stitching the Stars: The Story Quilts of Harriet Powers.* Scribner's, 1993. The famous quilts of Powers are reproduced here, accompanied by a narrative of her life. Powers was born into slavery in 1837.

Doreen Rappaport. *Escape from Slavery: Five Journeys to Freedom.* Illustrated by Charles Lilly. HarperCollins, 1991. Relates the escape stories of courageous African Americans who found freedom in the years before the Civil War.

Virginia Hamilton. *Many Thousand Gone: African-Americans from Slavery to Freedom.* Illustrated by Leo and Diane Dillon. Knopf, 1992. The stories of the many brave Blacks who struggled against slavery, from Harriet Tubman and Nat Turner to others less well known. Rich language lends itself to reading aloud.

William Loren Katz. *Breaking the Chains: African-American Slave Resistance.* Atheneum, 1990. Written and oral history accounts document the defiance and resilience of slaves before emancipation.

Julius Lester. *To Be a Slave.* Illustrated by Tom Feelings. Dial, 1968. Slave narrative accounts of auctions, plantations, and slave life.

Read fictional accounts to feel what it was like to live as a slave. The following books help students understand how hard it was to maintain stable families, to remember previous lives in Africa, and to accomplish something as simple as learning to read and write.

James Berry. *Ajeemah and His Son.* HarperCollins, 1992. Ajeemah and his son, in Ghana on their way to celebrate his marriage are kidnapped and sold as slaves in Jamaica. Atu, the son, kills himself, but Ajeemah doesn't give up hope. An excellent starting point for discussing the degradation of slavery and the different ways in which people responded to it.

Jennifer Armstrong. *Steal Away.* Orchard, 1992. Forty-one years after they ran away, a black woman and a white woman relive the year 1855, when they were thirteen and went north seeking freedom. (A good companion book to *Sweet Clara and the Freedom Quilt.*)

Deborah Hopkinson. *Sweet Clara and the Freedom Quilt.* Illustrated by James Ransome. Knopf, 1993. A young slave girl needs a map to guide her escape north. Because she cannot read or write, she stitches the escape information she has gleaned into a quilt. Illustrations carefully delineate specific people and places. Based on the Verona plantation, where the illustrator's ancestors were slaves.

Joyce Hansen. *Which Way Freedom?* Walker, 1986. After escaping from slavery, Obie serves in a black regiment and fights in the Civil War.

Delores Johnson. *Now Let Me Fly: The Story of a Slave Family.* Macmillan, 1993. Beginning with the capture of a young girl in Africa, the story follows her through harsh years of slavery as she works to help her family survive.

Jacob Lawrence. *Harriet and the Promised Land.* Simon and Schuster, 1993. Terse story of Harriet Tubman's life, dominated by dramatic paintings.

Mary Lyons. *Letters from a Slave Girl: The Story of Harriet Jacobs.* Scribner's, 1992. Fictionalized account of Jacobs's life. She tried to escape from North Carolina in 1842.

Mary Stolz. *Cezanne Pinto.* Knopf, 1994. Ex-slave Pinto, on his ninetieth birthday, looks back to his childhood on a Virginia plantation, his escape north, and his search for his mother.

Gary Paulsen. *Nightjohn*. Delacorte, 1993. Sarny, a young female slave, risks her life in order to be taught to read and write by a mysterious escaped slave. Gripping short novel of the power of literacy and the drive to resist.

Connie Porter. Addy Walker Series: *Meet Addy; Addy Learns a Lesson; Addy's Surprise.* American Girls Series. Pleasant Company, 1993. The life of a young African American girl growing up in the mid-1800s. The books start when Addy is a slave on a plantation in North Carolina. She and her mother run away to begin a new life in Philadelphia, where she attends a coeducational school.

Paula Fox. *The Slave Dancer.* Dell, 1973. Winner of the Newbery Award, this story tells of a boy who is forced to play his fife to make the slaves dance on the voyage from Africa to the United States to be sold. Recounts in vivid, gruesome detail a story of survival.

Faith Ringgold. *Aunt Harriet's Underground Railroad in the Sky.* Crown, 1992. Cassie from *Tar Beach* encounters a fantastic railroad and a woman, Harriet Tubman, who takes her back to the world of a slave plantation.

Patricia Beatty. *Who Comes with Cannons?* Morrow, 1992. A young Quaker girl goes to live with her aunt, uncle, and cousins in North Carolina. Their home is also a station on the Underground Railroad. Explores why people risked their lives to help slaves reach freedom.

Exploring Africa

Africa still holds a fascination due to its size, diversity, and long history. From Marcus Garvey to the elections in South Africa, Africa has exerted a powerful hold on the imaginations of American Blacks. Bring Africa into the classroom through stories, music, games, and pictures.

Put a map of Africa on the board. Can students name any of the countries? How big is it compared to the United States? To your state? What different languages are spoken on this continent? Why would some countries use English for their official language and others use French? These are languages they have to learn in school. Why don't they use the language they learn at home?

Talk about the diversity of Africa. What do the people look like? Display pictures to show the population: Arabs, South African whites, Asians (Indians), different African tribes. Locate these groups on the map. A reference book that students can use is *African Countries and Cultures: A Concise Illustrated Dictionary* by Jane Hornburger and Alex Whitney (McKay, 1981).

Learn what life is like in the different countries by listening to music and playing games. *African Children's Games,* from Howard University Press (1978), presents six games from West Africa. Caedmon Records has collections of songs from different regions, such as *Songs of the Congo.*

Read stories about different tribes and countries in Africa to illustrate the diversity of this enormous continent.

Virginia Kroll. *Masai and I*. Illustrated by Nancy Carpenter. Four Winds, 1992. Linda, an African American city girl, learns about the Masai in East Africa. She wonders how her life would be different if she lived there.

Margaret Sacks. *Themba*. Illustrated by Wil Clay. Dutton, 1992. Themba's father is expected home from working in the gold mines near Johannesburg. When he doesn't return, Themba leaves his Xhosa village to look for him.

Gregory Scott Kreikemeier. *Come with Me to Africa: a Photographic Journey*. Golden, 1993. This account of a trip through each country in Africa includes numerous photographs of people, animals, the countryside, and descriptions of how people live. This is an excellent resource for dispelling the myth that Africa is uniform. Shows how the different African tribes vary in appearance.

Catherine Stock. *Where Are You Going, Manyoni?* Morrow, 1993. The spectacular, detailed watercolors evoke the African veld of Zimbabwe showing a typical day in Manyoni's life as she gets up, walks through the countryside to the school, and plays with her friends. Illustrations have animals hidden in them to identify (listed at the back) and show the homes, school, and children's games so that students can point out similarities and differences. Useful for dispelling stereotypes and ignorance about the landscape and people of Africa. Uses a few unfamiliar words to give the flavor of foreignness. Definitions are provided.

Ifeoma Onyefulu. *A Is for Africa*. Cobblehill, 1993. Photos from Nigeria (by an Igbo) illustrate African "universals" such as *D* is for Drums, *W* is for Weaving, *Y* is for Yams. While the author claims that the photographs of Nigeria represent Africa as a whole because many influences are found in Nigeria, in fact the book encourages a homogeneous view of African tribal life and customs. Use this book to stimulate further exploration of different aspects of African culture and history.

Patricia and Fredrick McKissack. *The Royal Kingdoms of Ghana, Mali, and Songhay: Life in Medieval Africa*. Holt, 1993. The kingdoms of West Africa flourished for a thousand years. The great cities were centers for learning, medicine, and religion. Dispels the image of Africa as an empty, dark continent.

African Tales

All students will enjoy reading stories from various traditional African cultures. They will learn about the lives and values of the major African groups, from Ashanti to Zulu, and compare these cultures with their own.

Most short tales reflect common human problems and traits and are easily adapted to storytelling or creative dramatics. A typical story is *The Vingananee and the Tree Toad,* a Liberian tale retold by Verna Aardema (Warne, 1983).

Or you can read a story aloud and have students illustrate the characters and incidents. A good place to start is *The Crest and the Hide and Other African Stories* by Harold Courlander (Coward McCann, 1982). The famed collector not only includes a variety of stories but also offers important background on sources and related tales.

Students can also investigate a particular genre of folktale, for example, the trickster tales exemplified by West African stories about Anansi the spider.

More African tales to read:

Verna Aardema. *Anansi Finds a Fool*. Dial, 1992. An Ashanti story, one of many about Anansi.

Barbara Knutson. *How the Guinea Fowl Got Her Spots: A Swahili Tale of Friendship*. Carolrhoda, 1990. When a guinea fowl saves a cow from a lion, the cow reciprocates by giving her camouflage spots.

Gerald McDermott. *Anansi the Spider*. Holt, 1972. The six sons of Anansi combine their wits to save their father's life.

Gerald McDermott. *Zomo the Rabbit: A Trickster Tale from West Africa*. Harcourt Brace Jovanovich, 1992. The ancestor of Brer Rabbit, an African trickster tale.

Sheron Williams. *And in the Beginning*. Atheneum, 1992. Retelling of the myth, how the first man was created from the dark earth of Mount Kilimanjaro.

John Steptoe. *Mufaro's Beautiful Daughters*. Illustrated by John Steptoe. Lothrop, Lee, and Shepard, 1987. Based on a Shona folktale (Zimbabwe), this is a modern fable of two sisters, one proud and one humble.

What We Can Learn

After students have read a series of folktales from one culture or region, they will be ready to abstract concepts of human values and behavior from their study and apply them to a comparison of the other culture and their own. How did the people in stories behave? What kinds of problems did they face? Have students compare that to what they and their families would do. Would they have the same problems? What would they do instead? What can we learn from the problems and solutions in these stories that we could apply to our own lives? Students can write examples of similar problem stories, suggesting original solutions.

African Words

When Blacks were first brought to this country as slaves, they spoke many different languages. Because they could not understand each other, it was difficult to preserve their different native languages. It is not surprising, therefore, that few African words were borrowed into English. Even when a word appears to be originally African, it may be difficult to pin down the source language.

Prepare a bulletin board to reflect the African contribution to English. List some of the following:

tote—to carry	jubilant, jubilee (from "juba," a dance)
gumbo	goober—peanut (from "guba")
voodoo	cooter—tortoise (from "kuta")
hip—with it	OK (origin unknown—possibly from yaw kay)
guy—man	

Discovering Swahili

Students enjoy learning about another language. Offer them the challenge of learning Swahili, one of the major languages of Africa. These two books present Swahili for students:

Muriel Feelings. *Moja Means One*. Dial, 1971.

_____ . *Jambo Means Hello*. Dial, 1974.

Prepare task cards for students to use with the books. Include some of varied difficulty, ranging from matching the words *one* through *ten* with the corresponding Swahili words, to writing a paragraph using as many Swahili words as possible.

A recording of Swahili is also available from Folkways Records: *Jambo and Other Call and Response Songs and Chants* (includes a guide).

REFLECTIONS

We have been exploring ways to incorporate a global perspective on diversity in our teaching. Through looking carefully at conditions around them, students can develop an understanding of what it means to respect their heritage, to understand social forces of discrimination and prejudice, and yet to be free to be citizens of the world.

APPLICATIONS

1. Students identify with others of their own age. Begin to collect resources so that you can present a unit on childhood in other countries. You can include books that describe growing up in a particular country, names of possible speakers who could talk to your class about going to school in other countries, and examples of children's toys or games. (UNICEF is a good source of simple childhood games from different countries.) Identify suitable sources of information in the library so that older students can do their own research on this topic. Finish your unit by considering how you want students to present what they have learned from this study. Primary students could assemble a notebook of stories, letters, and pictures. Older grades might prepare a dramatization for other classes.

2. Read three to five folktales from a particular region or culture. What can they tell you about the people? Find out more about the history and culture of these people. What themes are repeated in the folktales? What basis do they have in the group's history? Develop a plan for teaching these tales to students. How are universal themes depicted? What cultural values are being promoted? Decide what you expect students to learn from studying these tales. Prepare a folktale for storytelling. *Fairy Tales, Fables, Legends, and Myths: Using Folk Literature in your Classroom* by Bette Bosma (Teacher's College Press, 1987) is a source of ideas and stories.

3. Develop a booklet of community resources for teaching about a local group. Many excellent sources of multicultural information are available right in your own community. Sometimes an organization has produced a list of possible contacts for materials, resources, or speakers. Your public library may have this information already compiled. If not, begin developing a list of your own. The best place to start is the telephone directory. Look for national organizations that have branches in a big city close to you. For example, names to look for include National Conference of Christians and Jews. Look also under group names to see what services are offered. Try Chicano, American Indian, Mexican American, Native American, La Raza, Black, African American, and so on.

Another important resource is the local college or university. Write or call them for information about possible ethnic studies departments or organizations for students of different ethnic backgrounds. Check the catalogs to see whether courses are taught in the history or culture of a particular group that might be of interest to your students. Sometimes the teachers of such courses can help locate more materials and information as well as perhaps provide contacts with other people in the community. They might also come to speak to the class.

Exploring Further

Kids Explore America's African American Heritage. Westridge Young Writers Workshop. Muir Publishing, 1993.

Molefi K. Asante and Mark T. Mattson. *Historical and Cultural Atlas of African Americans.* Macmillan, 1992.

Violet Harris, ed. *Teaching Multicultural Literature in Grades K–8.* Christopher Gordon, 1992.

Mary Ann Heltshe and Audrey Burie Kirchner. *Multicultural Explorations: Joyous Journeys with Books.* Teacher Ideas Press, 1991.

Lynne Jessup. *World Music: A Source for Teaching.* World Music Press, 1988.

William Anderson and Patricia Shehan-Campbell, eds. *Multicultural Perspectives in Music Education.* Music Educators National Conference, 1989.

A. P. Porter. *Africans in America.* Lerner, 1991.

R. P. Grossman. *Italians in America.* Lerner, 1992.

P. V. Hillbrand. *Norwegians in America.* Lerner, 1993.

Carla D. Hayden, ed. *Venture into Cultures: A Resource book of Multicultural Materials and Programs.* ALA, 1992.

Andrew Billingsley. *Climbing Jacob's Ladder: The Enduring Legacy of African-American Families.* Simon and Schuster, 1993.

Milton Meltzer. *Black Americans: A History in Their Own Words.* Trophy, 1988.

Darlene Clark Hine. *Black Women in America: An Historical Encyclopedia.* Carlson Publishing, 1993.

Joe Wood, ed. *Malcolm X: In Our Own Image.* St. Martin's, 1993.

David Gallen, ed. *Malcolm X: As They Knew Him.* Carroll and Graf, 1993.

Shirley Blumenthal. *Coming to America: Immigrants from Eastern Europe.* Delacorte, 1981.

G. J. Powell, ed. *The Psychosocial Development of Minority Group Children.* Brunner/Mazel, 1983.

Gladys Nadler Rips. *Coming to America: Immigrants from Southern Europe*. Delacorte, 1981.

Maxine Seller. *Immigrant Women*. Temple University Press, 1980.

Stephen Thernstrom, Ann Orlove, and Oscar Handlin, eds. *Harvard Encyclopedia of American Ethnic Groups*. Harvard University Press, 1980.

Dean Wood. *Multicultural Canada*. The Ontario Institute for Studies in Education, 1978.

HAPPY BIRTHDAY

Feliz Cumpleaños

Bonne Anniversaire

Χρονια Πολλα

Buon Compleanno

Geburtstagswünsche

STO LAT!

祝
生
日
快
樂

6

❖

Exploring Language and Linguistic Diversity

Every generation claims that the English of its time is being degraded by slang and other forces of change. Few people, except linguists, have the historical perspective to see that English would not be the language that they wish to preserve unless it had changed substantially along the way. In fact, language changes are normal.

As you present the English language to students, remember that so-called standard English is the product of influences from many different people and languages. The English that exists today bears the imprint of factory workers as well as scientists, children playing in the street as well as English professors in schools; and it contains the particular speech patterns of people from different cultural and linguistic backgrounds—African, Jewish, Latino. The grammar rules that are carefully presented in textbooks are not etched in stone but describe what is generally considered effective communication for a specific place and time.

Your job is to help students cope with these issues by explaining clearly the conventions that govern the written and spoken English they encounter in school. Since students who speak English already know a lot about the structure of English (the grammar), they need fewer lists of rules and more examples of writing from real texts (literature) as a source for discussion and analysis of what makes good writing.

The increasing number of students in the classroom who speak languages other than English is an area of great concern and controversy today. All teachers need to know how to teach this population effectively. Unfortunately, the labels usually associated with these students, such as ESL (English as a second language), LEP (limited English speaking), and NES (non-English speaking), focus our attention on what they cannot do, leading to language deficiency models and remedial instruction. In addition, many people confuse an inability to express oneself fluently in English with an inability to think clearly, so that students needing assistance only with English language skills are denied access to the full academic content of their grade level. An alternative approach, which we advocate in this chapter, is to view the students' native language as an asset, both in helping them learn a new language and also as a benefit to all students. New instructional strategies, such as Sheltered English in which teachers modify their delivery of lesson content to make new information more comprehensible, serve to make all students feel included and promote the goal of teaching multiculturally.

After reading this chapter, you should be able to:
- Help students appreciate the rich variety of forms of English.
- Promote the learning of other languages as an asset.
- Support the English learning of students for whom English is not a first language.

VARIETIES OF ENGLISH

The English that we speak, read, and write varies according to systematic factors. One of the most obvious is regional variation. People who come from different regions tend to speak differently. When people move from one region to another, they sometimes maintain their former habits of speech, which makes for interesting mixes of vocabulary and pronunciation habits. Although everyone speaks a dialect, some regional dialects are considered more prestigious than others. In addition, there are "social" dialects. People who live in the same neighborhood but inhabit different social spheres will talk differently. The speech pattern called Black English is an example of a social dialect. Finally, speech varies according to social context, or register. We use language differently when speaking to an audience, to a close friend, to a baby, to a person in the street. All of these differences make up the rich variety of English in this country. Moreover, quite different varieties of English are spoken in other countries. The English of England, Australia, India, and Nigeria is acknowledged to be the same language, yet we may have to struggle to understand people from those countries.

Exploring Regional Dialects

Many common objects have different names in different parts of the country. Early dialectologists (people who investigate regional differences in pronunciation and vocabulary) developed maps that showed the spread of words for particular objects. Conduct an experiment in dialectology and see how many different regional terms you can find. Ask students questions such as the following:

What do you say to stop a game?
  (time out, times, pax, time, fins)
What do you say you do if you don't come to school?
  (play hookey, ditch, bag school, bolt, lay out, lie out, play truant, skip class, cut school)
What do you call someone from the country?
  (hayseed, rube, hick, hoosier, yokel, hillbilly, yahoo, moss back, cracker, redneck, sodbuster)
What do you call a thick sandwich?
  (dagwood, hoagie, submarine, sub, grinder, hero, poor boy)

Have students ask their parents the same questions. If people give different responses, find out where they come from. Discuss the regional patterns you find. Do students from the same area use the same terms? Why or why not? Depending on how many different regions the students represent, can you divide the United States into several main dialect areas?

Students might be interested in seeing some of the dialect atlases that have been prepared for most areas of the United States. *The Linguistic Atlas of New England* (Hans Kurath) includes many interesting maps showing the distribution of regional differences in vocabulary and pronunciation.

We All Speak Dialects

It is important for students to realize that we all speak different dialects. Have students try pronouncing the following words as they compare the varied ways of saying them:

greasy	here	car
bath	dog	get
aunt	because	idea

Keep in mind the wide variation in pronunciation and draw students' attention to it as you work together in the classroom. It is particularly evident as the teacher pronounces spelling words. For words that present obvious difficulty, you might have a student or two pronounce the same word aloud.

Consider particularly the vowels in *Mary, merry,* and *marry.* Some students may pronounce these as three different sounds. Other students say them as two homonyms or even as three homonyms. Remember to allow for student differences in pronunciation when teaching spelling and reading rules.

Listening to Regional Dialects

Practice listening for regional variation with the record *Our Changing Language* (McGraw-Hill) by Evelyn Gott and Raven I. McDavid, Jr. (available from The National Council of Teachers of English, 1111 W. Kenyon Road, Urbana, IL 61801). On one side of this record high school students read a story that contains many words that are pronounced differently. Each student is from a different city in the United States, and the speech variation is fascinating. Students who are from these geographic regions will identify their own speech characteristics as they listen.

To demonstrate the difference in speech in your own classroom, have a number of children record the same passage onto a tape. Then play the tape. Discuss what kinds of variations are noted. Which words are pronounced differently? Have students compare their pronunciations of the following words:

right	bath	were	here
house	child	fire	log
fit	Mary	park	sorry

British-American Differences

The English spoken in Britain differs from the English of the United States in interesting ways. For example, mix these words up and challenge students to match the British word on the left with the American equivalent. Do they recognize any of these words from books they have read?

Food

biscuit	(cookie)
jelly	(jello)
tinned meat	(canned meat)
sweet	(candy)
tea	(light meal, supper)

Transport

pram	(baby stroller)
boot	(trunk of car)
lorry	(truck)
lift	(elevator)
underground, tube	(subway, metro)

Clothing

trainers	(sneakers)
vest	(undershirt)
jumper	(pullover sweater)

In many cases, the British words are familiar but less common. However, some words have very different meanings in Britain and the United States. A good example is football, which means soccer in Britain.

Spelling across the Atlantic

Write several of the following familiar words on the board for students to read and pronounce. Wait for students to notice something strange about these words. Tell them that these represent British rather than American spellings. Can they identify the differences?

theatre	colour	programme	civilise
kerb	practise	grey	behaviour
tyres			

Discuss the use of spelling conventions with the students. Why do we insist that everyone spell the same way?

You can also point out that some words are spelled the same way in the two countries but pronounced differently. Examples are *schedule* (pronounced *sh*edule) and *clerk* (pronounced *clark*). What are some of the implications of these differences? (Learning to read or spell, writing poetry-rhymes, etc.)

British English in Books

Have students search for additional examples of British English. Reading books written by British authors will bring out more items. Suggest titles by these British authors to upper-grade students:

Lucy Boston
  The Children of Green Knowe
  A Stranger at Green Knowe
Joan Aiken
  The Wolves of Willoughby Chase
  Black Hearts in Battersea

Students could also investigate the language used in familiar books such as *Mother Goose*. Ask students what *curds and whey* and *pease porridge* mean. *The Annotated Mother Goose,* by Martin Gardner, is a useful source for the origin of many of these phrases.

Standardized Spelling

Dictionary Day, October 16, commemorates the birth of Noah Webster. Students may be surprised to learn that the spelling they have so much trouble with was standardized only relatively recently. When Noah Webster was preparing the first American dictionary, he wanted to emphasize that American English was distinct from British English and thus further the Revolutionary cause. He set a standard against which we could measure our spelling. Previously, well-educated people could spell words as they chose. Because of Webster, we write *civilize* and *theater,* not *civilise* and *theatre,* as they do in England.

Is there any reason to have everyone spell the same way? Discuss with students the advantages and disadvantages of standardized spelling. (Students might be comforted to know that many spelling demons are reminders of how words used to be pronounced; for example, *night* was once pronounced with a hard *g*.) Organize a debate on spelling reform: Resolved—the English language should be spelled the way it sounds.

The Language in the Dictionary

If we all speak different dialects, whose dialect is the one represented in dictionaries? Students may look on dictionaries as the ultimate authority on language, not realizing that the editors of dictionaries have to select carefully which words and specific pronunciations are included in their pages. As students might predict, some dialects are more likely to be represented than others. How is this decided? Are the most prestigious dialects the most likely to be included? (What are "the most prestigious" dialects?) Can you tell how to pronounce a word by looking it up in the dictionary? Should we have different entries for different dialects? Ask students to propose arguments on both sides.

Before the 1960s, dictionaries generally professed to set a standard for "good" English, so they did not include slang, swear words, or "street" (informal) vocabulary. More modern dictionaries represent a more inclusive definition of language, aiming to describe English in its actual current form instead of a limited and idealized version of good English. If you have access to a fairly new dictionary, have students look up pronunciations. Do the entries match how they themselves pronounce these words? They can also look up slang words. Does this dictionary include slang words? Are there words that might not be included? Should dictionaries include all the words in English? After discussion, students may realize that this is impossible.

An excellent library resource for further investigation is the 1993 *New Shorter Oxford English Dictionary* (2 Vols), a new edition of the famous guide to the English language. This edition includes new words from fields such as computers (laptop), physics (quark), politics (political correctness), music (grunge), and the street (dweeb). Have students brainstorm a list of contemporary words that should be in the dictionary. They can research these words and report back to the class. Have them argue in favor of including these words in the dictionary. Note that because this dictionary comes from England, it reflects a different view of the language than that of a dictionary published in the United States. Can students find any British-American differences in this work?

English Borrowings

English is a mixture of many languages. Although English is historically related to German (see the Language Tree on page 169), it has been heavily influenced by French and has borrowed words from many of the other languages it has been in contact with. Words that were borrowed a long time ago are now considered part of English. Words borrowed recently usually show their foreign origins. When students look up word origins in the dictionary, point out that any word that does not come from Old English must have been borrowed into English at some time.

List a number of borrowed words for students. How many of the words do they know? Can they guess the language each word came from?

Language	Word
Malay	ketchup
Arabic	alcohol
German	kindergarten, sauerkraut
French	souvenir, menu, encore
Hindi	shampoo
Spanish	bonanza, mosquito
Dutch	cole slaw, sleigh
Native American	squash, raccoon
Italian	macaroni, piano
Yiddish	kosher
Japanese	kimono
Scandinavian	smorgasbord

Prepare a display showing the origins of the words. Use a map of the world pinned to the bulletin board with the words printed on cards placed near their country of origin. Or mount the Indo-European tree on the bulletin board and place the borrowed words on leaf shapes attached to the proper branches. Discuss how the display shows which languages have contributed most to the English language. Why are some languages represented more than others? Speculate on why these words might have been borrowed.

Why We Speak English

Although this country was settled by people from many different countries who spoke such languages as Spanish, French, and German, English became recognized as the national language. How did this happen? Discuss possible causes with the students and have them develop a list of hypotheses, such as the following:

- English speakers were the first settlers.
- England was the most powerful mother country.
- The settlers voted English the official language.

Students will be motivated to read and research further to determine the accuracy of their predictions. Once they have established the facts (there was no vote), they can come up with a more informed picture of what led to the acceptance of English.

Compare the development of the United States with that of Canada. How and why did Canada select two official languages (French and English)?

Students' Right to Their Own Language

The following is a statement prepared by the National Council of Teachers of English in response to the educational controversy over Black English. Read this to the students and discuss it. Do they agree with the position expressed? What do they think teachers should do?

> We affirm the students' right to their own patterns and varieties of language—the dialects of their nurture or whatever dialects in which they find their own identity and style. Language scholars long ago denied that the myth of a standard American dialect has any validity. The claim that any one dialect is unacceptable amounts to an attempt of one social group to exert its dominance over another. Such a claim leads to false advice for speakers and writers, and immoral advice for humans. A nation proud of its diverse heritage and its cultural and racial variety will preserve its heritage of dialects. We affirm strongly that teachers must have the experiences and training that will enable them to respect diversity and uphold the right of students to their own language.[1]

Considering Black English

Black English is a dialect of English spoken by many people in the United States, primarily urban African Americans. It has many distinctive features of grammar and vocabulary, and it serves as a significant marker of African American identity. As with all dialects, speakers vary in the ease with which they can switch to more standard dialects of English. A lawsuit in 1977 brought public attention to Black English as an educational issue when parents in Ann Arbor, Michigan, claimed that their children were called learning disabled because they spoke Black English. Although the structure of Black English as a legitimate variant to English has been known for many years, some people still associate it with poor grammar and lack of learning skills.

Speaking Black English (the black vernacular) doesn't prevent students from being able to learn in school. In fact, students' knowledge of black vernacular represents the same level of intellectual achievement as that of any child who has mastered the language of the home. At the same time, students speaking black vernacular will also benefit from access to the language of wider communication, in this case, standard English. Reassure students that they can learn to use standard English without losing the use of their familiar language that connects them to family and community.

Varied models for the teaching of standard English to speakers of black vernacular have included bilingual education and the teaching of (standard) English as a second language. We would like to suggest a model of code switching. All speakers switch among various registers of their language (or languages), using specific registers for different contexts. To be an effective communicator, a speaker of black vernacular needs to be able to use that form in casual talk with peers in the community but to switch to a more formal style when applying for a job.

What can teachers and students do to learn more about standard English and to master the skill of code switching?

Teachers can:
• Model standard English as part of formal speech in the classroom.
• Switch into Black English in specific situations of informal discussion.

Students can:
• Create a list of black vernacular expressions and translate them into standard English.
• Translate common phrases in standard English into black vernacular.
• Develop role-play exercises, setting up different situations that might require using different speech registers.
• Analyze the way black characters deliberately vary speech patterns on television programs.
• Read and retell stories in black vernacular and standard English.

Throughout these activities, establish shared goals with students. Your aim is to increase their exposure to standard English, to permit them to practice using standard English in safe, playful environments, and to direct their conscious attention to the differences between black vernacular and standard English.

Origins of Black English

Students may feel more pride in the way they speak if they investigate the origins of these speech differences. The source of Black English is disputed. Some linguists argue that it comes from Gullah, an early black creole still spoken by some people in the Sea Islands. Gullah developed when Africans were brought to America as slaves. Because they spoke different languages, they needed to develop a way to communicate. The resulting language, called a creole, used English words as a base but followed a structure more similar to many African languages. Almost all of the distinctive features of Black English resemble Gullah. In communities where Gullah still exists, some teachers may be trying to eradicate traces of Black English in children's speech while linguists are carefully studying every word of the same speech from the elders.

An alternative explanation for the development of Black English is even more curious. Some linguists have pointed out a similarity between this dialect's features and those of a regional English dialect spoken by early English settlers on the East Coast. Despite its differences from standard English, Black English is very similar to many other dialects spoken by European whites in parts of the United States and England.

See *The Story of English* by Robert McCrum, William Cran, and Robert MacNeil (Viking, 1986) for more information about Gullah.

Differences between Black English and Standard English: Summary

In talking of black vernacular, one must be careful to recognize that there are variations within the general term Black English. However, these generalizations may be helpful if Black English is unfamiliar to you.

1. *It* will often be used for *there* (e.g., "It's a book on the table" instead of "There's a book on the table").
2. The verb *to be* will tend to be missing where a contraction of it is commonly used in standard English, especially in the present tense (e.g., "I here" and "We going").
3. More than a single negative form is acceptable (e.g., "I don't take no stuff from nobody").
4. Two or more consonant sounds appearing at the end of words in standard English tend to be reduced (e.g., *tes* for *test* and *des* for *desk*). The reduction of consonant clusters affects words that end in *s* (e.g., plurals, third person singular forms, and possessives like *its* and *father's*). The reduction also affects verbs in the past tense ending in *-ed*.
5. Words in which a medial or final *th* appears often change pronunciation (e.g., *wit* or *wif* for *with* and *muver* for *mother*).
6. In words in which *r* and *l* appear in medial or final positions in standard English, these sounds are often absent.

In addition, a few more specific points might be helpful. Black English does not distinguish gender. The form *he* is used for "he, she, it." Black English has a verb form not found in standard English. *Be* is used to mean the habitual aspect. It does not change for person or tense. Singular and plural are often not distinguished in nouns in Black English. Instead, the pronoun can follow the noun to indicate number (e.g., The boy he. . . , Those guys them . . .).

There are a number of books that discuss Black English—its structure, use, history, and differences from standard English. The following are recommended resources:

Robbins Burling. *English in Black and White*. Holt, Rinehart and Winston, 1973.

J. L. Dillard. *Black English: Its History and Usage*. Random House, 1972.

ONE OF MANY LANGUAGES

English is only one of many languages in the world. Some languages, such as Spanish, Russian, and Hindi, are related to English because they share a common ancestor language; other languages, such as Vietnamese, Swahili, and Arabic are strikingly different. In addition, more than two hundred immigrant languages are represented in this country. Some were brought by recent refugees, some have been maintained as a part of cultural heritage for many generations, and some reflect early inhabitants of this country. Language diversity is great among Native Americans as well. Although only 1.9 million in number, they speak over two hundred languages, some as different from each other as English is from Chinese.

Linguistic Diversity in the United States

One in every fourteen U.S. residents over the age of five speaks a language other than English at home, according to the 1990 census. This represents a 35 percent increase over the figures for the 1980 census. Contrary to popular perception, however, 80 percent of these people speak English fluently as well. Not surprisingly, Spanish is the most common language next to English; 17.3 million people reported that they speak Spanish at home.

Spanish	17,339,172
French	1,702,176
German	1,547,099
Italian	1,308,648
Chinese	1,249,213
Tagalog	843,251
Polish	723,483
Korean	626,478
Vietnamese	507,069
Portuguese	429,860
Total	31,844,979

Determine what languages are represented in your classroom. Ask students not only what languages they speak but what languages their ancestors spoke. Students can learn about the history of this country as they find out what languages their families spoke before coming here and when their family started speaking English. Make a list of the languages represented and show on a map where they are spoken. Students can better understand the concept of ethnic diversity when they see how many of their parents and grandparents (and their friends' parents and grandparents) came from another country and had to learn to speak English when they arrived. Students will also identify more with the problems of recent immigrants when they realize how recently their own families arrived.

Compare the languages of your class with the data on the chart below, showing the distribution of speakers of other languages. Which states have populations speaking the languages found in your classroom? Why do New York and California have the most languages listed? Which states have no non–English-speaking populations listed? Why? Students will have to apply facts and concepts learned in social studies in order to answer these questions and to understand the implications of this list.

Note that these languages represent stable populations of state residents. Recent groups of immigrants, such as Indochinese, are not shown here.

LANGUAGE LOCATION

Location	Language
Arizona	Spanish, Uto-Aztecan
California	German, Italian, Spanish, Polish, Yiddish, French, Russian, Hungarian, Swedish, Greek, Norwegian, Dutch, Japanese, Chinese, Serbo-Croatian, Portuguese, Danish, Arabic, Tagalog, Armenian, Turkish, Persian, Malay (Indonesian), Scandinavian, Basque, Mandarin, Gypsy (Romani)

Location	Language
Florida	Spanish
Hawaii	Japanese, Tagalog, Polynesian
Idaho	Basque
Illinois	German, Italian, Spanish, Polish, Yiddish, Russian, Swedish, Greek, Norwegian, Slovak, Dutch, Ukrainian, Lithuanian, Czech, Serbo-Croatian, Danish, Balto-Slavic
Maine	French, Amerindian
Massachusetts	Italian, Polish, Yiddish, French, Swedish, Greek, Lithuanian, Portuguese, Celtic, Armenian, Albanian, Breton
Michigan	German, Polish, French, Hungarian, Dutch, Finnish, Arabic, Balto-Slavic, Near E. Arabic dialects, Amerindian, Iraqi, Algonquin, Gypsy (Romani)
Minnesota	Swedish, Norwegian, Finnish
Montana	Algonquin
New Hampshire	French
New Jersey	German, Italian, Polish, Yiddish, Russian, Hungarian, Slovak, Dutch, Ukrainian
New York	German, Italian, Spanish, Polish, Yiddish, French, Russian, Hungarian, Swedish, Greek, Norwegian, Slovak, Dutch, Ukrainian, Lithuanian, Czech, Chinese, Portuguese, Danish, Finnish, Arabic, Rumanian, Balto-Slavic, Celtic, Hebrew, Armenian, Near E. Arabic dialects, Turkish, Uralic, Albanian, Persian, Scandinavian, Amerindian, Dalmatian, Breton, Mandarin, Egyptian, Georgian, Gypsy (Romani), Athabascan
Ohio	German, Polish, Hungarian, Greek, Slovak, Czech, Serbo-Croatian, Slovenian
Pennsylvania	German, Italian, Polish, Yiddish, Russian, Hungarian, Greek, Slovak, Ukrainian, Lithuanian, Serbo-Croatian
Rhode Island	French, Portuguese
Texas	Spanish
Washington	Swedish, Norwegian, Scandinavian, Amerindian
Wisconsin	German

Source: Adapted from *Theodore Andersson and Mildred Boyer,* Bilingual Schooling in the United States. *U.S. Office of Education, 1970, pp. 26–27.*

Welcoming Vietnamese Students

Between 1975 and 1989, 800,000 Southeast Asian refugees arrived in the United States, half of them under the age of eighteen. As recent immigrants, Vietnamese students have had to struggle against fear and ignorance as they try to fit into the classroom environment and begin the task of learning English. Help them become accepted by sharing information about their country with the class. A book such as *The Brocaded Slipper, and Other Vietnamese Tales* by Lynette Dyer Vuong (Addison Wesley, 1982), with its familiar themes, will show students how much they have in common.

All students can empathize with Hoa in *Angel Child, Dragon Child* by Michele Maria Surat (Scholastic, 1989). This is the story of a young Vietnamese girl who is sad and lonely in school. She doesn't speak much English, the children call her Pajamas, and her mother is still in Vietnam.

Discussing the Value of Knowing More than One Language

Open discussions about languages in our country will aid students in recognizing the issues involved. Discuss the following topics.

- List the advantages of knowing a second language. List the disadvantages.
- How many different languages are spoken in your area? Do you know someone who speaks more than one language?
- What languages would you like to learn? Why?

A Fable

In a house there was a cat, always ready to run after a mouse, but with no luck at all.

One day, in the usual chase the mouse found its way into a little hole and the cat was left with no alternative than to wait hopefully outside.

A few moments later the mouse heard a dog barking and automatically came to the conclusion that if there was a dog in the house, the cat would have to go. So he came out only to fall in the cat's grasp.

"But where is the dog?"—asked the trembling mouse.

"There isn't any dog—it was only me imitating a barking dog," explained the happy cat, and after a pause added, "My dear fellow, if you don't speak at least two languages, you can't get anywhere nowadays."

Source: Reprinted from BBC Modern English, Vol. 2, No. 10, p. 34, December 1976.

The Language Tree

Prepare a bulletin board to provide information about the family of Indo-European languages, spoken by half the world's population, and the relationship of English to other languages. Construct a large tree out of construction paper, with eight branches representing the main groups:

- Albanian
- Armenian
- Balto-Slavic: Russian, Polish, Serbo-Croatian, Czech, Ukrainian, Bulgarian, Lithuanian
- Celtic: Irish, Scots, Gaelic, Welsh, Breton, Cornish
- Greek
- Indo-Iranian: Hindi, Urdu, Bengali, Persian
- Romance: French, Italian, Spanish, Portuguese, Rumanian

- Germanic: German, English, Dutch, Danish, Norwegian, Swedish
- Tocharian ⎫
- Hittite ⎭ extinct languages

Have students research what languages belong to each branch. Where does English fit in? Which are the most populous branches? In what countries are these languages spoken?

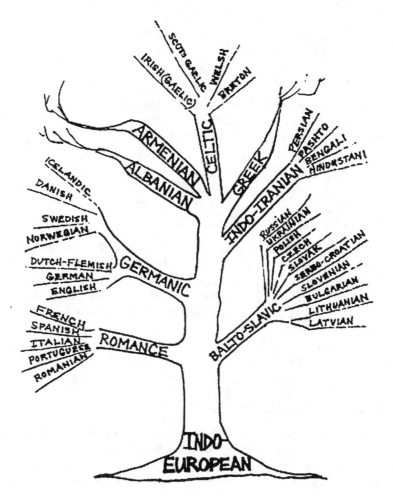

Exploring Different Languages

When the language tree is constructed and the branches labeled with the major languages, have students add life to the tree by discovering words in these different languages. Students can look up words or use words they have found in books. Provide "leaves" cut out of construction paper on which to write words to place on the tree according to the "branch" they belong to.

Exercises such as looking up the word for *ten* in many languages will help demonstrate to students the relationship among these languages, as well as their similarities and differences. Here are some examples to begin with:

English	ten	German	zehn
French	dix	Dutch	tien
Italian	dieci	Swedish	tio
Spanish	diez	Danish	ti
Portuguese	dez	Norwegian	ti
Rumanian	zece		

Other Language Families

Can students name languages that do not belong to the Indo-European language family? (Check names against the Indo-European family tree you constructed.) They may suggest some of the following names:

Language	*Family*
Chinese	Sino-Tibetan
Japanese	Japanese and Korean
Hebrew	Hamito-Semitic
Hungarian	Ural-Altaic

After the class has accumulated a list, have them look up the languages to find out which languages are related to one another. There are many language families besides the Indo-European, and some include languages with many speakers. Students may be surprised to learn that Chinese and Japanese are not related but belong to separate families. Many Native American languages belong to distinctly different language families as well.

So many different languages are spoken in Africa that it is difficult to classify all of them. Swahili, the best known, is the native language of some Africans but is learned by many others as a second language in order to communicate with neighbors.

English in Other Languages

Just as English has borrowed many words for new things, so other languages have borrowed words from English for objects or ideas that came from English-speaking people. Words that look or sound familiar to English speakers can be found in French, Japanese, Russian, Spanish, and many other languages. Ask students to guess what the following words mean.

le pique-nique	(French, picnic)
le coquetel	(French, cocktail)
el ampayer	(Spanish, umpire)
los jonroneros	(Spanish, homerun hitters)
jiipu	(Japanese, jeeps)
gamu	(Japanese, chewing gum)
garu-furendo	(Japanese, girlfriend)

parken   (German, to park)
hitchhiken   (German, to hitchhike)

Languages in the World

Ask students if they know which language has the most speakers in the world. Write several guesses on the board. Have students research how many people speak each language. They can prepare a chart of the most widely spoken languages in the world. Figures can be obtained by counting the populations of countries that speak a particular language, or you can use information on what languages people learn as a second language. Check figures in almanacs and encyclopedias. Because the population of China is large, more people grow up speaking Chinese than any other language. English is the most widely used second language.

Compare how many people in the world speak English and how many speak Spanish. Which languages in the world would be the most useful to learn as second or third languages? Why?

Languages in the Classroom

Bring other languages into the classroom by giving students a chance to hear what different languages sound like. Folk songs are an easy way to introduce students to other languages. Talk about what the words mean and why they sound different. Use the languages that are represented in your classroom. Have students teach the rest of the class how to say *hello, good-bye, please,* and *thank you* in their language.

Animals Speak in Different Languages, Too

What does a rooster say, or a dog, or a cat? Students may be surprised to find out that different languages have different ideas about the sounds animals make. Ask students who speak other languages to contribute examples. Share the book *Cock-a-Doodle Doo! What Does It Sound Like to You: Learning Sounds in Other Languages* written by Marc Robinson and illustrated by Steve Jenkins (Stewart Tabori Chang, 1993), which contains examples from such diverse languages as Portuguese, Russian, Greek, Hindi, Chinese, and Hebrew. It also includes a map showing where these languages are spoken.

Esperanto

The following paragraph is written in Esperanto. Write it on the board and read it to the class. (It is pronounced approximately like Spanish—follow the rules given in the chart on pages 178–180). See how much students can understand.

> La inteligenta persono lernas la interlingvon Esperanto rapide kaj facile. Esperanto estas la moderna, kultura lingvo por la internacia mondo. Simpla, flekselbla, praktika solvo de la problemo de universala interkompreno, Esperanto meritas vian seriozan konsideron. Lernu la interlingvon Esperanto!

Esperanto is an artificial language invented to be used as an international language. It is easy to learn and easy to understand because it is completely regular.

Bring books about Esperanto to the class. Students will enjoy practicing the new language and using it in interesting ways. They can write to each other in Esperanto and perform simple translation exercises. In addition, they will learn more about how their own language is constructed by comparing it with Esperanto.

Discuss why Esperanto was created. Is there a need for an international language? What are the advantages and disadvantages of Esperanto? Esperanto is only one of a large number of artificial international languages. Have students investigate the history of Esperanto and other artificial languages (Interlingua, for example).

A Language of Hands

Another special language is a silent language, the language of hands. This kind of language is used by deaf people and takes the place of speech. Although American Sign Language (ASL) uses signs that are equivalent to words, it also has signs for each letter (fingerspelling). Fingerspelling is sometimes called the manual alphabet. Anyone can quickly learn to fingerspell and the exercise helps practice English spelling. Students enjoy being able to signal each other secretly, across a noisy room, and without making a sound. Several books present fingerspelling for beginners. *Handtalk* by Remy Charlip, Mary Beth Ancona, and George Ancona (Parents Magazine Press, 1974) and *My First Book of Sign* by Pamela Baker (Gallaudet, 1986) include photographs of a person signing.

American Sign Language

Who uses ASL? Many people. Deaf people, their families, their friends, sign language interpreters, and deaf educators. Ask students if they or anyone they know uses sign language.

Discuss differences between sign language and spoken language. What are the advantages of sign language? What are the advantages of spoken language? What language is best when you are eating? Under water? On the phone? Students may not know that sign language is a "real" language. Present some of the following information about sign.

Facts about Sign Language

There are different sign languages used in different countries, just as there are spoken languages. People who use ASL cannot understand people who use British Sign Language.

ASL is not a word-for-word translation of English. Signed English is used for simultaneous translation and matches spoken English more closely.

Children who are deaf can learn ASL as a first language, similar to the way hearing children learn a spoken language. Signers (people who use sign) can express themselves as well in sign as hearing people can in a spoken language.

For more information, share with students *Communication* by Aliki (Greenwillow, 1993). The book's comic-strip format includes facts about deaf people and sign language.

Exploring Sign

Invite a hearing person who knows sign to speak to the class and demonstrate signing. (Try facilities for the deaf, teachers of sign language, and relatives of deaf people.) If students watch closely, they will be able to guess what some of the signs mean.

- Drink—fingers shaped around glass move to mouth
- See—two fingers move away from eyes
- Nose, Mouth—point to them on face

Find out what services are available for deaf people. Sometimes television news programs have simultaneous sign translations. Discuss with students why these services are necessary. Would printing the news on the screen as subtitles work? What does the "CC" on television programs mean? Can deaf people use telephones?

Deaf people are a neglected group in our discussion of the multicultural society. Too often included with the disabled, most deaf people do not want to be "fixed." They consider themselves a cultural and linguistic minority with their own heroes, history, and language. As with other language groups, deaf students can best be served by a bilingual education program. For more information on this educational controversy, see *The Mask of Benevolence* by Harlan Lane (Knopf, 1992).

Different Writing Systems

There are three basic types of writing systems. Alphabetic systems use symbols to represent individual sounds. Syllabaries have separate symbols for consonant-vowel pairs. Pictographic or ideographic systems represent entire words or ideas with a single symbol. Bring in examples of each type of writing (in print or handwritten) to show students how languages differ. Include some of the following:

- Alphabetic: *Cyrillic,* used for Russian and other Slavic languages, based on the Greek alphabet. *Hebrew,* an alphabet without written vowels, similar to *Arabic.*
- Syllabary: *Japanese,* despite adoption of some Chinese characters, still primarily uses *Kana,* syllable-based.
- Pictographic: *Chinese,* with large numbers of distinct characters, is difficult to memorize and write.

Discuss with students the implications of these different writing systems. Consider, for example, how dictionaries would be organized. How would Hebrew students read new words when they are written without the spoken vowels? The complex Chinese system works better for the Chinese than an alphabetic system. Speakers of different Chinese languages who cannot understand each other's spoken language can communicate through using the same writing system. How might these different writing systems make translation into English difficult? What would a keyboard look like in other writing systems?

Look for examples of Japanese writing, such as the illustration at the beginning of Chapter 8. A source for information about Japanese is the alphabet book *A to Zen* written by Ruth Wells and illustrated by Yoshi (Picture Book Studio, 1992). Note that this book reads from back to front, like books in Japanese.

Another interesting language to investigate is Hebrew, the national language of Israel. Although for many centuries Hebrew remained a purely religious language, today it is spoken on a daily basis by Jews, Arabs, and Christians. Note that many Jews in this country also speak Yiddish, if they came from Eastern Europe, or Ladino, if they came from the Mediterranean. A good introduction to Hebrew is *Alef-Bet: A Hebrew Alphabet Book* by Michelle Edwards (Lothrop, Lee and Shepard, 1992). Each page shows a letter in Hebrew, its Hebrew name, a Hebrew word, and the English pronunciation.

Cyrillic Alphabet

Letters	Names of Letters	Equivalent sounds in English
А, а	ah	*f*a*ther*
Б, б	beh	*b*et
В, в	veh	*v*at
Г, г	gheh	*g*o
Д, д	deh	*d*am
Е, е	yeh	*y*et
Ё, ё	yoh	*ya*wn
Ж, ж	zheh	plea*s*ure
З, з	zeh	*z*one
И, и	ee	*ee*l
Й, й	ee ᴋʀᴀʜᴛ-koh-yeh	bo*y*
К, к	kah	*k*ick
Л, л	el	*l*ow
М, м	em	*m*et
Н, н	en	*n*et
О, о	oh	*t*oy, sport
П, п	peh	*p*et
Р, р	er	*d*read (trilled *r*)
С, с	es	*s*ell
Т, т	teh	*t*ell
У, у	oo	*m*oon
Ф, ф	ef	*f*un
Х, х	khah	lo*ch*, soft sound *H*ugo
Ц, ц	tseh	ca*ts*
Ч, ч	chah	*ch*urch
Ш, ш	shah	*sh*ip
Щ, щ	shchah	prolonged *sh* sound
ъ	tv'ʏᴏʀ-dee znahk	indicates hard stress on previous consonant
ы	yeh-ʀᴇᴇ	s*i*t
ь	m'ʏᴀʜ-kee znahk	no sound, indicates soft emphasis
Э, э	eh (oh-boh-ʀᴏʜᴛ-noh-yeh)	*p*et
Ю, ю	yoo	*yu*le
Я, я	yah	*ya*rd

Where does the word *alphabet* come from? *Alpha* and *beta* are the first two letters of the Greek alphabet. Look at the Greek alphabet. Does it look anything like the alphabet we use? Where did our letters come from? Have students research the history of the English alphabet, from its origins in Greek and Phoenician letters, through Gothic, to its present form.

In an alphabetic writing system, each sound is represented by a symbol. Is this always true of English? What individual sounds in English are represented by pairs of letters? (Examples are *ch, sh, th*.)

The Birth of Writing, by Robert Claiborne and the Editors of Time-Life Books, 1974, is an excellent resource for more information on the origin of writing and the importance of knowing how to write.

Language Differences and Similarities: Background

One of the tasks of linguistics is to describe the structure of various languages. On the basis of language structure and history, languages are classified together into families. Examples of ways in which languages differ include the following:

1. Out of a limited number of possible sounds, no languages use precisely the same group of sounds. Some of these sounds do not occur in English and, therefore, sound strange to ears accustomed to English. The *th* sound in English is difficult for foreigners because it does not occur in many languages.

2. Some languages have a system for classifying nouns. Often this is called gender. Objects are arbitrarily assigned to one of two groups, called masculine and feminine (as in Spanish), or to one of three groups: masculine, feminine, and neuter (as in German and Russian). This use of gender is not equivalent to the division of humans into male and female. For example, in German, *Mädchen* (maiden) and *Fräulein* (young woman) are both neuter. Different languages may assign the same object different genders. The word for table is *Tisch* in German (masculine) and *mesa* in Spanish (feminine). In languages with gender, pronouns usually agree in gender with the nouns to which they refer. In addition, adjectives usually have different endings depending on the gender and number (singular or plural) of the noun modified. Note this example in French:

ils	préfèrent	les	tasses	blanches
they	prefer	*the*	*cups*	*white*
(3rd person, masculine, plural)	(3rd person, plural)	(plural)	(feminine, plural)	(feminine, plural)

In this sentence, the pronoun *ils* could refer to *les hommes* (men, masculine, plural) or to *les chats* (cats, masculine, plural) but not to *les femmes* (women, feminine, plural). Therefore, French speakers easily confuse the English he/she/it contrast and use he/she for inanimate objects. Examples of languages with a noun classification system not based on gender are the Bantu (African) languages. In these languages nouns are grouped into categories based primarily on the physical shape of the object; for example, long and thin, small and round.

3. The concept of *word* differs from language to language. The Japanese word *ikimasu*, for example, carries the potential meaning of these English words:

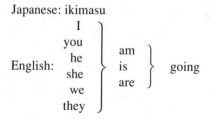

Japanese: ikimasu

English: I / you / he / she / we / they   am / is / are   going

Japanese speakers decide who is going from the context of the conversation.

An example of the concept of *word* taken from the Yana Indian language in northern California[2] is even more complicated:

yābanaumawildjigummaha'nigi

yā = several people move
banauma = everybody
wil = across
dji = to the West
gumma = indeed
ha' = let us
nigi = we

Try reading these definitions as a "sentence."

Even with the parts of the long word defined, we still do not understand it, because we arrange our thoughts differently and do not repeat words as the Yanas did. An English sentence that conveys the same meaning as the Yana word might go like this:

Let us each move to the West.

4. Word order differs in various languages. In English, adjectives usually precede the noun described. Compare these phrases in English and Spanish:

English	*Spanish*
the blue book	el libro azúl
	(the book blue)

5. Word order affects meaning in English, as is clear in these sentences:

The dog bit the man.
The man bit the dog.

In other languages special endings carry meaning so the words can be arranged in any order. For example, this Latin sentence says "Peter (subject ending *us*) sees Paul (object ending *um*)" no matter what the order.

Pet*rus* videt Paul*um*.
Paul*um* Pet*rus* videt.
Videt Paul*um* Pet*rus*.

While languages differ in vocabulary for cultural and historical reasons, all languages have the same expressive potential. There is no such thing as a primitive language, just as there is no such thing as a primitive people. All human languages and all human cultures are rich and complex and capable of adapting to different circumstances. A language may not express some concepts that are considered important in our society, but it can develop the vocabulary to express any of them if the speakers of the language consider it necessary. The use of formerly unwritten African languages to conduct all the affairs of law, government, and education is an example of the flexibility of language. Another example is

Hebrew, a language that was revived for use as a national language in modern Israel. All languages possess the capacity to adapt to such new uses.

Focus on Latinos: An Ethnolinguistic Group

In the 1990 census, 22,354,059 people in the United States identified themselves as being of Hispanic origin. Of these, 13,495,938 were of Mexican origin, 2,727,754 were Puerto Rican, and 1,043,932 were Cuban. The category "of Hispanic origin" refers to ethnic identity and is independent of racial identity. This Hispanic/Latino ethnicity is closely tied to Spanish, the shared language of their origin.

With people of Hispanic origin making up 9 percent of the U.S. population, it is not surprising then that the most commonly spoken language in the United States, after English, is Spanish. In many classrooms, Spanish speakers are in a majority. But not all Americans who come from Spanish-speaking backgrounds speak Spanish themselves, and many who do speak Spanish also speak English. So the most appropriate label for this group may be "ethnolinguistic" minority, to reflect the fact that some people who identify with the culture do not necessarily speak the language. In addition, the label Latino includes people who come from different countries and speak different varieties of Spanish. Today, people from communities with roots dating back to the settlement of California and the Southwest in the 1700s may feel they have little in common with the recent immigrants from El Sálvador.

It is not surprising, then, that there is much confusion over how to determine who is a member of this minority (Spanish-sounding last name, lack of knowledge of English, or birth in a Spanish-speaking country are some of the criteria that have been suggested) or what label to use to identify people (Latino, Hispanic, and Chicano have been some of the options). The Latino students that you have in the classroom may have lived in this country for a generation, immigrated from Mexico leaving many relatives still there, or arrived as war refugees with no option but permanent settlement in this country. These origins affect the extent to which the students have already learned English and also the family's desire to maintain Spanish at home.

We can serve all of our students best by exposing them to Spanish as a significant language in this country and a language of both historical and international importance. In addition, students who are able to contribute to the discussion through their own knowledge of this language will be able to take pride in their heritage.

Spanish on the Map

The importance of Spanish-speaking people in the history of this country can be easily seen in the names on the map. Project a copy of a U.S. map on the wall so that all the students can see the names marked on the map. Have students find examples of Spanish place names. Talk about how you can tell whether a name is Spanish or not. If the first word is *San* or *Santa* the name is probably a Spanish saint name. What would these names be in English? (San Francisco/Saint Francis, San Antonio/Saint Anthony, for example.)

Look at different areas of the country separately. Students will notice that more Spanish names occur in certain areas. Which areas have more Spanish names, and why?

As students search for Spanish names, they will notice other groups of foreign names. There are a number of French names in Louisiana, for example. Why? Ask students if they can think why the names used on the map might reflect the history of a region. Does the presence of Spanish names in an area necessarily mean that there are Spanish-speaking people living there?

Letter Names

What are the names of the letters of the alphabet? English-speaking children will be interested in learning how Spanish-speaking children say the alphabet. Have a child who speaks Spanish say these letters slowly for the group. This is more effective than reading or saying them yourself, for it makes the student aware that knowledge of Spanish can be important in school.

Spanish Letter Names

a	ä	n	ānā
b	bā	ñ	ānyā
c	sā	o	ō
*ch	chā	p	pā
d	dā	q	kü
e	ā	r	ārā
f	āffā	rr	ārrā (trilled)
g	hā	s	āsā
h	ächā	t	tā
i	ē	u	ü
j	hōtä	v	bā
k	kä	w	düblä bā
l	ālā	x	ākēs
*ll	āyā	y	ē grē·agä (Greek i)
m	āmā	z	sātä

Comparing Phonemes and Graphemes

After examining the alphabet letters that are used in writing Spanish, show students the phonemes used in speaking Spanish, some of which are similar to English but none of which are exactly the same. Also show them corresponding graphemes for these phonemes. Here they will notice many differences between Spanish and English, as shown in the chart that follows.

Consonants	Spanish	English
b	también	rib
	abrir	like v, but with lips almost touching
c	casa	case (before a, o, u)
	nación	cent (before e, i)

Table continues

*After 1994, these letters will no longer appear separately in the dictionary.

Consonants	Spanish	English
ch	chico	church
d	donde	down
	madre	the
f	familia	family
g	gente	like exaggerated h (before e, i)
	gordo	game
h	hacer	silent
j	jugar	like exaggerated h
k	kilómetro	kitchen
l	lástima	little
ll	llena	yellow
		million } (regional variation)
m	mañana	morning
n	nada	nothing
n	niño	canyon
p	piña	supper
q	queso	key
r	pero	rich
	rico	trilled r
rr	perro	trilled r
s	sala	sad
t	trabajar	time
v	enviar	like b in también
	la vaca	like b in abrir
w	Wáshington	wash
	examen	exam
	extranjero	sound
	México	hit
y	yo	yes
z	zapato	save

Vowels	Spanish	English
a	padre	father
e	es	they
i	nida	police
o	poco	poem
u	luna	spoon
	querer	silent after q

Dipthongs	Spanish	English
ai, ay	traiga	nice
au	auto	mouse
ei, ey	aceituna	tray
eu	deuda	ay plus oo
ia, ya	hacia	yonder

Table continues

Dipthongs	Spanish	English
ie, ye	nieve	<u>ye</u>s
io, yo	dios	<u>yo</u>lk
iu	ciudad	<u>yu</u>le
oi, oy	soy	b<u>oy</u>
ua	guante	<u>wa</u>nder
ue	vuelve	<u>wei</u>ght
y	y	<u>e</u>ven
ui, uy	muy	<u>we</u>
uo	cuota	<u>wo</u>e

Books in Spanish

Bring books in Spanish into the classroom. Students will enjoy exploring bilingual books, where they can compare stories in Spanish and English, as well as books in Spanish alone. Perhaps children who read Spanish can tell the other students about these books. Show students that knowing another language, such as Spanish, can be an asset. The following list of books in Spanish includes many excellent children's books that have been translated into Spanish. Other books are available from publishing companies in Mexico, Latin America, and Spain.

Sylvia Cavazos Pena. *Kikiriki: Stories and Poems in English and Spanish for Children.* Arte Publico, 1987. This book includes a variety of stories, poems, and riddles written by Latinos. Some selections are in English, some in Spanish.

Eric Carle. *La mariquita malhumarada.* (Translation of *The Grouchy Ladybug.*) Harper-Collins, 1993. This humorous picture book has widespread appeal. The illustrations can carry the story for students who don't understand the text.

Don Freeman. *Un bosillo para Corduroy.* (translation of *A Pocket for Corduroy*) Viking, 1991. Another book about Corduroy, the stuffed bear. Students can retell the story of Corduroy, the girl who owns him, and their adventures. Set in a multiethnic neighborhood.

Riki Levinson. *Mira como salen las estrellas.* (Translation of *Watch the Stars Come Out.*) Dutton, 1992. The story of a girl and her brother who make the long journey from Europe to America in the early 1900s to join their parents.

Ezra Jack Keats. *Silba por Willie.* (Translation of *Whistle for Willie.*) Viking, 1964. Classic universal story of a child in the city on a hot summer day.

Spanish Words We Know

Students may be surprised to see how many Spanish words they know. If Spanish is frequently used in the community, students should have no trouble recalling words seen on signs and heard in conversations. Have students list words they know as you write them on the board. Do they know what the words mean? They might suggest the following words:

amigos	fiesta	siesta
adíos	tortilla	piñata

Do any stores in the community have signs in Spanish? Where do the children hear Spanish spoken? What does "Aquí se habla español" mean? ("Spanish is spoken here.") Are there any Spanish place names or street names in the community?

Spanish Borrowings

English has borrowed extensively from Spanish, particularly in the Southwest. List examples of borrowings on the board. Do students know what these words mean? What kinds of words have been borrowed? Discuss why borrowings might take place. The following are examples of borrowings from Spanish:

arroyo	canyon	adobe	frijole
bronco	lasso	mustang	mesa
rodeo	chili	plaza	sierra
sombrero	avocado	stampede	tortilla
burro	vanilla		

Have students research Spanish borrowings. What do the original Spanish words look like? What happens to the words when they enter English?

Indian Borrowings

The Spanish spoken in Latin America is distinctively different from the Spanish of Spain because of the influence of the Native American languages. Many words borrowed into English from Spanish come originally from these languages. *Chocolate* was borrowed from Nahuatl, the Aztec language, into Mexican Spanish and then into English. As students research Spanish borrowings, have them notice examples of Native American words. The following are examples of words borrowed from Guaraní, a language spoken in Paraguay, into English: *tapioca, maracas, jaguar, jacaranda, tapir,* and *toucan.*

Spanish spoken in our country differs from the rest of Latin America because it has continued to borrow from the Native American languages and it has also been influenced by English.

Learning about Latinos and Their Heritage

Many books can be used to show students how others live. Select books carefully to avoid stereotyping. The best books include culturally specific details and promote respect for the diversity of the people. The following books introduce students to the lives of young Latinos, along with information about their culture and language.

Susan Kuklin. *How My Family Lives in America.* Bradbury, 1992. The story of three families from different cultures. Eric's family comes from Puerto Rico.

Tricia Brown. *Hello, Amigos!* Holt. 1986. A picture book, with photos of a seven-year-old Mexican American boy who lives in San Francisco and is celebrating his birthday. Includes many Spanish words that students will understand from the context.

Joan Hewett. *Hector Lives in the United States Now: The Story of a Mexican American Child.* Lippincott, 1990. Ten-year-old Hector was born in Mexico but lives in Los Angeles. The book describes his parents' application for citizenship through the amnesty in 1986.

Muriel Stanek. *I Speak English for My Mom.* Whitman, 1989. Reflects a common experience for many children. Lupe's mother works in a factory, but she begins taking English classes to get a better job.

Gary Soto. *The Cat's Meow.* Strawberry Hill Press, 1987. Nicol is "part Mexican." She is fluent in English and understands some Spanish. Her cat Pip, however, speaks Spanish.

Arthur Dorros. *Tonight Is Carnaval.* Dutton, 1990. Describes the preparations for the festival in Peru. Features local crafts, culture.

Omar Castañeda. *Among the Volcanoes.* Lodestar, 1991. A Mayan girl, living in a village in Guatemala, has to take care of her sick mother. She wants to become a teacher.

David Nelson Blair. *Fear the Condor.* Lodestar, 1992. The story of an Aymara Indian girl in Bolivia, set in the 1930s during the Chaco War over Indian rights and land reform.

Fran Leeper Buss. *Journey of the Sparrows.* Lodestar, 1991. The struggle of three young people from El Sálvador to come to the United States.

Varieties of Spanish

The information on Spanish presented in this book is very general. There are many varieties of Spanish spoken in the United States, depending on where the speakers live, how long they have lived in this country, and where they came from originally. Spanish in the Southwest is different from Spanish in the Midwest (Chicago), the Northeast, and Florida. Even in New York City, there are important cultural and linguistic differences between persons from Puerto Rico, Cuba, the Dominican Republic, Colombia, Ecuador, Peru, Mexico, Venezuela, Bolivia, and other South American communities.

The differences in the Spanish of Latin America are primarily vocabulary and pronunciation. Some vocabulary differences are due to influence from local Indian languages, others are due to independent development of Spanish.

The following are examples of different words used in Latin America for *boy:*

Mexico	chamaco	Panama	chico
Cuba	chico	Colombia	pelado
Guatemala	patojo	Argentina	pibe
El Sálvador	cipote	Chile	cabro

Pronunciation also varies regionally. The following are some of the differences found:

- Syllable final *s* becomes *h* or disappears—*estos* is [éhtoh] or [éto]
- *ll* becomes same as *y*—*valla* and *vaya* are alike
- Syllable final *r* sounds like *l*—*puerta* is [pwelta], *comer* is [komel]

Introduce vocabulary specific to local Spanish-speaking groups by having a variety of children's books available. Many books, written about members of particular groups, take pride in presenting common Spanish words that are special to that group.

Developing Pride in Latino History and Culture

Latino students need to see books that reflect their own lives and cultural experiences, just as children from any cultural background do. Choose books that represent a variety of regions and backgrounds, from Puerto Rico to Mexican Americans in the Southwest. These examples include rich cultural information and Spanish language in context.

Carmen Lomas Garza. *Family Pictures/Cuadros de familia*. Children's Book Press, 1990. The life of a young Mexican American girl who lives in south Texas. Excellent for details about Latino culture in the region.

Gary Soto. *Baseball in April*. Harcourt Brace Jovanovich, 1990. Short stories of growing up Chicano in central California, each featuring a different Mexican American child.

Pat Mora. *A Birthday Basket for Tía*. Macmillan, 1992. Cecilia wonders what to give her great aunt for her ninetieth birthday.

Arthur Dorros. *Abuela*. Dutton, 1991. A young girl imagines flying over the city of New York with her grandmother.

Denys Cazet. *Born in the Gravy*. Orchard, 1993. Margarita, born in Guadalajara, comes home from her first day in kindergarten in the United States and tells Papa all about it.

Ruth Sonneborn. *Friday Night Is Papa Night*. Puffin, 1987. A Puerto Rican family welcomes the hardworking father home on Friday night.

Lulu Delacre. *Vejigante/Masquerader*. Scholastic, 1993. In Puerto Rico, Ramon wants to sew a costume to march in the carnival parade and make his family proud. The book includes instructions so that students can make their own carnival masks. The text is in Spanish and English.

Gloria Anzaldua. *Friends from the Other Side/Amigos del otro lado*. Children's Book Press, 1993. Joaquín and his mother fear *la migra,* the Immigration Service.

Richard García. *My Aunt Otilia's Spirits*. Children's Book Press, 1987. A young boy remembers his aunt's strange visits to New York from Puerto Rico.

Cruz Martel. *Yagua Days*. Dial, 1976. On his first visit to Puerto Rico, a boy learns how children use the large yagua leaves to slide down a hill after a rainstorm.

Nicholasa Mohr. *Going Home*. Dial, 1986. Eleven-year-old Felita goes "home" to Puerto Rico for the first time and finds she doesn't fit in.

Rudolfo Anaya. *The Farolitos of Christmas: A New Mexico Christmas Story*. New Mexico Magazine, 1987. Luz is worried because his grandfather won't be able to light the fires to guide the shepherds on Christmas Eve, but he solves the problem. Illustrates the language and customs of Latinos in New Mexico and how people began lighting lanterns for Christmas Eve.

Omar Castañeda. *Abuela's Weave*. Lee & Low, 1993. This picture book shows the importance of respecting elders and maintaining the folk arts.

The Color Wheel

A Spanish color wheel is helpful to show students the names for colors they know. Make a large poster to display on the wall like that on the next page.

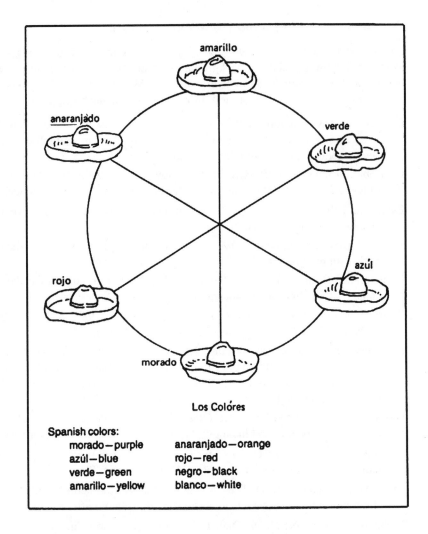

amarillo

anaranjàdo

verde

azúl

rojo

morado

Los Colóres

Spanish colors:
morado—purple
azúl—blue
verde—green
amarillo—yellow

anaranjado—orange
rojo—red
negro—black
blanco—white

This idea can be easily adapted for use with any language spoken by students in the class. With languages such as Tagalog and Navajo, it is often difficult to find printed materials for use with students. Prepare a variety of displays similar to the color wheel showing basic vocabulary. Include numbers, days of the week, and words used in the classroom.

Review Charts

Help students practice Spanish vocabulary they have learned or seen by preparing review charts. Construct a slip chart with common Spanish words written on the front. Students read the Spanish, say it aloud, give the English equivalent, and check their response by pulling the tab that shows the English word below each Spanish example. These are especially useful for practicing limited sets of words such as numbers and days of the week. (See example on the next page.)

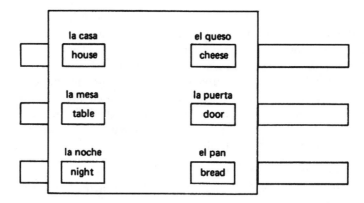

Charts can also be made with pictures of objects on the front. Students review by saying the name of the object in Spanish and then lifting the picture (attached at the top) to read the correct answer. Use these charts for independent student review or small group work. Both kinds of charts are useful for practicing English as a second language as well.

Famous Latinos

Help students break down stereotypes they may have about Latinos by sharing stories of famous people of Latino heritage. In addition, they will learn more about the diversity of people who have contributed to this country. Look for information about leaders in the local Latino community. Students will be encouraged to see examples of people who have become successful without giving up their Latino heritage.

Corinn Codye. *Vilma Martinez*. Raintree, 1990. This bilingual biography of the Mexican American attorney depicts her journey from poverty to leadership in the fight for Mexican American civil rights.

John Gillies. *Señor Alcalde: A Biography of Henry Cisneros*. Dillon, 1988. Students should know the name of Henry Cisneros, one of the most successful Latino politicians.

Janet Nomura Morey and Wendy Dunn. *Famous Mexican Amricans*. Cobblehill, 1989. This collection covers the stories of nine men and five women, among them César Chávez, Edward James Olmos, and Vilma Martinez. They share a determination to succeed despite obstacles of poverty and prejudice.

Joan Anderson. *Spanish Pioneers of the Southwest*. Lodestar, 1989. A photographic essay focusing on the people and history of mid–eighteenth-century New Mexico.

Milton Meltzer. *The Hispanic Americans*. Crowell, 1982. An old but still useful source of information about this people and their history.

Jane Pinchot. *The Mexicans in America*. Lerner, 1989. A survey of Mexican American life and Anglos' treatment of them.

Spanish Folklore

An important aspect of studying Spanish language and culture is Spanish folklore. This folklore reflects Spanish, English, and Indian influences and is unique to the Spanish-speaking culture as well as an important part of the American experience. Folklore includes stories (cuentos), sayings (dichos), songs, music, legends (leyendas), and drama. Special types of songs are corridos, mañanitas, and rancheros. Many legends center around La Bruja (the Witch) and La Curandera (the Healer).

Provide examples of different kinds of folklore and discuss the ritualized characteristics of each form. Encourage students to research more examples. Because all of the stories and songs are short, they are particularly suitable for presenting in front of the class. Several students can take turns telling stories that are spooky or humorous. You can also obtain records of traditional ballads and songs to play.

Folklore books for children

Pura Belpre. *Perez and Martina.* Viking, 1991. From the Puerto Rican storyteller, the tale of Perez the mouse and Martina the cockroach.

Gerald McDermott. *Papagayo the Mischief Maker.* Harcourt Brace Jovanovich, 1992. Papagayo the parrot annoys the night creatures when he keeps them awake with his noise. But he solves their problems for them when he shows them how to save the moon from being eaten up. Papagayo is the traditional trickster hero of the Amazon rain forest.

Lulu Delacre. *Arroz con Leche: Popular Songs and Rhymes from Latin America.* Scholastic, 1989. This collection includes twelve verses in Spanish and English, along with music.

Lulu Delacre. *Las Navidades: Popular Christmas Songs from Latin America.* Scholastic, 1990. This collection of songs and music for Christmas Eve to Epiphany includes information on the origins of the songs and descriptions of the traditions.

Suggested references and resources for exploring Latino folklore

Richard Dorson. *Buying the Wind: Regional Folklore in the United States.* University of Chicago Press, 1964.

Gilberto Espinosa. *Heroes, Hexes and Haunted Halls.* Calvin Horn, 1972.

José Espinosa. *Spanish Folk-Tales from New Mexico.* Kraus Reprint Co., 1969.

Luís Valdez and Stan Steiner. *An Anthology of Mexican American Literature.* Knopf, 1972.

Student Projects

Students can collect what they have learned and develop a book to share with other classes and schools. A model for this activity is *Kids Explore America's Hispanic Heritage* from the Westridge Young Writers Workshop (Muir Publishing, 1992). This book, written by students, includes information about and examples of dances, food, games, history, art, songs, and people.

Aspects of Spanish That May Cause Problems for Children Learning English: Summary

Many Spanish-speaking children make consistent mistakes as they learn English because they apply their knowledge of Spanish rules. The following points will help you to understand these mistakes and also to explain to students how English is different from Spanish.

1. Strong influence of the Spanish *ch* on the English *sh* is a common problem. When *sh* is introduced, because of its proximity in sound, the student may appear to say *share* for *chair* and *shoes* for *choose*.
2. In Spanish, *b* and *v* are exactly alike phonetically; each has two sounds. The use of one sound or the other is governed by accompanying sounds as follows:
   a. Sound one is made by the buzzing of both lips (e.g., *Ella botó la caja; Ella votó ayer*). The letters *b* or *v* surrounded by vowel sounds must be buzzed.
   b. Sound two is *b* as in boy (e.g., *El bote se caja, El vaso se caja*). Both sound like the *b* in boy. When *b* or *v* begins an utterance or is not surrounded by vowel sounds it is pronounced as the *b* in boy.
3. Spanish uses one word for *it is (es)* and for *there are* and *there is (hay)*. Examples: *It is* a nice day *(Es un día agradable)*. *There are* many children at school *(Hay muchos niños en la escuela)*. *There is* a teacher in the classroom *(Hay un profesor en la clase)*.
4. In Spanish, articles are placed in some positions where English does not require them: *Veo al* doctor Brown (I see *the* Dr. Brown); *Así es la vida* (That's *the* life).
5. In Spanish the adjective usually follows the noun and must agree with it in gender and number: *Yo tengo zapatos blancos* (I have shoes white).
6. There are five long vowels in Spanish, plus dipthongs. Spanish speakers tend to have difficulty distinguishing between long and short vowels in English, as in *leave* and *live*.
7. The adverb, not the direct object, usually comes right after the verb. Example: I immediately saw . . . *(Yo vi imediatamente . . .)*.
8. The consonant sounds *v, b, d, t, g, h, j, l, r, w, v,* and *z* are not pronounced the same in Spanish as in English. Knowledge of the point of articulation for the production of these sounds is necessary.
9. Beginning and ending sounds.
   a. Spanish words never begin with consonant clusters, identified in italics as follows: *sp*eak, *st*ay, *sch*ool, *st*reet, *spr*ing, *scr*atch, *sph*ere, *sl*ow, *sm*all, *sn*ail, *sv*elte. Speakers of Spanish add an initial vowel sound e as, for example, in *e*speak, *e*street.
   b. Spanish words can end in any of the five vowels—*a, e, i, o u*—or the consonants listed as follows:

l	*papel*	
d	*verdad*	*cara*
r	*señor*	*come*
z	*zariz*	*casi*
j	*reloj*	*todo*
y	*estoy*	*tu*
n	*son*	
s	*casas*	

   Note: Speakers of Spanish have difficulty with ending sounds such as *m, p, k, c, b, d, f, g, j, l, t, v,* and *x* (voiced *z*). They also have difficulty in pronouncing the 371 consonant-cluster endings used in English.

10. Some factors of intonation such as pitch and stress that can cause problems in communication are the following:
    a. *Stress*. Spanish words are stressed as follows:
        1) Stress on the last syllable: *pa pél, vi vi rás, te le vi sión, ciu dád*
        2) Stress on the next to last syllable: *cá sa, ma dé ra, clá ro*
        3) Stress on the third to last syllable: *jó ve nes, áng e les, te lé fo no*
        4) Stress on the fourth to last syllable: *llé va te los, mánd a se lo, có me te los*
        Most Spanish words are stressed on the last syllable (Group A words) or next to last syllable (Group B words). In contrast, English words are usually stressed on the first or second syllable; for example, *con*stant (*constante*, *te*lephone (*teléfono*). In English, long words may have two or even three stresses. Spanish uses only one stress except for adverbs ending in *mente (e.g., fácilmente, rápidamente).*
    b. *Tone system*. English and Spanish have four tone levels. Spanish normally operates on the lower three levels except in cases of extreme anger or alarm. Then the fourth (upper) pitch is used. English usually operates on all four levels.
11. Spelling differences. Although many Latin derivatives are common to Spanish and English, there are some interferences between spelling systems. Teachers should help students with the transfer of cognate vocabulary. Spanish does *not* use the doubled consonants or combination of consonants; that is, *bb, dd, ff, gg, mm, pp, ss, tt, zz, th, gh, ph, sh,* or *hn*.[3]

SUPPORTING SPEAKERS OF OTHER LANGUAGES AS ENGLISH LEARNERS

One of the most noticeable ways in which today's classrooms are heterogeneous is in the number of students who come from different language backgrounds and are learning English in school. Some of these children have parents who are working in this country for a limited time and expect to return to their home country. These parents often view learning English as an asset for their child and they continue to take responsibility for maintaining another language in the home. Other children may have been born in this country but grew up in communities where English was not a dominant language. Perhaps their parents do not speak English. In this case, teachers may encounter communication barriers that make it difficult to find out important information about the students. Another group of students are refugees. They may have undergone great hardships to come to this country and the student's family may be separated, making the position of parental responsibility unclear. In some cases, these students have not gone to school before, although they are older, and learning about school expectations may be the primary language task before they can participate in a class.

All of these situations place different demands on the teacher, who is usually not trained as a language teaching specialist. Nonetheless, we need to offer the best teaching we can to all students who are encountering English as an unfamiliar language. We can help students develop the oral fluency that provides a base for further language learning.

We can also structure activities that help students attend to the elements of the English language. Reading, writing, and many word games support the essential vocabulary development for students. Finally, we can make sure that all students feel included in the class because they know they make an important contribution.

Developing a Literacy Base

Students who come to school with little or no English-speaking proficiency need a solid foundation in basic areas to achieve literacy in either or both of their languages. In any program that starts with the student's first language and gradually introduces English in order to develop literacy skills, the following points are fundamental to success.

1. *Read aloud to students.* Students need to hear the special kind of language used in books. Have them respond by writing in the language they choose.
2. *Give students time to write everyday.* Beginning writers need frequent practice to develop fluency. Invented spelling and grammatical mistakes are evidence that students are applying hypotheses about how each language works.
3. *Publish some student writing.* This gives students an incentive to polish some of their pieces. As they revise and edit, they learn the conventions of written language. Use teacher-student writing conferences to focus attention on aspects of form and content.
4. *Provide many books and printed materials, particularly in the language other than English.* Students can transfer their literacy skills from one language to another. The more they read, the more they will learn about language.

Choral Speaking

Many students learning English as a second language (ESL) respond well to choral activities because they are not singled out or embarrassed by their mistakes. The class can learn a short piece to recite together, or a group of students can prepare a passage to present to the class. "The Old Woman Who Swallowed a Fly" is a traditional choice. Different parts can be spoken by different groups or parts of the class. Poems and prose with a strong rhyme and rhythm are easier to learn and more fun to recite. ESL students will learn oral skills such as pronunciation and intonation by participating.

In the following example, divide the class in half and ask each group to alternate lines.

If all the seas were one sea,
What a *great* sea that would be!
If all the trees were one tree,
What a *great* tree that would be!
And if all the axes were one ax,
What a *great* ax that would be!
And if all the men were one man,
What a *great* man that would be!
And if the *great* man took the great ax,
And cut down the *great* tree,

And let it fall into the *great* sea,
What a splish-splash that would be!
   (Old Nursery Rhyme)

For more examples, see *Presenting Reader's Theater: Plays and Poems to Read Aloud* by Caroline Bauer (Wilson, 1987).

Language Experience Stories

With this approach, even ESL students can write their own stories. Introduce students to the technique by composing a story as a group. After an experience shared by the class, begin writing about it on the board. As students make comments, write down the sentences they contribute. Prompt them to include more information if necessary. After the story is completed, read it back to the class so that they can see it is *their* story. Then have students copy the class story and read it themselves.

The same technique can be used for individuals. Students can dictate a story to the teacher or an aide, or write it themselves, in their own fashion, to read back later. ESL students can dictate stories into a tape recorder. After these stories are transcribed and typed, they can be read back to the students, showing the relation between the spoken and written language.

Reading through Dictation

Dictation helps develop student reading skills, particularly for the ESL student. Before reading a passage to the class, dictate a few lines for students to write. After each line, stop and discuss what students know about the story. Based on this information, what do they think will happen next? Continue this procedure for several lines and then have them read the rest of the story to find out what happened. This exercise promotes the ability to analyze and predict what could come next, which is an essential thinking skill for reading comprehension.

Tape-Assisted Reading

Tape-record several stories from a class reading textbook or other literature book. (Enlist parents, aides, or older students to help you with this, providing a variety of voices.) ESL students can listen to the stories on cassette as they follow along in the book. (If you use multiple headsets, a group of students can listen and read at the same time.) They will enjoy listening to these stories over and over again, and in the process, they will begin to make the connection between sound and symbol.

Draw the Word

Draw the word is a popular game with many students and adults. Adapt this game for classroom use, particularly for ESL students. One team draws a picture and the other team has to guess what the picture represents. You can set a time limit appropriate to the level of your class. Students can use this game to practice new vocabulary they are learning as well as to challenge each other with more difficult words. You can also increase the difficulty by making them spell the word correctly.

Oral Practice

The following techniques are particularly useful for ESL students but benefit all students by increasing oral fluency. Students need to listen carefully in order to produce the appropriate grammatical constructions.

Repetition:	Listen and repeat exactly as heard.
Teacher:	I see a dog.
Child:	I see a dog.

Analogy:	Repeat exactly with one change.
Teacher:	I am a man.
Anne:	I am a woman.
Fred:	I am a boy.
Sue:	I am a person.

Begin a PROGRESSIVE CONVERSATION so that all members of the group participate in this type of analogical replacement, thus:

Teacher:	I see a dog. What do you see, Jim?
Jim:	I see a cat. What do you see, Janet?
Janet:	I see a mouse. What do you see, Gerri?

Inflection:	Change the form of a word.
Teacher:	There is one girl.
Sue:	There are two girls.
Teacher:	There is one house.
Fred:	There are two houses.

Completion:	Finish the statement.
Teacher:	Susan is tall, but . . .
Jose:	Mary is taller.
Teacher:	John is big, but . . .
Carol:	Phil is bigger.

Expansion:	Add to the sentence
Teacher:	Steve is happy.
Chuck:	Steve is happy because he finished his work.
Teacher:	Milly is happy.
Ann:	Milly is happy because she has a new dress.

Transformation:	Change a given sentence to negative or interrogative form.
Teacher:	Judy is here today.
Carol:	Judy is not here today.
Teacher:	Judy is here today.
Fred:	Is Judy here today?

Restoration:	Student makes sentences from a group of words.
Teacher:	picture, wall, hanging

> **Chuck:** The picture is hanging on the wall.
> **Phyllis:** Is the picture hanging on that wall?
>
> *Response:* Answer or make a rejoinder.
> **Teacher:** It is chilly in this room.
> **Mary:** It feels fine to me.
> **Jim:** I think you are right.
> **Joan:** Shall I close the door?[4]

Pattern Books

ESL students of any age can learn about English grammar by reading primary/picture books that establish a syntactic pattern and then repeat it through many variations. For example, Wanda Gag's *Millions of Cats* provides excellent practice with number words and the plural ending. After the first couple of pages, students will have no trouble filling in the refrain: "Millions and millions of cats." *The Judge,* by Margot Zemach, focuses attention on the *-s* ending as it repeats verbs in the third person singular. And Marjorie Flack's *Ask Mr. Bear* is an excellent exercise for pronouns, especially the possessive adjective.

These books achieve their appeal through repetition, making them easy to memorize. Students learn the patterns quickly and practice important grammatical elements painlessly. Students will be motivated to "read" these books that they have memorized.

Traveling Sentences

Exercises that allow more than one right answer are especially important because they give the ESL student more chances to succeed. Begin by placing a simple sentence on the board and then go around the room, inviting students to add to it. Have them write the sentence on the board as it is revised. You can restrict the additions to one word each time, or you can require that each contribution make a complete sentence.

I	*II*
Manolo flew	Manolo flew.
Manolo flew kites	Manolo flew kites.
Manolo flew blue kites	Manolo flew kites in the park.
Manolo flew blue kites in	

Remind students that they can add words anywhere in the sentence, even in front.

Class Log

All students can participate in recording class activities and other information on a daily basis. They can make weather observations, write about special events, and note birthdays and other news. Students can take turns being secretary, making entries in a class log or diary by copying information off the board or from weather instruments. This is useful to refer to later and it is interesting to show to visitors as a record of the class year.

October 3

It was 76 degrees outside and partly cloudy at 10 A.M. Today a woman from the Police Department came to talk to us about bicycle safety. She gave us a list of rules and taught us how to lock up our bikes. We saw a filmstrip about life in the ocean. My favorite part was how the hermit crab lives in other shells.

Alliterative Sentences

This game stimulates students to make up sentences of words that begin with the same sound, thus reinforcing vocabulary development. Give students a name to start with, and see who can come up with the longest sentence.

Carmen:
Careful Carmen can't come.
Catty Carmen cut Conrad crushingly.

Students will also have to review the phoneme-grapheme relationship as they are forced to decide: Can I include *center?* What about *kangaroo?* Or *charming?*

Steven Kellogg's *Aster Aardvark's Alphabet Adventures* (Morrow, 1987) is an amusing alphabetical collection of alliterative sentences.

Scrambler

Play word games such as scrambled words to teach ESL students possible letter combinations in English and develop their vocabulary. If you write scrambled words on cards with the answer on the back, students will enjoy playing this game alone or in pairs. You can even have students develop their own cards.

A version for older students is to present a sentence out of order. Can they arrange the words to form a correct sentence? Be careful—sometimes there's more than one right answer. This exercise gives students practice in English word order patterns, groups of words that go together, and how the beginning of a sentence constrains the ending.

Students can also arrange mixed-up sentences to form a paragraph. They will enjoy creating examples to challenge their classmates. The skills involved in sorting out this mixed-up paragraph reinforce those required for successful reading and writing.

Students Can Help

Your English-speaking students can help you enormously to integrate the student with limited English skills into the class. Assign a "buddy" to each new student. This buddy can show the student where to go and what to do, as well as help explain what the teacher wants. Most significantly, the buddy, by speaking lots of English, provides important vocabulary and grammar input for the English language learner. And both participants in the pair receive rewards.

Peer tutoring, using a student in the same class, and cross-age tutoring, when a student in the upper grades helps a student in the lower grades, have proved helpful for language development of ESL students.

Guide for New Students

Encourage ESL students to prepare a guide to the school. It could include information useful for other ESL students as well as any new students. Have students take pictures of classrooms, student activities, and other important elements of school life. They can prepare captions ranging from a few words to a longer description of what is expected of a student. If you work with one particular language group, you might consider having the guide translated and sent out to incoming families as a bilingual introduction to the U.S. school system.

Older students can extend this project by preparing a guide to the community. It might include information about important resources for non–English-speaking families.

ABC Books

Challenge students to prepare their own ABC books. Limit the words to a certain category (animals or plants, for example) in order to stimulate a hunt for new words. ESL students will particularly benefit from this approach to vocabulary learning as they seek out dictionaries. Have students prepare "real" books—writing one example for each letter per page, illustrating it, and stapling the pages together. Encourage students to pass their books around and share their unusual discoveries. They can choose their favorite word in each book. Here are some examples of alphabet books that are also useful for vocabulary work:

Kate Duke. *The Guinea Pig ABC.* Dutton, 1986.

Marty Neumeier and Byron Glaser. *Action Alphabet.* Greenwillow, 1985.

Anne Rockwell. *Albert B. Cub and Zebra: An Alphabet Storybook.* Crowell, 1977.

Categories

Another vocabulary game that helps ESL students is the familiar "Categories." Most often used as a unit review, it consists of a word (the topic) written down the left side of a sheet and several categories across the top. Students fill in words under each category that begin with the letters of the topic word. For example, after discussing the subject of "space" for several days, give students this challenging exercise:

	Heavenly Bodies	*Colors*	*People/Professions*
S	Saturn	silver	scientist
P	Pluto	purple	pilot
A	Asteroid	azure	astronaut
C	Ceres	cocoa	chemist
E	Earth	emerald	engineer

This game works best if there is more than one possible answer. If you want to make it more difficult, you can give points for each letter and reward students who have the longest entries.

Individualized Dictionaries

Have primary-grade ESL students develop their own picture dictionaries. They can cut out or draw illustrations of all the new objects they encounter and copy the English word next to each one. Then students can refer to these dictionaries in class and even take them home for extra practice. Some older students may benefit from recording the pronunciation phonetically in their own language.

Intermediate and upper-grade students could construct a dictionary/notebook that focuses on signs and symbols. They could include examples such as the following:

Vocabulary Patterns

When you teach vocabulary, pay particular attention to teaching *morphemes*. (Morphemes are units of meaning that are put together to form words.) Demonstrate the power of morphemes by taking a familiar word such as *telephone* and exploring the meaning of each morpheme. *Tele* is a morpheme meaning *far,* and *phone* is another morpheme meaning *sound.* Ask students if they can list other words that contain one of these morphemes. Words they might know are *telegraph* and *phonograph.* They can look up more examples in the dictionary.

Based on the list, what do they think *graph* means? Did they guess it meant *write?* Once students learn that morphemes have meanings, independent of the words they are found in, and that they can be combined to form new words, students will be able to understand many more words.

Expanding Vocabulary

As students encounter new words, be sure to provide all the forms of the word (noun, verb, and adjective groups or the present, participle, and past forms for a verb). Draw students' attention to spelling and pronunciation changes, if any. This is particularly important for the ESL student, as it reinforces learning of regular patterns (ones that English speakers are already accustomed to) and exposes them to the common exceptions.

admire	(verb)
admirable	(adjective)
admiration	(noun)

(Note stress change in adjective form.)

creep	(present)
crept	(past)
crept	(participle)

Factors That Accelerate Language Learning: Summary

As you prepare your lessons, keep the following points in mind. Frequent application of these principles (based on extensive second language research) will maximize students' language-learning potential.

1. *Need to know.* Design lessons based on students' immediate needs and interests.
2. *Context.* Try to teach words as they occur in sentences, and grammatical constructions where they occur naturally in conversations.
3. *Inductive presentation.* Give examples and let students try to figure out the pattern or generalization.
4. *Manipulation.* Engage the physical aspect of learning by having students act out what they are learning.
5. *Relaxation.* Get students to talk (or write) without fear of making mistakes. They will absorb more and remember more.

REFLECTIONS

In school, students *learn* language, they learn *about* language, and they learn *through* language. As teachers, we need to recognize the central role that language plays in teaching and learning. For education that attempts to address multicultural issues of difference and diversity, language is the heart of the students' identity. We have the responsibility to bring language into the classroom in a way that acknowledges its importance in knowing who we are and what the world is about. We do this by reflecting on our own language, its history and variety, and by exploring other examples of languages and their uses.

APPLICATIONS

1. Investigate the children's literature available in the library and select several books that are based on patterns: refrains, repeated story lines, or questions and answers. Write lesson plans to show how you could use these books with students who need English as a second language support to help them develop oral fluency, to provide writing models, or to practice vocabulary.

2. Collect examples of writing in different languages. Try to find different scripts and different systems (pictographic, syllabary). Look for familiar children's books in different languages. Can you find *Winnie the Pooh* in French, Spanish, and Latin? Design a lesson plan to use these books to introduce children to different languages and their writing systems.

3. Look at different books that attempt to reproduce how people really talk (regional or social dialects, Black English). Are they accurate? What effect are they trying to produce? How would you read these aloud to students? Compare and analyze treatment of the same dialect in several books and make recommendations for the teaching of these books and the dialect.

4. Write a letter to parents explaining the language policy in your classroom. Describe the Students' Right to Their Own Language policy on p. 163 and how you support it. Outline what actions you expect to take to help their children develop their language abilities.

Endnotes

1. *Students' Right to Their Own Language* (NCTE, 1976).
2. J. N. Hook, *The Story of American English* (Harcourt Brace Jovanovich, 1972), p. 2.
3. Adapted from *Framework in Reading for the Elementary and Secondary Schools in California* (California State Department of Education, 1973).
4. Iris Tiedt, The Language Arts Handbook (Prentice-Hall, 1983). Used with permission.

Exploring Further

California Office of Bilingual-Bicultural Education. *Beyond Language: Social and Cultural Factors in Schooling Language and Minority Students.* Evaluation, Dissemination, and Assessment Center, Los Angeles, 1986.

California State Department of Education. *Schooling and Language Minority Students: A Theoretical Framework.* 1988.

Courtney Cazden. *Classroom Discourse: The Language for Teaching and Learning.* Heinemann, 1988.

Robert Claiborne. *Our Marvelous Native Tongue.* Random, 1983.

David Crystal. *The Cambridge Encyclopedia of Language.* Cambridge University Press, 1987.

Leslie Crawford. *Language and Literacy Learning in Multicultural Classrooms.* Allyn and Bacon, 1993.

J. L. Dillard. *Black English: Its History and Usage.* Random House, 1972.

Alan Dundes, ed. *Mother Wit from the Laughing Barrel.* Prentice-Hall, 1973.

Yvonne Freeman and David Freeman. *Whole Language for Second Language Learners.* Heinemann, 1992.

Eugene Garcia. *The Education of Linguistically and Culturally Diverse Students: Effective Instructional Practices.* National Center for Research on Cultural Diversity and Second Language Learning, Santa Cruz. 1991.

Shirley Brice Heath. *Ways with Words: Language, Life, and Work in Communities and Classrooms.* Cambridge, 1983.

Shirley Brice Heath and Leslie Mangiola. *Children of Promise: Literate Activity in Linguistically and Culturally Diverse Classrooms.* NEA, 1991.

Robert McCrum, William Cran, and Robert MacNeil. *The Story of English.* Viking, 1986. (See also the PBS video series of the same title.)

Suzanne Peregoy and Owen Boyle. *Reading, Writing, and Learning in ESL.* Longman, 1993.

Pat Rigg and Virginia Allen, eds. *When They Don't All Speak English: Integrating the ESL Student into the Regular Classroom.* NCTE, 1989.

Geneva Smitherman. *Talking and Testifying: The Language of Black America.* Houghton, 1977.

Catherine Wallace. *Learning to Read in a Multicultural Society: Social Context of Second Language Literacy.* Pergamon, 1988.

Education
enables all individuals
to come into
full possession
of all their
powers.

—John Dewey

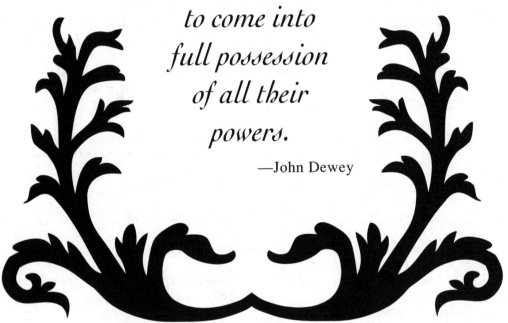

7
❖

Infusing Multicultural Education into Reading and Language Arts Programs

"As children and young people learn their language, they learn to think," wrote James Squire.[1] Language and literacy are foundational to learning across the curriculum. Oral language enables even young children to express their thinking, which later can be expressed in writing. Through oral language children first learn how language works. As they listen, they learn the grammatical structures that will be encountered in reading and used as they compose written sentences and paragraphs. Reading written language opens the door to independent encounters with literature that enable children to look into the lives of others. Learning to listen, speak, think, read, and write effectively is an essential part of education at any level.

The languaging processes must of necessity focus on some content. This chapter examines ways of learning about multicultural concepts and attitudes as students improve their use of the language processes. It also links the study of language and literature with multicultural education across the curriculum.

After reading this chapter, you should be able to:
- Introduce multicultural concepts through oral language experiences.
- Integrate multicultural concepts into literacy instruction.
- Select multicultural literature for individual and group study.
- Use questions to stimulate thinking about human concerns.
- Guide student responses to multicultural literature through such strategies as the dialectical or "double entry" journal.
- Design lessons that integrate sound theory and practice in language arts instruction with content from multicultural education.
- Organize a unit of study around a novel or a theme.

Because we live in a multicultural world, multicultural education is an integral part of instruction. Multicultural education extends to any area of study. Every teacher chooses consciously or unconsciously, to allow multicultural education either to exist only as the "hidden curriculum" that children absorb or to enhance explicit learning experiences designed to enlighten or to combat cultural misunderstanding. The language arts curriculum, including reading instruction, offers teachers numerous opportunities to present multicultural concepts. In this chapter we will focus on the following: the language arts and reading curriculum; oral language foundations; writing as a way of expressing thinking; and literature as a source of multicultural content.

THE LANGUAGE ARTS AND READING CURRICULUM

A comprehensive language arts program includes instruction that promotes development of basic language skills: listening, speaking, thinking, reading, and writing. In addition to these skills, however, language arts includes content about both language and literature.

A Curriculum Framework

We see the language arts curriculum as grounded in a strong oral facility with language, such as depicted in the schema on the following page.

Language arts instruction should integrate the development of skills and content so as to stimulate learning for real purposes. As students develop listening, speaking, and thinking skills, they can also learn information about the diverse population of the United States. Students can:

1. Discuss the problems of being poor.
2. Listen to Martin Luther King, Jr.'s "I Have a Dream" speech.
3. Argue about U.S. treatment of Native Americans.
4. Tape letters to young people living in China.

The possibilities are endless, and the topics generated lend stimulus to language and literacy instruction. Notice also that the suggested topics could well be presented in social studies classes, too, which suggests the integration of language arts and social studies instruction for a more powerful effect. We will continue this discussion in the next chapter.

Renewed concern about teaching writing is a second trend addressed in this chapter. Perceiving writing as another way of expressing thinking makes it a natural step following listening and speaking activities. A strong oral language foundation prepares the student to write successfully. Multicultural concepts and controversies provide food for thought, something to communicate to the world in writing.

Reading literature, an essential component of an outstanding language arts program, also plays a special part in teaching multicultural understandings. Good fiction enables the reader to "walk in another person's moccasins," to feel the humiliation or the joy experienced by a boy or girl of a different color. Well-written nonfiction provides background information about other countries and other cultures. Poetry gives students insight into the thinking of a writer who has a message to share about living. Multicultural literature provides vicarious experiences that lead students to recognize the commonalities they share with others.

Thus, English language arts and reading classes offer an unusual opportunity to introduce multicultural concepts to students at any age. Through selection of topics for discussion or literature to read, you can encourage students to think about other people who live next door or perhaps across the ocean. For those who may not be familiar with

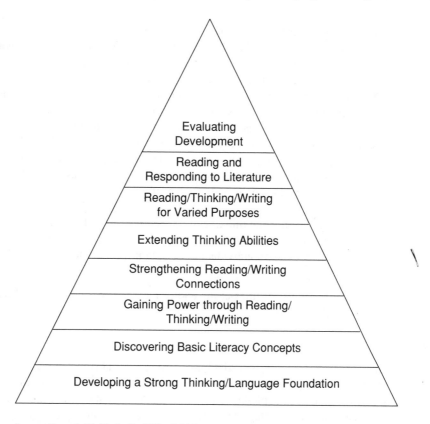

Source: From I. M. Tiedt, R. Gibbs, M. Howard, M. Timpson, and M. Y. Williams, *Reading/Thinking/Writing: A Holistic Language and Literacy Program for the K–8 Classroom* (Boston: Allyn and Bacon, 1989), p. 7.

the "cutting edge" of theory and practice in the language arts, we begin this chapter with a summary of what we know about teaching language and literacy skills. We will build on the ideas that were presented about teaching in Chapter 2.

What Research Tells Us

Studies of the language arts curriculum and instruction provide us with a knowledge base from which to begin planning a multiculturally-based language arts program. The following basic assumptions will guide the development of multicultural lessons to integrate into the language arts curriculum:

1. A strong thinking-language base is necessary for success in reading and writing. Thinking and language permeate all learning.
2. Reading and writing cannot be taught in isolation. Integrating the language arts reinforces learning efficiently and effectively.
3. Beginning readers need to learn basic phonics information, but they can best learn and then reinforce this learning through reading and writing whole language. Decoding (unlocking meaning from words presented in the English code) and encoding (spelling/writing words according to the English code system) should be presented as complementary processes applied during meaningful reading and writing activities.

4. Students learn to read, write, and think by engaging frequently in composing and comprehending activities that emphasize quality of the learning experience as well as quantity or frequency of practice. These experiences can involve learning in any subject area (e.g., multicultural concepts).

5. Literature must be an integral part of instruction across the curriculum at all levels. It should be presented as something to be read and also as an example of good writing by a real person who is sharing his or her thinking.

6. Both reading and writing entail a transaction between author and audience as they work together to construct meaning. The work of both reader and writer is influenced by prior knowledge—what each brings to the task of making meaning. All learners come to school with a store of prior knowledge, which includes cultural backgrounds.

7. Reading, writing, and thinking abilities grow uniquely for each individual. Instructional strategies should be selected to promote individual progress. Evaluation must also be adapted to fit individual growth with appropriate expectations established for each learner.

Refer to the list of titles at the end of the chapter if you would like to know more about studies in this area.

Recap

An integrated language arts curriculum is firmly rooted in oral language. Students progress developmentally, gaining independence as they experience success in making meaning first through observing, thinking, and listening. Emergent whole language approaches lead them naturally into reading ideas presented by others and expressing their own thinking through speaking and writing. In the following sections we will examine ways of working with oral language, writing, and reading literature.

ORAL LANGUAGE: FOUNDATION FOR LEARNING

As presented in the holistic model for language arts instruction, oral language—thinking, listening, and speaking—forms the foundation of all learning. Learning begins aurally and orally, and oral language continues to be an important way of communicating in adult life.

Unlike Japanese educators, who continue to stress oral communication, however, instruction in our classrooms tends to move quickly toward an emphasis on written language.[2] It is interesting to conjecture on our hesitancy to offer a strong oral language curriculum. Is it perhaps because studies that use the written language are more predictable and more easily controlled? Do teachers feel more comfortable with written exercises or reading assignments followed by workbook pages for which they know the answers? Is oral performance more difficult to evaluate?

Using Oral Language in the Classroom

Our contention is that we need to allocate more classroom time for learning with oral language than we do at present. In this section, we will explore ways of incorporating speaking and listening activities that promote multicultural thinking in language arts instruction. Focusing on multicultural concepts will, as noted previously, suggest the use of such approaches across the curriculum. This discussion will continue in Chapter 8.

Oral language is the foundation on which we base all language learning. Unless a child has a facility with a spoken language—Swahili, Tagalog, Spanish, English—he or she will not become a fluent reader or writer. Children who have difficulty with language, for example those who are learning English as a second language, need to spend more time working orally. Through oral language we develop an "ear for language" that enables us to construct grammatical sentences as we write and to interpret the meaning of sentences as we read.

Responding to Literature

Oral activities should be part of all daily learning experiences, for they assist children in continuing to learn more about the language they use. Prewriting and prereading motivation are usually oral. Sharing writing and responding to books offer further opportunities for bringing oral activities into the classroom. For instance, some of the following ideas will help students plan oral book reviews:

- Interview a character in the book. Two members of the class may share this review with one serving as the character to be interviewed.
- Give a first-person account of an event in the book read: Wilbur speaks, for example: "I tell you I was so lonesome I thought I'd die when suddenly I heard Charlotte's sweet voice. . . ."
- Tape a portion of the story after having practiced reading that part of the book aloud in order to achieve the best interpretation.
- Prepare a scroll theater presentation of important incidents in a book. Then tell the story briefly as the pictures are shown.
- Prepare a commercial to sell a book to fellow students. This activity might involve several students and could be correlated with art.

Role-Playing

Role-playing is a versatile oral activity that allows students to express their opinions in a realistic situation. They can literally stand in someone else's shoes as they speak in the role they have assumed. Ideas for role-playing come from all areas of the curriculum, for instance:

- A group of parents discussing a city problem.
- Children greeting a new student from Vietnam.
- A Japanese American family preparing to go to an internment camp.
- A Native American tribe holding a feast in 1700.

Role-playing may be performed by a group of three to five students as the others observe and take notes. After the performance, class discussion focuses on the strengths and weaknesses of the performance, for example, the language used and the appropriateness of the topics discussed. After this analysis, another group can perform with the same roles and situation.

At other times, the whole class can role-play a situation, such as plantation life in 1800. Before beginning this activity, of course, students need to study to determine what the various roles would be. Group activities in specific areas of the room might focus on the slave quarters, the barn where horses are shod, or a group of runaways in the woods. Simple costuming lends interest to this dramatic play.

Role-playing can lead to formal debate as students discuss the pros and cons of an issue. After arguing informally in role-play, students may be stimulated to search out more information to be presented in a panel discussion or debate. These oral activities lend interest to learning, and they provide a firm foundation for writing to express opinions. They also teach advanced thinking skills.

Philosophical Discussions

We often allude to discussion as part of classroom instruction. However, studies show that what is called discussion is often teacher-dominated, that is, the teacher asks questions to which students respond one by one. The percentage of student involvement revealing real thinking remains very low.[3]

Focusing on multicultural understanding offers an opportunity to deal with meaty concerns, matters of consequence. Introducing topics that are presented in fiction is a safe way to open up what we can identify as "philosophical discussions," the kind of talk in which informed adults frequently engage. Depending on the content of a particular book, a worthwhile discussion might involve students in talking about "experiences all children have had, such as being embarrassed by not knowing an answer. They may have wanted to talk about these experiences, but not in a personal way. By discussing what happens to the characters in a novel, they can talk about things in the third person: somebody else is the one involved."[4]

Classroom climate is crucial to developing a successful oral program. Once a climate of trust is built up, discussions may lead to sharing experiences or problems that individuals have faced. As students gain skill in such discourse, they can meet in small groups so that the percentage of participation for each student will increase. For some students a small discussion group is less inhibiting than a large group. A few conclusions from each group can then be shared with the larger group. Such discussion may serve as a prewriting stimulus as each student expresses his or her thoughts in writing about the topic discussed.

A Sample Lesson.   Following is a lesson that illustrates the kind of discussion that can follow the reading of almost any novel.

SAMPLE LESSON: THE NEED FOR FRIENDSHIP

Level of Difficulty: Grades 4–7

Outcomes

Students will:

1. Discuss the need for friends.
2. Identify problems that occur between friends.
3. Suggest solutions to problems that arise.

Description

After listening to the teacher's reading of *Always and Forever Friends,* students discuss Wendy's search for a friend. Through discussion they identify the need for friendship as a universal need that they share with all other human beings. In small groups they discuss problems that can arise between friends and possible solutions.

Procedures

Obtain a copy of *Always and Forever Friends* by C. S. Adler (Houghton Mifflin, 1988) or any similar book about friendship. Read the story aloud to the whole class, chapter by chapter, over a two-week period. Give students a chance to talk about the events depicted in each chapter following the reading. This lesson is designed to follow the completion of the whole book. It requires at least two class periods.

Stimulus

Present the following quotation from the book on a transparency:

> "The way I look at it," Honor continued earnestly, "you don't wind yourself around a friend like a strangler vine, and you don't expect friendship to be always and forever."
> "But Honor, if it doesn't last, what good is it?"
> "I didn't say it *wouldn't* last. All I'm saying is, we shouldn't expect it to because life's sure to change us, you and me. In high school, we'll be different people, and boys will come in the picture—for you anyway. I don't know if I'll have time for them if I'm going to be a lawyer. And if boys don't do us in, then after high school we'll go our separate ways, and that'll make it hard."

Ask students to state Wendy's view of friendship. Then ask someone to restate what Honor is saying.

Activity

Have students number off from 1 to 6 to form six cooperative learning groups. (Adjust these numbers to produce groups of four to six students.) Assign a Leader and a Recorder for each group, and give everyone copies of the following sheet. Give the recorder an extra copy.

---

1. Could you live without having friends?
2. Why do people feel the need of friends?
3. What are problems that make finding friends difficult?
4. What problems might break up a friendship?
5. What can we do to make a friendship last?

Directions

Take a few minutes for each person to read the questions and to write at least one response to each question.

Then discuss each question in turn. Each person should read one answer to the first question. Talk about the answers that were shared and agree on one answer for the whole group. After the Recorder has written the group answer on the Group Answer Sheet, go to question 2, and so on.

Follow-up

Working with the full class, have one person share the group response to each question in turn. After ideas have been shared, have each student write a paragraph about the importance of friendship in his or her life.

Evaluation

Have students meet in the same groups to share their paragraphs. After the group listens to a student's paragraph, group members in turn will identify one aspect of the writing they especially like. Then each student will make one suggestion for improving the writing of the paragraph.

Students will then rewrite their first drafts. The revised copies will be placed in a three-ringed notebook entitled *Friendship Forever.* After class members have had ample time to read it, place this class publication in the school library.

Recap

Oral language provides the foundation for all learning. From the time children acquire speech in the early years, they continue to use speaking and listening as the primary mode of communicating. Thinking is inextricably integrated with language learning. Effective teachers use oral language to support the development of literacy skills at all levels and in all subject areas. Listening, thinking, and speaking will support multicultural learning in the same way as they do all other learning.

WRITING "THINKING"

The most important development in working with written language is the discovery that *what we read is writing—an expression of a person's thinking.* Whole language approaches based soundly in the child's oral language encourage children to begin scribble writing their original stories as best they can, literally becoming authors. Only then do they gradually discover how to read their own writing. Thus, literacy emerges in a natural fashion akin to the way children learn oral language.

What We Know about Teaching Writing

Through a process of evolution, we have changed our approaches to teaching students how to write. Even though there is some resistance and clinging to traditional approaches, elementary and secondary teachers have received support for methodologies that demonstrate concern for students' self-esteem and that reduce the paper load for composition instructors. Following is a summary of beliefs compiled by K–12 teachers trained by the National Writing Project:

This We Believe . . .

    1. Writing is a process that involves thinking; it should not be defined as assignments or products.

2. Students need a prewriting warm-up, a stimulus that is often oral, before they begin to write. Oral language provides the foundation for both writing and reading.
3. Our first emphasis in a writing program should be on developing fluency. Students need to write daily and to experience a variety of forms and types of writing in order to write effectively.
4. Writers need to be aware of the audience for whom they are writing; this audience should not always be just the teacher.
5. Teachers should draw from a variety of theories and strategies for teaching writing.
6. An effective writing lesson includes (1) prewriting (talking, gathering ideas); (2) writing (organizing thinking, sharing, responding, editing, rewriting); and (3) postwriting (making the writing public).
7. Not every piece of writing goes through the full editing process; many will be short "finger exercises" designed to develop fluency and to break down writing apprehension.
8. A teacher should not expect to read or to grade every piece of writing that students do.
9. Teachers should write frequently with their students to model the writing process and to show value for writing as well as to share themselves.
10. Writing develops critical thinking skills and facilitates learning across the curriculum.
11. Evaluation of writing should be ongoing and should emphasize more than just the correct use of conventions. Students should engage in self-evaluation, peer evaluation, and conferences with the teacher.
12. Writing is the most difficult of the language skills, so we should appreciate what students are able to achieve.[5]

Kinds of Writing Students Can Try

Students will enjoy trying varied kinds of writing rather than writing the same forms repeatedly. James Moffett provides an interesting way of connecting thinking and writing processes and the forms of writing we use.[6]

Thinking Up (Imagination)
Fiction
Plays
Poetry

Looking Back
(Recollection)
Autobiography
Memoir

Noting Down (Notation)
Journal
Diary

Thinking Over, Thinking Through
(Cogitation)
Column
Editorial
Review
Personal Essay
Thesis Essay

Looking Into (Investigation)
Biography
Chronicle
Profile
Factual Article or Report

Here are eight forms of writing that young authors can use to express their ideas:

1. *Report of information.* The writer collects data from observation and research and chooses material that best presents a phenomenon or concept.
2. *Eyewitness account.* The writer tells about a person, group, or event that was objectively observed from the outside.
3. *Autobiographical incident.* The writer narrates a specific event in his or her life and states or implies the significance of the event.
4. *Firsthand biography sketch.* Through incident and description, the writer characterizes a person he or she knows well.
5. *Story.* Using dialogue and description, the writer shows conflict between characters or between a character and the environment.
6. *Analysis—speculation about effects.* The writer conjectures about the causes and effects of a specific event.
7. *Problem solving.* The writer describes and analyzes a specific problem and then proposes and argues for a solution.
8. *Evaluation.* The writer presents a judgment on the worth of an item—book, movie, artwork, consumer product—supported with reasons and evidence.

The types of writing specified reflect the intent of the author and ways of thinking rather than prescribed poetry or prose forms. For example, a report of information could be a résumé or a book review. A story might take the form of a fable or an extended dialogue. Thus the emphasis is not so much on producing a specific form as it is on the expression of students' ideas for a specific purpose.[7] Following are ideas for engaging students in writing.

Clustering: A Prewriting Technique

Clustering is a brainstorming technique that can be used individually or in a large group. It can be used to probe into a topic that students are planning to write or talk about. It can also be used as a preassessment tool to determine what students know or do not know about a topic to be studied. Clustering serves well to help students organize their thinking before they begin to write a report.

A good way to introduce clustering to a class is to create collectively a large clustering of ideas on the chalkboard. If, for instance, you are beginning a study of the Northwest, you might lead students through the clustering process, grouping ideas as shown on the next page.

Students quickly learn to use clustering as a way of collecting their thoughts before writing. Encourage them to spend five minutes clustering before writing anything, even the answer to a test question.

You can use clustering as an individual or group activity to assess student knowledge or attitudes before beginning a unit of study. The students may be surprised to discover how little they know about Black History or Alaska, our forty-ninth state. After a study has been completed, a second clustering should provide an interesting comparison as students see graphically how much they have learned. The clustering activity in the module on Chinese Americans is an example of preassessing the class's collective knowledge before beginning a study (see page 254).

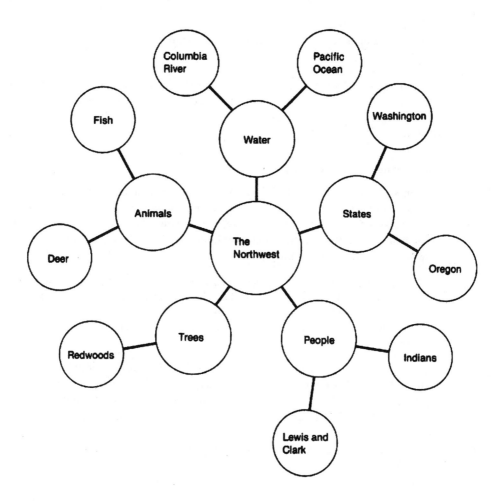

Writing a Report

The following lesson demonstrates just how to engage students in writing a report. In this case the report is the review of a multicultural book.

SAMPLE LESSON: INTRODUCING STUDENTS TO THE BOOK REVIEW[8]

Type of Writing: Report of Information

Level of Difficulty: Grades 3–8 (Adjust material and expectations.)

Outcomes

Students will:

   1. Read a book review.

2. Identify characteristic features of this form.
3. Write a book review that includes these features.

Procedures

Locate the review of a book that you would like students to know or perhaps an author you would like to introduce. Duplicate a class set of copies of the review. (You can write one yourself following the model presented here.) This lesson requires at least two class periods.

Book Review: *Where the Red Fern Grows*

Wilson Rawls was a country boy from the Ozarks. He spent much of his time roaming the hills with a blue tick hound, hunting and fishing, enjoying the out of doors.

It was natural, then, for him to write a book about a boy who wanted hunting hounds, a boy who also roamed the hills and river bottoms of the Cherokee country so familiar to Rawls. He describes the setting, thus:

> Our home was in a beautiful valley far back in the rugged Ozarks. The country was new and sparsely settled. The land we lived on was Cherokee land, allotted to my mother because of the Cherokee blood that flowed in her veins.
>
> It lay in a strip from the foothills of the mountains to the banks of the Illinois River in northwestern Oklahoma.

Where the Red Fern Grows is a story of love for family, for animals, and for this country. It is also a story of adventure as Billy achieves his greatest dreams.

Ten-year-old Billy wanted a pair of coon dogs, but hounds cost more money than the family could possibly afford. Determined, Billy began saving his money, storing it in an old K. C. Baking Powder can. After almost two years, he had fifty dollars, enough to buy the two redbone coon hound pups that would change his entire existence.

Billy, Dan, and Little Ann spent their lives together from the time he brought them home. As he said:

> It was wonderful indeed how I could have heart-to-heart talks with my dogs and they always seemed to understand. Each question I asked was answered in their own doggish way.
>
> Although they couldn't talk in my terms, they had a language of their own that was easy to understand. Sometimes I would see the answer in their eyes, and again it would be in the friendly wagging of their tails. Other times I could hear the answer in a low whine or feel it in the soft caress of a warm flicking tongue. In some way, they would always answer. (page 68)

The high point of the book is Billy's winning the gold championship cup in the annual coon-hunting contest. With the cup came a large cash prize that answered his mother's prayers for a new house.

Billy continued to hunt with his dogs until one night they met the "devil cat of the Ozarks, the mountain lion." His brave little dogs tried to save Billy from the lion whose "yellow slitted eyes burned with hate." Although Billy finally killed the huge animal with an ax, the dogs were badly wounded. Old Dan died from his injuries, and Little Ann soon died, too, of heartbreak at losing her hunting companion. Billy sadly buried the two dogs in a beautiful spot on the hillside.

As the family was leaving the Ozarks the following spring, Billy ran to this grave for one last farewell. It was then that he saw the beautiful red fern that had sprung up above the graves of the little dogs. He remembered the old Indian legend that "only an angel could plant the seeds of a red fern, and that they never died; where one grew, that spot was sacred." As they drove away, the family could see the red fern "in all its wild beauty, a waving red banner in a carpet of green."

Fast action, human interest, and believable characters make this a book for readers of all ages. A master storyteller, Wilson Rawls has shared a piece of himself.

—by Iris M. Tiedt

Stimulus (Prewriting)

Give students copies of the book review you have selected. Read the book review aloud slowly as students read their copies. (This is especially helpful for less able readers and ESL students, and it helps keep the class together for the purposes of the lesson.) Then have students return to the beginning of the review and direct them to identify the kinds of information the author included in the review. Begin a chart, Features of a Book Review, as students list such characteristics as the following:

Features of a Book Review

1. Includes quotations from the book
2. Comments about the content presented by the author
3. Tells something about the author, biography
4. Expresses personal reaction to the book
5. Includes the title and author of the book

Direct the students to bring a book that they have already read to class the next day.

Activity (Writing)

See that each student has a book to review. Display the Features of a Book Review list that the class compiled. Go through the features one by one with the class as students take notes based on the books they are reviewing. Tell students to complete the first draft of the new book review they have begun as homework.

Follow-up (Postwriting)

On the next day students should have the first drafts of their book reviews and copies of the book to be reviewed. Have students work in cooperative learning groups of three to five students. Each student is to read his or her book review aloud as the others listen to see if all features on the list have been included. After listening to a review, each member of the group should answer the following two questions for that writer:

1. What one aspect of this review was especially well written?
2. What one recommendation would help improve the writing?

Each student should mark with a big star the writing that was commended. The writer should also take notes on the suggestions for improvement to aid revision.

Students should complete a revision of this first draft as homework that night. They should bring both the first draft and the revision to class.

The next day revised versions of the book reviews can again be shared in the same editing groups. Each writer should point out exactly what changes were made from the first draft. Any further changes should be made, as needed.

Evaluation

Before completing the final draft of the book reviews, students should work as a class to determine just how these reviews will be evaluated. They might consider these types of evaluation:

- Pass or Fail (based on what is being taught)
  - 10 points   The completed book review contains all of the features listed.
  - 0 points   The completed book review does not contain all of the features listed.

- A Simple Rubric or Standard (some recognition for excellence)
  - 10   Uses excellent detailed description
    Shows clear personal involvement
    Includes important biographical information
    Speaks clearly to the audience
    Includes all features listed, very well presented
  - 5   Presents all features adequately
    Needs further revision
  - 2   Presents most features, very weak writing
    Needs extensive revision

Students who are involved in determining evaluation measures for their own work are assuming responsibility for their work. They also have clear ideas of what they need to do to get the top score, and they can help each other so that potentially everyone in each group can get the top score. Thus the teacher moves out of the authoritarian role of Grade Giver.

Students can also implement the scoring, reading each paper to see which scores it deserves. Students learn much about writing by reading one another's work. They are also engaged in thinking as they evaluate each other's writing.

When book reviews are fully revised, they can be published instantly in a three-ringed notebook that bears the title: Books We Recommend. Have someone decorate the cover. This collection, containing something by everyone in the class, should be available in the classroom for reading. Later it can be shared with others by placing the collection in the library.

Recap

Learning to write is an outcome that is an essential part of the curriculum at all levels and in all subject areas. In an effective writing program, students will:

Write frequently
Learn to write by writing
Learn to write by reading
Talk about the writing process
Write for varied purposes
Write to different audiences
See writing as a way of expressing "thinking"
Edit their own writing and that of others
Revise some writing selections to be made public
Be involved in evaluating their own progress
Confer with their instructor periodically[9]

Students in a multicultural education program will write about topics related to that area of study.

LITERATURE-BASED LANGUAGE ARTS INSTRUCTION

A second influential trend in literacy instruction is the strong move toward bringing literature into the mainstream in reading programs at the elementary school level. Trade books (library books, as opposed to textbooks) are appearing in publishers' series, and the books are being used directly as texts. We believe firmly that children should learn to read from real literature and that teachers' dependence on the basal reading series is turning students away from reading. Lessons focusing on multicultural literature offer students and teachers a wonderful way to share meaningful experiences. Most literature lessons also offer an opportunity to make connections with oral language and writing.

Responding to Literature

We can develop language skills and present language and literature concepts at the same time. Here are just a few suggestions for each skill:

Listening
Retell a folktale that the teacher has read aloud.
Act out an Indian coyote tale after hearing it at the Listening Center.

Speaking
Discuss the problems that Karana faced in *Island of the Blue Dolphins* by Scott O'Dell.
Prepare to tell a "flannel board story" to children in another room.

Reading
Select a poem to read aloud as part of a class presentation for Black History Month.
Read a book about someone your age who lives in another country.

Writing

Keep a process journal as you read a book by a Black American author.

Use mapping to outline the story of the life of a famous American woman.

Thinking

Tell how your life is like that of Peter in *The Snowy Day*.

Write the questions you would want to ask Katherine Paterson after reading her book *Bridge to Terabithia*.

Teaching Literature Concepts

The study of literature is a broad area that offers a wealth of material from which to choose. Literature concepts can be presented on a story chart.

A STORY CHART		
Who?	characters	dialogue
When?	setting	mood
Where?		
What?	plot	theme
Why?		problem
How?	conclusion	solution

Such concepts can be identified after reading James Houston's fine Canadian Eskimo trilogy—*Frozen Fire, Black Diamonds,* and *Ice Sword*—as well as other multicultural selections. The choices we make determine information that students will learn. Literature we choose to share in the classroom should always be by the very best authors, for example:

Primary Grades

Sherry Garland. *The Lotus Seed.*
Gerald McDermott. *Arrow to the Sun.*
Sharon Bell Mathis. *The Hundred Penny Box.*

Elementary Grades

Virginia Hamilton. *M. C. Higgins the Great.*
Mildred Taylor. *Roll of Thunder, Hear My Cry.*

Advanced Students

David Kherdian. *Road from Home.*
Gary Paulsen. *Night John.*

Many other books are listed in the Appendix. Ways of bringing multicultural literature into the classroom are also presented in Chapter 8.

Bibliotherapy

Universal Feelings Children and Adolescents Share. Sharing a good book can be a way of stimulating discussions about needs that students have in common. Read books aloud for this purpose; for example, *North Town* by Lorenz Graham for grades 4 and up, or *Stevie* by John Steptoe for primary grades. These two books happen to be about black characters, but children will identify with them as human beings who are experiencing emotions familiar to them.

Other good books that reveal universal needs and feelings include the following:

Primary Grades

Jan Brett. *Fritz and the Beautiful Horses.* Houghton, 1981. A gentle pony is excluded from the in-group.

Susan Jeschke. *Perfect the Pig.* Holt, 1980. The runt of the litter wishes for wings.

Patricia Lakin. *Don't Touch My Room.* Little, Brown, 1985. Adjusting to a new baby.

Phil Mendez. *The Black Snowman.* Scholastic, 1989. Jacob learns to believe in himself.

Norma Simon. *What Can I Do?* Whitman, 1969. A little Puerto Rican girl is looking for something to contribute.

Books for Older Students

Alice Bach. *The Meat in the Sandwich.* Harper and Row, 1975. Ten-year-old Mike creates a fantasy world to make his life more interesting.

Paula Fox. *Lily and the Lost Boy.* Orchard, 1987. Growing up.

Ruth Meyers and Beryle Banfield. *Embers.* Stories for a Changing World. Feminist Press, 1983. Collection of fiction, biography, and poetry about children struggling to overcome prejudice.

Laura Nathanson. *The Trouble with Wednesdays.* Bantam, 1987. Sexual abuse.

Emily Neville. *It's like This, Cat.* Harper and Row, 1963. Adolescent Dave Mitchell learns to get along with his father.

Cynthia Voigt. *Homecoming.* Atheneum, 1981. Growing up.

Linda Woolverton. *Running before the Wind.* Houghton, 1987. Incest.

Universal Problems Young People Face. Children today need to be able to talk about varied problems that were not so freely discussed ten years ago. Death and divorce are two topics that we can talk about in the classroom as an aid to students who are faced with these events in their lives. Books can often serve to provide a realistic perspective as well as to open up controversial topics for students and teachers who may find it difficult to introduce such topics. Many fine books written for young people handle these subjects sensitively.

Divorce or Single-Parent Families.

Primary Grades

Anne N. Baldwin. *Jenny's Revenge.* Four Winds, 1974.

Joan Lexau. *Me Day.* Dial, 1971.

Paul Zindel. *I Love My Mother.* Harper and Row, 1975.

Upper Elementary and Middle Grades

Charlotte Anker. *Last Night I Saw Andromeda*. Walck, 1975.

Sue Bridges. *Permanent Connections*. Harper, 1987

Barthe de Clements. *No Place for Me*. Viking, 1987.

Patricia MacLachlan. *Sarah, Plain and Tall*. Harper, 1985.

Mary Mahoney. *The Hurry-Up Summer*. Putnam, 1987.

Death and Relationships with Aged People.

Primary Grades

Jennifer Bartoli. *Nonna*. Harvey House, 1975.

John Burningham. *Grandpa*. Crown, 1985.

Miska Miles. *Annie and the Old One*. Little, Brown, 1971.

Helen Oxenburg. *Grandma and Grandpa*. Dial, 1984.

Charlotte Zolotow. *My Grandson Lew*. Harper and Row, 1974.

Upper Elementary and Middle Grades

Katherine Bacon. *Shadow and Light*. Macmillan, 1987.

Vera and Bill Cleaver. *Where the Lilies Bloom*. Lippincott, 1969.

Virginia Hamilton. *Cousins*. Philomel, 1990.

Penelope Jones. *Holding Together*. Bradbury, 1983.

Alfred Slote. *Hang Tough, Paul Mather*. Lippincott, 1973.

Doris B. Smith. *A Taste of Blackberries*. Crowell, 1973.

Phyllis Wood. *Then I'll Be Home Free*. Dodd, 1986.

An excellent resource to help you find more books like these is *Your Reading: A Booklist for Junior High and Middle School Students*, edited by A. P. Nilson (NCTE, 1991), which is categorized by subject.

Reader's Theater

Reader's theater involves students in reading various kinds of literature related to a theme, a unit of study in the social studies. You might, for example, divide the class in groups of five or six for planning reader's theater presentations. All may focus on a presentation for Black History Month, or each group might plan a presentation on one ethnic group in your school community. Several weeks are required for planning, searching for material, and giving the presentations to an audience. The work will follow these steps:[10]

Step 1: Planning. Talk with students about the idea of a reader's theater presentation. Explain that the presentation is read, not acted out. The presenters sit on stools or chairs and read their assigned parts. Choose a theme for the presentation and discuss the kinds of materials that might be used, for example:

- short stories (fables, myths, etc.) and excerpts from novels
- sayings, proverbs, quotations, poetry, song lyrics
- factual statements

Step 2: Searching for Material.   Plan a visit to the library as the groups search for material related to the selected theme. If you notify the librarian ahead of time, she or he will be able to locate appropriate sources for the class use. The material does not have to be written in play form for this kind of presentation, as you will see in the next step.

Step 3: Preparing the Script.   Duplicate copies of folktales or poems that students plan to use. These copies can then be marked and revised as the group deems appropriate. In narrative, roles are identified; for example, Anansi the Spider. There may be three or four roles to read plus one or more narrators who read the descriptive passages. Students can supply dialogue to add interest and to develop a character. Sometimes passages will be deleted.

Step 4: Rehearsing.   One student should be the director to signal the group when to stand and to sit. This person listens during rehearsals, ensures that students read clearly and effectively, makes suggestions for timing, and so on.

Poetry and nonfiction can be divided in various sections or verses. One or more persons may read to provide variety.

Step 5: The Presentation.   Select an audience for whom to perform the finished production. The audience may be the rest of the class, another class that is studying the same topic, or the whole school in an assembly. A reader's theater presentation can be given to the Parent Teachers' Association meeting to show parents what students are studying. A study of Japanese Americans and contemporary Japan might culminate with a reader's theater presentation based on student reading and research. Readings could be selected from books such as the following:

Sumiko Yagawa (translated by Katherine Paterson). *The Crane Wife*. Morrow, 1981.

Toshi Maruki. *Hiroshima No Pika*. Lothrop, 1982.

Nancy Luenn. *The Dragon Kite*. Harcourt, 1982.

Collections of Japanese folktales by Yoshiko Uchida include the following:

The Dancing Kettle and Other Japanese Folktales
The Sea of Gold and Other Tales from Japan

To enhance a presentation for their audience, students could add songs or dances. Pictures could be displayed with original student haiku. A filmstrip or film would add to a very impressive sharing time for both adults and children, which might be planned for May 5th, Children's Day in Japan. (See the Multicultural Calendar for other suggestions.)

Reading and Writing Poetry

Poetry is especially suitable for enhancing a social studies lesson. Your own enthusiasm will be contagious as students listen to you read (or recite) a favorite poem related to the current study. A wonderful collection of poems about people in history is *The Book of Americans* by Rosemary and Stephen Vincent Benet. *Bronzeville Boys and Girls* is a collection by Pulitzer Prizewinner Gwendolyn Brooks. Sample the work of a black poet, Langston Hughes; the composer of outstanding free verse, Carl Sandburg; and the well-polished haiku written by Japanese poets of the thirteenth century. To teach poetry effectively you must first know and enjoy poetry yourself.

Writing poetry is another way of involving students with expressing their ideas about social studies topics. Begin with unrhymed forms such as the cinquain (sank'en), a five-line poem like this:

Line 1: One word (which may be the title)
Line 2: Two words (describing the title)
Line 3: Three words (an action)
Line 4: Four words (a feeling)
Line 5: One word (referring to the title)

Indian,
Native American,
Gliding through forests,
Praising Great Spirit above,
Free.
    —Iris Tiedt

Use the work of Walt Whitman and Carl Sandburg to stimulate the writing of free verse. Students might study the life of one person before writing a poem to celebrate the contribution he or she made.

Have students write haiku as part of a study of Japan. Here are two examples of haiku translated from the original Japanese:

First cold showers fall.
Even little monkey wants
A wee coat of straw
    —*Bashō*

All sky disappears
The earth's land has gone away;
Still the snowflakes fall.
    —*Hashin*

Many poets have taken liberties with this versatile verse form which is in popular use today. American haiku have been written about a wide variety of topics, and lines have not always remained the prescribed length. Translator and poet Harry Behn comments, "Any translation into English should be, so I believe, what the author might have done if English had been his language." These rules that have grown out of Zen should be followed as much as possible in "the same packaging," but writing haiku is not a game. "It is not easy to be simple."[11]

An excellent source of information for the teacher who wants to know more about haiku is *An Introduction to Haiku* by Harold Anderson (Doubleday). Children are most successful with this brief verse form if emphasis is rightly placed on the thoughts they are expressing rather than on the confining form. The beauty of haiku for children is that they do succeed in producing charming examples that compare well with those created by adult writers. The following examples corroborate this point.[12]

The sun shines brightly.	The old cypress tree,
With its glowing flames shooting	So beautiful by the rocks,
It goes down at night.	Has been there for years.
—*Ricky*	—*Marjorie*

After first thinking about an idea they wish to express, the students are encouraged to write it on paper. They can then examine their own written thought to determine how it can be divided into three parts. Experimentation with word arrangement, imagery, changing the order of the lines, and choice of words used should be encouraged as the poem is developed. The deceptively simple form requires more delicate handling than does free verse. One way of introducing a class to haiku is through reading *Cricket Songs* by Harry Behn. After reading a number of these short poems aloud, provide each student with a duplicated sheet, containing several examples of haiku. Let them discover the haiku pattern, the subject treated, and other characteristics by rereading the poems, thus:

Count the number of syllables in each line. How many syllables does each line contain?

1 _____ 2 _____ 3 _____

Is this true of each poem? _____

What season of the year is indicated in each haiku?

_____

Japanese poetry makes us think of cherry blossoms or other spring blossoms. Use a twig of any flowering fruit tree to prepare an attractive display to motivate the writing of haiku. The flowers may be combined with pictures mounted on a bulletin board or music may be played to assist the development of a mood for haiku. Type haiku written by a class on a duplicating master or computer using two long columns so that the folded sheets will produce two long, slim pages. Cut the duplicated sheets to form pages of an attractive booklet, and make a decorative cover.

Motifs for booklet covers should be appropriate to the poetry. Students can experiment with brush stroking to simulate Japanese writing or the reeds, bamboo, flowers, and so on, associated with their art. The word *haiku* can be printed, using letters that have an oriental appearance. Investigate the following two films on haiku:

In a Spring Garden. Pictures by Ezra Jack Keats. Weston Woods Studios, 6 min., color, n.d.
    (See the book on which this film is based, too: *In a Spring Garden* by Richard Lewis.)
The Day Is Two Feet Long. Weston Woods Studies, 9 min., color, 1968.

A most rewarding art experience, which correlates well with the writing of haiku, is the blowing of ink with a straw. Washable black ink is applied in a swath near the bottom of an unlined file card (or any nonabsorbent paper). The wet ink is then blown with a straw to direct the ink in the desired direction. Blowing across the ink causes it to branch attrac-

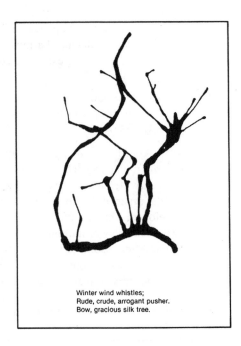

Winter wind whistles;
Rude, crude, arrogant pusher.
Bow, gracious silk tree.

tively. When the ink is dry, tiny dabs of bright tempera may be applied with a toothpick to add spring blossoms to the bare branch. The student then writes the haiku on the card below the flowering branch, and the card is used for display or as a gift for parents.

For an authentic presentation of haiku use rice paper (or thin onion skin or tissue paper) mounted inside colored paper. The poem is written (a felt pen will write on thin paper) together with an oriental motif—reeds, moon over water, flowering branch—and the author's name. The cover is folded so that the front flaps overlap slightly as in the sketch. A ribbon is then tied around the folder, which is ready for presentation as a gift, as shown.

Folded slightly overlapping . . .
. . . tied with ribbon

Tanka are five-lined Japanese poems that contain a haiku (the first three lines). Like the haiku, they are unrhymed and follow a well-defined syllabic pattern with a total of 31 syllables for the entire poem as in this example:

Line 1: 5 syllables
Line 2: 7 syllables
Line 3: 5 syllables
Line 4: 7 syllables
Line 5: 7 syllables

Silver raindrops fall;
A puddle of water stands.
  Ocean before me,
All the world is reflected.
Look hard and you see black mud.
                —*Irene Tabata*

A beautiful book on tanka is *The Season of Time,* edited by Virginia O'Baron and published by Dial Press.

Focus on Language: The Cloze Technique

The Cloze technique forces students to make closure by filling in missing words in sentences. To prepare materials for this purpose you can omit all adjectives or all verbs if you want to focus on the use of vivid language. In the example presented here, every fifth word is omitted, which focuses attention on grammatical constructions and comprehension. The selection is from the beginning of *The Slave Dancer* by Paula Fox.

There was nothing to __1__ to the slave Tituba __2__ this morning in November __3__ be unlike other mornings __4__ had known in Bridgetown. __5__ sun was out. The __6__ of Barbados lay like __7__ jewel sparkling in the __8__ . Its yellow-white coral __9__ coast line blazed in __10__ brilliant light. Tituba could __11__ part of the shore __12__ from the windows of __13__ Endicott's kitchen because the __14__ sat on the edge __15__ Carlisle Bay, just where __16__ made a wide inward __17__ .

The slave John, Tituba's __18__ , had been fishing and __19__ was showing her the __20__ snappers he had caught. __21__ had carried them into __22__ in a big __23__ woven basket. The basket __24__ a deep dark brown, __25__ as dark as his __26__ , and the fish as __27__ took them out of __28__ basket were silvery by __29__ . He had covered the __30__ with leaves to keep __31__ cool.

"Good eating," John __32__ , holding one of the __33__ fish up for Tituba's __34__ . He was a tall, __35__ built man with broad __36__ . He wore only a __37__ of white cotton trousers __38__ up to the knee. __39__ was barefooted. He leaned __40__ the basket and then __41__ up with a fluid, __42__ movement that made the __43__ on his back ripple __44__ the dark brown skin. __45__ smiled, and his face __46__ had looked dark and __47__ in repose was lightened __48__ brightened by the smile.

After students fill in all of the blanks, discuss the words they chose for each blank. Any answer that sounds right (is grammatical) is acceptable. Lead students to observe that almost everyone will have the same answer for space #5 while a variety of equally good ideas will fit space #20. Be sure to have several copies of this book on hand when you use the exercise because students will be motivated to read the book following this exposure to the beginning paragraphs.

Literature Promotes Awareness of the Conventions

La Dictée: A Dictation Method[13]

Following the method of teaching French students to write described by Rollo Brown in *How the French Boy Learns to Write* is an effective way of teaching writing by using multicultural literature selections. The procedures are simple and easily carried out by any teacher.

1. Select a good book that students can enjoy at the level you teach. Then choose one paragraph from the first chapter that contains sentences and vocabulary that you think your students should be able to write.
2. Introduce the book and author to your students. Read the first chapter aloud so that students know what the story is about and how the selected paragraph fits into the story.
3. Explain that you have selected a paragraph that you plan to dictate to them. Read the paragraph aloud as students listen. Then ask questions about the paragraph to help students understand the full meaning of words, images, and references.
4. Tell the class that you are now going to dictate the paragraph sentence by sentence. You will first read a sentence, and they will listen. Then they will begin writing. You will repeat the sentence once more, but no more than two times. Follow this procedure, giving students ample time to write before beginning the next sentence.
5. After students have written all sentences in this manner, read each sentence again as you help them correct their writing. You may choose to have several students write each sentence on the board before you discuss the necessary punctuation, capitalization, and spelling. Discuss any unusual features. Students will study these sentences in order to write them more correctly when you dictate them again the following day.
6. On the next day, repeat the same dictation passage. This time have students pass their papers to the person on the right as they correct each other's sentences.
7. You may have a third dictation. This can be conducted by a student who wrote the sentences correctly. You may wish to collect the third writing in order to assess the kinds of errors students are making.

The advantages of la dictée as a method of teaching writing are several: (1) it provides structure for student writing, adaptable to any grade level; (2) writing can be selected to introduce or reinforce any aspect of writing the teacher desires; (3) good literature is introduced, which may stimulate students to read the book; and (4) students are seeing the connection between reading and writing.

SAMPLE LESSON: LA DICTÉE BASED ON *FAREWELL TO MANZANAR* (JEAN WATSUKI HOUSTON AND JAMES HOUSTON)

Level of Difficulty: Grades 5–8 (Adapt by selecting different literature.)

Outcomes

Students will:

1. Learn multicultural concepts.
2. Learn writing conventions.

Procedures

Obtain copies of *Farewell to Manzanar* by Jeanne Watsuki Houston and James Houston. You can use this lesson over a two-week period. Tell the students something about Jeanne Watsuki Houston and her experiences:

> This book was written by a Japanese woman who was born just before World War II. Her family, up until the war, had been middle class. Her father owned his own fishing boat and carried on many of the Japanese traditions while integrating into the American culture. Jeanne had been raised primarily around Caucasians—in fact she had fears of Chinese children.
>
> With the onset of the war, her family was "moved" to a camp in Southern California in the desert. This story is about that move, the life they were forced to live, and the changing effects upon her life. Even after the war, Jeanne suffered the effects of the camp and its strain on her family.

Stimulus

Read the selected dictation passage aloud to the students:

> Mama took out another dinner plate and hurled it at the floor, then another and another, never moving, never opening her mouth, just quivering and glaring at the retreating dealer, with tears streaming down her cheeks. He finally turned and scuttled out the door, heading for the next house. When he was gone she stood there smashing cups and bowls and platters until the whole set lay in scattered blue and white fragments across the wooden floor.

Tell the students that this paragraph comes after the family has been told that they have to evacuate their home. Since their new home is much smaller and for an undetermined duration, the mother is forced to sell some of their precious items. The dealer has told her that all she can get for her heirloom china is $15, maybe $17.50 at the most. The value of the china is over $200. Mother's reaction, surprising as it was, was to throw the china on the ground in disgust.

Discuss the paragraph, emphasizing the emotions involved. Talk about the reaction of the mother, the dealer, and any witness, such as Jeanne.

Activity

Proceed to dictate the paragraph, one sentence at a time, as students write each sentence. You may have to divide some of the sentences at the natural breaks of the phrases.

Repeat the sentence only two times so students will listen carefully. Challenge them to do their best, but make it clear that what they write will not be graded.

Follow-up

Have several students write each sentence on the chalkboard. Discuss any errors and have each student correct his or her own copy. Make conventions clear to the students.

After students have a chance to correct their papers, have them work in pairs to see if they have correctly copied the paragraph.

Evaluation

Students study the dictation as homework. The dictation is then repeated. Correct a few papers until you find several that are written without errors. Appoint these students as Experts who note any errors on the remaining papers.

Students who made errors may take the dictation again, given by one of the Experts (or recorded on tape).

Additional Lessons

After this introductory lesson, build additional lessons as suggested here.

Activity 2

Talk again about the paragraph. Discuss the emotions. Brainstorm various emotions with your students (anger, love, sadness, happiness, loneliness).

Develop lists (the writing activity for the students) for two or three emotions of the type of things people do to display, for example, anger (slam door, hit fist, stick out tongue, shout, curse) or love (hold hands, kiss, help, buy gifts, bake cookies). Share these lists with a partner. Have students circle those things on their list that they thought were especially good.

Activity 3

Have students write in their journals about a time when they were angry. Point out that some of the actions on their list might be (should have been) ones that could be included in the paragraph(s).

Activity 4

Have the students read their copy of the paragraph to identify the strong verbs that were used. Discuss how these words create pictures. Give the students a copy of this paragraph:

> Again, Papa did not answer. They both knew what it would be. This time his long pause slipped into pure silence. Without the answer he could continue dabbling with the dream. Mama's eyes squinted shut. His fingers worked below her shoulder blades. He had found the knot, the tension node, and he homed in on it with a practiced knuckle. Mama rolled her head from side to side, pulling at the tendons in her neck, groaning loudly now, hissing with the painful pleasure of his cure.

Have the students underline the strong verbs. Then begin a list of strong verbs. Have students write sentences using some of their strong verbs.

Recap

Literature offers an outstanding way of promoting multicultural understandings. Selected novels present people of different cultures experiencing emotions and solving the problems they face. Student readers can respond to the ideas presented by each author as they gradually develop empathetic feelings for people and their needs through vicarious sharing.

REFLECTIONS

Language arts comprises a broad range of content and skills that can become part of any multicultural education program. Wise selections from language and literature will teach multicultural concepts and enhance the language arts classes. In summary, a teacher can strive to teach students how to (1) use language that is free of racist and sexist terms or labels; (2) recognize careless use of language and stereotyped perceptions of people that can hurt human beings and limit their potential; and (3) talk about people as individual human beings who have varied characteristics not limited by sex, race, class, or ethnic background.

You can lead students gradually to greater awareness without being preachy or hostile. Every teacher can, for example, (1) model appropriate behavior and usage of language; (2) initiate discussion of questionable practices or language to promote awareness; (3) plan lessons designed to break down stereotyped thinking; and (4) select nonstereotyped text materials.

The overall aim of the language arts curriculum is *communication*. In order to send messages, children speak and write. To receive them, they read and listen. In addition, we recognize the overriding language function: thinking, which is a part of any language activity. Our goal is to assist students in moving from the acquisition of language through listening and speaking to working effectively with written language and, above all, to learn to think about multicultural literature.

APPLICATIONS

1. Develop a unit of study about one of the lesser-known cultural groups in the United States. Begin by discovering as many books and other forms of literature as you can. You might, for example, explore Appalachia by searching for picture books by Cynthia Rylant, who comes from West Virginia. Look for:

When I Was Young in the Mountains. Harcourt, 1983.

Appalachia: The Voices of Sleeping Birds. Harcourt, 1991.

Best Wishes. Owen, 1992.

2. Working in a cooperative learning group (CLG), read a book appropriate for middle school students. Discuss the multicultural concepts presented and how you might develop a classroom study based on reading this book aloud together. You might consider studying titles such as the following:

Sherry Garland. *Song of the Buffalo Boy*. Harcourt, 1992. The story of a Vietnamese girl whose father was an American soldier. For more mature students.

Claudia Mills. *Dinah for President*. Macmillan, 1992. A middle school girl runs for president of the sixth grade. Humorous.

Patricia Beatty. *Jayhawker*. Morrow, 1991. A young Kansas abolitionist plays a dangerous role in fighting slavery.

Keep a double-entry journal as you read the book selected. Compare your notes with those collected by others in your CLG.

3. Explore the resources available in your local public library and any postsecondary institutions in your area. Look for the children's literature collection and explore pertinent magazines and journals, for example: *Book Links* published by the American Library Association, 434 W. Downer Place, Aurora IL 60506. This attractive magazine offers bibliographies and essays on current themes and suggests activities that bring children and books together in literature-based learning experiences.

4. Begin developing a unit of study related to one group in the United States; for example, Jews. Brainstorm topics or names of Jewish people you can research—Israel, synagogue, Golda Meir. Use the index of this book, encyclopedias, and the library subject cards to suggest avenues of investigation. Locate a copy of the *Children's Catalog* in the reference room of the library to see what kinds of books are listed. Outline the kinds of activities in which you could engage children as they learn more about the contributions Jews have made to the world.

5. Begin reading books that you can recommend to students or read aloud to a class. *The Children's Catalog,* the children's librarian, and other teachers can suggest titles. You might start with these outstanding authors:

Cynthia Rylant	Scott O'Dell	Ezra Jack Keats
Virginia Hamilton	Laurence Yep	Doris B. Smith

6. Plan three lessons that begin with a book as the stimulus and involve students in writing. Follow the lesson plan described on page 43–45.

7. 1984 was the year of the rat! (Check the Chinese calendar on page 262.) When you think of the rat, the images are usually very negative. Plan a lesson that introduces students to books that present the rat from different perspectives, for example:

Wayne Anderson. *Ratsmagic*. Pantheon, 1976.

James Cressey. *Fourteen Rats and a Rat-Catcher*. Prentice-Hall, 1976.

Julia Cunningham. *Dear Rat*. Houghton, 1961.

Kenneth Graham. *The Wind in the Willows*. Scribner's, 1922, 1953, 1961. Aeriel Books (Holt), 1981.

Thatcher Hurd. *Mystery on the Docks*. Harper, 1983.

Dorothy Ann Lovell. *Rufus the Seafaring Rat*. Faber and Faber, 1968.

Miska Miles. *Wharf Rat*. Little, Brown, 1972.

Edna Miller. *Pebbles, A Pack Rat.* Prentice-Hall, 1976.

Robert O'Brien. *Mrs. Frisby and the Rats of NIMH.* Atheneum, 1972.

E. B. White. *Charlotte's Web.* Harper, 1952.

Kaethe Zemach. *The Beautiful Rat.* Four Winds, 1979.

Endnotes

1. James Squire. "The Ten Great Ideas in the Teaching of English during the Past Half Century." Speech given at the CCCTE Conference, September 1982.
2. "Japanese Education." Cincinnati *Enquirer,* May 16, 1989.
3. James Marshall. "Classroom Discourse and Literary Response." In Ben F. Nelms, ed. *Literature in the Classroom: Readers, Texts, and Contexts.* National Council of Teachers of English, 1988, p. 45.
4. Mathew Lipman. "Some Thoughts on the Foundations of Reflective Education." In Joan B. Baron and Robert J. Sternberg, eds. *Teaching Thinking Skills: Theory and Practice.* Freeman, 1987, pp. 151–161.
5. South Bay Writing Project. "This We Believe." Training Institute, 1986.
6. James Moffett. "Thinking and Writing Connections." Address to Thinking Workshop, San Jose State University, June 15, 1985.
7. California State Department of Education. *Training Materials for Writing Consultants.* Training Institute, March 1987.
8. Iris McClellan Tiedt. *Writing: From Topic to Evaluation.* Allyn and Bacon, 1989, pp. 102–07.
9. Ibid., p. 40.
10. Adapted from Iris M. Tiedt, *The Language Arts Handbook* (Prentice-Hall, 1983), pp. 392–385. Used with permission.
11. Harry Behn. *Chrysalis: Concerning Children and Poetry.* Harcourt, 1938, p. 39.
12. Fourth-grade children at the Van Meter School, Los Gatos, California.
13. Iris M. Tiedt. "La Dictée: A Dictation Method." ERIC, July 1982.

Exploring Further

Gloria Blatt, ed. *Once upon a Folktale: Capturing the Folklore Process with Children.* New York: Teachers College Press, 1993.

Evelyn B. Freeman and Diane G. Person. *Using Nonfiction Trade Books in the Elementary Classroom. From Ants to Zeppelins.* National Council of Teachers of English, 1992.

Kenneth Goodman. *What's Whole about Whole Language?* Heineman, 1986.

Donald Graves. *Writing: Teachers and Children at Work,* Heineman, 1983.

Violet J. Harris. *Teaching Multicultural Literature in Grades K–8.* Norwood MA: Christopher-Gordon, 1992.

Julie Jensen, ed. *Composing and Comprehending.* National Council of Teachers of English, 1984.

James Moffett and Betty Jean Wagner. *A Student-Centered K–13 Language Arts and Reading Program,* Houghton Mifflin, 1991.

Marcia K. Rudman. *Children's Literature: Resource for the Classroom.* Christopher-Gordon, 1993.

Zena Sutherland, et al. *Children and Books.* Scott, Foresman, 1992.

Iris M. Tiedt, et al. *Reading/Thinking/Writing: A Holistic Language and Literacy Program for the K–8 Classroom.* Allyn and Bacon, 1989.

FRIENDSHIP FOREVER

8

❖

Multicultural Education across the Curriculum

Multicultural concepts and attitudes must be infused into learning activities across the curriculum over time if they are to have full effect. Both content and process, as discussed in Chapter 2, can be included in lesson plans for any subject at any level. In this chapter we examine possible ideas and resources for developing multicultural education in art, music, physical education and health, mathematics, science, and social studies. Then we look at four major instructional strategies that can be used across the curriculum—the Venn diagram, the I-Search paper, learning centers, and the unit of study.

After reading this chapter, you should be able to:
- Identify outcomes that reflect multicultural goals and those in a specific subject, both affective and cognitive.
- Describe methods for integrating multicultural concepts into instruction in a variety of subject areas.
- Select multicultural literature to support instruction in specific subject areas.
- Plan lessons that integrate multicultural and subject-specific objectives.

A basic assumption throughout this book is that multicultural education should not be presented in a single class, isolated from other instruction. As stated in Chapters 1 and 2, we believe that multicultural concepts should permeate all teaching. For example, a first-grade teacher might choose to read Ezra Jack Keats's *The Snowy Day,* a story about a young black child who plays in the snow. Following the reading, the class can cut out snowflakes and write a collaborative story about Peter's adventures in the snow and his attempt to save a snowball in his pocket. The intent is simply to show students that Peter and they have much in common.

A middle school or junior high history teacher might develop a unit of study around the shared reading of *The Good Earth* by Pearl Buck. Students will read other novels by the same author. They will study the geography and history of China—a vast country that is just opening up to us. They will collect clippings from the newspaper and record current linkages between China and the United States. Connecting literature and contemporary events with history instruction gives the study a reality that is missing from many history textbooks.

Notice that the examples above are necessarily also related to the language and literacy skills discussed in the preceding chapter, as well as to the other subject areas addressed in this chapter. Here we focus more directly on ways of introducing multicultural concepts into learning about various subjects.

PLANNING FOR MULTICULTURAL EDUCATION ACROSS THE CURRICULUM

In this section we will brainstorm ideas that you can apply at any level of instruction. Ideas presented under each subject heading are only suggestions for what you may develop. As you begin brainstorming, collect your ideas in a special notebook labeled, for example, Teaching Multicultural Concepts in Art. Scan through all the ideas presented throughout this chapter; an idea presented under science may relate to other subjects; or an idea under physical education may trigger an adaptation you could use elsewhere.

As you plan for instruction in any area, consider how students can learn multicultural concepts in the context of your subject-specific lessons. The following questions may lead you to discover additional multicultural applications:

Who creates what in this field?
Who has contributed to development in this field?
Are there specific stereotypes or biases in this field?
How does this field fit into the global village?
What is the future of this field?

In addition to your notebook, begin a file (perhaps a large cardboard box) of materials that will help you promote multicultural education in your classroom. Include pictures of men and women; quotations by scholars or practitioners; clippings from the newspaper about current events; publications (books, articles, art, records); lists of films; and realia.

Don't expect multicultural education always to be your primary emphasis in teaching. As you explore, however, you will find that multicultural concepts fit naturally into your plans. You can sometimes select literature by or about persons from different cultures, and you can point out the contributions of a great variety of people to the development of any field. Thus, you will be teaching multicultural concepts, both explicitly and implicitly.

Art

Art reveals historical development. Share information with students about the role art has played in human development over the years—the pictographs of the cave dwellers, the art of the Native Americans, painting developed through the years in Europe, American folk art, and so on. Point out the contributions of artists from diverse cultures.

Arrange a field trip to a local museum to view a special exhibit of Egyptian art or an exhibit from China. Share a slide presentation on the history of art or a specialized kind of art such as Appalachian basket weaving or quilt making.

The arts are an integral part of a humanities approach to instruction. Work with language arts, music, and history teachers to plan a humanities core program that integrates music, art, history, and literature. This approach works very well in junior high or middle school core plans, as well as in the self-contained elementary school classroom.

Children's books offer a special art form in their illustrations. Outstanding illustrators whose work you will enjoy sharing include the following:

Mitsumasa Anno. *Anno's U.S.A.* Japanese artist; many books.

Ezra Jack Keats. *In a Spring Garden.* Collection of haiku.

Jerry Pinkney. *Talking Easter Eggs.* Popular African American illustrator.

Maurice Sendak. *Outside over There.* Jewish author-illustrator; this book won the Caldecott Medal in 1987.

Also look for Paul Goble's books about Native Americans (e.g., *The Friendly Wolf*), which are beautifully illustrated. A Caldecott Medal winner, *Mufaro's Beautiful Daughters,* is an African tale illustrated by black author John Steptoe.

Art enhances instruction in other fields. Particularly in the elementary school, art activities can readily be tied into units of study in science or history. Encourage students to enhance information they have learned in other subject areas through various media, for example:

Papier maché figures
Masks as art or for performance
Dioramas to depict exploration, great discoveries, scenes from literature, animal habitats
Murals picturing westward expansion, scenes from a biography
Covers for books and reports—gadget printing, finger painting, crayon resist

Books to Explore

Literature can support understanding of art and artists. Explore the school and public library to ascertain what kinds of books are available. Search for nonfiction, fiction, and poetry. Biographies of artists are available in children's as well as adult literature. Look for some of the following titles:

Fiction

M. J. Rosen. *Elijah's Angels.* Harcourt, 1992. A story for Hanukkah and Christmas.

Elizabeth B. De Trevino. *I, Juan de Pareja.* Farrar, 1966. A slave in the household of Velasquez.

Zibby Oneal. *In Summer Light.* Viking, 1985. Girl wants to be a painter.

Autobiography and Biography

G. Everett. *Children of Promise.* Atheneum, 1992. Black artists.

Nathaniel Harris. *Leonardo and the Renaissance.* Bookwright, 1987. Painting and sculpture.

Milton Meltzer. *Dorothea Lange: Life through the Camera.* Viking, 1985. Photography.

Philip Sendak. *In Grandpa's House.* Harper, 1985. Illustrated by Maurice Sendak, son of the author of this autobiography.

Beverly Sherman. *Georgia O'Keefe: The "Wideness and Wonder" of Her World.* Atheneum, 1986. Painting.

Zheng Zhensun and Alice Low. *A Young Painter: The Life and Paintings of Wang Yani, China's Extraordinary Young Artist.* Scholastic, 1991.

SAMPLE LESSON: BEAUTIFUL WRITING

Level of Difficulty: Grades 3–8

Outcomes

Students will:

1. Learn an interesting art form.
2. Select quotations from diverse cultures.
3. Create an attractive display.

Procedures

Collect examples of quotations presented in calligraphy. Bring in books of quotations that students can use as resources.

Stimulus

Show students examples of quotations presented in calligraphy. Explain the history of calligraphy.

Teach students the rudiments of italic calligraphy, which is not unlike the manuscript or Danelian handwriting that they may have used in primary grades.

Activity

Have students select and print a quotation or saying they like from a specific culture.

Follow-up

Have each student frame the quotation. Framing can be done by mounting the quotation on a sheet of 9" x 12" red construction paper, or you may prefer to frame the quotations in simple black wooden frames that can be made or purchased.

Evaluation

Students should display their work in the classroom or in the library or another more public place where other students can view their art and the wise words depicted. No grades should be assigned for this project. Give credit or no credit for completing the task.

Music

Music is a part of every culture. Get assistance as you teach students some of the folk dancing representative of different countries. Students should experience a variety of music, either live or recorded—the blues, blue grass, classical—by members of many cultures. Introduce them to the fine musicians who have contributed to the world's musical heritage, for example, Rachmaninoff, Mozart, Sibelius, Benny Goodman, Mahalia Jackson, Pete Seeger, and others.

Music should be an integral dimension of units of study that focus on any group or country. Students should be made aware of music as a universal language that all can share. They can create their own music to express their ideas and emotions.

Books to Explore
Fiction

Jan Brett, *Berlioz the Bear.* Putnam, 1991.

Bruce Brooks. *Midnight Hour Encores.* Harper, 1986. Cellist.

Gillian Cross. *Chartbreaker.* Holiday, 1987. Rock band.

Karen Dean. *Stay on Your Toes, Maggie Adams!* Avon, 1986. Ballet.

Rumer Godden. *Thursday's Children.* Viking, 1984. Ballet.

Suzanne Newton. *I Will Call It Georgie's Blues.* Viking, 1983. Jazz piano.

Autobiography and Biography

Alan Blackwood. *Beethoven.* Bookwright, 1987.

Pete Fornatale. *The Story of Rock 'n' Roll.* Morrow, 1987.

Robert Love. *Elvis Presley.* Watts, *1986.*

Susan Saunders. *Dolly Parton: Country Goin' to Town.* Viking, 1985.

Catherine Scheader. *Contributions of Women: Music.* Dillon, 1985. Beverly Sills and four other women.

Wendy Thompson. *Franz Schubert 1797–1828.* Viking, 1991.

Nonfiction

Lulu Delacre, ed., *Las Navidades: Popular Christmas Songs from Latin America.* Scholastic, 1990.

John Langstaff, ed. *What a Morning! The Christmas Story in Black Spirituals.* McElderry, 1987. Singing plus piano accompaniment.

Nicki Weiss. *If You're Happy and You Know It.* Greenwillow, 1987. Picture book includes eighteen songs to sing together.

Physical Education and Health

Today there is much interest in health and fitness. Around the world, eyes watch the performance of the Olympic contestants who represent their countries proudly. All share the emotion as the national anthem is played for the gold medalist. Physical performance, the power and the grace, is another universal language we all understand.

We can help students become aware of the diverse cultures these athletes represent. Just listening or displaying pictures of the top performers such as gymnasts, tennis players, long distance runners, and skiers will demonstrate clearly the diversity of these athletes' family backgrounds. Students can discuss the fact that cultural origins do not dictate the success of an individual athlete, nor do they keep anyone from performing well.

Books to Explore

Fiction

Matt Christopher. *Red-Hot Hightops*. Little, Brown, 1987. Basketball.

Jeffrey Kelly. *The Baseball Club*. Houghton Mifflin, 1987. Baseball.

R. R. Knudson. *Rinehart Shouts*. Farrar, 1987. Racing shell.

Doris B. Smith. *Karate Dancer*. Putnam, 1987. Karate.

Cynthia Voigt. *The Runner*. Atheneum, 1985. Running.

Autobiography and Biography

Maury Allen. *Jackie Robinson: A Life Remembered*. Watts, 1987.

R. R. Knudson. *Babe Didrikson: Athlete of the Century*. Viking, 1985.

Herma Silverstein. *Mary Lou Retton and the New Gymnasts*. Watts, 1985.

Nonfiction

Dave Anderson. *The Story of Football*. Morrow, 1985.

Charles Cooms. *All-Terrain Bicycling*. Holt, 1987.

Edward F. Dolan. *Drugs in Sports*. Watts, 1986.

Jill Krementz. *How It Feels to Live with a Disability*. Simon & Schuster, 1992.

Margaret Ryan. *Figure Skating*. Watts, 1987.

Suggested Activities

Collage.   Have students create a collage focusing on one sport. They can collect pictures, clippings, and any materials related to the topic. Students present their completed collages to the class explaining the contributions of diverse cultures to this sport.

Teaching Games.   Assign a research project on games typical of different cultures. Each student writes a short report, including diagrams and other illustrations. Each person teaches a game to the group.

Reports on Diseases or Disabilities.   Have students research information about specific diseases or disabilities. Each should include an interview and a telephone investigation in their research. Completed reports are presented to the group and then included in a publication that can be placed in the library.

Mathematics

The use of numbers and mathematical concepts represents yet another universal language that we share around the globe. Students can study variations in applied mathematics around the world, for example:

> Monetary systems—compared worth of coins
> The abacus and its use

Metric system compared with U.S. weights and measures
The evolution of measurements over time
Computer use around the world
Math anxiety for women—causes and possible solutions
Calendars (see page 317)
Purchase of stocks; economic systems

Help students make connections between mathematics and other subjects or areas of interest. For example, how does math relate to art and music? What are the many relationships between math and the sciences? How are mathematics concepts displayed in nature, for example, Fibracci numbers?

Books to Explore

Counting Books for Children

P. Giganti. *Each Orange Had 8 Slices*. Clarion, 1992.

James Haskins. *Count Your Way through the Arab World*. Carolrhoda, 1987. Numbers related to concepts of geography and culture.

Nonfiction

Mitsumasa Anno. *Anno's Math Games III*. Philomel, 1991.

Laura Greene. *Careers in the Computer Industry*. Watts, 1983.

Christoher Lampton. *Computer Languages*. Watts, 1983.

Bruce McMillan. *Eating Fractions*. Scholastic, 1991.

Jack R. White. *How Computers Really Work*. Dodd, 1986.

Suggested Activities

Comparing Currency. Use the Task Card on the following page. Both the names of the coins or bills and their worth compared with the U.S. dollar (based on March 1993 figures) are given. On the other side of the card, students are directed to work with this informative chart. This kind of activity encourages reading, involves students in mathematics activities, and provides information about life in other countries. It is a worthwhile activity that provides valuable learning experience.

A Mathematical Dictionary. Have students prepare a dictionary of terms appropriate to their level of mathematical understanding. Include etymology of terms. Students will be surprised to discover the origins of words in math, for example, *algebra, algorithm,* or *googol.*

Women in Mathematics. Students can focus a special unit of study on the achievements of women in mathematics. Invite female mathematicians to visit your classroom. Discuss math anxiety and how or why these women were able to overcome it.

SIDE ONE

Money from Other Countries

Country	Currency	Worth in dollars*
Argentina	peso	1.01
Australia	dollar	.7055
Austria	schilling	.0856
Belgium	franc	.0291
Great Britain	pound	1.4335
Canada	dollar	.8029
Chile	peso	.00258
China	yuan	.1712
Colombia	peso	.00155
Denmark	krone	.1562
Ecuador	sucre	.000556
Egypt	pound	.2994
France	franc	.1773
Germany	deutschmark	.6020
Hong Kong	dollar	.1293
Israel	shekel	.3658
Italy	lira	.00062
Japan	yen	.0085
Mexico	peso	.32258
Netherlands	guilder	.5332
Norway	krone	.1409
Peru	sol	.565
Portugal	escudo	.0065
South Africa	rand	.2169
Spain	peseta	.0084
Sweden	krone	.129
Switzerland	franc	.657
Uruguay	peso	.00027
Venezuela	bolivar	.0119

*March, 1993.

SIDE TWO

Money Around the World

Have you ever heard of a guilder?
    In which country would you find this coin?
        (Look at the chart on the other side of this card.)
    How much is a guilder worth compared with our dollar?

Do other countries use dollars besides the United States?
    Which countries use dollars?
    Are these "dollars" worth the same amount?
    Which "dollar" is worth the most?

Every day this list of currencies appears in the newspaper. See if you can find it in the financial or business section. Compare the values for each coin to see how it has changed since this list was published.
    Why might values of coins or bills go up or down?
    See if you can find information about what determines the
        value of a piece of currency.

Pretend you are traveling to several different countries. As you enter each country, you exchange $10 for the currency of that country.
    How many pesos would you get in Mexico?
    How many francs would you get in France?
    How many pounds would you get in Great Britain?
    How many rands would you get in South Africa?

Find pictures of some of these coins. Perhaps someone you know has money from different countries.

Science

Literature selections frequently provide science backgrounds, for science appears in both fiction and nonfiction. Science fiction has long fascinated students, especially when they read older fiction (by Jules Vernes, for example) and note that much has come to pass in the present. Conversely, they may see science fiction published in the twentieth century and into the twenty-first century as predicting the future. You can encourage them to read such writers as Isaac Asimov, a biochemist who writes scientific texts as well as fiction; Arthur C. Clarke; Ray Bradbury; and many other contemporary writers of good science fiction today.

Naturalist Jean Craighead George authors titles for the middle grades that portray the interaction of humans and animals. Her Newbery Award-winning *Julie of the Wolves* tells us of the habits of wolves, serving to break down the stereotyped thinking of the wolf as a ferocious, mean animal. She tells of a crow's imprinting on a human in *Talking Crow* and the plight of whales in *Water Sky. Shark Beneath the Reef* focuses on sharks, depicting Mexican fishermen in Baja, California, and a young boy's decision making.

Science is also related to humanities approaches. Following is a commentary published in a "A Naturalist's Perspective," which comments on the history of the Midwest and uses a selection from literature to help describe the imagined scene.

> Two hundred years ago, Southwestern Ohio was at the "edge of civilization," home and hunting land for Miami and Shawnee, a mystic land of wealth and opportunity to land-hungry settlers to the east and south, and the new U.S. Government's answer to its revolutionary war debts. By 1788, Kentucky was already home to 70,000 settlers, but almost none ventured north of the Ohio River, primarily because the Miami, Shawnee, Wyandot, and Delaware were determined that they would not be pushed farther west by endless streams of white settlers. Southwestern Ohio was then a forested wilderness.
>
> Oh, what I would give to be able to travel back in a time machine to see that land of endless trees! Conrad Richter in his historical novel *The Trees* takes us back:
>
>> They rounded a high ridge. A devil's racecourse cleared the area of limbs below. Here was something Worth had not told them about . . .
>>
>> Then she saw that what they looked down on was a dark, illimitable expanse of wilderness. It was a sea of solid treetops broken only by some gash where deep beneath the foliage an unknown stream made its way. As far as the eye could reach, this lonely forest sea rolled on and on till its faint blue billows broke against an incredibly distant horizon (Richter, 1978).
>
> When the Ohio country was first settled, 25 million acres of 10,000-year-old hardwood forest covered 95% of the state. It had a continuous forest canopy of trees 50 to 100 feet tall, and up to 14 feet in diameter! Sycamores large enough to stable horses within their hollow centers grew beside the stream! In the bottoms grew cottonwood, black willow, green ash, pin oak, box elder, silver maple, American elm, honey locust, and river birch. On the uplands climax forests of American beech, sugar maple, oaks, and hickories could be found. Where the Indians had burned away the timber to clear land, open, young forests of eastern red cedar, wild cherry, red maple, sassafras, ash, redbud, and sumac stretched toward the sunlight. Through these dark and massive forests, enormous bands of squirrels migrated, as did passenger pigeons, bison, wolves, deer, and more.[1]

Books to Explore

Fiction

James Lincoln Collier. *When the Stars Begin to Fall*. Delacorte, 1986. Pollution.

Midas Dekkers. *Arctic Adventure*. Orchard, 1987. Whales.

Jean G. Howard. *Bound by the Sea: A Summer Diary*. Tidal Press, 1986. Science diary.

Gary Paulsen. *Hatchet*. Bradbury, 1987. Wilderness survival.

Autobiography and Biography

Nathan Aaseng. *More with Less: The Future World of Buckminster Fuller*. Lerner, 1986.

Steve Parker. *Marie Curie and Radium*. HarperCollins, 1992.

Ethlie Ann Vare. *Adventurous Spirit: A Story about Ellen Swallow Richards*. Carolrhoda, 1992.

Nonfiction

Gilda Berger. *Crack: The New Drug Epidemic!* Watts, 1987.

Robert Cattoche. *Computers for the Disabled*. Watts, 1986.

Anne Ehrlich and Paul Ehrlich. *Earth*. Watts, 1987.

Dorothy Francis. *Computer Crime*. Dutton, 1987.

Kathlyn Gay. *The Greenhouse Effect*. Watts, 1986.

Noel Simon. *Vanishing Habitats*. Gloucester, 1987.

Bernie Zubrowski. *Mirrors*. Morrow, 1992.

Social Studies

Concern about cultural literacy has focused heavily on student knowledge of geography and history. Integrating such studies with multicultural education may lend impetus to lively studies that will correct this deficiency. Recognizing that social studies is a broadly inclusive term, we choose to focus on geography and history as those aspects of social studies that are more commonly taught within the P–8 curriculum.

Geography

The study of geography provides a sense of place—where we are in relation to others and how we fit into the huge global village. As such, its content is related to every other study in the curriculum. Familiarity with maps and mapping can begin with the earliest years as children develop a sense of the layout of a classroom, the setting for a story, the school building, and the local community. Using a globe clarifies their understandings about the location of the United States and its immediate neighbors as well as the relative distances between the United States and the areas from which our ancestors came.

Suggested Activities

Discussion Topics.   Children can study and discuss topics like the following: Why do we use the term *global village* today? Why has the creation of a new country—Israel—been difficult? Middle-grade students might read the novel, *The Boy from over There* by Tamar Bergman (translation from the Hebrew by Hillel Halkin, Houghton Mifflin, 1988).

Mapping.   Have students locate different kinds of maps, e.g., a Guide to World Time Zones. Discuss and compare the perspective of new world maps to other maps you may have.

Assessing Class Knowledge.   After discussing the general definition of geography (the study of the earth's surface, climate, continents, countries, peoples, industries, and products), have the class divide into small groups to assess their knowledge about one of these subdivisions of the topic. Have each group present its information to the class, using maps and charts. Other members of this group can add to the knowledge. Cooperatively, the class can compose a compendium of *What We Know about Geography*. This knowledge can be referred to during multicultural studies, with each group assuming an Expert role.

Mapping the Origins of the Members of the Class.   Create a large outline map of the world by enlarging a map from a text with the opaque projector. Have students interview their parents to ascertain general information about where grandparents and earlier ancestors came from. Students can then locate these places and outline the trail of their individual origins on the map with colored pens. Each student can then tell his or her story and show the trail on the map.

An unusual book, *The World in 1492* (Holt, 1992), was written by six noted children's authors. Each author presents an overview of a continent in a combination of geography and history.

History

The hope of history instruction is that "education can help us to see that not all problems have solutions, to live with tentative answers, to accept compromise, to embrace responsibilities as well as rights—to understand that democracy is a way of living, not a settled destination."[2] History lessons can lead even young students to appreciate that it is difficult to preserve our way of life and that we cannot take democracy for granted. Students of all ages can begin to answer the following questions:

1. What conditions—geographic, military, economic, social, technological—have nurtured democratic society, and what happens when conditions change?
2. What ideas, values, and educational forces have promoted freedom and justice for us in the past, and can we take these for granted now?
3. What have Americans in each generation actually done to extend democracy, and what needs doing still?[3]

Timely topics in this field can be debated. More advanced students need to be involved in thinking about the pro and con positions about real concerns as they learn to be active, informed citizens living in a global village. Contemporary history, for example, suggests the following topics related to learning to get along with the diverse people in the world:

1. Democracy's solutions for war-related problems at home and abroad and the strains on democracy produced by them.
2. The tragedy of Vietnam.

3. The dramatic advances made by women and minorities in civil rights and in political and economic life.

4. The emergence of new economic and environmental problems that affect democratic society in the technological age.[4]

Books to Explore

Throughout the extensive list of books in the Appendix are books that increase students' understanding of geography and history, contemporary and ancient. Historical novels, folklore, nonfiction, biography, poetry—all forms of literature add to each student's cultural literacy. Representative newer titles are listed below:

Fiction

Paula Fox. *The Moonlight Man*. Bradbury, 1986. Nova Scotia.

Rudolf Frank. *No Hero for the Kaiser*. Lothrop, 1986. Germany, 1914.

Ellen Howard. *When Daylight Comes*. Atheneum, 1985. Virgin Islands.

Liza Murrow. *West against the Wind*. Holiday, 1987. California gold rush.

Scott O'Dell. *The Serpent Never Sleeps*. Houghton, 1987. Jamestown.

Yoko Kawashima Watkins. *So Far from the Bamboo Grove*. Lothrop, 1986. Korea; autobiographical.

Autobiography and Biography

Linda Atkinson. *In Kindling Flame: The Story of Hannah Senesh, 1921–1944*. Lothrop, 1985. Hungary.

Ida Cowen and Irene Gunther. *A Spy for Freedom: The Story of Sarah Aronsohn*. Dutton, 1984. Palestine.

Dorothy Hoobler and Thomas Hoobler. *Nelson and Winnie Mandela*. Watts, 1987. South Africa.

Margy Knight. *Talking Walls*. Tilbury House, 1992.

Nonfiction

David M. Brownstone. *The Jewish-American Heritage*. Facts on File, 1988. Part of America's Ethnic Heritage series.

Renata Von Tscharner and Ronald Fleming. *New Providence: A Changing Cityscape*. Harcourt, 1987.

Ted Wood with Wambli Numpa Afraid of Hawk. *A Boy Becomes a Man at Wounded Knee*. Walker, 1992.

Recap

Multicultural education belongs in every classroom. Teachers who are aware of the importance of teaching multiculturally will find it easy to bring in the contributions of people from diverse cultures to any field of study. Literature—fiction, nonfiction, poetry, autobiography, and biography—contributes to students' understanding of people from varied cultures. Emphasis can be placed on the universality of such studies as art and music, which speak alike to people who cannot communicate verbally. In the same way, science and mathematics are "spoken" around the world. The studies of geography and history provide a foundation for young people's recognition of the earth as a global village.

SELECTED TEACHING STRATEGIES ACROSS THE CURRICULUM

Teachers need to step down from the podium, to decrease the use of lecture methods in favor of teaching strategies that permit students of all ages to become involved with the subject of study. We need to select methods that engage students in thinking, in making choices and decisions, and in solving problems. Multicultural teaching should guide students to make connections, to personalize learning in a way that will lead to greater human understanding.

In this section we describe just four methods that will enhance your teaching (1) the Venn diagram, (2) the I-Search paper, (3) organizing a learning center, and (4) creating a unit of study.

The Venn Diagram

Developed by John Venn in the nineteenth century, the Venn diagram is used in mathematics to compare two sets. This diagram can be used to compare two concepts or two books in a very effective social studies lesson.

After each student has read a novel about young people living in different lands, ask each one to complete a Venn diagram that compares his or her life with that of the book character, thus:

> Title and author of the book: *Seven Daughters and Seven Sons* by Barbara Cohen (Atheneum, 1982).

> Brief description: This book is based on an Iraqi folktale that demonstrates the worth of daughters. Buran disguises herself as a man to help her family, and all kinds of adventures follow. It's really an exciting story.

In sections 1 and 2 of the Venn diagram unique characteristics are listed for each person. In section 3, the student lists adjectives that describe both, showing how they are alike. After completing the Venn diagram, each student writes a five-paragraph essay following this pattern:

> Paragraph 1: Introduction
> Paragraph 2: Description of herself or himself
> Paragraph 3: Description of the book character
> Paragraph 4: Summary of how the two are alike
> Paragraph 5: Concluding paragraph

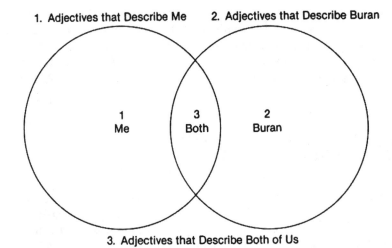

1. Adjectives that Describe Me   2. Adjectives that Describe Buran

| 1 | 3 | 2 |
| Me | Both | Buran |

3. Adjectives that Describe Both of Us

This exercise may lead students to observe that people are more alike than different, particularly when they consider their personal characteristics and problems.

Once students know how to use this diagram, you can use it to guide comparisons of more complex topics, for example, two ethnic groups, two religions, or two forms of government.

The I-Search Paper

The I-Search paper begins with the identification of something a student really wants to know. It ends with a formal presentation of what the student discovered through independent research. Because the topic is student-selected, the project has genuine purpose. The I-Search paper is recommended for most students in place of the traditional research paper. The students are guided through these four developmental stages:

Stage 1: Identification of a Problem to Study.   Students should make a list of three to five questions they have or things they would like to know; for example:

> I would like to know
>> what Benjamin Franklin was really like
>> how a slave family lived
>> how the underground railroad worked
>
> I would like to know
>> what our town was like a hundred years ago
>> how my grandfather lived when he was my age
>> the story of my great-aunt who died before I was born

By writing several ideas, students will be able to select one that they would really like to work on. After choosing the question for investigation, students should write a paragraph outlining the problem to be researched and reasons for selecting that particular topic. This piece of writing, called the Statement of the Problem, will be the first part of the report compiled at the end of the study.

Stage 2: Conducting the Study.　Talk with the students about the resources available to them as they search for information. Plan a visit to the school or public library to show them reference tools they may not know, for example, atlases, almanacs, the *Reader's Guide to Periodical Literature*, and catalogs (card or on-line).

Ask the librarian to help plan for this visit so that students will be able to use their time to advantage.

List on the chalkboard all the other ways of gathering information that students can name, for instance, telephoning (yellow pages), writing letters, and interviewing people.

Plan class instruction to assist students in using these techniques effectively. Discuss the interview process and interview a person in the classroom before students work individually. Prepare an interview schedule consisting of the questions to be asked with space for recording the answers. Letter writing and notetaking lessons will also assist students in gathering information.

As students begin their search, they should keep a log containing dated entries describing the process they are experiencing. This process journal will also include their notes from reading or interviewing. The log will become part of the final report as The Procedures.

Stage 3: Reporting the Findings.　After the data have been compiled, students should reread their notes. They can plan a presentation of the information they have gathered. This presentation will be written in paragraphs, but it may also include pictures, graphs, or other ways of sharing the information in an interesting way. Students may compile their work in an attractive booklet with a specially designed cover. The findings comprise the main portion of the final report.

Stage 4: The Summary.　The last part of the report is the summary, which notes the significance of the study. The students might state their plans for using the information or doing additional research. Their personal feelings about the study can be included. After students complete their research and the final reports, discuss ways of sharing the results. Students should have a chance to tell others in the class about their studies. They may also share them with another class and with their parents.

After having students try the I-Search paper, you will observe distinct advantages of this type of research. When students begin with a problem that interests them, they are less likely to copy pages directly from the encyclopedia. The final report is the product of more thought and represents the student's own work. Since the focus is on the process as much as the result, the reports need not be extremely long. The satisfaction comes from finding out just what each one wanted to know, a process that students can transfer to other learning experiences.

Organizing a Learning Center

A learning center is a portion of the classroom, large or small, devoted to the study of a specific topic or set of skills. For example, you might have a language center, a United Nations center, a center for the study of Native Americans, or a center for the study of prejudice. Here are collected books, pictures, and other items related to the center focus. Here, too, teaching materials and equipment are placed to aid students working in the center as they engage in varied learning experiences.

How to Develop a Center

Plan with your students. First, decide what kind of center is needed. This depends, of course, on the focus of study in your classroom. Give the center a name that can be printed on a large sign to place above the space allocated for this learning center. You may have several centers operating at any one time.

Use your ingenuity to create a suitable place in which to focus activities. A reading table can be used to collect materials together. You may have students construct a kind of cubicle, as shown below. The bottom and sides of a large carton, placed on a table, form the back of the center; varied shapes and sizes of tables are appropriate. This particular center focuses on Americans from Scandinavia. Feature any types of information pertinent to the study.

A corner of the room is easily transformed into a center focusing on Alaska as shown on the following page. In this case you might include a map of Alaska, the number of people living in Alaska, and other information.

Invite students to participate in collecting all kinds of pertinent information and materials that might be useful—clothing, postcards, magazine articles. Brainstorm possible activities, people to contact, and places to visit as you develop the study together. Provide paper, pencils, and other materials that may be needed as students engage in work

A Cozy Corner

at the center. Depending on the type of study being developed, you might consider the following materials and equipment for the center:

- Tape or cassette recorders
- Typewriter
- Stapler
- Scissors
- Rulers

- Various papers: lined and unlined, drawing paper, colored construction paper, cardboard, posterboard, and corrugated cardboard for construction
- Computers

In addition to pictures and information displayed to make the center attractive and inviting, there will be a variety of activities. Planned activities should range from easy to more difficult as well as involve using varied skills—listening, speaking, reading, and writing. Included, too, can be activities that draw from different subject areas and those that stimulate student creativity in music and art. In the following sections of this chapter we will explain how to produce two useful kinds of teaching materials for the learning center—the task card and the learning module.

How to Use the Learning Center

After you and your students have created one or more learning centers, you need to talk about using them. Discuss how many students can work at each center at any one time. The number of seats provided is a good way to indicate how many can work at a center. As a seat is vacated, someone else may come to the center. Students may need to sign up for a particular center.

A good way to begin work at learning centers is to post a schedule giving each student a specific assignment for the day. You can prepare the schedule for a week, two weeks, or a month, depending on how long the study will take and how many centers are available. Working in the library could be one center activity that would accommodate a number of students. Your schedule for ten days might look like this:

Name	M	T	W	TH	F	M	T	W	TH	F
Felipe	1	1	2	2	L	3	3	4	4	L
James	1	1	2	2	L	3	3	4	4	L
Kentu	1	1	2	2	L	3	3	4	4	L
Sandra	2	2	L	3	3	4	4	L	1	1
Hope	2	2	L	3	3	4	4	L	1	1
Harold	2	2	L	3	3	4	4	L	1	1
Marisa	3	3	4	4	L	1	1	2	2	L

Enlarging specific centers to provide more activities and seating space will permit additional students to participate. Sometimes, activities can be completed at the student's desk. Adding other learning centers also expands the capacity.

Keeping track of materials at each center is another important part of planning. Here are several tips that may help you.

1. Package all the parts of a game in one large envelope. Label the envelope in big print, thus:

2. Color-code everything that belongs at one center. If the center on France is blue, then mark games, task cards, modules, and so on, with a blue felt pen. Students soon learn to replace task cards or games at the appropriate center.

3. Hang activities in envelopes or plastic bags on the wall where they are visible. Pegboard is ideal for this purpose, but you can improvise with cork bulletin boards or strips of wood in which hooks can be placed. If you have a specially marked hook for each item, you can quickly tell when something is missing at the end of the day.

Whenever there are problems regarding classroom operations, have a class meeting to thrash out the problems and possible solutions. If students decide on the solution, their decision is more likely to carry weight, and they will enforce it, not you!

As teacher, your role in working with learning centers is to help students organize their work toward a goal and specific objectives. You facilitate and guide the learning experiences and serve as a resource, a person to be consulted when help is needed. You guide the students in assessing their own growth and learning as well as in checking their own work. Avoid playing the undesirable role of corrector or grader. Instead, use your talents and expertise to respond to student needs, to plan strategies for stimulating further learning, and to explore new resources and materials that come your way.

Developing Task Cards

The task card is one of the most useful and versatile forms of presenting learning activities. Especially appropriate for the learning center and individualized instruction described in the preceding section, task cards can also be used in conjunction with whole class presentations. Developing sets of cards is well worth the time invested, for the cards can be used repeatedly and in various ways. In this section we will suggest ways of working with task cards.

How to Make Task Cards.   Task cards are sometimes called job cards or activity cards. They come in various sizes, from small (about 3" × 5") to large (about $8\frac{1}{2}$" × 11"). The size you choose depends on the age of the students who will use the cards (young children can handle large cards more easily) and on your instructional purpose.

Making Small Cards.   Small cards work well for "idea files" to which students refer individually. For example, a set of cards might be designed for a file called Choice. The ideas on these cards would stimulate creativity as well as develop understandings about different people of the world. In addition, you might use small cards for sets focusing on the following:

- *Acting Out.* On each card a problem situation is described that calls for role-playing. Activities could be for small groups.
- *Books to Read.* Each card lists the title and author of a book as well as a short synopsis of the story. Students use this file as they are searching for a book to read about Mexico, living in New York City, or any other topic you want to include.

Have students themselves develop these sets of cards. If you prepare just a few cards to show the kinds of ideas that can be included, the students will soon generate a useful set. Each person can prepare a card, for example, about the book he or she has read. This activity serves a dual purpose—the students have a purpose for reading, and they create a set of cards about books other students will find interesting. Preparing "acting out" situations gives students a purpose for writing a short paragraph. Then the students use the set of cards for further educational experience. Sets of cards can be made easily with purchased, unlined file cards.

Making Large Cards.   Large cards are usually constructed of sturdy poster board, so they are stiff and durable. These cards are used to present an activity that one or more students will undertake at different times. Directions must be clear if students are to work independently in an individualized approach.

On page 236 is a task card for upper-grade students that focuses on the money used in various countries. When material is prepared for you like this, simply copy the material presented. The information about currencies can be typed. If available, use a primary typewriter to facilitate reading. Directions can also be typed. If they are short, however, printing with a felt pen is effective. Throughout this book you will find informative material and activities that can be presented in similar fashion on task cards.

Make these cards more durable by covering them with clear contact paper or laminate them if you have access to a laminating machine. This kind of coating makes it possible to have students write on a card with a grease pencil. The writing can then later be wiped off.

Cards for a Specific Learning Center: Focusing on French Origins

French Canadians and Americans with French backgrounds will be interested in a learning center that focuses attention on the French language and France as the country of origin. Such a study should also be of interest to students who know nothing about France, the French language, or French Canada (Québec).

Create a Center.   Varieties of learning centers are shown in this chapter and elsewhere in this book. On the following page is one possibility. It can be quickly set up and put into use. Use a reading table, the bigger the better. Create a display like the one shown that

focuses on whatever aspect of this study you wish to emphasize, for example, Traveling in Québec, Flying to France! or Parlez-Vous Français? For an attractive display consider using a map of the area, pictures, postcards, and/or items from the newspaper. Students can add to the display as the study progresses.

Making Cards for the Center.   Develop a variety of learning experiences that will lead students to discover facts about France. Make cards that direct students to discover facts about France or to draw their own map of France, as shown on these examples:

FACTS ABOUT FRANCE

1. List as many things as you can that you already know about France.
2. List any words you know that we have borrowed from the French language.
3. Use the encyclopedia to find the answers to these questions:
   How big is France?
   Which other countries touch its borders?
   For what products is France best known?
   (Add more questions to guide student research.)

Display a map of France on the bulletin board to aid students in drawing their own maps as directed on this card. Divide the map in fourths to assist them.

TRAVELING THROUGH FRANCE

As you prepare to take a trip to France, draw your own map. Use a large sheet of paper.

Step 1: Draw light pencil lines to divide your paper in fourths. This will help you make the map the right size. Then draw the outline of France; notice the harbors and seaports.

Step 2: Locate the larger cities and rivers. Try to place them accurately. The pencil lines will help you.

Step 3: Print in the names of the countries and bodies of water that touch France on all sides. Locate the mountains.

Now choose one of the cities on your map to investigate. Find out as much as possible about it. You may be able to find a book that takes place there. Be ready to tell something about your city. We will record each person's talk on a cassette.

Create a set of small cards that will help students learn French-English vocabulary. Begin with basic vocabulary such as numbers, objects around the room, expressions students can use, for example:

Numbers

1	un	*uhn*
2	deux	*duh*
3	trois	*twah*
4	quatre	*kat truh*
5	cinq	*sank*
6	six	*sees*
7	sept	*set*
8	huit	*weet*
9	neuf	*nuhf*
10	dix	*dees*

Colors

red	rouge	*roozh*
yellow	jaune	*zhone*
blue	bleu	*bloo*
green	vert	*vair*
white	blanc	*blahnk*
black	noir	*nwahr*

Family

mother	mère	*mehr*
father	père	*pehr*
sister	soeur	*suhr*
brother	frère	*frehr*

Expressions

hello	bonjour	*bohn zhoor*
good-bye	au revoir	*oh ruh vwahr*
thank you	merci	*mair see*
please	s'il vous plait	*seel voo pleh*

Any standard high school French book will provide an ample vocabulary to introduce to your students. Note that the suggested pronunciations above are only approximate, as many French sounds cannot be directly translated into English. We suggest that you find a French teacher, or perhaps a parent who can pronounce the words on a tape for you and your students if you do not know French yourself.

Students can use these cards in numerous ways. They will enjoy just using them as flash cards to test each other. For this purpose prepare the cards with the French word or words on one side and the translation in English on the other, as shown here:

maison
(may zohn)

house

To encourage students to use these vocabulary cards, construct a gameboard. To give the gameboard a French motif, glue pictures from travel brochures around the board. Spaces are colored with alternate colors such as blue and white. Cover the board with clear contact paper or have it laminated. Use a die to determine the number of moves a student is to make. If the student lands on blue, he or she draws a card from the French pile (French words are on top, and the student must supply the English). If the player lands on a white space, he or she draws from the English pile (English words are up, and the player must supply the French word). Students who are unable to answer correctly move back three spaces. Before they move, however, they read the correct answer, and the card is placed at the bottom of the pile.

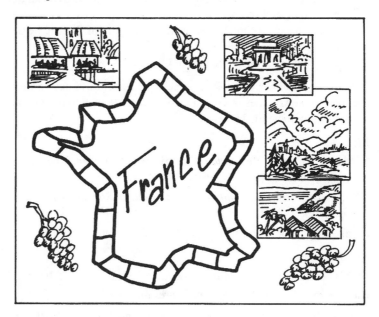

Focus a learning center on the Canadian province of Québec, which touches our states of Maine, New Hampshire, Vermont, and New York. The largest of the provinces,

its capital is Québec City. Québec is especially interesting because of its French origins; 80 percent of its population is French Canadian. You might develop task cards that involve students in the following activities:

- Draw a map of Québec. Identify its cities and waterways.
- Reproduce Québec's flag on paper or cloth.
- Write letters to obtain information about such places of interest as Montréal, the Gaspé Peninsula, The Citadel in Québec City, the St. Lawrence River. (Address: Canadian Government Travel Bureau, Ottawa, Ontario, Canada KIA OH6).
- Make a poster featuring facts about Québec—the provincial tree, the flower, coat of arms, flag, and so on.
- Develop a class time line showing the history of Québec beginning with its discovery by Jacques Cartier in 1534.
- Read a book set in some part of Québec.

Have a number of books available for student use during this study. In addition to the appropriate volumes of encyclopedias, include both nonfiction and fiction. Following is a list of recommended titles:

Fiction

C. Marius Barbeau. *The Golden Phoenix and Other French-Canadian Fairy Tales*. Retold by Michael Hornyansky. Walck, 1958.

Natalie S. Carlson. *The Talking Cat and Other Stories of French Canada*. Harper and Row, 1952.

Natalie S. Carlson. *Jean-Claude's Island*. Harper and Row, 1963.

Nonfiction

Morris G. Bishop. *Champlain: The Life of Fortitude*. McClelland, 1963.

Hazel Boswell. *French Canada: Pictures and Stories of Old Québec*. Atheneum, 1967.

Anne F. Rockwell, ed. *Savez-Vous Planter les Choux? and Other French Songs*. World, 1969.

Joseph Schull. *Battle for the Rock: The Story of Wolfe and Montcalm.* Macmillan, 1960; St. Martin's, 1960.

J. Fred Swayze. *Frontenac and the Iroquois: The Fighting Governor of New France.* Macmillan, 1959.

William Toye. *Cartier Discovers the St. Lawrence.* Oxford, 1970; Walck, 1970.

This study of French-speaking Americans or those who have French backgrounds could also include a New Orleans or Louisiana learning center. Another center might focus on French in our language—the many English words borrowed from French (*ballet, adroit*), place names that are French, or French expressions that we use (R.S.V.P.). In this truly interdisciplinary approach to teaching, students study concepts from the various social studies, mathematics, and literature and develop such skills as reading, writing, painting, and singing.

Notice, too, that you can develop similar learning centers that focus on any group, its locations within the United States, and the country or countries of origin:

Swedish Americans—Minnesota (Sweden); Irish Americans—New York City (Ireland); Italian Americans—San Francisco (Italy); Spanish-speaking Americans—California, Texas, the southwest, Florida (Spain, Mexico, Puerto Rico, Cuba).

Simply follow the steps described in developing a center focusing on Americans who have French backgrounds. Use some of the same activities. Interspersed throughout the chapters of this book you will find additional suggestions for different groups. Check the index as well as the special listing of activities and information related to specific groups.

Creating a Unit of Study

The most effective way of teaching multicultural studies is through an integrated study that involves students in thinking, reading, writing, speaking, and listening for a purpose. The theme or subject to be studied varies according to your curriculum. The unit developed here focuses on China and Chinese Americans.

Introducing the Study

Begin with a preassessment exercise. Have each student cluster around the word *China.* Each writes all the words he or she associates with China. Save this preassessment activity for examination later after the students learn more about the land and people. Comparison should show growth and perhaps changed viewpoints. Clusters will look something like the one on page 254.

Saturate your classroom with books, pictures, and other items of interest related to China. Use these materials as a basis for discussion designed to get students involved in the topic to be explored.

You might begin your study by reading a folktale from China, for example, *Tikki Tikki Tembo,* the story of a little boy who had such a long name that he almost drowned because his little brother had so much trouble repeating the name. This book is also recommended because it is illustrated beautifully by Blair Lent. A film and filmstrip of the story are available from Weston Woods, Weston, Connecticut, 06880.

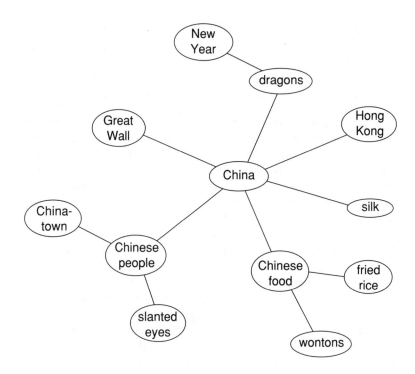

Retold by Arlene Mosel, this story is a good example of a *pourquoi* tale, a story that explains why something happened, in this case why the Chinese have such short names. After hearing this story, students of all ages can write original pourquoi (the French word for *why*) tales to explain, for example:

- Why our clock has twelve numbers.
- Why cherries have pits.
- Why corn has a tassel on top.
- Why we have stoplights on city streets.

After students have written their pourquoi tales, have them collected in a book entitled: *Pourquoi? ¿Porque? Why?* Place the book on the reading table where everyone can read it.

Collecting Resources

Explore your school library as well as the local public library to see what kinds of resources are available. To accommodate a wide range of reading abilities, include both easy and more difficult fiction. Also bring in the China entries from several encyclopedias, which also vary in reading difficulty. You can find other nonfiction written for young people. Here is a selection of titles to look for. Ask the assistance of your librarian in discovering other resources.

Fiction

Easy Books

Eve Bunting. *The Happy Funeral.*

Thomas Handforth. *Mei Li.*

Yen Liang. *Happy New Year.*

Kurt Wiese. *Fish in the Air.*

Short Stories and Myths

Arthur Chrisman. *Shen of the Sea.*

Alice Ritchie. *The Treasure of Li-Po.*

Laurence Yep. *Dragon of the Lost Sea.*

Books for Older Students

Meindert De Jong. *The House of Sixty Fathers.*

Adrienne Jones. *Ride the Far Wind.*

Jean Merrill. *The Superlative Horse.*

Katherine Paterson. *Rebels of the Heavenly Kingdom.*

Nonfiction

Cornelia Spencer. *The Land and People of China.*

Cornelia Spencer. *The Yangtze, China's River Highway.*

Betty Lee Sung. *The Chinese in America.*

Creating a Center of Focus

Create a learning center something like the one shown here to serve as the center of focus for the study of China and Chinese Americans. Have students help develop the center for the study of China.

You can feature any pertinent information to add interest to the center. Here we have presented facts designed to pique student curiosity, such as the fact that 600 million people speak Chinese or that China is the third largest country in the world. The gameboard, Challenging the Dragon, can be presented as part of the module or as a separate activity with the directions displayed where students can read them easily. Place the modules, varied supplies, and numerous resources such as books at this work center.

Preparing a Module for Students

We find it helpful to prepare learning modules that guide students through the study, stressing activities that are stimulating and informative. A learning module, as defined here, is a booklet, usually 8½" × 11", that focuses on a single topic. Rather short, five to twenty pages, the module is designed to teach two to three objectives that are part of an overall goal. Both goal and objectives are stated clearly. The module begins with a simple pretest and concludes with a posttest or culminating activity that aids student self-evaluation. The learning module is self-contained and speaks directly to the student. A teacher's guide is usually included with suggestions for use and such teaching aids as test answers, additional enrichment activities, and recommended resources. Read through the sample module that follows so that you have a clearer picture of how a module can be used.

The U.S. Bicentennial, 1976, was the year of the dragon, as was 1988; the dragon will come again in the year 2000. 1990 was the year of the horse. The title of the module could be modified according to the symbol for the year in which you plan to present this unit of study to provide a more contemporary flavor. The dragon, however, is still a useful motif for the gameboard at any time.

Copy the module directly on duplicating masters so that you can produce a number of booklets at one time. Enlarge drawings by projecting them with an opaque projector. Prepare a simple construction paper cover that bears the title and perhaps the head of the dragon. Or the cover might be decorated with a Chinese ideograph (a symbol used for a word or idea).

DISCOVERING CHINA

Discovery *

*Derived from symbols dated 1523–1028 B.C. during the Shang dynasty in China, now the People's Republic of China.

The Year of the Dragon—2000

THE YEAR OF THE DRAGON:
A STUDY OF CHINA AND
CHINESE AMERICANS

The Cover of the Module

Module Activity 1: Gifts from China

The chart on the next page shows that we have received many gifts from China. China's civilization developed long before that of the United States. Our country is an infant compared to such countries that trace their history to the years before Christ (B.C.).

Since China existed so many years before we did, naturally many things we take for granted today came originally from China. Can you name three things that we use today that were gifts from China?

1. _____

2. _____

3. _____

Module Activity 2: Your Own Book about China

Begin a book about China. You can put everything you do in this study in your book. Choose a title for the book. Select a piece of colored construction paper to use as the cover. Use a brush and black tempera paint to create a Chinese ideograph to decorate the cover. You may find some ideas in your encyclopedia or other books about China. Follow the directions given in Module Activity 3. Make a page for the table of contents. You can add titles to this page gradually as you make new pages for your book. Make a page now about

CHINA'S GIFTS TO THE WEST

CHINA*		THE WEST*
Silk, about 1300		
Folding umbrella (?)	—300 B.C.—	
Lodestone, 240	—200 B.C.—	
Shadow figures (?)	—100 B.C.—	
	Birth of Christ	
Lacquer		
Paper, 105	—A.D. 100—	Peach and apricot
	—200—	
Tea, 264–273		
Word for porcelain	—300—	
first used		
Sedan chair	—400—	
	—500—	
Kite, 549		Silk, 552–554
	—600—	
Playing cards, Dominoes	—700—	
Gunpowder (?)		
Porcelain described, 851	—800—	
First printed book, 868	—900—	
Movable type, 1041–1049	—1000—	
Compass		Orange
Zinc in coins, 1094–1098	—1100—	
Explosives, 1161		Paper, 1150
	—1200—	Compass, 1190
	—1300—	Gunpowder and cannon, 1330
		Playing cards, 1377
	—1400—	
		Block printing, 1423
		Gutenberg's Bible, 1456
Chaulmoogra oil and ephedrine	—1500—	Zinc described
described, 1552–1578		Kite, 1589
	—1600—	Sedan chair, tea, folding umbrella, 1688
	—1700—	Wallpaper manufactured, Porcelain, 1709
		Lacquer produced, 1730
The use of the following also		Zinc in industrial production, 1740
originated in China in early times,	—1800—	"German silver" production
but cannot be accurately dated:		Chrysanthemum, tea rose, camellia,
peach, orange, apricot, lemon,		azalea, China aster, grapefruit,
pomelo, Chrysanthemum, tea rose,		Shadow figures, gingko, tung oil,
camellia, azalea, China aster,		soy bean, ephedrine, chaulmoogra oil
gingko, "German silver," wallpaper,		
goldfish.	—1900—	

*Dates in the "China" column indicate approximate date of origin; "The West" column indicates the approximate date of receiving item described.

Source: From Derk Bode, *China's Gift to the West,* American Council on Education, Washington, D.C., 1978.

Gifts We Received from China. You can make a chart like the preceding one or you can simply list the things we received from China. You can add pages of your own to this book, too. Perhaps you would like to include a picture from a magazine or a newspaper clipping. If you like to draw, you may include some of your own illustrations.

Module Activity 3: Chinese Brush Painting

Combine art with reading and the study of the Chinese culture. Try your hand at the beautiful figures used in classic Chinese writing. Use white art paper (9" × 12"), a brush, and black tempera to create the words shown here. To explore further, find *You Can Write Chinese* by Kurt Wiese in your library.

man   **beautiful**   **country**

Module Activity 4: Exploring China

Find articles about China in an encyclopedia, newspapers, or magazines. See what you can find out about: the people of China; the land—its boundaries, size comparison with the United States, mountains and rivers; China's government; the languages of China.

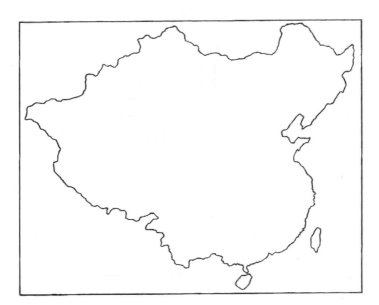

Study the map of China. Make an outline of this country like the one shown on the previous page. First divide your paper in fourths with light pencil lines. This helps you draw the map in proper proportion. The lines can be erased later.

Locate provinces, major cities, and rivers. Print the names of countries that border China. Identify the bodies of water that touch China.

Module Activity 5: The Puzzling Pagoda—Chinese Crossword Puzzle

After reading about China and drawing a map of this country, you should be able to complete the crossword puzzle. If you can't think of an answer, refer again to the encyclopedia.

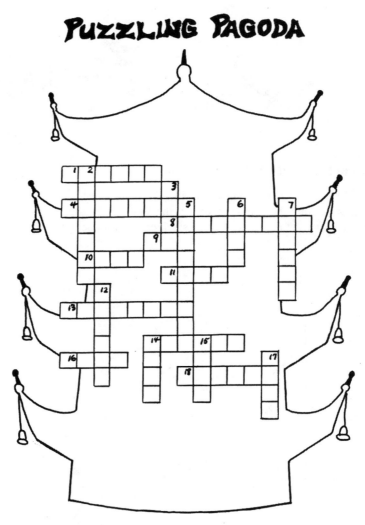

Definitions (For answers see page 272.)

Across	*Down*
1. The capital of China	2. Tallest mountain
4. People's _____ of China	3. Common cereal
8. Chinese philosopher and scholar	5. Kind of government
9. Jewel	6. Fishing boat
10. Luxurious cloth	7. Country larger than China
11. Basic Chinese coin	12. Large woody plant
13. Largest city in China	14. Common fish eaten
14. Useful cloth produced	15. Prized lumber
16. Leader: _____ En-lai	17. Precious stone
18. Unique building	

Module Activity 6: Chinese Folktales

Every country has its share of stories, tales that have been passed down through the years. Here is an interesting fable that comes to us from China.

The Mussel and the Bird

Once upon a time there was a Mussel who lived in the cliffs along the edge of the ocean. After a long winter, sunshine at last reached the rocks, and the Mussel drowsily opened its shell to the warmth. A Bird dropped suddenly from the sky swooping down on the Mussel to snatch a meal from the shell. The Mussel quickly snapped shut, closing tightly on the Bird's beak. The Mussel squeezed the Bird's beak, but no matter how hard the Mussel squeezed the Bird wouldn't leave.

Finally the Bird spoke to the Mussel: "Mussel, if you don't open your shell soon, not in one day, not in two days, but in three days surely you will die." The Mussel made no reply.

Eventually the Mussel spoke to the Bird: "Bird, if you don't take your beak out of my shell, not in one day, not in two days, but in three days surely you will die." The Bird would not heed the Mussel.

Then along came a child on her way to play in the ocean. The Bird saw the child, but still it would not remove its beak. The Mussel also saw the child, but still it would not open its shell. The child spotted the Bird and the Mussel locked together, picked them up, and carried them away for the family stew pot.

—*Retold by Pamela Tiedt*

Can you think of a moral for this story?

Moral: _____

_____

_____

Find another folktale from China. Read it together with a friend. Plan how you can act the story out for others in the class. Invite other people to join you if you need their help.

Module Activity 7: The Chinese Calendar

The Chinese calendar is quite different from the one we usually refer to. It is based on ancient traditions. An animal symbol is identified for each year, and persons born in that year are supposedly ruled by this symbolic animal and have characteristics associated with the animal. Twelve symbols are repeated continuously. Examine this chart showing the symbols for the twentieth century. What is your symbol? Do you think the characteristics listed fit you?

IN WHICH YEAR WERE YOU BORN?

Ox (1913, 1925, 1937, 1949, 1961, 1973, 1985, 1997) You have a calm patient nature. Friends turn to you because you are that rarest of creatures—a good listener. Love bewilders you so many people wrongly consider you cold.

Tiger (1902, 1914, 1926, 1938, 1950, 1962, 1974, 1986, 1998) You are a person of great extremes, a sympathetic and considerate friend, a powerful and dangerous enemy. In your career you are both a deep thinker and a careful planner.

Hare (1903, 1915, 1927, 1939, 1951, 1963, 1975, 1987, 1999) You are blessed with extraordinary good fortune and will inevitably provide financial success. This luck of yours not only extends to your business interests, but also to games of chance.

Dragon (1904, 1916, 1928, 1940, 1952, 1964, 1976, 1988, 2000) Your reputation as a fire-eater is based on your outward show of stubbornness, bluster and short temper. But underneath you are really gentle, sensitive, and soft-hearted.

Serpent (1905, 1917, 1929, 1941, 1953, 1965, 1977, 1989, 2001) You Snake people have more than your share of the world's gifts, including basic wisdom. You are likely to be handsome, well formed men and graceful, beautiful women.

Horse (1906, 1918, 1930, 1942, 1954, 1966, 1978, 1990, 2002) Your cheerful disposition and flattering ways make you a popular favorite. Great mental agility will keep you in the upper income.

Ram (1907, 1919, 1931, 1943, 1955, 1967, 1979, 1991) You are a sensitive, refined, aesthetic type with considerable talent in all the arts. Indeed success or failure will depend upon whether you can shepherd your ability and energy into a single field.

Monkey (1908, 1920, 1932, 1944, 1956, 1968, 1980, 1992) In today's parlance you are a swinger. And because of your flair for decision making and sure-footed feel for finance, you are certain to climb to the top.

Rooster (1909, 1921, 1933, 1945, 1957, 1969, 1981, 1993) You either score heavily or lay a large egg. Although outspoken and not shy in groups, you are basically a loner who doesn't trust most people. Yet you are capable of attracting close and loyal friends.

Dog (1910, 1922, 1934, 1946, 1958, 1970, 1982, 1994) You are loyal and honest with a deep sense of duty and justice. You can always be trusted to guard the secrets of others.

Boar (1911, 1923, 1935, 1947, 1959, 1971, 1983, 1995) The quiet inner strength of your character is outwardly reflected by courtesy and breeding. Your driving ambition will lead you to success.

Rat (1912, 1924, 1936, 1948, 1960, 1972, 1984, 1996) You have been blessed with great personal charm, a taste for the better things in life, and considerable self control which restrains your quick temper.

Module Activity 8: Chinese Celebrations

Through the years many Chinese have immigrated to the United States, especially to the West Coast. San Francisco and Los Angeles have large sections called Chinatown where you can eat Chinese food and visit Chinese shops.

Many Chinese Americans still celebrate the traditional holidays and festivals of China. There is nothing so festive and exciting as a Chinese New Year's parade with the flamboyant dragon leading the way down the streets of Chinatown. Chinese New Year falls on a variable date depending on the moon. It is celebrated as each person's birthday with fireworks, gongs and cymbals, and of course, wonderful delicacies.

Here are some other traditional Chinese holidays:

Spring Festival. Honors the planting season.

The Dragon Boat Festival. Sometimes called the Double Fifth, this holiday falls on the fifth day of the fifth month of the Chinese calendar. On this day dragon-shaped boats race, and inhabitants of Chinatown eat *jung,* three-cornered rice dumplings, in the local teahouses.

Ch'ung Yang Festival. This summer holiday, celebrated with kite flying, originated with a legend. The story goes that a fortune teller foretold disaster for a certain farmer on the ninth day of the ninth month, so he took his family to a high windy hill. Upon returning home, they found that, indeed, their animals had all perished.

Festival of the Moon. This harvest festival is celebrated privately at night. This romantic celebration is the women's festival. They prepare large moon cakes made of flour and brown sugar to resemble the moon and its palaces.

Double Ten Festival. On the tenth day of the tenth month, the dragon appears again to celebrate the Chinese Revolution and the fall of the Manchu Empire in the early twentieth century.

Ching Ming Festival. Also called the Festival of the Tombs, it falls on the 106th day after the winter solstice. At this time the Chinese go to private cemeteries to honor the dead.

Winter Festival. A family celebration, this holiday usually occurs in December shortly before Christmas.

See if you can find out more about Chinese celebrations. Try one of these means of gathering information:

- Interview someone whose family originated in China. Find out if they celebrate these holidays, and if so, how the celebration is carried out.
- Read about Chinese holidays in a book in your library.
- Go to Chinatown to observe a celebration.
- Write to a tourist agency or the Embassy of China to request information.

Write a short report of your findings.

Module Activity 9: Chinese Come to America

People of Chinese origins have made major contributions to the development of the United States. Many are doctors, college professors, and business executives. As immigrants, however, their life was difficult.

Read this list of events that are significant in the history of Chinese Americans from the first immigration to the present.

1785 First record of Chinese in the United States. Three Chinese seamen from the ship *Pallas* were left stranded in Baltimore.

1815 First record of a Chinese in California. Ah Nam, a cook for Governor de Sola, was baptized as a Christian on October 27, 1815. (California was not yet a part of the United States.)

1849 In the year of the gold rush, Chinese in San Francisco recorded as 54; in 1850 there were 787 men and 2 women. First anti-Chinese riot at Chinese camp, Tuolumne County, California.

1850 First laundry business begun in San Francisco by a Chinese person.

1852 First Chinese opera performed in San Francisco. First Chinese theater built in San Francisco. Columbia Resolution expelled Chinese from gold mines in Tuolumne County; followed by a similar action in other counties.

1854 First Chinese newspaper in America, *Gold Hill News.*

1869 Completion of Transcontinental Railway. Chinese labor used by Central Pacific. Chinatown established in Deadwood, South Dakota, with discovery of gold. Chinese followed development of the mining industry as well as agriculture, and fishing; resentment by whites.

1871 Chinese massacre in Los Angeles.

1877 Special Report by joint Committee of Congress investigated the "Chinese Question." Labor agitation; anti-Chinese movement.

1879 California Constitution contained anti-Chinese legislation prohibiting employment of Chinese by corporations and government agencies.

1882 Chinese Exclusion Act passed by U.S. Congress; ten-year ban on immigration; anti-Chinese riots.

1892 Geary Act extended exclusion for another ten years; required aliens to register.

1893 Anti-Chinese riots grew numerous; Fresno, California; Napa, California; Redlands, Tulare, Visalia, Ukiah, California.

1894 Vacaville, California, riot; Chinese driven to cities where they formed Chinese ghettos, called Chinatowns.

1902 Exclusion laws extended indefinitely.

1907 Vancouver, British Columbia, riot.

1943 Repeal of Chinese Exclusion Act: Chinese aliens in U.S. may become citizens. Chinese immigration quota set at 105 per year.

1965 Quota system repealed. Permits up to 20,000 Chinese to enter United States each year.

Work with others in your class to prepare a time line on a long strip of paper that looks something like this:

```
1780  1800  1820  1840  1860  1880  1900  1920  1940  1960  1980  1990  2000
```

Add illustrations and other information related to the history of Chinese immigration into the United States.

Module Activity 10: Challenging the Dragon—Making a Game

Directions to the Student.   Here is a fiery dragon whose breath can destroy you or bring you fortune. Which will it be? (See pages 266–267.)

This dragon guards a Treasure Chest that you can reach only by performing the many tasks required by the fearsome beast.

At each step roll the dragon's Curious Cube to see how many tasks you must perform. To learn what the tasks will be, draw forth a Cardinal Card for each task. If you perform the required tasks, the dragon will permit you to move to the next perilous step. If you fail even one of the tasks, you must slide back to the previous step.

You have only a limited time to perform each task. As you complete each task, place the Cardinal Card under the great pile of Arduous Tasks. That task may be assigned to another unlucky challenger who dares to challenge the dragon.

Making the Curious Cube.   Copy the pattern shown here to make the cube that will tell how many of the Arduous Tasks you must perform. After cutting the cube pattern from heavy red paper, print the numbers indicated with a felt pen. Then fold the pattern on each line, folding in the same direction each time. Form the six-sided figure and tuck the flaps in after applying glue on each.

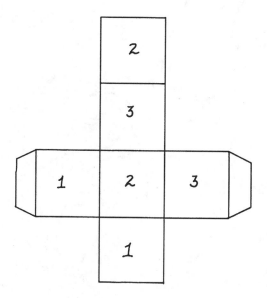

Preparing the Arduous Task Cards.   Cut the cards apart. Mount each one on red (cardinal) construction paper that is 3" × 4" so the color frames the card. (See tasks on p. 268.)

Playing the Game Alone.   This is a good game to play individually as you challenge the dragon alone. You may need a person to serve as Timer and Checker to see if your answers are acceptable. Use any means to discover the correct answer within the time limit, for instance, a dictionary.

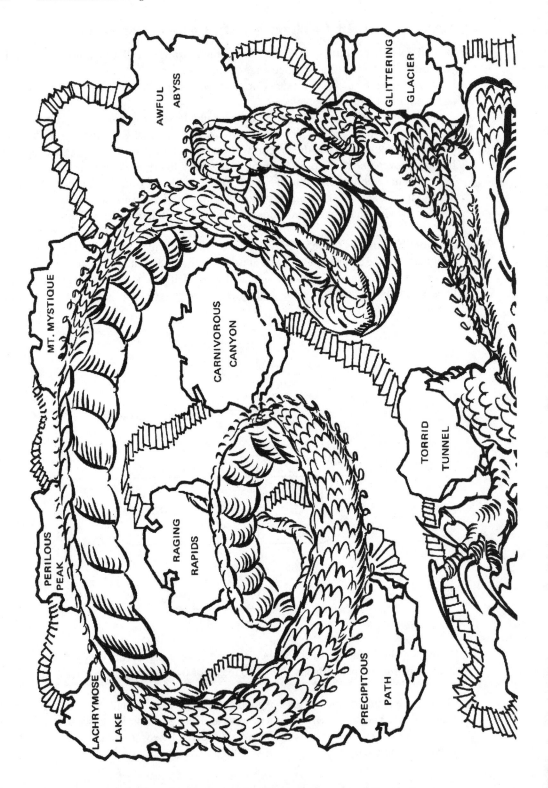

Playing the Game with a Friend.   You may wish to play this game with a friend or two. In this case do not wait for each person to finish the tasks assigned. If one player finishes a task in a short time, he or she can move to the next step, throw the Curious Cube, draw the Cardinal Cards and work on the tasks assigned. In this way, each person moves ahead individually depending on the number of tasks received each time and how quickly they are completed. You will want to hurry, of course, if you are to reach the Treasure before someone else gets it away from the Dragon!

1. About how many people live in China?	6. Name the tallest mountain in China.

2. Name the 3 largest countries in the world.	7. Identify the following:
	    a. pagoda
	    b. junk
	    c. carp

3. What kind of cloth was a gift from China?	8. Where did Chinese immigrants first settle?
4. What city is the capital of China?	9. Which of these names is likely to be Chinese? Martin Chang Yomura
5. Which city is the largest in China?	10. Name two countries that border China.

Module Activity 11: Exploring Your Community

What do you know about Chinese Americans in your own community? Begin a survey by turning to your local telephone book to answer the following questions:

- How many persons are listed under several common Chinese names such as Wong, Chang, or Yee? What other names might you try?
- How many listings begin with the word *Chinese*, for example, Chinese Alliance Church?
- How many Chinese restaurants are listed in the yellow pages under *Restaurants*?
- How many doctors under the entry *Physicians and Surgeons* in the yellow pages have Chinese names?

Write a summary of your findings. Then write a paragraph explaining your conclusions about the Chinese in your community.

Do your findings surprise you? How can you find out more about Chinese Americans in your community?

Module Activity 12: A Writing Lesson

SAMPLE LESSON: LA DICTÉE, A DICTATION METHOD[5]

Level of Difficulty: Grades 1–12 (Adapt materials selected.)

Outcomes

Students will:

   1. Listen to sentences read aloud.

2. Write each sentence dictated.

3. Discuss spelling and mechanical errors.

Procedures

Select a paragraph from a good book that students have already heard or one that you would like to introduce. Choose a paragraph that includes interesting sentence structures, varied uses of punctuation and capitalization, and new vocabulary. (Choose a less complex paragraph for the first experience with la dictée.) In this lesson we will use a paragraph from *Dragonwings* by Laurence Yep (Harper), a story of the Chinese in California during the early twentieth century.

Stimulus

Introduce the book and author to your class, for example:

> *Dragonwings* was written by a California author, Laurence Yep, who was inspired by the account of a Chinese immigrant who built a flying machine in 1909. This is how the story begins:
> "Ever since I can remember, I had wanted to know about the Land of the Golden Mountain, but my mother had never wanted to talk about it."

Invite students to conjecture about what the Land of the Golden Mountain is. Tell them that the main character, Moon Shadow, lives in China with his mother and grandmother, but his father, Windrider, lives in San Francisco's Chinatown.

Then share the interesting paragraph you have selected for the la dictée exercise, for example:

> Mother had talked quite a bit about him and so had Grandmother; but that too was not the same. They were speaking about a young man who had lived in the Middle Kingdom, not a man who had endured the hardships and loneliness of living in the demon land. I knew he made kites; but as marvelous as his kites were, he and I could not spend the rest of our lives flying kites. I was afraid of the Golden Mountain, and yet my father, who lives there, wanted me to join him. I only knew that there was a certain rightness in life—the feeling you got when you did something the way you knew you should. I owed it to Father to obey him in everything—even if it meant going to such a fearful place as the Golden Mountain. And really, how really frightening could it be if Hand Clap wanted to go back? I turned to Mother and Grandmother. "I want to go," I said.

Talk about the passage the students have heard. Ask them questions such as the following:

1. Who is talking?

2. What characters are mentioned in this paragraph?

3. Who is Hand Clap?

4. What is this fearful place, The Golden Mountain? Where is it? How did it get that name?

5. Why was Moon Shadow afraid? Why did he decide to go?

Activity

Tell the students that you are going to dictate this paragraph to them, sentence by sentence. You will read each sentence only twice: The first time they are to listen without writing; the second time will be after they have begun writing. Challenge them to write each sentence as well as they can without help.

Follow-Up

After you have completed the dictation exercise, have students correct any errors together. Ask two students to write the first sentence on the chalkboard. Ask if any changes need to be made in spelling, punctuation, or capitalization. Tell students to correct any mistakes they made on their own papers.

Students should study this passage in preparation for writing the same passage again on the next day.

Evaluation

Have students compare the results of the two dictations. Have each one write several sentences summarizing what they learned from doing this exercise.

Have them staple the three papers together to place in their writing portfolios. Schedule la dictée lessons once a week for a period of time. After four weeks have each student examine his or her packet of dictation exercises to analyze how this learning experience is working, perhaps noting what he or she might do to improve performance on this task.

Related Learning Activities

Extend student learning by providing instruction related to the literature you have introduced, as described in these examples.

1. *Repetition of the same dictation.* Dictate the same passage to students a month later to see if they have retained the knowledge. Students who have repeated difficulty can work together in pairs, dictating one sentence at a time to each other. This is a good exercise for ESL students.

2. *Exploring sentence patterns.* Choose a sentence from the passage to serve as a model for students. Show them how to identify the structural features of the sentence that form a pattern, thus:

_____ had _____ and so had

_____ ; but that _____

Students can generate sentences that follow this pattern, like this one:

John had lied and so had Mildred; but that didn't make any difference now.

3. *Responding to literature through writing.* This passage suggests a number of topics that middle-grade students might identify, for example:

How would you feel if you were Moon Shadow? Would you have made the same decision?

Write the dialogue that you think might have taken place between Moon Shadow and his father, Windrider, when they met in San Francisco.

Module Activity 13: What Do You Know Now?

Write three things that you know about China or Chinese Americans now that you did not know before you began this study:

1. _____

2. _____

3. _____

Examine the answers you gave to the questions on the first page of this module. Would you change any of them now?

Choose one of the following activities to complete your work on this study:

- Write a poem or story about a person from China.
- Act out a story set in China that you have read. (You may work with several students on this task.)
- Plan a reader's theater presentation of a folktale from China. (Work with several students.)
- Make a diorama of a scene from China.
- Make a table-size relief map of China. (Work with another student.)

Module Activity 14: Sharing Information

Your class may want to share your information about China and Chinese Americans with other classes or the whole school. How can you do this?

Notes to the Teacher

Preparing the Gameboard

If you choose to prepare the gameboard yourself as a stimulating extra activity for this study, begin by enlarging the drawing with an opaque projector. Have students help you as much as possible because involvement pays off. Examine this part of the module again before reading the following directions so you will understand the instructions.

Duplicate or copy the directions to the student on page 265. Mount these directions on a heavy piece of colored cardboard. Cover the directions with a sheet of clear contact paper to protect the sheet as it is used repeatedly. Pressing the direction board (covered with a sheet of clean paper) with a warm iron will make the protective sheet adhere well.

Have a student construct the Curious Cube as instructed (page 265). Have several other students finish the Cardinal Cards (see page 268). You will need to prepare additional cards similar to the examples given if a number of students wish to play at once.

Answers to Cardinal Cards (page 268):

1. 600 million
2. Russia, Canada, China
3. silk
4. Peking
5. Shanghai
6. Mt. Everest
7. a. special kind of building
   b. Chinese boat
   c. kind of fish
8. California
9. Chang
10. Russia
    North Korea
    North Vietnam
    Laos
    Burma
    India
    Bhutan
    Sikkim
    Nepal
    Pakistan
    Afghanistan
    Mongolia

Answers to the Pagoda Puzzle (page 260)*

Across	*Down*
1. Peking	**2.** Everest
4. Republic	**3.** Rice
8. Confucius	**5.** Communist
9. Gem	**6.** Junk
10. Silk	**7.** Russia
11. Yuan	**12.** Bamboo
13. Shanghai	**14.** Carp
14. Cotton	**15.** Teak
16. Chou	**17.** Jade
18. Pagoda	

Additional Activities

As students are working on the study of China, you might wish to interject additional interesting activities that can involve the whole group or may be designed for small group interaction. Here are a few suggestions:

- Invite a parent who was born in China to visit your class to tell about China as they remember it, childhood experiences, coming to the United States, what his or her life here is like. Students then write these stories together.
- Prepare a simple Chinese meal of rice and a combination of vegetables—celery, onions, green peppers, canned water chestnuts, soy sauce. See *Eating and Cooking Around the World; Fingers before Forks* by Erich Berry (Day).
- Read a version of "Cinderella" that comes from China. See: *Favorite Children's Stories from China and Tibet* by Lotta C. Hume (Tuttle).
- Write a Chinese play or produce one that is available in the library. See *7 Plays and How to Produce Them* by Moyne R. Smith (Waick).
- Learn how the Chinese New Year is celebrated. See *Holidays Around the World* by Joseph Gaer (Little, Brown).
- Explore Chinese poetry. See *Chinese Mother Goose Rhymes* edited by Robert Wyndham (World); *The Moment of Wonder* edited by Richard Lewis (Dial).
- Read stories aloud that are set in China, for the well-told story adds much to our understanding of another culture. You might choose, for example, *Seven Magic Orders: An Original Chinese Folktale,* beautifully illustrated by Y. T. Mui (Lippincott).

Chinese Children in Your Classroom

Presenting a study related to the country of origin for students in your class gives them a good feeling of belonging. They can often contribute special information and personal experiences. Their parents may be willing to share in the study, too. The students will learn as they participate in the study. Students who may have arrived recently from China or Hong Kong will be very much interested in finding out about Chinese Americans in the community and in the United States.

*Sources for the Pagoda Puzzle were *China,* edited by Thomas W. Chinn, and *California, A Syllabus.* The Chinese Historical Society of America, 17 Adler Place, San Francisco, CA 94133.

As you work with Chinese-speaking children, it is helpful to be somewhat aware of the problems they may experience as they learn English.

ASPECTS OF THE CHINESE LANGUAGE THAT MAY CAUSE PROBLEMS FOR CHINESE STUDENTS LEARNING ENGLISH

1. The verb has only one form. Unlike the English verb, the Chinese verb is not conjugated to indicate tense. Tenses are indicated by the use of auxiliaries placed before or after the stable verb form.
2. Nouns are not inflected to indicate plural forms. Plurality is indicated by the use of auxiliaries in the form of specific or general number indicators placed before a noun (e.g., three book, many boy).
3. The Chinese article *a* is very specific and complex. It refers to the noun that it modifies and varies according to that noun. It is used as a unit of measure rather than as a general article (e.g., a book, a building, a string, a coat, a horse, a pencil).
4. Word order may not be manipulated to change meaning as is done in English. In Chinese the word *is*, for example, may not be repositioned to convert a statement into a question (e.g., "She is a nurse" may not be repositioned to "Is she a nurse?").
5. Spoken Cantonese and spoken Mandarin have an identical spoken sound to represent the pronoun he and she; but the written forms for these and three other singular pronouns in the third person are very distinct when genders are indicated basically by word-radical forms: She (feminine); he (masculine); it (inanimate object); it (animate object); and He (deity).
6. In a Chinese dictionary, words are not arranged in alphabetical order. Instead, they are listed by the number of strokes each character has.
7. There is a tendency for Chinese speakers to drop, glottalize, or add a vowel sound to English endings in the consonants *t, d, s, l, p, b, k, f, g, r,* and *v*.
8. A tone system is used in Chinese as a device for distinguishing word meanings. Words having the same pronunciation may have four different meanings. These meanings are, in turn, represented by four written forms.
9. There is a distinction between *n* and *l* in spoken Chinese; but some speakers, especially the Cantonese, use the letters interchangeably. The difference in pronunciation is particularly distinct in Mandarin.

Source: Framework in Reading for the Elementary and Secondary Schools of California. California State Department of Education.

Recap

Multicultural education, taught across the total curriculum, should lead students to better understand themselves and others as they also learn content from varied fields. In order to integrate multicultural concepts into the curriculum effectively, we choose teaching strategies that engage students in interactive learning, for example, researching and writing an I-Search paper on a topic of their choice. We also develop the curriculum around broad themes that invite students to explore cultural diversity from many perspectives together. As we work with children from different cultures, we need to be aware of language differences that may impede their learning English easily.

REFLECTIONS

Multicultural education fits well into the total curriculum. Teachers need to confer as a faculty to determine just how they can best promote the understanding of diversity in any particular school. If each teacher agrees to present multicultural literature or to use a lesson that teaches a multicultural concept at least once a month, student empathy will gradually grow, reinforced by instruction in all classrooms. Teachers in self-contained classrooms can readily plan integrated units of study that incorporate multicultural studies in all areas of the curriculum.

APPLICATIONS

Begin exploring on your own. Consider the ways you can use the resources listed in this chapter. Try several of these ideas.

1. Choose one state to study in detail. Think chiefly about the people who now live in that part of our country. Find out their backgrounds and how they came to settle there. As you focus on the people, you will discover how they make their living, the cities and towns in which they live, and the issues that concern them. Use the library as a resource, but also watch the daily newspaper and talk with people who have lived in that state.

Begin a file of books that you or your students might read to learn more about the state. If you choose Hawaii, for example, you might list the following:

Marcia Brown. *Backbone of the King: The Story of Paka and His Son Ku.* Scribner's, 1966. Middle-grade students will enjoy this story written by an outstanding author.

Eleanor Nordyke. *The People of Hawaii.* The University of Hawaii Press, 1981. This book tells you about the multiethnic population on the islands.

Ruth Tabrah. *Hawaii: A Bicentennial History.* Norton, 1980. Written for the bicentennial, here is a good overview of Hawaiian history up to the present.

Vivian Thompson. *Hawaiian Myths of Earth, Sea, and Sky.* Holiday, 1966. Students can act out the tales of the Hawaiian gods as a way of learning more about the people of Hawaii.

If each person in your class develops a collection of resource material about one state, you can duplicate them for sharing so that everyone will have a rich packet to use in the classroom.

2. Outline a study of religious groups in the United States. How might you guide students to learn more about the various beliefs? Include a list of the many groups in the United States, and begin listing books that could be used with a study of comparative religions, for example:

Eileen Weiman. *Which Way Courage.* Atheneum, 1981. A story about the Amish.

Ann the Word; The Life of Mother Ann Lee, Founder of the Shakers. Little, 1976. Information about the Shakers, founded in 1776 by a woman of great faith.

Also refer to the list of materials about Jews in America on pages **396–399** and Edward Rice's *American Saints and Seers: American-Born Religions and the Genius behind Them* (Four Winds, 1982).

3. Plan a letter-writing unit of study in which each student writes to request free or inexpensive materials available from different companies and organizations. Here is a list that you can add to; also see addresses, p. 350. After students receive the materials that were requested, they can share them orally.

Agency for Instructional TV. Box A, 1111 V. 17th St. Bloomington, IN 47401. "Trade Offs."

Cooperative Extension Service. Box U-35, The University of Connecticut, Storrs, CT 06268. *Mexican Foods and Traditions.*

Delmonte Teaching Aids. Box 4007, Clinton, IA 52732. *The Big Four Daily Countdown (Basic Foods). Consuma diariamente los cuatro alimentos básicos.*

Frito-Lay Tower. Dallas, TX 75235. *Tasty Recipes from Frito-Lay, Inc.*

National Dairy Council. Chicago, IL 60606, *Una guía par comer bien*—Chart.

Procter & Gamble. Box 599, Cincinnati, OH 45201. "Consumer."

Texas Education Agency. 201 East 11th St., Austin, TX 78701. *El corrido de Gregorio Cortez.* (Send blank tape, cassette size.)

World Research, Inc. 11722 Sorrento Valley Rd., San Diego, CA 92121, "The Inflation File."

4. Design a module for use in teaching a specific unit of study. Plan an integrated study that will last for three to four weeks. Draw from the entire text of *Multicultural Teaching* for ideas that fit your topic. Modules can be produced for any subject area. You must first decide, of course, on what you want to teach. Modules can focus on groups of people, geographic areas, or broad concepts related to multilingual/multicultural studies. Examples of good topics for presentation in modular form are prejudice in America, Native Americans today, Americans from Puerto Rico, breaking down stereotypes, and the people in New York City.

Endnotes

1. "A Naturalist's Perspective." *Nature Center News* (September 1988): 4.
2. Paul Gagnon. "Why Study History?" *Atlantic Monthly* (November 1988): 43.
3. Ibid., p. 45.
4. Ibid., p. 64.
5. Iris McClellan Tiedt. *Writing: From Topic to Evaluation.* Allyn and Bacon, 1989, pp. 145–148.

Exploring Further

Evelyn B. Freeman and Diane G. Person. *Using Nonfiction Trade Books in the Elementary Classroom: From Ants to Zeppelins.* National Council of Teachers of English, 1992.

Mary Ann Heltshe and Audrey B. Kirchner. *Multicultural Explorations: Joyous Journeys with Books.* Teachers Ideas Press, 1991.

Kenneth Jackson. *Building a History Curriculum: Guidelines for Teaching History in Schools.* Bradley Commission on History in Schools, 1988.

James Lynch. *Multicultural Education in a Global Society.* Falmar, 1989.

Miller-Lachmann. *Our Family, Our Friends, Our World: An Annotated Guide to Significant Multicultural Books for Children and Teenagers.* Bowker, 1992.

James Moffett. *Active Voice: A Writing Program across the Curriculum.* Boynton-Cook, 1981.

P. G. Ramsey et al. *Multicultural Education: A Sourcebook.* Garland, 1989.

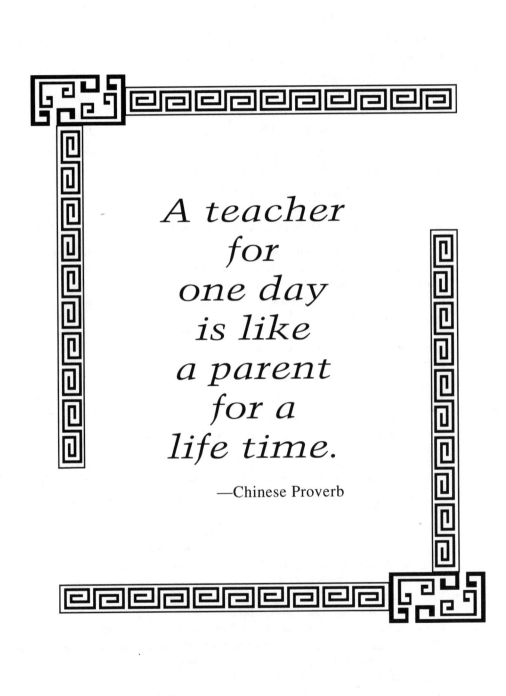

*A teacher
for
one day
is like
a parent
for a
life time.*

—Chinese Proverb

9
❖
Teaching Multiculturally around the Year

In Chapters 1 and 2 we explained why multicultural understanding must be integrated into your teaching throughout the school curriculum. This chapter provides information and examples to show how you can teach multiculturally around the school year. We need to take all the opportunities we can to make sure that our students learn about other cultures as well as their own. Developing multicultural understandings in students requires more instructional attention than just presenting a unit on African Americans in February or a unit on Mexico in September. Multicultural understandings can develop only when students are constantly involved in exploring and discussing the differences and similarities among people and the way that the presence of many cultures in this country affects the students' own identity.

This chapter is divided into three parts. The first section includes information on preparing a multicultural calendar for your class and suggestions for units of study based on the calendar. The second part is organized around a monthly calendar beginning with September (and including the summer months), so that you can incorporate information and discussions that build these multicultural understandings into your teaching plans as you move through the school year. The notes on each day and the suggested activities are intended to serve only as a base upon which your class can build its own Multicultural Calendar, personalizing it as appropriate with student birthdays and events of local significance. The third section of the chapter includes information on calendars and time in various cultures so that you can provide this background for the students as they work with the calendar. In addition, events such as religious holidays are presented here, as they follow a different measure of time.

After reading this chapter, you should be able to:
- Incorporate multicultural perspectives into all content areas of your teaching.
- Show students how many different racial, ethnic, and other groups have contributed significantly to the history and identity of this country.

- Build on student knowledge about different racial, ethnic, and other groups and the history of their treatment in this country.
- Stimulate student interest in and appreciation for the value of different perspectives.
- Encourage students' pride in and awareness of their own heritage.

PREPARING THE CALENDAR

Challenge students to decide on the most effective way to prepare the calendar for the class. Have them brainstorm ideas and alternatives for displaying the months. Students can work in teams to construct a display. While some students mount a frame for the month, others can be researching and collecting quotations, pictures, and other items to supply background information. The materials collected for each month can be assembled in a class notebook for students to consult throughout the year as they work on other projects.

The Multicultural Calendar should always be the result of the effort and interest of the whole class. Although you may want to keep the materials developed from year to year, each class will need to create its own version, reflecting students' own perspectives and discoveries.

Displaying the Calendar

You can reproduce the calendar directly on a large bulletin board. Divide the display space into squares or rectangles using thick, colored yarn or strips of colored construction paper as shown here:

Make the spaces as large as possible. (Challenge several students to solve this measurement problem!) Cut large block letters for the days of the week and the names of the months. Cut a set of numbers from 1 to 31. Both letters and numbers can be made easily if you use graph paper. Use different colors for variety.

Developing the Calendar

Older students can type or print the names and dates on slips of colored construction paper or unlined file cards to mount in the appropriate block for each month. Be sure that they check the current calendar so that the number 1 is placed under the correct day of the week; the rest of the dates will then fall in place accordingly. Add events that occur locally or dates of personal interest to your students. Include pictures and quotations wherever possible.

Quotations are of special interest for the multicultural calendar. Find as many as possible for people whose names appear for that month. Begin with the quotations presented throughout this book. Additional sources of quotations include the following:

Joseph Robert Conlin. *The Morrow Book of Quotations in American History.* Morrow, 1984.

Gorton Carruth and Eugene Ehrlich. *The Harper Book of American Quotations.* Harper, 1988.

Angela Partington. *The Oxford Dictionary of Quotations,* 4th ed. Oxford University Press, 1992.

Advanced readers will enjoy poring over these books, which they probably have not yet explored.

Pictures add a special dimension to the calendar. Let other teachers know that you are searching for multiethnic pictures for this purpose. Keep your eyes open as you look at the daily newspaper or magazines; it is surprising how many suitable pictures you will find. If you have a large bulletin board on which to display the calendar, you might place a ring of pictures around the calendar. Challenge students to identify the people and events pictured.

Encourage students to add to the calendar. As they read, they can take notes on information to include in the calendar. They can even do research in particular areas for this purpose as they search the newspapers, their textbooks, library reference books, and fiction. Students can become investigators as each one takes responsibility for exploring a specific topic.

Students can also decorate the bulletin board by adding appropriate designs, symbols, or illustrations. Snowflakes for the winter months, leaves for the fall, and flowers for the spring add interest and individuality to the calendar. Other popular seasonal motifs include pumpkins, kites, butterflies, and hearts. Avoid symbols associated with stereotypes, such as shamrocks or Indian headdresses.

Strategies for Using the Calendar

Sometimes a more extensive study is triggered by a single event or even a series of dates on the calendar. The following sample unit titles cross subject areas as well as periods of time and require students to use affective and cognitive abilities.

- Childhood in Other Countries
- Ethnic Groups in Our Community
- Native Americans Yesterday and Today

- Religions of the World
- Holidays and Celebrations
- Women in Sports

Almost any topic that you study in the elementary and middle school classroom will lend itself to a multicultural approach. Point to the contributions of various groups—ethnic, religious, young and old, male and female—as a strength of our society. Described here are representative strategies that will add stimulus to your curriculum.

Great Interviews

Students practice significant skills as they interview a personality from the past or present. Two or more students will need to develop this activity together as they plan the best questions and appropriate responses. Students can also interview several people, perhaps from different times. Encourage students to play these roles as realistically as possible.

In the Words of . . .

Students could pretend to be someone from the past who has suddenly arrived in your community. For example, how might George Washington Carver or Frederick Douglass react to the problems of today? What would they think of New York City? How would they react to being introduced to Sandra Day O'Connor, Clarence Thomas, or Ruth Bader Ginsburg? Students could then write a diary for the person from the past, which would include an account of such personal reactions. Naturally, students should be allowed to select the topics or situations that interest them.

Letters

Encourage students to develop their ideas in the form of letters. They can write letters to the local newspaper when there is an issue on which they have an opinion. They can also write letters to people from whom they would like information—members of Congress, authors of articles or books, leaders of groups or movements, and so on.

Collage

Have students choose one person or group represented on the multicultural calendar about which to develop a collage. They might choose César Chávez and his activities, black women in the United States, author Alex Haley, or Japanese Americans. Pictures, words, maps, poetry, small objects—almost anything can be included in this composite picture. Students can present their collage to the class, explaining what they learned.

Illustrated Lecture

Upper-grade students can prepare a formal lecture to present to the class. Students select a subject from the calendar to research. They prepare the lecture, including appropriate illustrations to make their presentation more effective, for example, pertinent newspaper clippings mounted on a poster, a time line displayed on the bulletin board, transparencies showing statistics, or a list of words that might be new to their listeners. If these lectures are presented over a period of months, the selection of topics will be larger and the class will not get tired of hearing "lectures." Students should concentrate on making the presentation informative and stimulating.

THE MONTHLY CALENDAR

In this section you will find ideas for celebrating multicultural understandings every day of the year. The activities presented in this section provide opportunities for students to ask and answer questions, to discuss fundamental issues such as race and identity, and to begin to develop the skills and information essential to live in a complex world.

   The calendar includes:

- Birthdays of historical and contemporary Americans from major ethnic groups
- Important dates in the history of different groups
- Religious and cultural holidays and festivals

   The individuals mentioned here are the exceptional few whose achievements have been recognized by history. We want to honor them without limiting ourselves to their example. Encourage students to come up with their own suggestions for notable entries. In every community there are people who have made significant contributions to the welfare of the group. One way to acknowledge and appreciate their efforts is to present them on the multicultural calendar.

   Following each month is a short list of suggested activities for incorporating the calendar information into your everyday teaching.

   To facilitate presentation, we have not prepared the calendar for one specific year. You will need to make slight adaptations to correct the dates accordingly. For each month, too, there are certain special weeks or holidays that occur on variable dates. July and August are included so that you can present this information during the rest of the school year.

   We begin with September and the opening of the school year.

September Activities

In this month we recognize the contributions of Americans of Latino heritage. What events occur during September that are particularly associated with Latinos? Local celebrations of Latino Heritage Month give teachers an excellent opportunity to collect ideas and materials to be used in classrooms throughout the year. In addition, Chapter 6 includes an extensive feature on Spanish-speaking Americans.

September 16.   Prepare the class for Mexican Independence Day by featuring Mexico in the classroom. Use all available materials to create an atmosphere of Mexico. Travel posters, clothes, and objects from Mexico will contribute a festive appearance. Display books about Mexico. Older students can write reports on different aspects of Mexico to put around the room. Use a map of Mexico as a focus for featuring facts about Mexico. Have students research information to construct a time line of significant events in Mexican history. Why is Mexican Independence Day important? What are other dates that are cele-

SEPTEMBER

1	2	3	4	5	6	7
Liliuokalani, 1838–1917, last sovereign of Hawaii		Prudence Crandall, 1803–?, first to admit Black girls to her school	Richard Wright, 1908–1960 Henry Hudson discovered Manhattan, 1609	Harriet E. Wilson published first novel by Black American		
8 International Literacy Day	**9** Sarah Douglass 1806–1882, Black teacher and abolitionist Mao Zedong died, 1976	**10** Alice Davis, 1852–1935, Seminole tribal leader	**11**	**12** Henry Hudson named Hudson River, 1609	**13** Maria Baldwin, 1856–1922, Black educator and civic leader	**14**
15 Porfirio Díaz, President of Mexico, 1830–1915	**16** Mexican Independence day, 1810 Mayflower Day (Pilgrims left England, 1620)	**17** Citizenship Day Constitution Day Steuben Day Constitution Week	**18** Quebec surrendered to English, 1759	**19** Lajos Kossuth, Hungarian patriot, 1802–1915	**20**	**21**
22 First French republic established, 1792 Martha Corey hung for a witch, Salem, 1692	**23**	**24** Francis Watkins Harper, 1825–1911, Black author and reformer	**25** Balboa discovered Pacific Ocean, 1513 Columbus began second trip to America, 1493	**26**	**27** American Indian Day	**28** Confucius birthday (National holiday, Taiwan)
29	**30**					

I am a red man. If the Great Spirit had desired me to be a white man he would have made me so in the first place. He put in your heart certain wishes and plans, in my heart he put other and different desires. Each man is good in his sight. It is not necessary for eagles to be crows.

–Sitting Bull

brated in Mexico? Make task cards such as the one shown below for individualized approaches.

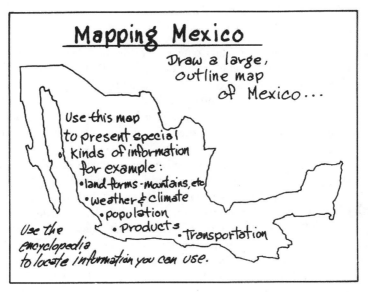

Sample Task Card

September 17.   The importance of citizenship is recognized on the anniversary of the signing of the Constitution (1787). Do students know what it means to be a citizen of a country? Ask them what a citizen can do that a noncitizen cannot.

While immigrants can live in this country legally for many years without being citizens, once they become citizens they gain the right to vote, to hold public office, and to serve on juries. This process is called naturalization. If possible, arrange for an immigrations lawyer to visit the class to explain how aliens (noncitizens) become citizens.

Find out what countries the people who want to become citizens come from.

September 27.   American Indian Day is an appropriate time to assess student knowledge of Native Americans. Ask students how many tribes they can name. Check your library for books about various Indian tribes. Look for books by Paul Goble, such as *Her Seven Brothers* (Bradbury, 1988), beautifully illustrated stories that cross grade levels.

In celebrating American Indian Day, take time to combat stereotyped images that students may have picked up about Native Americans from television or other sources. Instead of featuring generalized symbols such as the tepee or war bonnet, concentrate on showing how the tribes differ in clothing, housing, food, and other aspects of life. Have students discover what tribe(s) once lived in your area. How did they live? How do they live now?

October Activities

This month has been heralded as Native American Month, in recognition of the impact of Columbus's arrival on the "first Americans." See Chapter 4 for suggestions for a unit on

Native Americans to feature this month. Also watch for opportunities to extend student understanding through television programming and newspaper/magazine articles during this month.

October 2. The Pan American Conference recognized that the countries of the Americas have shared needs and should support one another. Display a map of North, Central, and South America, showing the names of the countries and their capitals. Illustrate it with the flags of the different countries. Discuss what these countries have in common. They were all colonized by Europeans, for example, although descendants of the original inhabitants still live in all the countries. Ask students what languages are spoken in these countries.

Are students aware of the major languages spoken in these countries? French and English are the official languages of Canada. Spanish is the language of much of Central and South America, along with Guaraní (a native Indian language) in Paraguay and Quechua (the language of the Incas) in Peru and Bolivia. Portuguese is the language of Brazil. In addition, many countries of North, South, and Central America contain great linguistic diversity, including the languages of indigenous populations and those of substantial immigrant groups. Do students know what languages are most common in the United States? (See pages 166–167) Which of these languages are represented in your classroom?

October 12. Columbus Day celebrates the landing of Columbus at San Salvador in 1492. Locate San Salvador on the map. Trace Columbus's journey from Spain to the New World. Where did he go after San Salvador? Why did he call the people he met "Indians"? People usually refer to Columbus as the discoverer of America. Is that true? After all, the Indians were there first. What was their world like when Columbus arrived? Read aloud *Morning Girl* by Michael Dorris, an eye-opening account of the life of a Taino sister and brother (natives of the Bahamas) in 1492. They had no reason to fear the visitors in the strange clothes and no way to foresee how their lives would be changed.

October 18, 27. Less than forty years elapsed between the first baptism of a Chinese in California (before California was part of the United States) and the performance of a Chinese opera. Have students read accounts of the Chinese immigration to this country in order to see how this rapid change occurred. How did the discovery of gold and the building of the railroad affect Chinese immigration?

The Chinese Exclusion Act, signed in 1882, meant that Chinese were forbidden to immigrate to the United States. Any Chinese already in the country were not allowed to become citizens. This law was not repealed until 1943.

Elicit from students statements about special characteristics of the early Chinese immigrants. Here are some possible examples:

- They were primarily single, young men.
- They maintained close ties with their family back in China.
- They saved their money and sent it home.

OCTOBER

1	2	3	4	5	6	7
Mohandas K. Gandhi, 1869–1948; First Pan American Conference—Washington, D.C., 1889				Tecumseh (Shawnee) died, 1813	Faith Ringgold, 1930–; Fannie Lou Hammer 1917–1977, Black Civil Rights leader	Imanu Amiri Baraka (LeRoi Jones), 1934–; Marian Anderson, first Black to sing at Metropolitan Opera, 1954
8	**9** Leif Erikson Day; Mary Shadd Cary, 1823–1893, Black teacher, journalist, lawyer	**10** Shawnees defeated in Battle of Point Pleasant (WV), 1774, ends Lord Dunmore's War; Chinese Revolution began, 1911	**11** Eleanor Roosevelt, 1884–1962; Pulaski Memorial Day	**12** Columbus lands at San Salvador, 1492; Día de la Raza (Latin America)	**13**	**14** Eamon de Valera, Irish president, 1882–1975; William Penn, 1644–1718
15 3rd Week, Black Poetry Week; World Poetry Day	**16** Sarah Winnemucca died, 1891, Paiute Indian leader; Alaska Day Festival	**17** Albert Einstein came to U.S., 1933	**18** First Chinese opera performed in U.S.—San Francisco, 1852; Helen Hunt Jackson, 1831–1885, author of *Ramona*	**19**	**20**	**21** UN founded in San Francisco, 1945; Alfred Nobel, 1833–1896
22 4th Week, United Nations Week	**23** Hungarian Freedom Day, 1956; Pélé, Brazilian Soccer star, born, 1940	**24** United Nations Day	**25**	**26** Mahalia Jackson, 1911–1972	**27** Ah Nam, first Chinese in California, baptized, 1815	**28**
29	**30**	**31** Black Hawk died, 1838, Sauk Indian leader; Roberta Lawson, 1878–1940, Delaware civic leader; National UNICEF Day				

There is a sufficiency in the world for man's need but not for man's greed.
—*Mohandas Gandhi*

Discuss the consequences of these facts. Include some of the following:

- Families in San Francisco's Chinatown now occupy single rooms that were built as dormitories for the original bachelor immigrants.
- Many Chinese who live in all-Chinese ghettos (Chinatowns) do not speak English.

October 31—Halloween around the World. Popular Halloween customs draw on many of the world's cultures. In Egypt they set out oil lamps and delicacies in honor of Osiris, the god of the dead. The Romans established November 1 and 2 for similar rituals. October 31, All Hallows Eve, became a Christian holiday in 1006. In the British Isles, Samhain (the Celtic festival of the dead) meant candles lit in carved turnips. For the autumn festival of Bon, the Japanese dressed up in disguise and hung paper lanterns to guide the spirits of their ancestors home. In Mexico, El día de los muertos (the Day of the Dead) is celebrated with special sweets to feed the spirits and with masks and skeletons to scare them away.

November Activities

November 5.

> I have been discriminated against far more because I am a female than because I am black.
> —*Shirley Chisholm*

Here is a provocative quote for students to discuss. Why would her statement be true? Shirley Chisholm was the first black woman elected to the House of Representatives. Read portions from her autobiography, *Unbossed and Unbought* (Houghton Mifflin, 1970) showing her struggles to overcome racial and sexual discrimination.

Shirley Chisholm was elected in 1968. Now there are more Blacks, men and women, in the House of Representatives. Do students think that racial prejudice still affects whether people are elected to Congress? If not, why are there not *more* Blacks in Congress (or women and members of other ethnic minorities)?

November 20. The Incas were one of the major indigenous civilizations encountered by the first Spanish explorers of the Americas. Have students investigate the Incas and their culture. The Spaniards were amazed at the achievements of the Incas. How were the Incas more advanced than the Spaniards? How did the Spanish treat the Incas, and what happened to them? Have students make a model of the mysterious Inca city, Macchu Picchu. In what South American country are the ruins of Inca culture found?

November 26. In 1851, Sojourner Truth said:

> The man over there says women need to be helped into carriages and lifted over ditches, and to have the best place everywhere. Nobody ever helps me into carriages or over puddles or gives me the best place . . . ain't I a woman? Look at my arm! I have ploughed and planted and gathered into barns and no man could head me—ain't I a woman? I could work as much and eat as much as a man—when I could get it—and bear the lash as well! And ain't I a woman? I have born 13 children and seen most of 'em sold into slavery, and when I cried out with my mother's grief, none but Jesus heard me . . . and ain't I a woman?

NOVEMBER

1 Sholem Asch, 1880–1957	**2** Haile Selassie crowned Emperor of Ethiopia, 1930 Father Junípero Serra, Spanish explorer, 1713–1784	**3**	**4**	**5** Shirley Chisholm, first black woman elected to House of Representatives (NY), 1968 Guy Fawkes Day (Canada)	**6**	**7** William Harrison defeated the Shawnee Prophet at Tippecanoe (IN), 1811 Marie Curie, 1867–1934
8 Edward Brooke, first black U.S. senator in 85 years, elected (MA), 1966	**9** W. C. Handy, 1873–1958 Benjamin Banneker, 1731–1806	**10** Martin Luther, 1483–1546	**11** Remembrance Day (Canada)	**12** Dr. Sun Yat-sen, 1866–1925	**13**	**14** Freedom for Philippines, 1935 Jawaharlal Nehru, 1889–1964
15	**16** Chinua Achebe, 1930– Brother and Sister Day (India, Nepal)	**17** Opening of Suez Canal, 1869	**18** First Thanksgiving, Pilgrims and Massasoit, chief of Wampanoags, 1777	**19** Indira Gandhi, 1917–1984	**20** Atahualpa, Inca of Peru, filled room with gold for Pizarro, 1532	**21**
22	**23**	**24**	**25** St. Catherine's Day (Canada)	**26** Sojourner Truth died, 1883	**27**	**28**
29	**30** Shirley Chisholm, 1924–					

To understand is hard. Once one understands, action is easy.
—*Sun Yat-sen*

Who was Sojourner Truth? Investigate her life with the class. Ask students why we do not know her birthdate, when we know the birthdates of the white women she worked with. Look up information on the life of women and of Blacks at that time. Why did Sojourner Truth fight for the women's movement and women's right to vote? What might she say to women today? A biography for young students is *Sojourner Truth, Fearless Crusader* by Helen Stone Peterson.

Older students will appreciate *Sojourner Truth: Ain't I a Woman* by the award-winning African American author, Patricia McKissack.

Thanksgiving: A Celebration of Arrival. Thanksgiving, for many years a popular holiday to celebrate in schools, has become controversial as people become more aware of the Native American perspective on the Pilgrims' arrival. Instead of conventional classroom activities such as making turkeys and Pilgrims, consider this an appropriate time to celebrate the diversity of this country. Because we all, even Native Americans, came from some other place, make Thanksgiving a holiday of arrival, a day to honor the many immigrants to this country. How and why did the students, their parents, or their ancestors come to this country? By choice, by force (African Americans as slaves), or by migration (Native Americans)? To seek better jobs, to flee religious or political persecution, for educational opportunities? How has each group of newcomers been treated by the previous inhabitants of this country?

Read *Coming to America,* by Eve Bunting, a book for primary-grade children about a family forced out of their island country by the military and subjected to many hardships as they travel by boat to reach the United States and freedom. When they arrive, they find that everyone is celebrating Thanksgiving and they join in gratefully. This book suggests the conditions that have driven many to leave their own countries, and children will be able to sympathize with the struggles of this immigrant family. As Eve Bunting notes, whether you arrive by boat or by airplane, you share the pain of leaving the familiar and the challenge of making a home in the new land.

Molly's Pilgrim by Barbara Cohen, a book for intermediate-level students, teaches everyone a lesson about diversity. A simple Thanksgiving assignment to dress a doll like a Pilgrim has unexpected consequences. Molly's mother doesn't know about the Pilgrims, but she does understand why people come to the United States for religious freedom and she dresses the doll to represent herself, a Russian Jewish immigrant woman. At first, Molly is embarrassed in front of her classmates because her doll looks "different." But the teacher explains how Molly's "Pilgrim" fits the meaning of Thanksgiving.

December Activities

Many religions and cultures celebrate the midwinter solstice (December 21, the shortest day of the year). Involve students in discovering the origins and meaning of many common customs associated with this time of year. What are some of the traditions in your region? Do students know how children celebrate in other countries? What countries gave us the following: the piñata, the Christmas tree, the Yule log?

Christmas, Hanukkah, and now Kwanzaa are major celebrations and winter holy days. Share the stories of Christmas, the Festival of Lights, and Kwanzaa with all students so that everyone can participate in the special spirit of the holidays, no matter what tradi-

DECEMBER

1	2	3	4	5	6	7
Rosa Parks arrested, 1955	Monroe Doctrine, 1823 Pan American Health Day	Myrtilla Miner opened first Colored Girls School, Washington D.C., 1851	Phillis Wheatley died, 1784, Black poet	Feast of St. Nicholas Columbus discovered Haiti, 1492		Bombing of Pearl Harbor by Japanese, 1941
8	**9**	**10**	**11**	**12**	**13**	**14**
2nd Week, Human Rights Week Diego Rivera, 1886–1957		U.S. acquired Cuba, Guam, Puerto Rico, Philippines, 1898; Human Rights Day; Universal Declaration of Human Rights ratified, 1948	Aleksandr Solzhenitsyn, 1918– UNICEF established, 1946		Yehudi Menuhin makes NY debut, 1927	
15	**16**	**17**	**18**	**19**	**20**	**21**
Bill of Rights day, Bill of Rights ratified, 1791 Sitting Bull killed, 1890		Maria Stewart died, 1879, Black teacher and lecturer	Ratification of 13th Amendment ended slavery, 1865	Bernice Pauahi Bishop, 1831–1884, Hawaiian leader	Cherokees forced off their land in Georgia because of gold strike, 1835 Sacajawea died, 1812, Shoshoni interpreter	María Cadilla de Martinez, 1886–, early Puerto Rican feminist Pilgrims landed at Plymouth (MA), 1620
22	**23**	**24**	**25**	**26**	**27**	**28**
Teresa Carreño, 1853–1917, Venezuelan American concert pianist	First Chinese theater built, San Francisco, 1852 Madame C. J. Walker, 1867–1919, Black businesswoman		Christmas Day	Mao Zedong, 1893–1976		
29	**30**	**31**				
	Pocahontas rescued Captain John Smith, 1607 Gadsden Purchase signed with Mexico, 1853	Ellis Island, New York Harbor, became immigrant receiving station				

Congress shall make no law respecting an establishment of religion, . . . or abridging the freedom of speech, or of the press . . .
Amendment 1, U.S. Bill of Rights

tions are practiced at home. No one should feel left out. Read, for example, *Latkes and Applesauce: A Hannukkah Story,* by Fran Manushkin, illustrated by Robin Spowart (Scholastic, 1990). There are no traditional holiday latkes (potato pancakes) or applesauce because of the snow, and the children wonder if they will be able to have Hanukkah. *The Polar Express* by Chris Van Allsburg is an engaging story that captures the wonder and magic of Santa Claus for young children. *Imani's Gift at Kwanzaa*, written by Denise Burden-Patmon and illustrated by Floyd Cooper (Simon and Schuster, 1992), explains the customs of Kwanzaa (December 26) as Imani learns to share with others.

December 10.   Human Rights Day celebrates the proclamation of the Universal Declaration of Human Rights by the United Nations (1948). This day provides an opportunity for students to discuss what human rights are. Ask each one to complete this sentence: Every human being has the right to . . .

December 15.   Related to human rights is the Bill of Rights, the first ten amendments to the U.S. Constitution. A group of students can present the Bill of Rights as part of a special program. They can prepare it as a reader's theater presentation.

UNITED STATES BILL OF RIGHTS

Amendment 1

Congress shall make no law respecting an establishment of religion, or prohibiting the free exercise thereof; or abridging the freedom of speech, or of the press; or the right of the people peaceably to assemble, and to petition the government for a redress of grievances.

Amendment 2

A well-regulated militia being necessary to the security of a free State, the right of the people to keep and bear arms shall not be infringed.

Amendment 3

No soldier shall, in time of peace, be quartered in any house without the consent of the owner; nor in time of war but in a manner to be prescribed by law.

Amendment 4

The right of the people to be secure in their prisons, houses, papers and effects, against unreasonable searches and seizures, shall not be violated, and no warrants shall issue but upon probable cause, supported by oath or affirmation, and particularly described the place to be searched, and the persons or things to be seized.

Amendment 5

No person shall be held to answer for a capital or otherwise infamous crime, unless on a presentment or indictment of a grand jury, except in cases arising in the land or naval forces, or in the militia, when in actual service in time of war or public danger; nor shall any person be subject for the same offense to be twice put in jeopardy of life or limb; nor shall be compelled in any criminal case to be witness against himself, nor be deprived of life, liberty, or property, without due process of law; nor shall private property be taken for public use, without just compensation.

Amendment 6

In all criminal prosecutions the accused shall enjoy the right to a speedy and public trial, by an impartial jury of the State and district wherein the crime shall have been committed, which district shall have been previously ascertained by law, and to be informed of the nature and cause of the accusation; to be confronted with the witnesses against him; to have compulsory process for obtaining witnesses in his favor, and to have the assistance of counsel for his defense.

Amendment 7

In suits at common law, where the value in controversy shall exceed twenty dollars, the right of trial by jury shall be preserved, and no fact tried by a jury shall be otherwise reexamined in any court of the United States than according to the rules of the common law.

Amendment 8

Excessive bail shall not be required, nor excessive fines imposed, nor cruel and unusual punishments inflicted.

Amendment 9

The enumeration in the Constitution of certain rights shall not be construed to deny or disparage others retained by the people.

Amendment 10

The powers not delegated to the United States by the Constitution, nor prohibited by it to the States, are reserved to the States respectively, or to the people.

December 18.

Thirteenth Amendment: Neither slavery nor involuntary servitude, except as a punishment for crime whereof the party shall have been duly convicted, shall exist within the United States, or any place subject to their jurisdiction.

The ratification of the Thirteenth Amendment meant the official end of slavery. Begin reading a book such as *The Slave Dancer* by Paula Fox (Bradbury, 1973), which won the Newbery Award in 1974, an excellent historical novel for grades 5–9.

Mr. Lincoln had told our race we were free, but mentally we were still enslaved.
—*Mary McLeod Bethune*

Discuss this quote. What does *mentally enslaved* mean? Is it possible to change people's thinking by passing a law? What factors made it difficult to change? (education, jobs)

December 25. Point out that many words associated with Christmas come from other languages, for example:

- *Noel,* French (from Latin *natalis*)
- *Carol,* Greek *choros* (dance) and *arelos* (flute)
- *Crèche,* French (crib)
- *Angel,* Greek *angellos* (messenger)
- *Poinsettia,* red flower native to Mexico, brought to United States by Joel Poinsett, minister to Mexico

- *Yule,* Norse *jol* (feast)
- *Xmas,* Greek letter chi (χ) stands for Christ

December 26.   Kwanzaa is a festival that is rapidly spreading among African Americans as a way to honor their heritage. Begun in 1966 in Los Angeles, Kwanzaa, which is Swahili for "first fruits of the harvest," is a nonreligious celebration of Black culture, community, and family that lasts from December 26 to January 1. Each day participants light a candle and discuss one of the seven principles to live by all year: Umoja (unity), Kujichagulia (self-determination), Ujima (collective work and responsibility), Ujamma (cooperative economics), Nia (purpose), Kuumba (creativity), and Imani (faith).

Merry Christmas around the World

Joyeux Noel — France, Belgium, Switzerland
Kala Hrystoughena — Greece
Glaedelig Jul — Norway
Fröhliche Weihnachten — Germany, Austria
Buon Natale — Italy
Feliz Navidad — Spain, Mexico
God Jul — Sweden
Merry Christenmass — Scotland
Um Feliz Natal — Portugal
Nodlaig Mhaith Dhuit — Ireland
Boldog Karacsony Unnep — Hungary
Wesolych Swiat — Poland
Kung ho shen tan — Chinese
Vrolyk Kerstmis — Holland
S Rozhdestvom Christovom — Russia
Happy Christmas — England

January Activities

The name of this month comes from the Roman god Janus, who had two faces and looked back into the past and forward into the future. It is very appropriate, therefore, to take time at the beginning of the year to consider where we have been and where we are going. Talk with the class about the history of this country. Have them list ways in which the country has changed: inventions, attitudes, and people. Then ask them to face forward and think

JANUARY

1	2	3	4	5	6	7
Emancipation Proclamation, 1863 Commonwealth of Australia established, 1901	Emma, 1836–1885, Queen of Hawaii	Alaska admitted to Union, 1959 (49th state)	Louis Braille, 1809–1852 Selena Sloan Butler, 1872, founded first Black PTA in country	George Washington Carver Day, 1864–1943 Sissieretta Jones, 1869–1933, Black singer	Celebration of King's Day—Pueblo Dances Lucy Laney, school for Negro children, 1886	Harlem Globetrotters played first game (Illinois), 1927
8 World Literacy Day	**9** Joan Baez, 1941–	**10** League of Nations founded, 1920, Geneva	**11** Eugenio de Hostos, 1839–1903, Puerto Rican patriot	**12** Adah Thoms, 1863–1943, Black nursing leader	**13** Charlotte Ray, 1850–1911, first Black woman lawyer First Black Cabinet member, Robert Weaver, becomes Secretary of HUD, 1966	**14** Carlos Romulo, Philippine leader, 1901–? Albert Schweitzer, 1875–1965
15 Martin Luther King, Jr., 1929–1968, Black minister and civil rights leader Human Relations Day	**16**	**17**	**18**	**19**	**20**	**21** Fanny Jackson-Coppin died, 1913, Black educator Eliza Snow (Smith), 1804–1887, "Mother" of Mormonism"
22 Sam Cooke, 1932–1964	**23** 24th Amendment barred poll tax in federal elections, 1964 Amanda Smith, 1837–1915, Black evangelist	**24** Eva del Vakis Bowles, 1875–1943, Black youth group leader	**25** Florence Mills, 1895–1927, Black singer and dancer	**26** Republic of India established, 1950	**27** Vietnam War ended, 1973	**28** Louis Brandeis, first appointment of American Jew for U.S. Supreme Court, 1916
29	**30** Mohandas Gandhi (India) assassinated, 1948	**31** Jackie Robinson, 1919–1972				

It may be true that the law cannot make a man love me, but it can keep him from lynching me, and I think that's pretty important . . .

—*Martin Luther King, Jr.*

about what might change in the future. What would they like to see happen? Will people be any different? Use the excitement of speculating about the future to show the importance of finding the roots of the future in the past.

The Chinese New Year and Tet, the Vietnamese celebration of the lunar New Year, occur in January or February, depending on the lunar calendar. Share a book with your students to introduce this holiday, popular in the Asian community. Discuss the holiday customs to combat stereotypes students may have about unfamiliar celebrations. *Chinese New Year* by Tricia Brown (Holt, 1987), set in San Francisco, and *Lion Dancer: Ernie Wan's Chinese New Year* by Kate Waters and Madeline Slovenz-Low (Scholastic, 1990), set in New York, both feature photographs of the preparations and the festivities.

January 1.   Australia has a special fascination because of its antipodean location. Have students discover as much as possible about this island continent in a class search that begins in the library. Teach them a song from Australia such as "Waltzing Matilda." Discuss the words and phrases presented in this song. Would you call this English? Why might people speak English differently in different countries?

Waltzing Matilda

Once a jolly swagman camped by a billabong
Under the shade of a coolibah tree,
And he sang as he watched and waited till
his billy boiled,
"You'll come a-waltzing Matilda with me!"

Chorus:
Waltzing Matilda, Waltzing Matilda,
You'll come a-waltzing Matilda with me!
And he sang as he watched and waited until his billy boiled,
"You'll come a-waltzing Matilda with me!

Down came a jumbuck to drink at the billabong,
Up jumped the swagman and grabbed him with glee,
And he sang as he stowed that jumbuck in his tucker bag,
(Chorus)

> Up rode the squatter, mounted on his thorough-bred,
> Down came the troopers, one, two, three,
> "Where's that jolly jumbuck you've got in your tucker bag?"
> (Chorus)
>
> Up jumped the swagman, sprang into the billabong,
> "You'll never catch me alive," said he,
> And his ghost may be heard as you pass by that billabong.
> (Chorus)

January 15.   Discuss with students the quotation by Martin Luther King, Jr., on page 293. What do they think was the context of this statement? Martin Luther King, Jr., was a leader in the civil rights movement. What point of view was he arguing for and what was he arguing against? What does civil rights mean?

Happy Birthday, Dr. King, written by Kathryn Jones and illustrated by Floyd Cooper (Simon and Schuster, 1994), features a boy puzzled by a school assignment to celebrate King's birthday. But after talking with his family, he learns about the civil rights movement and King's achievements.

Ask students what they would do if they wanted to change someone's behavior or opinion. What methods work best, and when? Do any laws protect them from other people? What about classroom rules—do they protect anyone? Discuss problems the students might have with a bully or a liar. Have them write possible strategies to resolve the conflict.

In 1964, Martin Luther King, Jr., received the Nobel Peace Prize, an international award in recognition of his work for human relations. Why would people in other countries think that his work was important? Is Martin Luther King, Jr., a hero just for African Americans, or is he an inspiration for other people as well? Read *Martin Luther King: The Peaceful Warrior* by Edward Clayton (Archway, 1989) to find out.

January 27.   The Vietnam War is a powerful memory for many people today, but what do students know about Vietnam?

Explore the following books:

Nguyen Ngoc Bich (translated by) with Burton Raffel and W. S. Merwin. *A Thousand Years of Vietnamese Poetry.* Knopf, 1975.

David D. Cooke. *Vietnam: The Country, the People.* Norton, 1968.

Betty Jean Lifton and Thomas Fox. *Children of Vietnam.* Atheneum, 1972.

Huynh Quang Nhuong. *The Land I Lost: Adventures of a Boy in Vietnam.* Harper, 1982.

Jon Nielsen with Kay Nielsen. *Artist in South Vietnam.* Messner, 1969.

January 30.   Although Gandhi lived in another country, students should know something about his life and his ideas because he influenced so many people in the United States. Feature several quotations from Gandhi:

Ahimsa ("harmlessness" or nonviolence) means the largest love. It is the supreme law. By it alone can mankind be saved. He who believes in nonviolence believes in a living God.

All humanity is one undivided and indivisible family, and each one of us is responsible for the misdeeds of all the others. I cannot detach myself from the wickedest soul.

All amassing of wealth or hoarding of wealth above and beyond one's legitimate needs is theft. There would be no occasion for theft and no thieves if there were wise regulations of wealth, and social justice.

My nationalism is intense internationalism. I am sick of the strife between nations or religions.

Discuss his ideas. Gandhi is credited with forcing the British to give India its independence. How have his methods of nonviolence (demonstrations) and passive resistance (sit-ins and hunger strikes) been translated to this country? How effective have they been?

Gandhi and his ideas were very powerful, yet he led a simple life. Students can read a biography such as *Mohandas Gandhi* by Glenn Alan Cheney (Watts, 1983).

Read selections from an excellent book written for adults in which people who knew Gandhi describe his life: *Mahatma Gandhi and His Apostles* by Ved Mehta (Viking, 1977).

February Activities

February is African American History Month so you can look forward to programs, articles, speeches, and discussions about the history and current status of Black Americans, Formerly Black History Week, this celebration is sponsored by the Association for the Study of Negro Life and History, founded by historian Carter G. Woodson. The week was first observed in 1926 and it included the birthdays of Abraham Lincoln (12) and Frederick Douglass (14). However, the whole month is rich in the birthdays of exceptional Black Americans. Request from the association a publication list of materials to be used at this time: 1538 Ninth St., NW, Washington, DC 20001.

Use an activity such as Celebrating Black Americans found on page 298. Feature some of the following books about the achievements of Black Americans:

Virginia Hamilton. *W. E. B. Du Bois; a Biography.* Crowell, 1972.

Robert Hayden. *Eight Black American Inventors.* Addison-Wesley, 1972.

Patricia McKissack and Frederick McKissack. *Frederick Douglass.* Children's, 1987.

See Chapter 5 for more suggested activities and resources about African Americans.

A special activity for this month would be to learn James Weldon Johnson's song "Lift Every Voice and Sing," also known as the Negro National Anthem. The song is featured in the picture book *Lift Every Voice and Sing,* written by James Weldon Johnson and illustrated by Elizabeth Catlett (Walker, 1993). Students will be interested in learning more about the man who wrote this song. Offer them the biography *James Weldon Johnson* by Harold Felton (Dodd, 1971), which also includes the song.

February 1. Feature the poetry of Langston Hughes. An attractive collection is *Don't You Turn Back* compiled by Lee Bennet Hopkins (Knopf, 1969). Langston Hughes's poetry lends itself to graphic presentation. Have students create posters featuring a selection from a poem. Encourage them to use calligraphy and art on the poster in order to celebrate the

FEBRUARY

1	2	3	4	5	6	7
Langston Hughes, 1902–1967 National Freedom Day Treaty of Guadalupe Hidalgo, 1848	Candlemas Day		Philippine Rebellion against U.S. began, 1899	Constitution Day (Mexico)	Senate ratified treaty ending Spanish-American War, 1899	
8	**9**	**10**	**11**	**12**	**13**	**14**
		Leontyne Price, 1927– End of French and Indian War, 1763		Fannie Williams, 1855–1944, Black lecturer, civic leader Thaddeus Kosciusko, Polish patriot, 1746–1817 Abraham Lincoln, 1809–1865 Chinese Republic, 1912		Frederick Douglass, 1817–1895 Valentine's Day
15	**16**	**17**	**18**	**19**	**20**	**21**
Galileo Galilei, 1564–1642 Susan B. Anthony, 1820–1906		Marian Anderson, 1902–1993 Chaim Potok, 1929–	Toni Morrison, 1931–	Nicolaus Copernicus 1473–1543		Malcolm X Day, 1925–1965 Barbara Jordan 1931–
22	**23**	**24**	**25**	**26**	**27**	**28**
Gertrude Bonnin, 1876–1938, Sioux author and reformer Ishmael Reed, 1938–	W.E.B. Du Bois, 1868–1963		First Black in Congress, Hiram Revels (Ms.), 1870 José de San Martín (the great liberator), 1778–1850		Marian Anderson, 1902–1993	
29	**30**					
Emmeline Wells, 1828–1921, Mormon leader and feminist Mother Ann Lee, 1736–1784, Founder of the Shakers						

If a race has no history, if it has no worthwhile tradition, it becomes a negligible factor in the thoughts of the world and it stands in danger of being exterminated.

—*Carter G. Woodson*

Celebrating Black Americans

Fill in the last names of famous Black Americans to solve this puzzle. The first name is given as a clue.

_ _ _ _ N _ _ _ _   Duke _____

_ _ _ _ _ E   Ralph _____

_ _ _ _ _ _ _ G _ _ _   Booker T. _____

_ _ _ _ R _ _ _   Marian _____

_ _ O _ _ _ _   Carter G. _____

_ _ _ H _ _ _   Mary McLeod _____

_ _ I _ _   Bessie _____

_ _ _ _ _ _ S _ _ _   Dizzy _____

_ _ _ T _ _ _   Sidney _____

_ _ _ _ _ O _ _   Shirley _____

_ _ R _ _   Lena _____

_ _ Y _   Willie _____

_ _ _ _ W _ _   James A. _____

_ _ _ _ E _   Nat _____

_ _ _ _ E _   Langston _____

K _ _ _   Martin Luther _____ , Jr.

1) Find out why each person is famous.
2) List 5 other Black Americans who are known in their fields.

Source: Reading Ideas, February 1977.

Answers to Celebrating Black Americans: Ellington, Bunche, Washington, Anderson, Woodson, Bethune, Smith, Gillespie, Poitier, Chisholm, Horne, Mays, Baldwin, Turner, Hughes, King.

poem. Begin reading his biography on this date; for example: *Langston Hughes, Poet of His People* by Elizabeth Myers (Garrard, 1970). Play the recording *Langston Hughes Reads and Talks about His Poems* for students (Spoken Arts).

February 5. Celebrate Mexico's Constitution Day. Create a learning center on Mexico. (Let students contribute ideas.) Explore your library for nonfiction and fiction about Mexico as well as stories about Mexican Americans or Chicanos, for example, *Viva Chicano* by Frank Bonham (Dutton, 1970) and *Graciela: A Mexican-American Child Tells Her Story* by Joe Molnar (Watts, 1972).

Develop task cards that focus on Mexico for reading in the content areas.

February 12. Have students prepare a bulletin board display about Abraham Lincoln, a president who has become a folk hero. He symbolizes the poor boy who rose to leadership, the president who freed the slaves. Feature quotations by Lincoln around his picture, for instance:

> The ballot is stronger than the bullet.

> Any people anywhere, being inclined and having the power, have the right to rise up and shake off the existing government, and form a new one that suits them better. This is the most valuable, a most sacred right—a right which we hope and believe is to liberate the world.

> A house divided against itself cannot stand. I believe this government cannot endure, permanently half *slave* and half *free*.

> As I would not be a *slave,* so I would not be a *master.* This expresses my idea of democracy. Whatever differs from this, to the extent of the difference, is no democracy.

Have students prepare "The Gettysburg Address" for choric speaking. Plan a short program using this address, quotations, and poetry about Lincoln. One or two students might tell a story about Abe.

February 22. *Brotherhood Week.* Celebrated during the week that includes George Washington's birthday (22), this week was initiated by Father McNenamin of Denver, Colorado, in 1929. It is sponsored by the National Conference of Christians and Jews, 43 W. 57th St., New York, NY 10019. Feature books about promoters of peace and understanding such as Martin Luther King, Jr., or Eleanor Roosevelt.

Explore different ways to present quotations in your classroom. Students might use quotations related to the topic of brotherhood to form a heart (see page 300). Other topics will suggest appropriate forms, such as the silhouette of Washington or Lincoln made of quotations related to freedom or patriotism, or a cornucopia formed from quotations related to thankfulness.

Quotations for Brotherhood Week

We have committed the Golden Rule to memory; let us now commit it to life.
  —*Edwin Markham*

No man is an Island, entire of itself.
  —*John Donne*

Whoever seeks to set one race against another seeks to enslave all races.
  —*Franklin D. Roosevelt*

If our brothers are oppressed, then we are oppressed. If they hunger, we hunger. If their freedom is taken away, our freedom is not secure.
—*Stephen Vincent Benet*

The world is my country;
All mankind are my brethren.
—*Thomas Paine*

No one can make you feel inferior without your consent.
—*Eleanor Roosevelt*

March Activities

Women's history is celebrated this month, in honor of March 8, International Women's Day. As you collect materials for use in the classroom this month and throughout the year, aim for a diverse perspective: women of the past and women of today, women who represent different ethnic and other groups, stories of both women and men who have actively combated stereotypes about both sexes. The National Women's History Project (7738 Bell Road, Windsor, CA 95492-8518) offers books, posters, and other resources for the classroom. See Chapter 3 for activities and information to feature this month.

March 8. Celebrate the achievements of American women. Here is an opportunity to point out the achievements of women of all races and creeds. Make a point of including lesser-known persons. An excellent resource is *Notable American Women* by Edward T. James, ed. (Belknap Press, 1974), 3 volumes.

Discuss the role of women today. What kinds of work do women do? Talk about women the students know. Whom do they admire? Bring in women who have unusual jobs to talk to students. Older students can write letters to the local newspaper, describing women they admire and explaining why.

March 9. Our country is named after Amerigo Vespucci. What other countries does *America* refer to? North, Central, and South America are all called the *Americas*. Who is an American? People living in Mexico call U.S. citizens "norteamericanos."

The name of a country is important. Ask students if they can suggest reasons why this country is called "The United States of America." What other names might have been proposed at different times? (Columbia, New India) Invite students to propose a new name for this country and to justify their choice.

March 10. Harriet Tubman led an active and dangerous life. Although she could not read or write, she was able to escape slavery and flee to the North where she was free. Instead of remaining safe in the North, she returned to slave holding territory many times to guide other slaves to freedom. Read about her exploits and have students choose several crucial events to dramatize. They can prepare a play by writing dialogue and narration and using a few props. This play can be presented for other classes to watch. A good biography of Harriet Tubman was written by Ann Petry.

March 17. Although highly stereotyped, St. Patrick's Day offers an opportunity to recognize Irish Americans and the many Irish customs with which we are familiar. What Irish folk beliefs can students name? Students can look up the origins and real versions of these symbols and beliefs and report their finding to the class.

Read aloud Irish folktales from such collections as the following:

Padraic Colum. *The King of Ireland's Son*. McGraw-Hill, 1966.

Eileen O'Favlain (retold by). *Irish Sagas and Folktales*. Walck, 1954.

MARCH

1	2	3	4	5	6	7
Ralph Ellison, 1914–1994 Black author Peace Corps est., 1961 St. David's Day (Wales)	Texas declares independence from Mexico, 1836	Doll Festival (Japan)	Knute Rockne, 1888–1931		Fall of the Alamo, 1836	Tomáš Masaryk (Czech patriot), 1850–1937
8	**9**	**10**	**11**	**12**	**13**	**14**
Week of March 8, National Women's History Week International Women's Day	Amerigo Vespucci, 1451–1512, Italian navigator	Harriet Tubman's death, 1913 Hallie Q. Brown, 1850–1949, Black teacher and women's leader		Gabriele d'Annunzio, 1863–1938		Albert Einstein, 1879–1955
15	**16**	**17**	**18**	**19**	**20**	**21**
		St. Patrick's Day	Hawaii admitted to Union, 1959 (50th state)	St. Joseph's Day (Italy)	Harriet Beecher Stowe's *Uncle Tom's Cabin* published, 1852 Holocaust Remembrance Day	Benito Juárez, Mexican leader, 1806–1872 Namibia became independent, 1990
22	**23**	**24**	**25**	**26**	**27**	**28**
Emancipation Day (Puerto Rico)			Seward's Day (Alaska)	Kuhio Day (Hawaii)	Marconi sends first international wireless message, 1899	
29	**30**	**31**				
	15th Amendment Right to Vote passed, 1870 U.S. purchased Alaska from Russia, 1867	First treaty U.S.–Japan, 1854 U.S. took possession of Virgin Islands from Denmark, 1917 Octavio Paz, 1914– Elizabeth Greenfield died, 1876, Black singer				

All novels are about certain minorities: the individual is a minority.
—*Ralph Ellison*

Virginia Haviland (retold by). *Favorite Fairy Tales Told in Ireland*. Little, Brown, 1961.

Have students prepare stories for dramatization, assigning parts and rewriting the dialogue.

March 22.   Have students research the history of Puerto Rico's relationship to the United States and the significance of this Emancipation Day. Read stories aloud. A story for younger children about Puerto Ricans in the United States is *Friday Night Is Papa Night* by Ruth Sonneborn (Viking, 1970). A book for older students is *Magdalena* by Louisa Shotwell (Viking, 1971).

April Activities

April 9, 12.   Someone once said that the Civil War is the longest war in history because it began in 1861 and is still going on today. Discuss this with students. Do they agree? What does it mean to say the war is still going on? What kind of "war" is it? Are people being killed?

> You can't hold a man down without staying down with him.
> —*Booker T. Washington*

Discuss this quotation with students. Who is being held down? How can oppressing someone hurt the oppressor?

April 20.   This day for remembering the Holocaust has been celebrated since 1980. The opening of the Holocaust Museum in Washington, D.C., in 1993 has added to public awareness of the immensity of the tragedy in which innocent men, women, and children were killed simply because they were Jewish. To share Jewish life and culture with students, read selections from *My Grandmother's Stories: A Collection of Jewish Folk Tales* by Adele Geras (illustrated by Jael Jordan, Knopf, 1990).

April 7, 15, 25, 26. Black Blues.   Four important female blues singers were born this month: Ma Rainey, one of the first blues performers; Bessie Smith, a major influence on all subsequent blues singers; Billie Holiday, whose distinctive voice and tragic life exemplified the blues; and Ella Fitzgerald, a contemporary singer with a repertoire that includes the blues. The blues is an important part of American history, particularly of African American history.

Ask students what the term *the blues* means to them. Discuss the following quotation:

> The whites just *startin'* to get the blues
> —*John Lee Hooker*

He's not just talking about blues music. What does he mean?

Bring records of the blues to school to play for students. What are some recurring themes in these songs? Is it significant that most performers are Black?

After students have talked about what makes blues different, suggest some books about blues people for them to read.

Hettie Jones. *Big Star Failin' Mama; Five Women in Black Music*. Viking, 1974. Includes Ma Rainey, Bessie Smith, Mahalia Jackson, Billie Holiday, and Aretha Franklin.

Sharon Bell Mathis. *Ray Charles*. Crowell, 1973.

Elizabeth Rider Montgomery. *William C. Handy: Father of the Blues*. Garrard, 1968.

APRIL

1	2	3	4	5	6	7
Spring Corn Dances (Pueblos)	Ponce de León landed in Florida, 1513 International Children's Book Day		Martin Luther King, Jr., assassinated, 1968	Booker T. Washington, 1856–1915 Pocahontas married John Rolfe, 1614	Peary and Henson reached North Pole, 1909 Joseph Smith founded Mormon Church, 1830 Alexander Herzen, 1812–1870	Billie Holiday, 1915–1959
8	**9**	**10**	**11**	**12**	**13**	**14**
First synagogue in America founded in NYC, 1730 Buddha's birthday (Japan)	Civil War ended, Treaty of Appomattox, 1865	Joseph Pulitzer 1847–1911 Dolores Huerta 1940–		Civil War began, 1861, Ft. Sumter Yuri Gargarin, cosmonaut, became first person to orbit earth, 1961	Lucy Laney, 1854–1933, Black educator	Pan American Day Abraham Lincoln assassinated, 1865 Carlos Romulo, Philippine leader, 1899–1985
15	**16**	**17**	**18**	**19**	**20**	**21**
Bessie Smith, 1894–1937, Black blues singer	Mary Eliza Mahoney, 1845–1926, first Black nurse	World Health Day		Revolutionary War began, 1775	Day of Remembrance (Holocaust)	Spanish-American War began, 1898
22	**23**	**24**	**25**	**26**	**27**	**28**
Earth Day	César Chávez died, 1993		Ella Fitzgerald, 1918– UN founded, 1945	Gertrude (Ma) Rainey, 1886–1939, Black blues singer Syngman Rhee, 1875–1965	Coretta Scott King, 1927– Eritrea becomes independent from Ethiopia, 1993	
29	**30**					
Emperor's birthday (Japan) Duke Ellington, 1899–1974	Louisiana Territory purchased, 1803 Loyalists and Negroes attacked Shrewsbury, NJ, 1780					

The wisest among my race understand that the agitation of questions of social equality is the extremest folly, and that progress in the enjoyment of all the privileges that will come to us must be the result of severe and constant struggle rather than of artificial forcing.

—*Booker T. Washington*

May Activities

This month has been set aside to recognize the contributions made by people of Asian and Pacific Island heritage. During this month, we can acknowledge the diversity of Asian and Pacific Island immigrants, and the rich cultural and linguistic heritage that they hope to maintain.

May 3. Golda Meir taught school in Milwaukee, Wisconsin, before going to live in Palestine. She later became prime minister of Israel, one of the first women in the world to hold such a position. Read a biography, *The Golda Meir Story* by Margaret Davidson (Scribner's, 1981), to learn more about this unusual woman, the American immigrant experience, and the founding of the state of Israel.

May 5. Today, Japanese children fly carp kites. Students can make their own gaily decorated fish to hang like streamers. Each student can draw a model, or you can provide one for everyone to trace onto construction paper. (See model on below.) They should have two fish shapes, one right side and one reversed. After the children color and cut out the fish, they glue the two pieces together around the edges (except for the mouth) and gently stuff with tissue paper for a three-dimensional effect. These fish can be hung around the room with thread tied to the back, or attached to a stick (fishing pole) by the mouth, If you have Japanese-speaking children in the class, this is a good opportunity to have them teach the class how to count in Japanese.

ichi—one	san—three	go—five	shichi—seven	ku—nine
ni—two	shi—four	roku—six	hachi—eight	ju—ten

One, two, three,
    (echo)
Listen to me,
    (echo)
I can count to ten,
    (echo)
In Japanese,
    (echo)
Ichi, ni, san, shi, go
    (echo)
I can count to five
    (echo)
Let's try four more.
    (echo)
Roku, shichi, hachi, ku,
    (echo)
I can count to nine,
    (echo)
Let's try one more,
    (echo)
(together) JU!

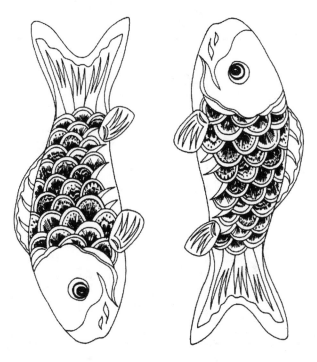

MAY

1	2	3	4	5	6	7
Loyalty Day Law Day Agrippa Hull, free Black, began six years of army service, 1777	Golda Meir, 1898–1978			Children's Festival (Japan) Gwendolyn Brooks won Pulitzer Prize for Poetry, 1950 Cinco de Mayo	Chinese Exclusion Act passed, 1882 Rudolph Valentino, 1895–1926	Rabindranath Tagore, 1861–1941
8	**9**	**10**	**11**	**12**	**13**	**14**
Chinese expelled from mines, Tuolemme County (CA), 1852 V-E Day, 1945		Chinese labor helped complete Transcontinental Railroad, Utah, 1869	Joan of Arc Day (France)		Joe Louis, 1914–1972 Congress declared war on Mexico, 1846	State of Israel proclaimed, 1948 Jamestown established, 1607
15	**16**	**17**	**18**	**19**	**20**	**21**
		Supreme Court declared racial segregation in schools unconstitutional, 1954	Hispanic Society of America founded, 1904	Malcolm X, 1925–1965 I Am an American Day Lorraine Hansberry, 1930–1965		
22	**23**	**24**	**25**	**26**	**27**	**28**
		Ynes Mexia, 1870–1938, Mexican-American botanical explorer	African Freedom Day	Susette LaFlesche Tibbles died, 1903, Omaha Indian rights advocate	Victoria Matthews 1861–1907, Black author and social worker Buddha's birthday (China)	
29	**30**					
John F. Kennedy, 1917–1963	Hernando de Soto landed in Florida, 1539 Countee Cullen, 1903–1946 Joan of Arc burned, 1431					

What other countries have taken three hundred years or more to achieve, a once dependent territory must try to accomplish in a generation if it is to survive.

—*Kwame Nkrumah (Ghana)*

Count Your Way through Japan by Jim Haskins (Carolrhoda, 1987) is a good book for students, with numbers in Japanese accompanied by pictures of the country.

May 5.   Cinco de Mayo marks the victory of Mexican forces over the French at Puebla, Mexico, on May 5, 1862. It is celebrated today in Mexican American communities in the United States as the occasion for a fiesta, with a parade, dancing, and other activities. You can hold a fiesta in your room. Bring records of Mexican popular music, folk songs, or Mexican Indian music. Let the students prepare food such as tortillas, guacamole, or buñelos. Students can decorate the room appropriately by using poster paint or felt pens to create murals that evoke Mexico and Mexican American life. Possible subjects include food, sports, clothing, arts and crafts, and historical figures.

May 14.

> Forgiveness is the key to action and freedom.
> —*Hannah Arendt*

> The motto should not be: Forgive one another; rather, Understand one another.
> —*Emma Goldman*

When Israel was established in 1948, few countries would admit the large numbers of European Jewish refugees. From what were they fleeing? Read some books with older students about children's responses to the Holocaust.

Linda Atkinson. *In Kindling Flame.* Lothrop, 1984.

Miriam Chaikin. *A Nightmare in History.* Clarion, 1987.

Anne Frank. *The Diary of a Young Girl.* Doubleday, 1952.

Johanna Reis. *The Journey Back.* Crowell, 1976.

———— . *The Upstairs Room.* Crowell, 1972.

Aranka Siegal. *Upon the Head of a Goat: A Childhood in Hungary 1939–1944.* Farrar, Straus, and Giroux, 1981.

Talk about feelings of helplessness that students have had. In this case, who was the enemy? Is it more difficult when the enemy is faceless? Does it help if you learn to forgive or understand your enemy?

May 25.   African Freedom Day offers an opportunity to discuss the origins of African Americans. Explore books such as the following:

Primary Grades
Marc Bernheim and Evelyn Bernheim. *In Africa.* Atheneum, 1973.

Muriel Feelings. *Jambo Means Hello; Swahili Alphabet Book.* Dial, 1974.

Upper Grades
Ashley Bryan. *Lion and the Ostrich Chicks, and Other African Tales.* Atheneum, 1986.

John Chiasson. *African Journey.* Bradbury, 1987.

A. Okion Ojigbo. *Young and Black in Africa.* Random House, 1971.

Students can investigate early African civilizations. Too many books picture Africa as a land of barbaric people who were captured and taken to the "civilized" world. Show students that Africa was not dark and uncivilized before the Europeans arrived. Pictures of people from different African countries will teach that not all Africans look alike.

Even the youngest students can learn a few words of Swahili, a widely spoken African language. Refer to *Jambo and Other Call-and-Response Songs and Chants* (Folkways Records, 1974).

June Activities

June 11.   Discover Hawaii, the fiftieth state, with your students. One of the state's attractions is its multicultural, multilingual heritage. Investigate the history of Hawaii. How and when did it become a state? People from many different countries are represented in Hawaii. What are some of them? Are there native Hawaiians?

Ask students to find examples of unusual words used in Hawaii, for example, words for different foods. Here are a few words used commonly in Hawaii:

ae	(eye)	yes
aloha	(ah *loh* hah)	greetings
hale	(*hah* lay)	house
haole	(*how* lay)	foreigner (white person)
hula	(*hoo* lah)	dance
kamaaiana	(*kah* mah ai nah)	oldtimer
kane	(*kah* neh)	man
kaukah	(*kow* kow)	food
keiki	(*kay* kee)	child
lani	(*lah* nee)	sky
lei	(lay)	wreath
luau	(loo ah oo)	feast
mahalo	(mah *hah* loh)	thanks
malihini	(*may* lee *hee* nee)	newcomer
mauna	(*mou* nah)	mountain
moana	(moh *ah* nah)	ocean
nani	(*nan* nee)	beautiful
ohana	(oh *hah* nah)	family
peheaoe	(pay *hay* ah *oy*)	How are you?
wahine	(wha *hee* nay)	woman

Students can assemble a dictionary of Hawaiian words or expressions and their meaning.

June 19.   News of the January 1863 Emancipation Proclamation freeing the slaves did not reach African Americans in Texas until June 1865. Juneteenth (June 19) has become a community celebration of African American heritage, featuring picnics and music.

June 20.   Investigate Alaska, the forty-ninth state. Only half a million people (587,000 in 1992) inhabit this huge area. Who are they? Read about Alaska in such books as *Julie of the Wolves* by Jean George (Harper and Row, 1972), the story of an Eskimo girl.

JUNE

1	2	3	4	5	6	7
Brigham Young, 1801–1877 First Week, National Flag Week		DeSoto claimed Florida for Spain, 1539 Roland Hayes, 1887–1977		English colonists massacre Pequot village in Pequot War, 1637 Kaahumanu died, 1832, Hawaiian ruler Socrates born c. 470 B.C.	Evacuation of Japanese Americans into concentration camps completed, 1942 Sarah Remond, 1826–1887, Black lecturer and physician	Gwendolyn Brooks, 1917– , Black poet Paul Gauguin, 1848–1903 Mohammed died, 632 AD Nikki Giovanni, 1943–
8	**9**	**10**	**11**	**12**	**13**	**14**
			Kamehameha Day (Hawaii) Addie W. Hunton, 1875–1943, Black youth group leader	Philippine Independence Day		Hawaii organized as territory, 1900 Harriet Beecher Stowe, 1811–1896
15	**16**	**17**	**18**	**19**	**20**	**21**
	Flight of Valentina Tereshkova (first woman in space), 1963	Susan LaFlesche Picotte, 1865–1915, Omaha physician James Weldon Johnson, 1871–1938	War of 1812 declared against Great Britain, 1812	Statue of Liberty arrived in New York Harbor, 1885 Juneteenth—Emancipation reaches Texas, 1865	Start of French Revolution, 1789 Announced purchase of Alaska from Russia, 1867	
22	**23**	**24**	**25**	**26**	**27**	**28**
Slavery abolished in Great Britain, 1772	U.S. entered Korean War, 1950 William Penn signed treaty with Indians, 1683	San Juan Day (Puerto Rico)	Crazy Horse (Sioux) defeated Custer—Battle of the Little Bighorn, 1876	Pearl S. Buck, 1892–1973 UN Charter signed, 1945	Paul Dunbar, 1872–1906, Black writer Joseph Smith, Mormon prophet, killed, 1844 Helen Keller, 1880–1968	World War I began, 1914 Peace Treaty signed, 1919
29	**30**					
First African church in the U.S. (Philadelphia), 1794 Azalia Hackley, 1867–1922, Black singer José Rizal, 1861–1896						

. . . We could never learn to be brave and patient, if there were only joy in the world.

—*Helen Keller*

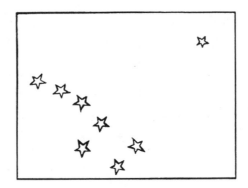

Alaska's flag was designed by Benny Benson, a thirteen-year-old schoolboy. The flag is deep blue with seven gold stars, which represent the gold found in Alaska, forming the Big Dipper. The eighth star is, of course, the North Star, which symbolizes Alaska's northern location close to the North Pole.

June 27.   Read the poem by Paul Laurence Dunbar that begins, "We wear the mask that grins and lies." Use this selection to stimulate a discussion about feelings—how we express them and why we hide them. Ask students if people always show what they feel on their face. Why or why not? Have they ever seen people pretend to be happy when they're sad inside? How do we show our feelings? With our eyes? Mouth?

After discussing expressions, have the students make papier-mache masks that illustrate a particular feeling (through eyes, mouth, color). They can write a story about a time when they wanted to show their true feelings or hide them. Then they can use the masks to tell the story.

July Activities

July 1, 3.   Recognize Canada on Canada Day. Display its symbol, the maple leaf, with pictures of Canada from travel folders. (See pages 251–253 for ideas specific to Québec.) Can students name some famous Canadians? Display a map of Canada. Look at the names of the provinces. What do they indicate about the ethnic influences on Canada and where the early settlers came from? How is the history of Canada different from that of the United States? How is it similar?

O Canada, a picture book by the well-known Canadian artist Ted Harrison (Tickner and Fields, 1993), based on the Canadian national anthem, is an excellent introduction to this diverse land and its peoples.

Read aloud some poems from the prize-winning collection by Mary Alice Downie and Barbara Robertson, comp., *The New Wind Has Wings: Poems from Canada* (Oxford/Merrimack, 1985).

July 4.   Independence Day for the United States can be recognized in many ways. Prepare a program that includes songs such as "America," "The Star-Spangled Banner," "America, the Beautiful," and "Columbia, the Gem of the Ocean." Students can read some

JULY

1	2	3	4	5	6	7
Canada Day	Thurgood Marshall, 1908–1993	Champlain founded Québec, 1608	Edmonia Lewis, 1845–?, Black-Cherokee sculptor; Lucy Slowe, 1885–1937, Black teacher and administrator; Giuseppe Garibaldi 1807–1882			
8	**9**	**10** Mary McLeod Bethune, 1875–1955	**11**	**12**	**13** Wole Soyinka, 1934–	**14** Bastille Day (France), 1789
15 Maggie Walker, 1867–1934, Black insurance and banking executive; Ch'iu Chin died, 1875–1907	**16** Ida Barnett-Wells, 1862–1931, Black journalist and civic leader; Mary Baker Eddy, 1821–1910, Founder, Christian Science	**17** Spain transferred Florida to U.S., 1821; S. Y. Agnon, 1888–1970	**18** Miguel Hidalgo, 1753–1811, Father of Mexican independence; Yevgeny Yevtushenko, 1933–	**19** Alice Dunbar Nelson, 1875–1935, Black author, teacher	**20**	**21**
22	**23** Simón Bolívar, 1783–1830; Mormons settled Salt Lake City, 1847	**24**	**25** Puerto Rico became a commonwealth, 1952	**26**	**27** Korean War ended, 1953	**28**
29	**30**	**31** Sarah Garnet, 1831–1911, Black educator and civic worker				

The drums of Africa still beat in my heart. They will not let me rest while there is a single Negro boy or girl without a chance to prove his worth.
—*Mary McLeod Bethune*

of the great poetic prose written by the patriots who drew up the Constitution as well as the eloquent words of Lincoln in "The Gettysburg Address":

> Four score and seven years ago our fathers brought forth on this continent, a new nation, conceived in liberty, and dedicated to the proposition that all men are created equal.
>
> Now we are engaged in a great civil war, testing whether that nation, or any nation so conceived and so dedicated, can long endure. We are met on a great battlefield of that war. We have come to dedicate a portion of that field, as a final resting place for those who gave their lives that the nation might live. It is altogether fitting and proper that we should do this.
>
> But, in a larger sense, we can not dedicate—we can not consecrate—we can not hallow—this ground. The brave men, living and dead, who struggled here, have consecrated it, far above our poor power to add or detract. The world will little note, nor long remember, what we say here, but it can never forget what they did here. It is for us the living, rather, to be dedicated here to the unfinished work which they who fought here have thus far so nobly advanced. It is rather for us to be here dedicated to the great task remaining before us—that from these honored dead we take increased devotion to that cause for which they gave the last full measure of devotion—that we here highly resolve that these dead shall not have died in vain—that this nation, under God, shall have a new birth of freedom—and that government of the people, by the people, and for the people, shall not perish from the earth.

Younger students can talk about words associated with the Fourth of July, such as democracy, independence, equality, liberty, and fraternity.

What do these words mean? Where do they come from? Analyze the words by looking at the morphemes (prefixes, suffixes, and roots). Show how knowing the meaning of the morphemes can help you predict the meaning of unfamiliar words.

July 10.   Who was Mary McLeod Bethune? The featured quote by her suggests her concern with education. Challenge students to find out about her life and achievements. Students can read *Mary McLeod Bethune* by Patricia McKissack (Children's Press, 1985) or write to The Bethune Museum Archives, 1318 Vermont Avenue, NW, Washington, D.C. 20006, for further information.

Talk about the words *segregation* and *desegregation*. Do students know what these words mean? At one time (during slavery) it was illegal to teach Blacks to read and write. Why would people be afraid of literacy? Discuss the consequences of segregated schools. What are some of the solutions?

August Activities

August 2.

> The fear I heard in my father's voice . . . when he realized that I really *believed* I could do anything a white boy could do, and had every intention of proving it, was not at all like the fear I heard when one of us was ill or had fallen down the stairs or strayed too far from the house. It was another fear, a fear that the child, in challenging the white world's assumptions, was putting himself in the path of destruction.
> —*James Baldwin*

James Baldwin grew up in Harlem, New York, and became a writer, but he had to leave this country in order to develop his writing abilities. He settled in Paris, as had other Black

AUGUST

1 James Baldwin, 1924–1987	**2** Columbus started first voyage, 1492	**3** Anne Frank captured, 1944	**4**	**5** U.S. bombed Hiroshima, Japan, 1945	**6** Ralph Bunche, 1904–1971	**7**
8 U.S. bombed Nagasaki, Japan, 1945 Roberto Clemente, 1934–1973	**9** Janie Porter Barrett, 1865–1948, Black social welfare leader	**10**	**11** Alex Haley, 1921–1992	**12** U.S. annexed Hawaii, 1898	**13** Spanish conquered Aztecs, 1521	**14** Japan surrendered, World War II, 1945
15	**16**	**17** Charlotte Forten (Grimke), 1837–1914, Black teacher and author V. S. Naipaul, 1932–	**18**	**19** Mammy Pleasant, 1814–1904, Black California pioneer	**20** Bernardo O'Higgins Chilean patriot, 1778–1842	**21**
22	**23**	**24** Lucy Moten died, 1933, Black educator	**25**	**26** Women's Equality Day	**27** Rose McClendon, 1884–1936, Black actress	**28**
29	**30**	**31** Josephine Ruffin, 1842–1924, Black leader				

The wonder is not that so many Negro boys and girls are ruined but that so many survive.
—*James Baldwin*

exiles. What do the quotes indicate about Baldwin's opinion of the position of Blacks in American society? Why would someone like Baldwin leave the United States? What does "going into exile" mean?

August 7.

> I was offered the ambassadorship of Liberia once, when the post was earmarked for a Negro. I told them I wouldn't take a Jim Crow job.
> —*Ralph Bunche*

Ralph Bunche was a famous diplomat and the first African American to win the Nobel Prize. What did he have to overcome to win recognition for his abilities? Ask students whether they know what a "Jim Crow" job is. Can they guess? Why would the ambassador to Liberia be expected to be Black? What would it feel like to go to Africa, after being treated as an inferior in this country, and find people like yourself in positions of power?

Collect and display pictures of Africans in different jobs and positions of responsibility. Show students what the world looks like when people aren't denied opportunities because of their skin color.

August 13. Who were the Aztecs and why did the Spanish conquer them? Pose such questions to the students and have them search for the answers. The Aztec civilization is particularly interesting because it was so advanced, and yet we know very little about it because the Spanish destroyed most of the records. Investigate the Spanish treatment of the Aztecs and compare it with the way the English settlers treated the Native American groups they met.

Have students research the Aztec circular calendar. The Aztecs were excellent astronomers and developed a calendar that was more accurate than the one the Spaniards used, yet they had not invented the wheel. Prepare a display featuring the accomplishments of the Aztecs.

Students who are fascinated by pyramids might work cooperatively to make a sand table model of a pyramid. This project can stimulate extensive research on the Aztecs and make this ancient civilization come alive for all students.

Variable Dates

Listed here are holidays or events that fall on different dates each year. Add them to the appropriate months.

United States Holidays or Special Days. Note that many holidays are celebrated on a Monday or Friday to provide a holiday weekend.

Mother's Day	second Sunday in May
Armed Forces Day	third Saturday in May
Memorial Day	last Monday in May
Father's Day	third Sunday in June
Labor Day	first Monday in September

Election Day	first Tuesday after first Monday in November
Veterans' Day	fourth Monday in October
Thanksgiving Day	fourth Thursday in November

Jewish Feasts and Festivals.   Because the Jewish calendar (described in the next section) is lunar, the dates of Jewish holidays vary each year. The following chart gives the names and dates for the holidays by year and shows the corresponding Jewish calendar year under Rosh Hashanah, when the new year begins. Note that each holiday actually begins at sundown on the preceding day.

Year	Purim (Feast of Lots)	Pesach (Festival of Freedom)	Shavuot (Feast of Weeks)	Rosh Hashanah (New Year)	Yom Kippur (Day of Atonement)	Succot (Feast of Tabernacles)	Hanukkah (Feast of Dedication)
1994	Feb. 25	Mar. 27–Apr. 3	May 16–17	Sept. 6–7	Sept. 15	Sept. 20–26	Nov. 28
1995	Mar. 16	Apr. 15–22	June 4–5	Sept. 25–26	Oct. 4	Oct. 9–15	Dec. 18–25
1996	Mar. 5	Apr. 4–11	May 24–25	Sept. 14–15	Sept. 23	Sept. 28–Oct 4	Dec. 6–13

CULTURES AND TIME

The calendar itself is an object of interest in the multicultural classroom. Although students may assume that the calendar and the way people count time has always been the same, you can introduce the idea of cultural diversity in time measurement as you work with the Multicultural Calendar. In addition, the calendar has changed over time, due to political as well as scientific considerations. And once students begin to look at the calendar as an object of study, they will be interested to learn the origins of the names of the months and the days of the week. Students will enjoy discovering the amazing diversity of contemporary and historical methods of telling time.

Marking Time—Background

As we begin an exploration of calendars, we might first discuss ideas about marking time in general. For example, students may be surprised to find that not every culture has the same concept of day as we do. We accept the concepts of day, hour, minute, and second—as well as week, month, and year—with little question. Let us examine a few ideas that you might discuss as examples of varied ways of considering time within different cultures.

What is a day? Our idea of day is a 24-hour period that includes both light and darkness. Is it not strange that we count a day from the middle of a night to the middle of the next night? In some cultures there is no word that means just that. Many ancient cultures recognized a single event such as dawn, the rising of the sun, and spoke of so many dawns or suns. Other cultures used the night and spoke of "sleeps." Gradually the light period was broken up with terms related to the sun: daybreak, sunrise, noon, afternoon, twilight, and sunset. The crowing of cocks, the yoking of oxen, and the siesta are other examples of ways of marking the time of day. For some peoples day begins with dawn, but, for example, Hebrew days begin in the evening. Dividing the day into hours is a modern concept brought about by industrialization.

Beginning the day at midnight and having two sets of times designated one to twelve are arbitrary decisions that are not always followed. Many students will have heard of 24-hour clocks, which are used in many countries and in some cases (such as military organizations) in the United States. They might not know, however, that astronomers begin their day at twelve noon in order to use the same date for observations made at night.

Our determination of months and weeks is also an arbitrary decision. Months roughly correspond to the cycle of the moon, which is $29\frac{1}{2}$ days. Early societies noted the phases of the moon and used them as measures of time from new moon to full moon. The moon is still the basis for some calendars, as we will discuss in the next section. Today, we use a calendar that divides the year into months of 28 to 31 days to fit the solar year, so the phases of the moon occur at different times of the various months.

The seven-day week is another interesting phenomenon, which began when people who were trading needed some regular arrangement. The week, as the interval between trading or market days, has varied from four to ten days. It is thought that the selection of seven days as the "magical" number does, indeed, have something to do with the significance of the number *seven*. This hypothesis is supported by our use of the names of gods and goddesses to name the days of the week, thus:

Latin Name	French Name	Saxon Name	English Name
Dies Solis	Dimanche	Sun's day	Sunday
Dies Lunae	Lundi	Moon's day	Monday
Dies Martis	Mardi	Tiw's Day	Tuesday
Dies Mercurii	Mercredi	Woden's day	Wednesday
Dies Jovis	Jeudi	Thor's day	Thursday
Dies Veneris	Vendredi	Frigg's day	Friday
Dies Saturni	Samedi	Seterne's day	Saturday

The Saxon names, which reflect Norse mythology, are carried into our English names. In the French and Latin names, which are related, you can find Mars, Mercury, Venus, and Jupiter (Jove).

Although we now take for granted the knowledge of astronomy on which we base our year, this concept of year is a relatively new idea. Gradually, ancient peoples found a need for longer designations of time than market days or lunar months. This need was chiefly to count the ages of people and to compare these ages. Some of the following measures were used:

- Family generations
- Momentous events—plague, famine, war
- Reigns of monarchs or chiefs
- Cycles of seasons
  monsoons
  wet and dry periods (rains)

summer and winter (summers, snows)
agricultural changes
animal migration

Folklore provides a wealth of information related to these concepts of time. Encourage students to search out such ideas. They might begin with expressions or beliefs related to time, for example, Friday is a bad day, and Friday the thirteenth is the worst of all days! *Blue Monday and Friday the Thirteenth* by Lila Perl (Clarion, 1986) explores the origins of many beliefs.

Students might pursue the study of cultural beliefs and superstitions in such books as *Cross Your Fingers, Spit in Your Hat* by Alvin Schwartz (Lippincott, 1974).

How Calendars Developed

Encourage students to investigate the history of calendars. They can learn, for example, the origins of the word which goes back to the Latin *calendarium,* which means *account book*. Calendars are associated, therefore, with the payment of debts, marking times when payments were due. A calendar, as generally used, is a system for recording the passage of time. Congress, for example, has a calendar, or schedule of events.

Before we had formal ways of measuring time, humans marked time by observing the rising and setting of the sun, the different phases of the moon, and the passage of the seasons. The first calendars, created by the Babylonians, were based on moons (months), the periods of time when the moon completed its full cycle of phases. Twelve moons make a 354-day year. When it was observed that every four years the year needed an adjustment to make the calendar fit the seasons, the Babylonians added another moon, or month. This calendar was adapted by the Egyptians, Semites, and Greeks.

The Egyptians modified this calendar by basing their calculations on the regular rising of the Nile River, which occurred each year just after Sirius, the Dog Star, appeared. They developed a calendar that more nearly matched the solar year, using 365 days, which was still a little off from the $365\frac{1}{4}$ days we now consider accurate. Considering that they created this system around 4000 B.C., however, they were amazingly exact. They worked with 12 months of 30 days each and simply added 5 days at the end of the year.

The Roman calendar, introduced by Romulus around 700 B.C., was derived from that used in Greece. The Romans had ten months: Martius, Aprilis, Maius, Junius, Quintilis, Sextilis, September, October, November, and December. The names of the last six months correspond to the Latin numbers—five, six, seven, eight, nine, and ten. One king, who wanted to collect more taxes, added two more months, Januarius and Februarius. Needless to say, the calendar soon became very confused and did not correspond with the solar year.

Then came the Julian calendar, which Julius Caesar created in 46 B.C. to correct the inaccuracy of the Roman calendar. He divided the year into 12 months of 30 and 31 days except for February which he gave 28 days plus one every fourth year, so his year was a few minutes longer than the solar year. He changed the beginning of the year to January 1st instead of March 1st and renamed the month of Sextilis August, after Emperor Augustus. The month Quintilis was renamed Julius in his honor. Thus, we have the origins of our names for the twelve months. The Julian calendar was used for more than 1,500 years. The Gregorian calendar was created to correct the error in the Julian calendar, which was off by ten days in 1580. The Gregorian calendar was adopted gradually until it became stand- ard throughout much of the world.

Students might investigate further efforts to reform the calendar. The thirteen-month calendar would contain thirteen months of equal length. The perpetual calendar is another topic to explore.

The Christian Calendar

The calendar that Christians use is the Gregorian calendar, which was developed by Pope Gregory around 1580. Students may know a version of the old verse that helps them remember the number of days in each month according to this calendar:

> Thirty days has September,
> April, June, and November.
> All the rest have thirty-one
> Excepting, February, alone,
> And that has twenty-eight days clear
> And twenty-nine in each leap year.

This Christian calendar is based on the year Jesus Christ was born. Dates before his birth are marked as B.C. (before Christ). Dates after his birth are marked as A.D. (*anno domini*—in the year of our Lord). Also used are the markings B.C.E. (before the Common era) and C.E. (Common era). On this Christian calendar there are certain fixed dates, such as Christmas. Movable feast days include Easter and Thanksgiving.

Christian Holidays

	Ash Wednesday	*Easter Sunday*
1994	February 16	April 3
1995	March 1	April 16
1996	February 21	April 7

Easter falls on the first Sunday following the arbitrary Paschal Full Moon, which does not necessarily coincide with a real or astronomical full moon. The Paschal Full Moon is calculated by adding 1 to the remainder obtained by dividing the year by 19 and applying the following:

1—April 14	6—April 18	11—March 25	16—March 30
2—April 3	7—April 8	12—April 13	17—April 17
3—March 23	8—March 28	13—April 2	18—April 7
4—April 11	9—April 16	14—March 22	19—March 27
5—March 31	10—April 5	15—April 10	

Thus, for the year 2000 the key is 6, or April 18. Since April 18 in the year 2000 is a Tuesday, Easter Sunday is April 23. *Caution*—If the Paschal Full Moon falls on a Sunday, Easter is the following Sunday. The earliest Easter can fall is March 23 and the latest is April 25.

Lent begins on Ash Wednesday, which comes forty days before Easter, excluding Sundays.

The Hebrew Calendar

Another calendar that is still widely used today is the Hebrew, or Jewish, calendar, based on the Creation, which preceded the birth of Christ by 3,760 years and 3 months. The Hebrew year begins in September rather than January. From the fall of 1995 to the fall of 1996, therefore, the Hebrew year will be 5756.

Based on the moon, the Hebrew year usually contains twelve months. Periodically, an extra month is inserted to adjust this calendar, as shown here:

Months in the Hebrew Calendar

Tishri	Nisan
Heshvan	Iyar
Kislev	Sivan
Tevet	Tammuz
Shevat	Av
Adar	Elul
(Veadar or Adar Sheni) added in leap years	

Encyclopedia Britannica distributes a series of three filmstrips called *Jewish Holidays* (1984) covering Rosh Hashanah, Yom Kippur, Hanukkah, and Passover.

The Islamic Calendar

Also based on the moon, the Islamic calendar dates from Mohammed's flight from Mecca, called the Hegira, which took place in A.D. 622. The year has only 354 days so that its New Year moves with respect to the seasons. It makes a full cycle every $32\frac{1}{2}$ years. The names of the Islamic months are:

Muharram	Rabi II	Rajab	Shawwal
Safar	Jumada I	Shaban	Zulkadah
Rabi I	Jumada II	Ramadan	Zulhijjah

Clarify terminology for students who may be confused as they read news reports from the Near East. Followers of Mohammed are called Muslims and Islam means surrender to the will of Allah (God). Islam is the second largest religion in the world, after Christianity, and there are approximately 2.6 million Muslims in North America.

Other Calendars of the World

Students who are interested in calendars can research other systems that have been developed. The Chinese calendar, consisting of a twelve-year cycle based on Jupiter's positions in relationship to the constellations, is discussed on page 262. Other calendars that students can investigate include Hindu, Assyrian, Greek, and Maya.

REFLECTIONS

We have presented information in this chapter to encourage you to begin your teaching for multicultural understanding immediately. With the help of these activities and resources, you can introduce diversity into any curriculum and any classroom. But we believe that multicultural teaching means more than just "heroes and holidays." As you read the entries for each month, you will note opportunities to mention the contributions of varied groups throughout the year. In addition, calendar-based discussions of people, issues, and events will lead to students' greater appreciation of their own cultural heritage as well as better understanding of others.

APPLICATIONS

1. Choose a holiday such as St. Patrick's Day, Easter, or New Year's Day that is often celebrated in popular culture. Use this as a base for a unit on multicultural understanding. Possible topics include how this holiday is celebrated in different regions or different countries, the origin of the customs associated with this holiday, and underlying themes that promote multicultural concepts.

Develop a bibliography of books and other resources to help you build your unit. Plan lessons that integrate writing, discussion, and thinking skills. Present your unit to the class.

2. Focus on birthdays. Find out how to say "Happy Birthday" in one hundred languages. How do people celebrate birthdays in different cultures? Make a list of ways to create a multiethnic atmosphere (food, music, decorations) in the classroom and to make the children feel special.

3. Choose a group (ethnic, religious, or regional) to be responsible for and research names, dates, events, and other kinds of information to include in a multicultural calendar. Try to find special holidays celebrated by this group, names of significant individuals, and important contributions by the group.

Where would you look for this information? What kind of information is most difficult to find? Why?

Prepare lessons to present this information to students.

Exploring Further

Alex Ayers, ed. *The Wisdom of Martin Luther King, Jr.* Meridian, 1993.

June Behrens. *Hannukkah: Festivals and Holidays*. Children's Press. 1983.

Joyce Armstrong Carroll. *Books for Special Days: Integrated Teaching of Reading, Writing, Listening, Speaking, Viewing, and Thinking*. Jackdaws Series No. 4. Teacher Ideas Press, 1993.

Mary Ann Heltshe and Audrey Burie Kirchner. *Multicultural Explorations: Joyous Journeys with Books*. Teacher Ideas Press, 1991.

Leon Litwack and August Meier, eds. *Black Leaders of the Nineteenth Century.* University of Illinois Press, 1988.

Myra Cohn Livingston. *Celebrations.* Holiday House, 1985.

Milton Meltzer. *The Black Americans: A History in Their Own Words, 1619–1983.* Crowell, 1985.

Thomas Sowell. *Ethnic America: A History.* Basic Books, 1981.

EDUCATION
BRINGS DAYBREAK;
IGNORANCE,
A LONG, LONG NIGHT.

—Maya Angelou

10
❖
Reflecting on Multicultural Education

According to Maya Angelou, "Education brings breaking; ignorance, a long, long night."[1] Now that we have completed our exploratory journey together, it is time to reflect on what you have learned about multicultural education. Recognizing that multicultural concepts are assimilated over a period of time, it is helpful to assess where you are today as you begin making plans for how you might progress tomorrow.

In this text we have endeavored to present a wide variety of information, attitudes, and teaching strategies, enough to challenge the most experienced teacher. On the other hand, the ideas presented should enable even novice teachers to make a difference in the lives of the children in their classrooms. In this chapter we review what we have discussed in this text. We acknowledge the problems and issues that we must surmount to move forward, examining the pros and cons of the issues involved and preparing to face the dragon of controversy. Adding a positive note, we summarize a number of promising practices currently supporting multicultural education in the schools and in teacher education. At the end of the chapter we provide a checklist that may help you to assess your development as a teacher of multicultural education.

After reading this chapter, you should be able to:
- Identify the problems and issues you must address if you are to carry out successful multicultural education programs.
- Describe progressive thinking and promising practices that support effective multicultural education.
- Evaluate the assumptions underlying multicultural education as presented in this text.

PROBLEMS AND ISSUES TO BE ADDRESSED

As a teacher, you need to continue developing your multicultural knowledge base, and you need to continue working toward the outcomes we have identified for student learning. Now we would like to identify problems and issues that you may need to address in your school or district as you work toward developing a full-fledged multicultural program that offers equity for all students.

Knowledge about Multicultural Education

Prior to 1978, *multicultural education* was not even listed as a category in the *Education Index,* which indicates that few articles were being written in pedagogical journals about this topic. An entry for *Mexican Americans* first appeared in the 1963–1964 volume. At that time multiethnic topics were referred to as *Intergroup Education.* All references to Blacks were entered under *Negroes* until 1978. References to Asian Americans were listed under *Orientals* until 1980. Only within the past decade do we find a substantial number of books and articles on multicultural education. (The first edition of this text, *Multicultural Teaching,* appeared in 1979.)

Given the lag that typically occurs between the development of a theory and its impact on practice, these findings make it clear that we have not yet sufficiently emphasized teaching about cultural diversity in teacher education programs. Few classroom teachers and professors of teacher education today were educated to teach multicultural concepts. Members of the public educated years ago, too, still frequently use the melting-pot metaphor with well-meaning, but mistaken, intent and effects; and such terms as *culture* are often misused in textbooks and public dialogue.

Standards listed in 1987 by the National Council for Accreditation of Teacher Education (NCATE) include multicultural education. Teacher education programs are therefore now examined to see that multicultural concepts are present in class syllabi. The expected "multicultural perspective" is defined as

> . . . a recognition of (1) the social, political, and economic realities that individuals experience in culturally diverse and complex human encounters and (2) the importance of culture, race, sex and gender, ethnicity, religion, socioeconomic status, and exceptionalities in the education process.[2]

Teachers need to know accurate definitions, terminology, and concepts that can be shared with students at all levels of instruction. They need to know literature that will inform such instruction. They also need to accept the responsibility for teaching to enhance empathy in all classrooms.

The solution to this problem lies in both preservice and inservice staff development. This text is designed to add to the knowledge base for future teachers as well as those already in the field. Throughout the text we have presented numerous up-to-date references that you can explore to extend your knowledge base. We have also recommended experiences and activities that will enhance your ability to teach for diversity as you work with young learners.

Stereotyped Thinking and Prejudice

All of us grew up within a culture surrounded by beliefs and behaviors that we accepted without question. As young children, we probably associated with persons from the same culture, and tended to consider our way of thinking and behaving as the "right" one. Thus, stereotyped thinking may begin, and thus we may become prejudiced against those who think or behave differently.

Education, however, informs us. As we encounter people from broader circles, we learn that thinking and behavior differ. Gradually, we learn to accept diverse thinking as a normal state of affairs. Mobility, television, the newspaper, literature—all serve to broaden our perspectives. If their minds are open to new ideas, teachers, students, and parents will revise stereotyped thinking as they learn to accept differences and to realize that "different" does not connote "deficient" or "wrong."

Yet we continue to hear crude ethnic jokes or references in the speech of supposedly educated people. Children's rhymes and stories often contain stereotyped references children may or may not understand. Women and the elderly continue to be discriminated against. Education still has work to do.

Teachers and others in the community have a responsibility to intervene when students or other adults demonstrate stereotyped thinking and prejudice. It is essential for us not to remain passively listening; inaction can be seen as acceptance of and agreement with derogatory comments or jokes shared within our hearing. Instead we can simply state, "I'm sorry, but I don't think that joke is funny." Although each incident may seem a small matter, such culturally sensitive behavior serves to educate children and other adults. In the classroom, of course, we have the opportunity of following up with appropriate learning experiences. Addressing stereotyped thinking is discussed in several chapters of this text.

The Prescribed Curriculum

Those who influence curriculum development are not always well informed. For example, former education secretary William Bennett, a highly literate man schooled in the classics, published a list of literature for K–8 classrooms in his report entitled *James Madison Elementary School: A Curriculum for American Students.*[3] He included only a few titles with multicultural content. In fact, of a total of 200 books listed by title, only 6 percent can be identified as multicultural. One title, *Sylvester and the Magic Pebble,* by William Steig, contains stereotypes of (1) a totally stereotyped female housekeeper/wife/mother and (2) police portrayed by this author-illustrator as pigs. (Such a book could be recommended only as a basis for a lesson on how stereotyped thinking permeates our society.) At best, Bennett's list of publications reveals a lack of information, if not concern. It is clear that "multicultural representation" was not one of the criteria for the selection of these books.

We must select instructional materials that include a greater percentage of quality literature by and about members of different ethnic groups as well as the many identity groups that have special needs and concerns. We must also find time in the already burgeoning curriculum for multicultural education. Multicultural concepts belong in every classroom and should therefore be written into the objectives of every lesson. From self-esteem to immigration to the contributions of men and women of every race and religion to the history of the United States, lessons must reinforce the worth of every person who makes up our diverse population.

The curriculum is prescribed in many ways, for example:

Textbooks selected
Commercial tests used by school districts
State departments of education—course of study
Specialty organizations—NCTE, NMA, NAEYC, IRA
Critics, researchers, authors

You may wish to explore this topic in the following resources:

William Bennett. *James Madison High School and James Madison Elementary School.*
U.S. Government, 1988.
E. D. Hirsch. *Cultural Literacy.* Houghton Mifflin, 1988.
Mary Ellen Van Camp, ed. *Testing.* Support for the Learning and Teaching of English,
NCTE, December 1988.

Fear of Handling Controversy

Teachers and textbook publishers have a tendency to avoid topics that invite controversy
in the classroom. Teachers feel uncomfortable with the expression of real emotion—fear,
anger, or conflict. Publishers deliberately excise multicultural issues from reprinted materials. An example of the latter is noted in reprinting *Sound of Sunshine, Sound of Rain* by
Florence Heide. The climax of this outstanding short novel, a racial confrontation that
provides insight into the development of a major character, is deleted from both the reprint
in a basal reader and the filmed version of this well-written book.[4] Without this realistic
scene, the quality of the author's work is diminished because the character development
remains one-dimensional; and the students have missed an effective multicultural learning
experience about humanity.

Dealing with real topics in the classroom adds vitality and stimulates student involvement in learning. Children who are confronting racism and dealing with the pain of
conflict in their own lives benefit from classroom discussions that acknowledge the reality
of what they face. Reading and discussion, for example, may suggest ways that others have
found to deal with problems students encounter. Teachers need to seek ways of engaging
students in multicultural topics even if these subjects may be controversial. Such literature
as that cited throughout this text can help you present controversial issues and human
feelings through a kind of simulation that is not threatening. Authors who include sensitive
topics in well-written novels, dramas, or essays have created useful texts from which
students can learn multicultural concepts. All educators share the responsibility for knowing and making skillful use of instructional options beyond the less inspiring textbook to
support multicultural education.

Communicating with Parents

Teachers need to apprise parents of the expected learning outcomes students are working
toward in their classrooms. Parents also need to become directly involved in their children's learning, providing encouraging support for school-initiated learning. You can suggest ways, too, for parents to extend their children's learning of content and skills. You
might send home a short list of reasonable activities for them, for example, taking their
children to the local library or just talking and listening with respect to their children's
conversation. Such practices support the child's development of self-esteem and a positive
attitude toward learning.

On occasion, you will have a parent who objects to the content of the curriculum you
are presenting or to a specific classroom activity. This opposition might center on multicultural content or activities. For example, many parents object to a curriculum that works

toward developing self-esteem, which they equate as "teaching values." It is wise to discuss such an objection with your principal to determine proper handling of the matter and to obtain administrative support for your decisions. The principal should be able to clarify any legal aspect to be considered as well as to suggest appropriate interpersonal tactics. The law demands, for example, that we respect parental religious beliefs. As with all planning, our concern should remain student-centered as we attempt to avoid making a child feel ill at ease as a result of this parent-school interaction.

Censorship Efforts

Censorship may involve parental objections, discussed above, but censorship is such a complex and frequent concern that it deserves special attention. This topic could well be the subject of staff development within your district or a discussion for your school staff, including the principal. For example, you can determine together just how to handle requests to eliminate books from a reading list or from the school library. Having a procedure in place is very helpful for all staff members.

You might begin by obtaining material from various professional organizations. Many groups have an organizational stance that they will share with you. They may also suggest procedures and provide sample forms that are useful. Such information also provides the authority of a large, respected professional group to support your school practices. For example, the National Council of Teachers of English (NCTE) will give you one free copy of its position statement *Censorship: Don't Let It Become an Issue in Your Schools,* written by its Committee on Bias and Censorship in the Elementary School and published in 1978. It will also provide one free copy of a new statement related to nonprint media, *Guidelines for Dealing with Censorship of Nonprint Materials,* published in 1993. Address requests to NCTE, 1111 Kenyon Rd., Urbana, IL 61801. (You might also request a copy of their latest catalog, which lists other helpful teaching materials.)

Homophobia's Impact on Schooling

The broad issue of human rights in contemporary society includes awareness of homosexuality, gay rights, and lesbianism. These topics are frequently in the newspapers and on television, so they cannot be ignored. Whatever your personal stance, you need to be prepared to deal with questions from students and/or parents. You may also be involved in decision making at the school or district level regarding faculty hiring or firing, the purchase of instructional materials, and curriculum planning. This controversial topic requires discussion at all levels within the school district.

Questions in this area often also relate to censorship, as many school districts have discovered. For example, when New York City adopted a multicultural program entitled *The Rainbow Curriculum,* which included materials related to homosexual lifestyles, parents demanded that children's literature titles dealing with this topic be removed from the library. They also questioned inviting lesbian parents to the classroom or any similar recognition that a child had same-sex parents. Imagine how children who have same-sex parents feel when the school district appears to support the homophobia found in society as a whole.

As has been true with any controversial topic in children's literature, for example, death, titles presenting homosexual lifestyles are gradually appearing. Note that this topic is not brand new. You may wish to examine the following:

Frances Hanckel. *A Way of Life: A Young Person's Introduction Into What It Means to Be Gay.* Lothrop, 1979.

John Donovan. *I'll Get There; It Better Be Worth the Trip.* Harper, 1969.

Norma Klein. *Now That I Know.* Bantam, 1988.

George Shannon. *Unlived Affections.* Harper, 1989.

The "English Only" Movement

As mentioned in Chapter 1, the "English only" movement became a national concern in the 1980s, led by S. I. Hayakawa, then Senator from California. A number of states jumped on this bandwagon, declaring English the official state language. Today there is an active national organization that seeks to extend this effort. NCTE discusses the drawbacks of this policy in its position statement *The National Language Policy: A Position Statement from the Conference on College Composition and Communication* (one copy free from NCTE, 1111 Kenyon Rd., Urbana, IL 61801).

The English-only movement runs counter to efforts to support instruction in children's native languages. Yet, current research recommends that a child learn to read and write in the native language first while English is being acquired. Such professional organizations as Teachers of English to Speakers of Other Languages (TESOL) bring thousands of teachers together at annual conferences to address the complex issues involved. They publish a newsletter and varied instructional materials to support bilingual education. Inquire about their publication list and sample publications at 1600 Cameron St., Alexandria, VA 22314. NCTE offers a free position statement on this topic, *TESOL and Bilingual Education,* prepared by the Committee on Issues in ESL and Bilingual Education. Teachers at all levels should be well informed regarding issues related to language development and literacy instruction.

Assessment, Testing, and the Effect of Bias

All methods of assessment are being critiqued on the basis of equity. To provide for diverse learning styles, students need to experience varied methods of assessing mastery. A new assessment strategy that is receiving much attention is portfolio assessment, a method that is highly individualized.

More pertinent to this textbook is the concern about cultural bias in tests. Test authors are being asked to review all tests to determine whether they contain cultural bias. Are there underlying assumptions about common knowledge that place some students at a disadvantage?

The American Association for Higher Education (1 Dupont Circle, Washington, D.C. 20036) has published the following excellent summary of assessment practices, "Principles of Good Practice for Assessing Student Learning":

1. **The assessment of student learning begins with educational values.**

   Assessment is not an end in itself but a vehicle for educational improvement. Its effective practice, then, begins with and enacts a vision of the kinds of learning we most value for students and strive to help them achieve. Educational values should drive not only *what* we choose to assess but also *how* we do so. Where questions about educational mission and values are skipped over, assessment threatens to be an exercise in measuring what's easy, rather than a process of improving what we really care about.

2. **Assessment is most effective when it reflects an understanding of learning as multidimensional, integrated, and revealed in performance over time.**

   Learning is a complex process. It entails not only what students know but what they can do with what they know; it involves not only knowledge and abilities but values, attitudes, and habits of mind that affect both academic success and performance beyond the classroom. Assessment should reflect these understandings by employing a diverse array of methods, including those that call for actual performance, using them over time so as to reveal change, growth, and increasing degrees of integration. Such an approach aims for a more complete and accurate picture of learning, and therefore firmer bases for improving our students' educational experience.

3. **Assessment works best when the programs it seeks to improve have clear, explicitly stated purposes.**

   Assessment is a goal-oriented process. It entails comparing educational performance with educational purposes and expectations—these derived from the institution's mission, from faculty intentions in program and course design, and from knowledge of students' own goals. Where program purposes lack specificity or agreement, assessment as a process pushes a campus toward clarity about where to aim and what standards to apply; assessment also prompts attention to where and how program goals will be taught and learned. Clear, shared, implementable goals are the cornerstone for assessment that is focused and useful.

4. **Assessment requires attention to outcomes but also and equally to the experiences that lead to those outcomes.**

   Information about outcomes is of high importance; where students "end up" matters greatly. But to improve outcomes, we need to know about student experience along the way—about the curricula, teaching, and kind of student effort that lead to particular outcomes. Assessment can help us understand which students learn best under what conditions; with such knowledge comes the capacity to improve the whole of their learning.

5. **Assessment works best when it is ongoing, not episodic.**

   Assessment is a process whose power is cumulative. Though isolated, "one-shot" assessment can be better than none, improvement is best fostered when assessment entails a linked series of activities undertaken over time. This may mean tracking the progress of individual students, or of cohorts of students; it may mean collecting the same examples of student performance or using the same instrument semester after semester. The point is to monitor progress toward intended goals in a spirit of continuous improvement. Along the way, the assessment process itself should be evaluated and refined in light of emerging insights.

6. **Assessment fosters wider improvement when representatives from across the educational community are involved.**

   Student learning is a campus-wide responsibility, and assessment is a way of enacting that responsibility. Thus, while assessment efforts may start small, the aim over time is to involve people from across the educational community. Faculty play an especially important role, but assessment's questions can't be fully addressed without participation by student-affairs educators, librarians, administrators, and students. Assessment may also involve individuals from beyond the campus (alumni/ae, trustees, employers) whose experience can enrich the sense of appropriate aims and standards for learning. Thus understood, assessment is not a task for small groups of experts but a collaborative activity; its aim is wider, better-informed attention to student learning by all parties with a stake in its improvement.

7. **Assessment makes a difference when it begins with issues of use and illuminates questions that people really care about.**

   Assessment recognizes the value of information in the process of improvement. But to be useful, information must be connected to issues or questions that people really care about. This implies assessment approaches that produce evidence that relevant parties will find credible, suggestive, and applicable to decisions that need to be made. It means thinking in advance about how the information will be used, and by whom. The point of assessment is not to gather data and return "results"; it is a process that starts with the questions of decision-makers, that involves them in the gathering and interpreting of data, and that informs and helps guide continuous improvement.

8. **Assessment is most likely to lead to improvement when it is part of a larger set of conditions that promote change.**

   Assessment alone changes little. Its greatest contribution comes on campuses where the quality of teaching and learning is visibly valued and worked at. On such campuses, the push to improve educational performance is a visible and primary goal of leadership; improving the quality of undergraduate education is central to the institution's planning, budgeting, and personnel decisions. On such campuses, information about learning outcomes is seen as an integral part of decision making, and avidly sought.

9. **Through assessment, educators meet responsibilities to students and to the public.**

   There is a compelling public stake in education. As educators, we have a responsibility to the publics that support or depend on us to provide information about the ways in which our students meet goals and expectations. But that responsibility goes beyond the reporting of such information; our deeper obligation—to ourselves, our students, and society— is to improve. Those to whom educators are accountable have a corresponding obligation to support such attempts at improvement.

Resistance to Multicultural Education

Related to the expressed concerns about censorship and the handling of controversial topics is the recognition that certain individuals and groups resist or actively combat multicultural education, because they do not believe that this emphasis is appropriate in our schools. They argue for assimilation into the so-called majority culture and the use of English as the only language in the United States. They bemoan the use of culturally sensitive terminology for groups and tag such efforts as "political correctness," a term that has acquired strong negative connotations in the media.

Daniel Boorstin, Pulitzer Prize–winning historian and former librarian of Congress, states: "The menace to America today is in the emphasis on what separates us rather than on what brings us together—the separations of race, or religious practice, of origins, of language." He sees the idea of a "hyphenated American" as "un-American" and will not use such terms as African American, stating that we are all Americans. He does not support bilingual teaching, citing his own Jewish heritage as an example of appropriate assimilation in the new world. Author of numerous texts on the American experience through history,[5] he advocates an emphasis on community rather than diversity, and he favors accommodating immigrants as an aspect of American humanism. If such a respected, prominent writer and thinker speaks against multicultural approaches in education and the celebration of diversity, just think of the numbers of lesser-known people who share this viewpoint!

Objections often come from religious groups who rely on "freedom of religion" to support their objections to practices in the schools. You might like to read the January 1994 issue of The Association of Supervision and Curriculum Development's journal, *Educational Leadership,* which presents ten articles explicating aspects of this contemporary issue under the title "Public Schools and the Christian Fundamentalists." This issue is also explored in a special report, *Church, State, and the Religious Right,* published by Americans United for Separation of Church & State, 8120 Fenton Street, Silver Spring, MD 20910.

Those who disagree with multicultural approaches to education will never totally disappear from our society despite our best efforts. As teachers, you must be aware of such opposing viewpoints and prepare to combat criticism of sound theories and practices that the schools are trying to implement. You need to have a clear understanding of your stance and the rationale for including multicultural education in the schools in order to argue persuasively.

The Relationship of Violence to Multicultural Education

Children of all ages are exposed to violence in their lives. More than one-third of the first and second graders in our nation's capital have seen dead bodies. Forty-five percent report that they have witnessed muggings, and thirty-one percent report having witnessed shootings.[6] Recently, the National Medical Association, comprising 16,000 black doctors, addressed "violence reduction in the African-American community." The association's president, Dr. Leonard Lawrence, stated "We've really got to teach our young people that there are alternative ways of problem solving" and noted that "there is some value in being disciplined," being in charge of one's behavior. Lawrence advocated teaching students "the positive aspects of discipline at a very early age, teaching them how to achieve, how to learn, how to interact with other people." He also encouraged adults to spend time with young people, to serve as models and mentors to boys and girls growing up under difficult circumstances.[7]

Violence and abuse touch all of our lives. People of all national origins and cultural backgrounds cause violence and abuse, and all are at some time the victims of such attacks on human rights, even if only indirectly. Teaching for diversity addresses concerns that may help bring violence under control. Teaching students "how to get along," for example, stresses self-esteem, empathy, and equity, which should help alleviate the same conditions that lead to stereotyping and discrimination as well as violence and abuse. Thus, as we work toward achieving one goal, we will also be working toward achieving the second.

Working with students at risk, discussed in some detail in Chapter 2, should also help to reduce violence and abuse, particularly in relation to adolescents. We need to address the problems that follow from having young people who drop out of school, especially males, on the street with nothing constructive to do. The long summer school vacation may also prove to be a problem if students have nothing to occupy them and do not have supervision during those months.

Recap

Teachers must recognize the controversial nature of issues related to multicultural education. Each of us has to reflect on the rationale for what we teach and how we provide for the good of each learner in our classrooms. We need to be prepared to discuss issues that will almost certainly arise throughout a teaching career.

Once we acknowledge the existence of the issues presented in this section, we can address them and strive to find solutions. Multicultural education can become a reality.

PROGRESSIVE THINKING AND PROMISING PRACTICES

Today we see visible efforts to deal with issues related to multicultural education. However, a difference of opinion remains. We need to support progressive thinking and to recognize exemplary practices that can be replicated across the country.

Self-Esteem—The Bottom Line

Humanistic educators wrote of self-image and self-concept in the 1960s, and affective education became a goal for many teachers.[8] Benjamin Bloom recognized both cognitive and affective domains in writing objectives for education.[9] Concern for the student as the center of the curriculum was expressed by such theoreticians as James Moffett in the first edition of *The Student-Centered Curriculum*.[10]

Currently there is renewed interest in the student's role in the learning process. We talk of student self-esteem as the foundation for learning; we recognize that all students need a sense of worth—an "I can" attitude—if they are to strive to achieve. We are concerned about the classroom climate as we try to build an attitude of trust between student and teacher. We try to let students know that making mistakes is an essential part of real learning, so that they will dare to take risks as they brainstorm and solve problems together. We need citizens who have genuine self-esteem, for they are the people who can reach out confidently to others with empathy and caring. Self-esteem undergirds the effort to save at-risk students—a topic of national concern that we discuss later in this section.

You may wish to explore this topic in the following resources:

Jack Canfield and Harold Wells. *100 Ways to Enhance Self-concepts in the Classroom.* Prentice-Hall, 1976.

C. Combs. *Humanistic Education.* Allyn and Bacon, 1974.

Matthew McKay and Patrick Fanning. *Self-Esteem.* St. Martin's, 1987.

Eileen Tway, ed. *Reading Ladders for Human Relations,* 6th ed. National Council of Teachers of English, 1981.

Writing "Thinking"

Many educators recognize the need for instruction in K–12 classrooms (as well as at preschool and adult levels) that encourages students to think. Whereas some educators focus only on "critical thinking," which they associate with the scientific method, others also recognize the importance of stimulating creative and reflective thinking.

Focus on the writing process, as advocated by National Writing Project consultant-teachers across the country for the past decade, is closely tied to the development of thinking skills. Thinking leads to writing as one way of expressing ideas, and the process of writing these ideas extends thinking. Thus, the writing of "thinking" is a generative process that engages students in dealing with real issues and concerns. Students who have self-esteem express their ideas confidently, and their successful writing supports the growth of self-esteem, which is another interlocking learning process that should be in any classroom.

You may wish to explore this topic further in the following resources:

Julie Jensen, ed. *Composing and Comprehending.* ERIC Clearinghouse on Reading and Communications Skills, 1984.

Judith Langer and Arthur Applebee. *How Writing Shapes Thinking: A Study of Teaching and Learning.* National Council of Teachers of English, Research Report No. 22, 1987.

Carol Olson. *Thinking/Writing: Fostering Critical Thinking Skills through Writing.* University of California at Irvine, 1984.

James Squire, ed. *The Dynamics of Language Learning.* National Conference on Research in English, 1987.

Iris M. Tiedt. *Writing: From Topic to Evaluation.* Allyn and Bacon, 1989.

Iris M. Tiedt et al. *Teaching Thinking in K–12 Classrooms.* Allyn and Bacon, 1989.

Literature-Based Reading Instruction

A developing trend is the use of literature or trade books to support instruction in all subject areas. The use of library books instead of the usual textbook humanizes the curriculum and lends a vitality to learning that has not heretofore been present. Studies point out that the usual history textbook, for example, presents a sterile summary of events compared to a well-written trade book.[11] Furthermore, literature (including nonfiction, narrative prose, and poetry) sets historical events in a rich context that may more effectively engage student interest in learning. Students who read Scott O'Dell's novel, *Sarah Bishop,* for example, will have an affective knowledge of the War for Independence that is not produced by the sterile prose of most history textbooks for young adults.

Use of literature presumes that we will dismiss the necessity to "cover a textbook" in favor of guiding students to choose selections that provide different perspectives of the same period of history or the geography of a country. This approach also presupposes a different way of teaching—employing discovery methods that lead students to question and to think as they analyze, evaluate, and reflect. This approach presupposes, too, a confident teacher who can facilitate student learning and who does not need to lean on textbooks that provide questions at the end of each chapter and an answer key to ease the task of grading. We need a way of teaching that leads students to construct their own meaning based on knowledge gathered from varied sources. Literature study offers such a way, a way that also engages students in a humanistic experience that may lead to the empathy we are attempting to achieve through multicultural education.

Whole-language instruction, a popular theory of teaching in the elementary school, uses literature for instruction and the development of literacy skills. Based on sound theory, a whole-language program encourages students to use both oral and written language, real language for real purposes. This approach includes listening to many stories read aloud and also reading many books. As they write and read, children also learn to connect sounds (phonemes) and symbols (graphemes), popularly termed "phonics," as they work with words in context. They respond to the stories they hear through active discussions, acting out, retelling; through literature they learn varied content about many interesting topics. They also begin to author books themselves, putting their books on the shelf beside those of other writers. Above all, they learn to enjoy reading and writing.

Kenneth Goodman. *What's Whole about Whole Language?* Heineman, 1989.

Janet Hickman et al. *Children's Literature in the Classroom: Extending Charlotte's Web.* Christopher-Gordon, 1993.

Heidi Mills et al. *Looking Closely: Exploring the Role of Phonics in One Whole Language Classroom.* National Council of Teachers of English, 1992.

Zena Sutherland et al. *Children and Books.* Scott, Foresman, 1992.

Educating Teachers for Empowerment

Increasing attention is being paid to the quality of teaching and the professionalization of teaching as a respected career. Respondents to a 1988 nationwide study by the Association of Supervision and Curriculum Development recommended emphasizing the following to improve the quality of instruction and to provide a more professional role for teachers at all levels:

- Empowerment: Teachers need more control and autonomy in the classroom and in determining what is taught in general.
- Recruitment: We need to work to attract top-quality people to choose teaching as a career.
- Retention: We also need to work to retain top-quality teachers in the field.
- Roles: Teachers need support as they assume new roles, for example, in management of the inclusive classroom.
- Training: Teachers need more professional staff development opportunities.[12]

The establishment of The National Board of Teaching represents a positive effort to upgrade the status and ability of teachers in the field. Funded by the Carnegie Foundation and grounded in the work of Lee Shulman, the board provides a performance-based test as a basis for national certification as a master teacher. It is expected that many top teachers will opt to acquire this national recognition.

Site-based management is another positive approach to involving teachers in decision making about how education is carried out at the local level. Although not an easy process to initiate, some principals and their staffs are committed to the necessary study and effort required. The emphasis is on collaboration rather than top-down direction; everyone needs to be informed. Such promising practices add to a sense of empowerment for teachers involved.

Activism results from teacher empowerment as teachers become advocates for school change. Informed teachers are needed to take a position and speak on children's behalf. Ask yourself what you truly believe about teaching. What do you have to say about teaching to provide equity for diverse learners?

True empowerment of the teacher comes from within. It is not something that an external task force can fund or a legislature can enforce. We all, however, have a responsibility to nurture this sense of empowerment, which is akin to self-esteem and self-confidence. The teacher who has this sense of power is best able to teach multiculturally, addressing controversy with equanimity and sharing leadership with young learners in the classroom.

Teacher education can empower novice teachers by providing them with basic knowledge in the foundations, liberal studies, and pedagogy, including multicultural education. Such teachers have confidence in their knowledge base, but above all they know how to apply this knowledge in the classroom. Furthermore, the teacher who possesses a sense of empowerment is best able to nurture that same feeling in students. You may wish to explore this topic further in the following resources:

James A. Banks and Cherry Banks. *Multicultural Education: Issues and Perspectives.* Allyn and Bacon, 1993.

Louis Harris. *The Second Year: New Teachers' Expectations and Ideals, A Survey of New Teachers Who Completed Their Second Year of Teaching in Public Schools in 1992.* Metropolitan Life Insurance Co., 1992.

Bruce Joyce et al. *The Self-Renewing School.* Association of Supervision and Curriculum Development, 1993.

Seymour B. Sarason. *The Case for Change: Rethinking the Preparation of Educators.* Jossey-Bass, 1993.

Schools as Centers of Inquiry

Gradually, teachers are recognizing that direct, teacher-dominated instruction is not as effective as discovery methods that engage students in inquiry. We need to consider the goals of education in terms of student learning, the expected outcomes that we identify. The testing of student achievement should then reflect what we really mean to teach. The evaluation of teacher performance should in turn reflect our expectations for student learning.

In direct instruction the teacher typically lectures, perhaps addressing questions to individual students one by one; only a small percentage of students are actively involved at any one time, and there is little student interaction. This is the quiet, orderly classroom; learning follows predictable lines and is easily evaluated. In this type of teaching, the teacher generates the questions, and the kind of question asked has one correct answer, which of course the teacher knows. This has been the traditional mode of instruction for many years.

When inquiry approaches are used, however, the students generate questions to which they need to know the answers. There is self-motivation as each one works 100 percent of the class time on a self-selected problem or project. Metacognitive approaches guide students to awareness of the thinking processes in which they are engaged. They talk and write to express thinking and test it against the thinking of other students in pairs or small groups. They accept ownership for the learning that is going on because they selected a topic in which they have an interest. Far from abdicating their role, teachers plan extensively in order to set up discovery learning situations; often they plan directly with students. They facilitate and support the learning process and serve as resource persons.

Evaluation of progress is part of the inquiry—a process shared by teacher and student. In this kind of classroom students have an opportunity to learn more than is presented in a single textbook, and they naturally develop self-esteem. Thus, what they learn is both cognitive and affective, but it may not always be easily measured by tests used by school districts. Because such approaches are more sensitive to individual student needs, they fit with the outcomes we have identified for multicultural education. They also show promise in supporting the at-risk students, an identified group that needs special attention in our schools.

You may wish to explore this topic further in the following resources:

Kenneth Goodman et al. *Report Card on Basal Readers.* National Council of Teachers of English, 1988.

Robert J. Marzano et al., eds. *Dimensions of Thinking: A Framework for Curriculum and Instruction.* Association for Supervision and Curriculum Development, 1988.

James Moffett and Betty Jean Wagner. *The Student-Centered Curriculum.* Houghton Mifflin, 1991.

Iris M. Tiedt et al. *Teaching Thinking in K–12 Classrooms.* Allyn and Bacon, 1989.

Reflection (Thinking), an Essential Aspect of Learning

Opportunities for thinking of all kinds, but especially reflection, need to be integrated throughout instruction at all levels. The child is a thinker from birth, an active learner observing what is happening in the world, asking questions as a way of learning, processing information. The child's acquisition of language is an example of the amazing discovery process in action as the newborn human gradually abstracts the complexities of a grammar system from language heard in the environment. Constructing hypotheses and developing theories about how the language works, growing children test these hypotheses by communicating. Never afraid of making errors, children talk, talk, talk, trying out what they have learned.

Only recently have we recognized the need to relate what we know about the infant's acquisition of speech to the later acquisition of literacy abilities. While acknowledging the limitations of this way of learning more complex content and skills, we realize that learner-generated questioning and the construction of hypotheses are natural and essential aspects of thinking and learning that we need to continue to encourage. This approach has much to offer multicultural education, too, as children probe into new areas of study.

Teachers are stimulated by the challenge of teaching thinking skills. Engaging students in thinking activities encourages the students to generate the questions rather than the teacher. This kind of student-centered instruction can involve learners in problem solving and interacting with other students as they study concepts related to racism, stereotyping, and prejudice. Multicultural literature offers an opportunity to explore a wide variety of thought-provoking topics. Analysis, synthesis, and evaluation are the kind of advanced thinking skills even the youngest students can employ when led by a competent teacher.

You may wish to explore this topic further in the following resources:

Beau F. Jones et al., eds. *Strategies for Teaching and Learning: Cognitive Instruction in the Content Areas.* Association of Supervision and Curriculum Development, 1987.

Iris M. Tiedt et al. *Reading/Thinking/Writing: A Holistic Language and Literacy Program for the K–8 Classroom.* Allyn and Bacon, 1989.

Iris M. Tiedt et al. *Teaching Thinking in K–12 Classrooms.* Allyn and Bacon, 1989.

S. R. Yussen and M. C. Smith, eds. *Reading across the Life Span.* Springer-Verlag, 1993.

Early Childhood Education

We have long known that attitudes and values are firmly rooted in what is learned during a child's early years. What is not learned at this time, furthermore, constitutes a great loss that may never be overcome. Although we now recognize and can work to correct it, children who do not have good learning opportunities during these early years enter kindergarten and first grade with a handicap.

Early childhood intervention instruction for children may alleviate any discrepancy an individual child may have. Such projects as Head Start and other organized preschool programs strive to build a strong experiential and knowledge base before children enter the formal school system, so that children are better prepared for success in formal schooling from the outset.

As we are making special efforts to prepare children to enter school, we are also rethinking the concept of "readiness." Rather than making the student "ready" for literacy instruction, for example, we are now considering how the school can better meet the needs of each individual child. This fits with our emphasis in this text on teaching for diversity to provide equitable education that accommodates individual learning styles and abilities.

The ungraded primary is not a new idea, but it has come into its own in many contemporary schools that recognize the importance of individualizing instruction. In an ungraded structure, the emphasis is on achieving specific outcomes rather than moving through the grades. We know that some children require more time (and some less) to achieve the basic foundation for learning on which upper-grade teachers can build. Giving children more time without branding them "failures" by "holding them back" increases children's success rate and their sense of self-esteem. Thus, they have a much better chance of success throughout their elementary school years.

Vivian Paley, an experienced kindergarten teacher in New Orleans, New York City, and Chicago's Laboratory School, focused on the ethics of play with young children. To avoid exclusionary attitudes and behaviors, she established this rule: "You can't say, you can't play." Children quickly learn to accept the rule as fair, although many discussions ensued related to its implications. Paley notes that in her early years of teaching she tried to ignore children's unfairness, hoping it would work itself out. It was only when she was almost sixty years old that she undertook to assume a more active leadership role as a teacher. She has written a number of books about her experiences, including *You Can't Say You Can't Play* (Harvard University Press, 1992). As she states optimistically, "If every kindergarten in the country were to promote this idea and it would continue year by year by year, in twenty years, when everybody got out of college, we would have a nicer world."[13]

You may wish to explore this topic further in the following resources:

G. Robert Carlsen and Anne Sherrill. *Voices of Readers: How We Come to Love Books.* National Council of Teachers of English, 1988.

V. Hildebrand. *Introduction to Early Childhood Education.* Macmillan, 1986.

N. Peterson. *Early Intervention for Handicapped and At-Risk Children.* Love, 1987.

B. Spodel et al. *Foundations of Early Childhood Education.* Prentice-Hall 1987.

Join the Early Childhood Education Network—Contact S. M. Childs, Teaneck Public Schools, One Merrison St., Teaneck, NJ 07666.

The journal *Young Children* is published by the National Association for the Education of Young Children (NAFYC), 1834 Connecticut Avenue, NW, Washington, D.C. 20008.

Dimension is published quarterly by Southern Association on Children under Six (SACUS), Box 5403, Brady Station, Little Rock, AR 72215.

Growing Concern for At-Risk Students

Within the past decade, various studies are pointing out that the United States faces an economic crisis. In the next century we will not have the educated work force that we need in order to compete in the world. The reason is clear: A high percentage of our students are dropping out of school long before graduating from high school. Instead of a trained work force, we will have a welfare-dependent segment of society that does not contribute to the nation's economy. Instead, these uneducated young people will drain the national income.

School districts and whole communities are addressing the problem of these at-risk students. This group includes the hundreds of thousands of young girls who become pregnant each year, the young adolescents on the streets involved in drugs and crime, and the little children who come into our schools with limited knowledge and experience. Multicultural education, with its emphasis on empathy, offers a hope of reaching these students before they drop out of school and out of mainstream society.

James Comer stresses the need for emphasizing relationship issues and the social condition—"interaction between teacher and student, between parent and student, between parent and teacher." In carrying out his School Development Program, he argues for providing support for "the kind of development that all children need." He also emphasizes the need to recognize the influence of poverty, which is an alarming reality in our large cities."[14] The Children's Defense Fund reports that the percentage of children under eighteen living in poverty is over 40 percent in Detroit, Laredo, New Orleans, Flint, Miami, Hartford, Gary, Cleveland, Atlanta, and Dayton. What is appalling is that the percentage of children living in poverty in the United States, the "land of plenty," is more than double that of Canada, Britain, France, the Netherlands, Sweden, and West Germany.[15] We need to continue efforts to support children who are in our schools.

You may wish to explore this topic further in the following resources:

Dianne Applemen and Johanna McClear. *Teacher, the Children Are Here.* Scott, Foresman, 1988.

Association for Supervision and Curriculum Development, 1250 N. Pitt St., Alexandria, VA 22314. Audiocassette series; five tapes by educators from large urban school districts describing how they are handling the problem of at-risk students.

James S. Coleman. "Families and Schools." *Educational Researcher,* August/September, 1987: pp. 32–38.

James Comer. "Dr. James Comer's Plan for Ensuring the Future." *Black Issues in Higher Education,* May 20, 1993, pp. 42–47. (See also the same author's *Beyond Black and White: Black Child Care, School Power,* and *Maggie's American Dream.*)

Michael Harrington. *Who Are the Poor? A Profile of the Changing Faces of Poverty in the United States.* Justice for All, 1987.

Dianne W. Hayes. "Learning in Poverty: Children in Crisis." *Black Issues in Higher Education.* June 17, 1993, pp. 21–25.

International and Global Issues

Global and international issues are directly related to multicultural education at the world level of interaction. Americans need to learn how to operate in a rapidly changing world scene. U.S. foreign policies must change, and the citizens of this democracy must understand and support such change. Professor Richard Gardner outlines global issues in a 1992 report sponsored by the United National Development Programme (UNDP). He sees the following as being threats to the welfare of the world, including the United States:

1. Environmental degradation: Lack of emphasis on environmental concerns in the U.S., saving the planet.
2. Energy productivity: U.S. failure to deal with the energy problem; the limits of natural resources.
3. Population growth: Failure to lead efforts to control population explosion; problems related to hunger and poverty.
4. People on the move: Handling of refugee and immigration problems, particularly in terms of human rights.
5. Humanitarian crises: Intervention in other countries to assure human rights; what is our responsibility and our role.
6. Drugs: More effort put into controlling the demand for drugs rather than focusing on the supplier; the U.S. is the big consumer.[16]

Students might well discuss any of these issues, generating questions about U.S. policy and how it might be changed. It is interesting to consider, too, the factors that prevent such changes from taking place. Any one of these concerns offers an opportunity to seek out information and to become involved in effecting change in your community.

An executive speaking for the international division of a large conglomerate includes the following among the projected corporate needs for the year 2000:

> Employees who are not predominantly ethnocentric in their view of the world.
>
> People who are able to work and live abroad effectively, who are comfortable with expatriation and repatriation and have the potential for linguistic success for studying foreign languages.
>
> Employees who understand that the United States is competing on an even playing field in the next century . . . that the competition is as good as, often better than, that offered by U.S. organizations.
>
> Employees who are willing to take risks—to try and maybe have setbacks, but who can get up, learn from adversity and try again. . . .
>
> Employees who do not rely on English only sources of information. . . . [17]

This statement supports the need for educating students to live in a multicultural world. It extends the empathy we are trying to achieve among persons living in the United States to the global village that we share. Children who are brought up with limited perspectives of the world will be handicapped, unable to move beyond the narrow environs in which they were raised.

You may wish to explore this topic further in the following resources:

Carnegie Endowment National Commission Report. *Changing Our Ways.* Brookings Institute, 1992. (Order from the institute, Box 029, Washington, D.C. 10042 for $12.95, including shipping.)

Paulo Freire and Donaldo Macedo. *Literacy: Reading the Word and the World.* Bergin and Garvey, 1987.

June Jordan. *On Call: Political Essays.* South End Press, 1987.

M. Trow. "Comparative Reflections on Leadership in Higher Education." *Journal of Education,* 20: pp. 143–59.

M. Tsukada. "A Factual Overview of Education in Japan and the United States." In W. K. Cummings et al., ed. *Educational Policies in Crisis: Japanese and American Perspectives.* Praeger, 1986.

Outcome-Based Education

Similar to competency-based education, outcome-based education (OBE) supports efforts to teach for diversity. Adopted in such states as Minnesota, OBE promises to ensure the greater success of all students, and it permits individuals to work at different paces to achieve the same outcome. As discussed in Chapter 2, in planning a lesson we begin by identifying the expected outcomes for any learning experience; at the same time we select the appropriate assessment processes to be used. Individual students who know just what they have to achieve and the performance criteria they need to meet have a clear sense of direction. They can work on any outcome for as long as it takes to achieve success, and they can get appropriate assistance.

Related to OBE is multi-age grouping, which is similar to the ungraded primary. Typically used in the elementary school, multi-age grouping permits children to learn at an individual pace. Under this plan they are grouped and regrouped for different purposes—interests, ability, outcomes. Emphasis is placed on what they do achieve, not on failure, so individual self-esteem remains intact while children move from one learning experience to another. Slower learners receive the help they need while students who are academically talented can move ahead.

Recap

As we consider multicultural education, it is important to note progressive thinking and practices that stand out as exemplary. Across the country, teachers and school districts are making sincere efforts to reach multicultural goals from different perspectives. Grounded in the principle of achieving self-esteem for all students and leading to understanding of others, these programs may address the needs of preschool children or adolescent at-risk students; they may be directed toward preparing the teacher; or they may deal directly with selection of content or methods of delivering the curriculum. Increasing support can be identified for practices that support multicultural education.

REVIEWING THE STUDY OF MULTICULTURAL TEACHING

In this book we have presented a philosophy of teaching that is grounded in humanity and a sincere desire to make the world a better place in which to live. We believe that education, particularly in the early years, offers the only route to the empathy for others that is necessary to achieve cooperative planning and harmonious living on our planet. We live in an interdependent world. It is our belief that multicultural education is subsumed in the meaning of democracy as we aim to carry it out in the United States. We hope to educate teachers who will bear this message.

Multicultural teaching is a broad topic that cannot be taught in one single course. Therefore, we have presented multicultural studies as a spiraling curriculum comprising concepts and understandings that evolve over years of schooling. Threading its way through all instruction, multicultural education is a lifelong endeavor. For the purposes of review and assessment, we list again here the assumptions on which we have based our presentation, presented in Chapter 1. As we revisit these assumptions, we will consider the implications of each one in terms of practice. You can use this self-assessment as you plan for your professional development as a multicultural teacher. Where are you in your ability to carry out multicultural teaching?

Assumptions Underlying Multicultural Teaching

MULTICULTURAL EDUCATION: THEORY AND PRACTICE

Well prepared	Adequate	Needs study	
			1. The United States is a multiculture, a society comprising many diverse cultures. All of living, including schooling, involves contact between different cultures and is, therefore, multicultural. No one culture can be considered more American than any other.
			2. The United States is gradually moving away from its expressed goal of assimilation or making everyone alike (the melting-pot metaphor) toward recognizing and appreciating the diversity in our society (the "tossed salad," or mosaic, metaphor). Educators play a role in disseminating this knowledge and acting on its implications.
			3. Multicultural education is too complex and pervasive a topic to be encompassed in a single course for teacher educators. All of education must reflect multicultural awareness. Curricula for grades P–8 must be designed to teach content about our multiculture and to provide equity for all learners in all subjects.
			4. We should not pretend or even aim to be creating teaching materials that are bias-free. Instead, we should guide students to recognize the biases from which they and all people operate.
			5. We need to clarify our use of such terms as *culture, ethnicity,* and *race.* We also need to be aware of accepted labels for groups of people within our population, speaking out against insensitive usage whenever appropriate.
			6. Although every child grows up within a given culture, he or she is shaped over the years by additional influences, such as education and personal interactions with others. Education can guide students to become more aware of and appreciative of their individual cultures, their heritage. Children can also learn to avoid ethnocentrism by being open to the cultural ideas of others.
			7. All children enter school with a store of prior knowledge, closely aligned with their individual cultural backgrounds, on which teachers can build.
			8. Education can guide all students to become more aware and appreciative of the many cultures that people contributed to what is now the United States. Because of our history, we cannot identify a single "American" culture; rather we all comprise a giant multiculture composed of a diverse national population, a chracteristic that makes our country unique. Diversity should be viewed as a strength, not as disunity.

Well prepared	Adequate	Needs study	
			9. Teachers need to be aware of their own cultural backgrounds and biases. They need to be aware of how these biases might influence their expectations of students and how they interact with others. Open dialogue with students will acknowledge these cultural influences as common to us all. Both teachers and students can learn together about different ideas and ways of thinking.
			10. Multicultural teaching is exciting because it is grounded in reality. Through active, constructivist learning strategies, students can become directly involved in their learning. At the same time, teachers may find such multicultural approaches more difficult because they may include controversy and emotion. Open discussion may lead to expression of anger or hostility, pain, and guilt. Since such discussions do not usually result in identification of "right answers," resulting ambiguity may cause students to feel unsettled.
			11. Multicultural education, global studies, and internationalization of the curriculum are related in their focus on human concerns. Thus, a study of universal needs suggests topics that overlap so that the three are not completely separate areas to be added to the school curriculum.
			12. Multicultural education deals with values and attitudes as well as knowledge. We can guide students to be aware of their own thinking and that of others. We guide them to make choices based on expressed reasoning, problem solving, and decision making. Because changes in values and attitudes and the development of empathy take time, assessing such changes quickly is not possible.

Where are you in your development as a multicultural teacher? In which areas do you feel the most need for additional study? It is important to remember that multicultural education will continue for all of us throughout our lives. We all have much to learn about "getting along" with others.

REFLECTIONS

As Dewey writes, education can empower, and teachers are the enabling agents who can make it happen. In this chapter, we have reflected with you on the beliefs that we have shared in this book, restating what we believe about teaching. We have also recognized problems and issues that may impede multicultural teaching and have identified ways in which education for understanding might realistically come about. We have concluded on a positive note with a discussion of progressive thinking and promising practices that are already in effect. We hope that you will find support for your endeavors to implement multicultural education in your classrooms.

Now that we have come full cycle in our study of multicultural education, we are reminded of the words of the noted author Aldous Huxley, which appeared in an interview in the *New York Times* in 1926:

> So the journey is over and I am back again, richer by much experience and poorer by many exploded convictions, many perished certainties. For conviction and certainties are too often the concomitants of ignorance . . . I set out on my travels knowing, or thinking I knew, how men should live, how be governed, how educated, what they should believe. I had my views on every activity of life. Now, on my return, I find myself without any of these pleasing certainties . . . The better you understand the significance of any question, the more difficult it becomes to answer it. Those who attach a high importance to their own opinion should stay at home. When one is traveling, convictions are mislaid as easily as spectacles, but unlike spectacles, they are not easily replaced.[17]

As we reflect on our journey, consider how your thinking has changed. What convictions have you lost along the way?

APPLICATIONS

1. Begin a clipping file of multicultural issues that appear in your local newspaper for a period of at least a month. Write a summary statement about multicultural concerns in your local area; these may reflect national or worldwide concerns.
2. Focus on one obstacle to the implementation of multicultural education enumerated in this chapter. Discuss this problem in a cooperative learning group. Share your group's thinking with the full class.
3. Begin interviewing local educators to identify one exemplary practice related to multicultural education in your area. Write a review of this idea or program and attempt to obtain newspaper coverage for this outstanding instructional practice.
4. Write a letter to the editor of your local newspaper, pointing out the accomplishments of one minority group in your community.

Endnotes

1. Maya Angelou. Speech at Moorhead State University, Moorhead, Minnesota, October 11, 1992.
2. National Council for Accreditation of Teacher Education. *Standards, Procedures, and Policies for the Accreditation of Professional Teacher Education Units.* NCATE, 1987.
3. William Bennett. *James Madison Elementary School: A Curriculum for American Students.* U.S. Government Printing Office, 1988.
4. Florence Heide. *Sound of Sunshine, Sound of Rain.* Parents, 1970.
5. Daniel Boorstin. Speech at Moorhead State University, April 17, 1993.
6. Bob Herbert. "Children the Victims of Violence." *The Forum* newspaper, Fargo, ND. August 21, 1993, p. A4.
7. Leonard Lawrence. Speech to the National Medical Association, December, 1992.
8. Arthur Combs. Chair of the Committee, ASCD Yearbook, *Perceiving, Behaving, Becoming.* ASCD, 1962. Mario Fantini and Gerald Weinstein. *The Disadvantaged.* Harper, 1968. William Glasser. *Schools without Failure.* Harper, 1969.
9. Benjamin Bloom. *All Our Children Learning: A Primer for Parents, Teachers and Other Educators.* McGraw, 1981.

10. James Moffett. *Student-Centered Language Arts and Reading Curriculum, K–13*. Houghton Mifflin, 1976.

11. The Bradley Commission. *Reforming the History Curriculum*. The Commission, 1989.

12. ASCD, Survey, 1988.

13. Mary Beth Marklein. "Learning to Play by New Rules: Teacher Adds Ethics of Play to Preschool Curriculum." *National Retired Teachers Association Bulletin*. September, 1993, p. 24.

14. James Comer. *Black Issues,* October, 1992.

15. Carnegie Endowment National Commission. *Changing Our Ways*. Brookings Institute, 1992. (Report available for $12.95, including shipping, from Box 029, Washington, D.C. 10042.)

16. Michael Copeland. International Divisions, Procter & Gamble Company. Letter to Dr. Leon Boothe, president, Northern Kentucky University.

17. Aldous Huxley. "Interview." *New York Times*. September 17, 1926.

Appendix

Developing a Knowledge Base for Multicultural Education

As you work with information presented in the ten chapters of *Multicultural Teaching,* you will find these extensive lists of books helpful as you develop units of study.

After you have completed this textbook, the lists will prove invaluable to you to support your teaching in any P–8 classroom.

EXTENDING YOUR RESOURCES

While using this detailed list of resources, you will want to continue expanding the list in areas that particularly interest you. For example, if you plan a broad study of Japan and Japanese Americans, you will want to explore *Japanese Education Today,* a 1987 publication from the U.S. Department of Education. Each new publication that you locate will refer you to other resources to extend your knowledge.

MULTICULTURAL UNDERSTANDINGS: INTERGROUP RELATIONS, ETHNIC STUDIES, GLOBAL EDUCATION

The books listed here will extend your knowledge and understanding about the diverse cultures and groups that make up the population of the United States. At the same time, you will become aware of the universal concerns that transcend national borders. Multicultural education begins with a study of the individual and expands to a study of the world and its interdependent peoples.

James A. Banks. *Multiethnic Education: Theory and Practice.* 2nd ed. Allyn and Bacon, 1988.

James A. Banks. *Teaching Strategies for Ethnic Studies.* 4th ed. Allyn and Bacon, 1987.
A good overview with many suggestions for the adult reader; suggests books that will provide information about specific ethnic groups.

Christine Bennett. *Comprehensive Multicultural Education: Theory and Practice.* Allyn and Bacon, 1986.

Francelia Butler and Richard W. Rotert. *The Triumph of the Spirit in Children's Literature.* Shoestring, 1986.

California State Dept. of Education. *Studies of Immersion Education: A Collection for U.S. Educators.* The Department, 1984.

Robert A. Carlson. *The Quest for Conformity: Americanization through Education.* Wiley, 1975. Explains hostility toward nonconformity; gives historical perspective.

Ruth Kearney Carlson. *Emerging Humanity; Multi-Ethnic Literature for Children and Adolescents.* Brown, 1972. Describes values and criteria for multiethnic literature; suggestions for use.

H. T. Collins and S. B. Zakariya, eds. *Getting Started in Global Education.* NAESP, 1982. Good overview of this viewpoint.

Arthur Combs. *A Personal Approach to Teaching: Beliefs That Make a Difference.* Allyn and Bacon, 1982.

Francesco Cordasco, ed. *American Ethnic Groups: The European Heritage.* Arno, 1980.

CIBC. *Violence, the Ku Klux Klan and the Struggle for Equality.* Council on Interracial Books for Children, 1981. Information specific to this group and racism, with ideas for giving students an educated viewpoint.

CIBC Racism and Sexism Resource Center for Educators. *Human and Anti-Human Values in Children's Books: Guidelines for the Future.* The Council, 1976. Analyzes over 200 books and explores "hidden messages" transmitted to young readers.

Maxine Dunfee and Claudia Crump. *Teaching for Social Values in Social Studies.* Association for Childhood Education International, 1974.

Henry Ferguson. *Manual for Multicultural Education,* Intercultural Press, 1987.

Jack D. Forbes. *The Education of the Culturally Different: A Multi-Cultural Approach.* Far West Laboratory for Educational Research and Development, 1969. Explains educational disadvantages of monocultural orientation.

Nina Gabelko and John Michaelis. *Reducing Adolescent Prejudice—A Handbook.* Teachers College, 1981.

Patrick Gallo, Jr. *Old Bread, New Wine: A Portrait of the Italian Americans.* Nelson, 1981.

Ricardo J. Garcia. *Education for Cultural Pluralism: Global Roots Stew.* Phi Delta Kappa, 1981.

———. *Fostering a Pluralistic Society through Multi-Ethnic Education.* Phi Delta Kappa, 1978.

———. *Teaching in a Pluralistic Society: Concepts, Models, Strategies.* Harper, 1982.

William Goodykoontz, ed. *Prejudice; The Invisible Wall.* Scholastic, 1968.

Andrew Greeley. *The Irish Americans: The Rise to Money and Power.* Harper, 1981.

Angela Grunsell. *Let's Talk about "Racism."* Gloucester, 1991.

Merrill Harmin, Howard Kirschenbaum, and Sidney B. Simon. *Clarifying Values through Subject Matter: Applications for the Classroom.* Winston, 1973.

Robert C. Hawley and Isabel L. Hawley. *Human Values in the Classroom.* Hart, 1975.

J. Joseph Huthmacher. *A Nation of Newcomers: Ethnic Minority Groups in American History.* Dell, 1981.

R. Johansen. *The National Interest and the Human Interest.* Princeton University Press, 1980.

Charlotte Matthews Keating, comp. *Building Bridges of Understanding.* Palo Verde, 1967. An annotated bibliography of minority groups.

————. *Building Bridges of Understanding Between Cultures.* Palo Verde, 1971. Annotations are listed by age level in each minority group; companion volume to above listing.

Ernece B. Kelly. *Searching for America. NCTE, 1972.* Contains critiques of twelve English textbooks; provides insights into distortions and exclusions in literature at all levels.

Louis Knowles and Kenneth Prewitt. *Institutional Racism in America.* Prentice, 1969. Explains ideological roots of racism; illustrates perpetuation of institutional racism.

Gil Loescher. *The World's Refugees: A Test of Humanity.* Harcourt, 1982. An overview suitable for older students.

Margaret MacDonald. *The Storyteller's Sourcebook: A Subject, Title, and Motif Index to Folklore Collections for Children.* Neal Shuman, 1982.

Joan Morrison and Charlotte Zabusky. *American Mosaic: The Immigrant Experience in the Words of Those Who Lived It.* Dutton, 1981. Oral history.

John Naisbitt. *Megatrends.* Warner, 1984. Exciting ideas about future interdependence of all people.

J. Rosenau. *The Study of Global Interdependence.* Nichols Publishing Co., 1981.

William Ryan. *Blaming the Victim.* Pantheon, 1971. Exposes myths and racism and social science; well written.

Andrew Scott. *The Dynamics of Interdependence.* University of North Carolina Press, 1982.

Steven Steinberg. *The Ethnic Myth: Race, Ethnicity and Class in America.* Atheneum, 1981.

Melvin Steinfield. *Cracks in the Melting Pot: Racism and Discrimination in American History.* Glencoe, 1970. A collection of readings providing insight into racist practices at many levels.

Madelon D. Stent, William R. Hazard, and Harry N. Rivlin. *Cultural Pluralism in Education: A Mandate for Change.* Appleton, 1973. Excellent collection of papers given at a Chicago conference by prominent educators and leaders from various cultural groups.

Robert W. Terry. *For Whites Only.* Eerdmans, 1970. Good analysis of the processes of racism; strategies for bringing about changes in the society.

Stephen Thernstrom et al. *Encyclopedia of American Ethnic Groups.* Harvard University Press, 1980.

M. Donald Thomas. *Pluralism Gone Mad.* Phi Delta Kappa. 1981.

Pierre Van den Berghe. *The Ethnic Phenomenon.* Elsevier, 1981.

Eileen Tway, ed. *Reading Ladders for Human Relations.* 6th ed. National Council of Teachers of English, 1981. An outstanding annotated booklist on relevant themes; updated periodically.

David A. Welton and John T. Mallan. *Children and Their World: Teaching Elementary Social Studies.* Rand McNally, 1976.

Background Information about the World

If you are near a large city, visit the embassies of specific countries. If not, you can write on school stationery to request free information.

Africa

Ghana: Press Attaché, Embassy of Ghana, 2460 16th St., NW., Washington, D.C. 20009.

Tunisia: Embassy of Tunisia, 2408 Massachusetts Ave., NW., Washington, D.C. 20008.

Union of South Africa: Information Service of South Africa, 655 Madison Ave., New York, NY 10021.

Asia

Australia: Australian News and Information Bureau, 636 Fifth Ave., New York, NY 10020.

Burma: Embassy of the Union of Burma, 2300 S St., NW., Washington, D.C. 20008.

China: Embassy of the Republic of China, 552 National Press Building, Washington, D.C. 20004.

India: Information Service of India, 2107 Massachusetts Ave., NW., Washington, D.C. 20008.

Indonesia: Embassy of the Republic of Indonesia, 2020 Massachusetts Ave., NW., Washington, D.C. 20006.

Iraq: Embassy of the Republic of Iraq, 1801 P St., NW., Washington, D.C. 20036.

Israel: Consul General of Israel, 105 Montgomery St., San Francisco, CA 94104.

Japan: Information Section, Embassy of Japan, 2514 Massachusetts Ave., NW., Washington, D.C. 20008.

Jordan: Embassy of the Hashemite Kingdom of Jordan, 2319 Wyoming Ave., NW., Washington, D.C. 20008.

Korea: Embassy of Korea, 1145 19th St., NW., Suite 312, Washington, D.C. 20036.

Malaysia: Embassy of Malaysia, 2401 Massachusetts Ave., NW., Washington, D.C. 20008.

New Zealand: New Zealand Embassy, 19 Observatory Circle, NW., Washington, D.C. 20008.

Pakistan: Embassy of Pakistan, 2315 Massachusetts Ave., NW., Washington, D.C. 20008.

Russia: Russian Embassy, 1706 18th St., NW., Washington D.C. 20009.

Sri Lanka: Embassy of Sri Lanka, 2148 Wyoming Ave., Washington, D.C. 20008.

Turkey: Turkey Tourism & Information Office, 500 5th Ave., New York, NY 10036.

Canada

Canadian Government Travel Bureau, Ottawa, Ontario, Canada K1A OH6.

Alberta: Alberta Government Travel Bureau, 1629 Centennial Building, Edmonton, Alberta, Canada T5J 4L6.

British Columbia: Dept. of Travel Industry, Govt. of British Columbia, 1019 Wharf St., Victoria, British Columbia, Canada V8W 2Z2.

Greater Vancouver Visitors and Convention Bureau, 650 Burrard St., Vancouver, British Columbia, Canada V6C 2L2.

Manitoba: Manitoba Tourist Branch, Dept. of Tourism and Recreation, Winnipeg 1, Manitoba, Canada.

Yukon: Yukon Tourism, Travel and Information Branch, Govt. of the Yukon, Box 2703, Whitehorse, Yukon, Canada.

New Brunswick Tourism, Post Office Box 12345, Fredericton, New Brunswick, Canada E3B 5C3.

Ontario Travel, Queen's Park, Toronto, Ontario, Canada M7A 2E5.

Québec Tourisme, C.P. 979, Québec, Canada 83C ZW3.

Saskatchewan Tourism, 1919 Saskatchewan Drive, Regina, Saskatchewan, Canada S4P 3V7.

Europe

Denmark: Danish Information Office, 280 Park Ave., New York, NY 10017.

Finland: Embassy of Finland, 1900 24th St., NW., Washington, D.C. 20008.

France: French Government Tourist Office, 972 Fifth Ave., New York, NY 10021.

Germany: German Information Center, 410 Park Ave., New York, NY 10022.

Ireland: Irish International Airlines, 564 Fifth Ave., New York, NY 10036.

Italy: Italian Government Travel Office-ENIT, 630 5th Ave., New York, NY 10020.

Netherlands: Royal Netherlands Embassy, 4200 Linnean Ave., NW., Washington, D.C. 20008.

Norway: Norwegian Embassy Information Service, 825 Third Ave., New York, NY 10022.

Portugal: Casa de Portugal, Portuguese National Tourist Office, 570 Fifth Ave., New York, NY 10036.

Spain: Spanish Embassy, Cultural Relations Office, 1629 Columbia Rd., NW., Washington, D.C. 20009.

Switzerland: Swiss National Tourist Office, 661 Market St., San Francisco, CA 94105.

Yugoslavia: Yugoslav State Tourist Office, 509 Madison Ave., New York, NY 10022.

South America

Colombia: Information Services Staff, Foreign Agricultural Information Division, U.S. Dept. of Agriculture.

Ecuador: Embassy of Ecuador, 2535 15th St., NW., Washington, D.C. 20009.

Venezuela: Embassy of Venezuela, Institute of Information and Culture, 2437 California St., NW., Washington, D.C. 20008.

United States

Here is a list of addresses and phone numbers for requesting tourist information from the 50 states and the District of Columbia. Postcards are best for mail requests; toll-free numbers are sometimes answered in other states, and calls to toll numbers may get better results.

Alabama: Bureau of Tourism and Travel, Post Office Box 4309, Montgomery, AL 36103; (800) 252-2262 or (205) 242-4169.

Alaska: Division of Tourism, Post Office Box 110801, Juneau, AK 99811; (907) 465-2010.

Arizona: Office of Tourism, 1100 West Washington Street, Phoenix, AZ 85007; (800) 842-8257 or (602) 542-8687.

Arkansas: Tourism Office, 1 Capitol Mall, Little Rock, AR 72201; (800) 628-8725 or (501) 682-7777.

California: Office of Tourism, Post Office Box 9278, Van Nuys, CA 91409; (800) 862-2543 or (916) 322-2881.

Colorado: Tourism Board, Post Office Box 38700, Denver, CO 80238; (800) 265-6723 or (303) 592-5510.

Connecticut: Department of Economic Development, 865 Brook Street, Rocky Hill, CT 06067; (800) 282-6863 or (203) 258-4355.

Delaware: Tourism Office, 99 Kings Highway, Box 1401, Dover, DE 19903; (800) 441-8846 or (302) 739-4271

District of Columbia: Convention and Visitors Association, 1212 New York Avenue, NW, Washington, D.C. 20005; (202) 789-7000.

Florida: Division of Tourism, 126 West Van Buren Street, Tallahassee, FL 32399; (904) 487-1462.

Georgia: Department of Industry and Trade, Box 1776, Atlanta, GA 30301; (800) 847-4842 or (404) 656-3590.

Hawaii: Department of Tourism, 2270 Kalkaua Avenue, Suite 801, Honolulu, HI 96815; (808) 923-1811.

Idaho: Department of Commerce, 700 West State Street, Boise, ID 83720; (800) 635-7820 or (208) 334-2470.

Illinois: Bureau of Tourism, 100 West Randolph, Suite 3-400, Chicago, IL 60601; (800) 223-0121 or (312) 814-4732.

Indiana: Division of Tourism, 1 North Capitol, Suite 700, Indianapolis, IN 46204; (800) 289-6646 or (317) 232-8860.

Iowa: Department of Tourism, 200 East Grand, Des Moines, IA 50309; (800) 345-4692 or (515) 242-4705.

Kansas: Travel and Tourism Division, 400 Southwest Eighth Street, Fifth floor, Topeka, KS 66603; (800) 252-6727 or (913) 296-2009.

Kentucky: Department of Travel Development, 2200 Capital Plaza Tower, Frankfort, KY 40601; (800) 225-8747 or (502) 564-4930.

Louisiana: Office of Tourism, Post Office Box 94291, L.O.T., Baton Rouge, LA 70804; (800) 334-8626 or (504) 342-8119.

Maine: Office of Tourism, 189 State House Station 59, Augusta, ME 04333; (800) 533-9595 or (207) 289-5711.

Maryland: Office of Tourism Development, 217 East Redwood Street, Baltimore, MD 21202; (800) 543-1036 or (410) 333-6611.

Massachusetts: Office of Travel and Tourism, 100 Cambridge Street, 13th floor, Boston, MA 02202; (800) 447-6277 or (617) 727-3201.

Michigan: Travel Bureau, Post Office Box 30226, Lansing, MI 48909; (800) 543-2937 or (517) 373-0670.

Minnesota: Office of Tourism, 375 Jackson Street, 250 Skyway Level, St. Paul, MN 55101; (800) 657-3700 or (612) 296-5029.

Mississippi: Department of Tourism, Post Office Box 22825, Jackson, MS 39205; (800) 647-2290 or (601) 359-3297.

Missouri: Division of Tourism, Post Office Box 1055, Jefferson City, MO 65102; (800) 877-1234 or (314) 751-4133.

Travel Montana, Room 259, Deer Lodge, MT 59722; (800) 541-1447 or (406) 444-2654.

Nebraska: Division of Travel and Tourism, 301 Centennial Mall South, Room 88937, Lincoln, NE 68509; (800) 228-4307 or (402) 471-3796.

Nevada: Commission on Tourism, Carson City, NV 89710; (800) 638-2328 or (702) 687-4322.

New Hampshire: Office of Travel and Tourist Development, Post Office Box 856, Concord, NH 03301; (603) 271-2343.

New Jersey: Division of Travel and Tourism, 20 West State Street, C.N. 826, Trenton, NJ 08625; (800) 537-7397 or (609) 292-2470.

New Mexico: Tourism and Travel Division, Post Office Box 20003, Santa Fe, NM 87503; (800) 545-2040.

New York: State Department of Economic Development, 1 Commerce Plaza, Albany, NY 12245; (800) 225-5697 or (518) 474-4116.

North Carolina: Division of Travel and Tourism, 430 North Salisbury Street, Raleigh, NC 27603; (800) 847-4862 or (919) 733-4171.

North Dakota: Parks and Tourism Department, Capitol Grounds, Bismarck, ND 58505; (800) 435-5663 or (701) 224-2525.

Ohio: Division of Travel and Tourism, Post Office Box 1001, Columbus, OH 43266; (800) 282-5393 or (614) 466-8844.

Oklahoma: Tourism and Recreation Department, 500 Will Rogers Building, Oklahoma City, OK 73105; (800) 652-6552 or (405) 521-3981.

Oregon: Tourism Division, 775 Summer Street N.E., Salem, OR 97310; (800) 547-7842 or (503) 373-1270.

Pennsylvania: Office of Travel Marketing, Post Office Box 61, Warrendale, PA 15086; (800) 847-4872 or (717) 787-5453.

Rhode Island: Tourism Division, 7 Jackson Walkway, Providence, RI 02903; (800) 556-2484 or (401) 277-2601.

South Carolina: Division of Tourism, Post Office Box 71, Room 902, Columbia, SC 29202; (800) 346-3634 or (803) 734-0122.

South Dakota: Department of Tourism, 711 East Wells Avenue, Pierre, SD 57501; (800) 843-1930 or (605) 773-3301.

Tennessee: Department of Tourism Development, Post Office Box 23170, Nashville, TN 37202; (615) 741-2158.

Texas: Department of Commerce, Tourism Division, Post Office Box 12728, Austin, TX 78711; (800) 888-8839 or (512) 462-9191.

Utah: Travel Council, Council Hall, Capitol Hill, Salt Lake City, UT 84114; (801) 538-1030.

Vermont: Travel Division, 134 State Street, Montpelier, VT 05602; (800) 528-4554 or (802) 828-3236.

Virginia: Division of Tourism, 1021 East Cary Street, Richmond, VA 23219; (800) 847-4882 or (804) 786-4484.

Washington: State Tourism, Post Office Box 42513, Olympia, WA 98504; (800) 544-1800 or (206) 586-2012.

West Virginia: Division of Tourism and Parks, 1900 Washington Street East, Building 6, Charleston, WV 25305; (800) 225-5982 or (304) 345-2286.

Wisconsin: Division of Tourism Development, Post Office Box 7606, Madison, WI 53707; (800) 432-8747 or (608) 266-2161; in state (800) 372-2737.

Wyoming: Division of Tourism, I-25 at College Drive, Cheyenne, WY 82002; (800) 225-5996 or (307) 777-7777.

Newsletters and Journals

Each month a number of newsletters and journals report promising practices related to multicultural education. These same periodicals often publish lists of books and other instructional materials of interest to teachers. Request sample copies and information about subscribing to those that have something to offer your staff.

The Booklist and Subscription Books Bulletin: A Guide to Current Books. American Library Association. 60 E. Huron St., Chicago, IL 60611.

Booknotes. World Affairs Council of Northern California, 312 Sutter St., Suite 200, San Francisco, CA 94108.

The Bulletin. Council of Interracial Books, CIBC Resource Center, Room 300, 1841 Broadway, New York, NY 10023.

Bulletin of the Center for Children's Books. University of Chicago Press, Box 37005, Chicago, IL 60637. Reviews new books and makes recommendations about purchasing; includes those you should not purchase.

Canadian Ethnic Studies. The University of Calgary, Calgary, Alberta, Canada.

Civil Rights Digest. United States Commission on Civil Rights, 1121 Vermont Ave., NW, Washington, D.C. 20425.

Colloquy. School Program, World Affairs Council, 312 Sutter St., San Francisco, CA 94108. Excellent source of up-to-date information and publication lists.

Education and Society. Anti-Defamation League, 823 United Nations Plaza, New York, NY 10017.

Explorations in Ethnic Studies. Journal of the National Assn. of Interdisciplinary Ethnic Studies, California State Polytechnic University, 3801 W. Temple Ave., Pomona, CA 91768.

The Horn Book Magazine. Park Square Bld., Boston, MA 02116. Good articles; lists information about new books and authors.

Integrated Education. Integrated Education Associates, School of Education, University of Massachusetts, Amherst, MA 01003.

Journal of Comparative Cultures. National Bilingual Education Assn., 9332 Vista Bonita, Cypress, CA 90630.

Journal of Ethnic Studies. Western Washington State University, Bellingham, WA 98225.

Journal of the National Association for Bilingual Education. 1201 16th St., NW., Washington, D.C. 20036.

Kirkus Reviews. 200 Park Ave. S, New York, NY 10003. (Bimonthly.)

Language Arts (with membership in NCTE). 1111 Kenyon Rd., Urbana, IL 61801. Articles on all aspects of language instruction; reviews books for children and professional materials; often features authors with full-page photo.

Melus: The Multi-Ethnic Literature of the United States. Dept. of English, University of Southern California, Los Angeles, CA 90007.

NABE: Journal of National Association of Bilingual Educators. Alma Flor Ada, ed. Los Angeles Publishing Co., 40-22 23rd St., Long Island City, New York, NY 11101. Subscription free with membership, quarterly publication.

The Negro Educational Review. Box 2895, General Mail Center, Jacksonville, FL 32203.

New York Times Book Review. 229 W. 43rd St., New York, NY 10036.

School Library Journal. 1180 Avenue of the Americas, New York, NY 10036.

Social Education. National Council for the Social Studies, 3501 Newark St., NW., Washington, D.C. 20016.

TESOL Newsletter, TESOL Quarterly. Teachers of English to Speakers of Other Languages, 455 Nevits, Georgetown University, Washington, D.C. 20057.

STUDYING SPECIFIC GROUPS

As we work with students in the classroom, we can develop units of study focused on one specific group. At that time students can read fiction and nonfiction to learn more about one part of our American culture.

Included here are lists of books for adults, information for students, bibliographies of available materials, and sources of additional up-to-date information and resources. Although these lists are not exhaustive, they do provide titles to get you started. Always consult your local librarians and the library catalog to locate other materials. Also refer to such reference tools as *Children's Catalog, The High School Catalog, Education Index,* and *Reader's Guide to Periodical Literature* (all published by Wilson Publishing Company) to continue locating new books and articles that may help you.

Exploring the Backgrounds of Asian Americans

This section explores books and resources that provide information about Americans who have Chinese, Japanese, Korean, or Vietnamese backgrounds.

General Resources

Frank Chin et al., *Aiiieeeee! An Anthology of Asian-American Writers.* Howard University, 1974.

Russell Endo et al. *Asian-Americans: Psychological Perspectives.* Science and Behavior Books, 1980.

Brett Melendy. *Asians in America: Filipines, Koreans, and East Indians.* Twayne, 1977.

Don Nasanishi, ed. *Asians and the American Educational Process.* Oryx Press, 1982.

Franklin Odo. *In Movement: A Pictorial History of Asian America.* Visual Communications, 1977.

Linda Perrin. *Coming to America.* Delacorte, 1980.

Amy Tachiki et al., eds. *Roots: An Asian American Reader.* University of California at Los Angeles, 1971.

Periodicals

Amerasia Journal (irregular). Asian American Studies Center, 3232 Campbell Hall, UCLA, Los Angeles, CA 90024.

Asian American Review (irregular). Asian American Studies, 3407 Dwinelle Hall, Berkeley, CA 94720.

Bridge: An Asian American Perspective (quarterly). Box 477, Canal Station, New York, NY 10013.

Bulletin of Concerned Asian Scholars (quarterly). Box W, Charlemont, MA 01339.

Intercom (3–5 times a year). The Center for War/Peace Studies, 218 E. 18th St., New York, NY 10003. Articles on issues, resources, and guides for teachers on subjects related to Asia.

Additional Sources

Asia Society. 725 Park Avenue, New York, NY 10021.

Asian Writers' Project/Asian Media Project. *Sojourner.* Berkeley Unified School District.

UNICEF. *Children of Asia.* 331 E. 38th St., New York, NY 10016.

Visual Communications. Asian American Studies Central, 1601 Griffith Park Blvd., Los Angeles, CA 90026.

Exploring the Backgrounds of Chinese Americans

General Resources

China Books & Periodicals, Inc. 2929 Twenty-fourth Street, San Francisco, CA 94110. (Subscriptions to magazines published in China; English language).

China International Travel Service. 6 East Chang'an Avenue, Beijing, People's Republic of China.

The China Project (SPICE). Hoover Bldg., Rm. 200, Stanford University, Stanford, CA 94305.

East/West: The Chinese American Journal (weekly). 838 Grant Avenue, Suite 307, San Francisco, CA 94108.

U.S.–China Peoples Friendship Association. 50 Oak Street, San Francisco, CA 94102.

Bibliographies

Cecelia Mei-Chi Chen, comp. *Books for the Chinese-American Child; A Selected List.* Cooperative Children's Book Center, 1969. A list of books included for their literary quality and honesty.

Anna Au Long et al. *The Chinese in Children's Books.* New York Public Library, 1973.

Arlene Posner and Arene J. dekeijzer, eds. *China: A Resource and Curriculum Guide.* University of Chicago Press, 1972. An annotated guide to books about China. Includes films, slides, tapes, records, periodicals, and organizations.

Teaching Materials

Center for Teaching about China. 407 So. Dearborn St., Suite 945, Chicago, IL 60605.

The China Project. Hoover Bldg., Stanford University, Stanford, CA 94305.

Don Wong and Irene Collier. *Chinese Americans Past and Present: A Collection of Readings and Learning Activities.* Association of Chinese Teachers, San Francisco, 1977.

Ed Young and Hilary Beckett. *The Rooster's Horns.* World, 1978. (Directions for producing a puppet play.)

Fiction

Maxine Hong Kingston. *China Men.* Ballantine Books, 1980.

———. *The Woman Warrior: Memoirs of a Girlhood among Ghosts.* Vintage, 1976.

Books for Students

You will also learn much by reading the books students read.

Fiction

Eve Bunting. *The Happy Funeral.* Harper, 1982.

Kathleen Chang. *The Iron Moonhunter.* Children's Book Press, 1977.

A. B. Chrisman. *Shen of the Sea: Chinese Stories for Children.* Dutton, 1968. Short stories.

M. DeJong. *The House of Sixty Fathers.* Harper and Row, 1956.

Demi. *Liang and the Magic Paintbrush.* Holt, 1980.

Eleanor Estes. *The Lost Umbrella of Kim Chu.* Atheneum, 1979.

M. Flack and K. Wiese. *The Story of Ping, A Duck Who Lived on a Houseboat on the Yangtze River.* Viking, 1933.

Julianna Foget. *Wesley Paul, Marathon Runner.* Lippincott, 1979.

Ina R. Friedman. *How My Parents Learned to Eat.* Houghton Mifflin, 1984.

*T. Handforth. *Mei Li.* Doubleday, 1938.

*E. Lattimore. *Little Pear: The Story of a Little Chinese Boy.* Harcourt Brace Jovanovich, 1931.

E. Lewis. *Young Fu of the Upper Yangtze,* rev. ed. Holt, Rinehart and Winston, 1973.

Bette Bao Lord. *In the Year of the Boar and Jackie Robinson.* Harper, 1984.

R. L. McCune. *Pie-Biter.* Design Enterprises of San Francisco, 1983.

J. Merrill. *The Superlative Horse.* Young Scott Books, 1961.

Manus Pinkwater. *Wingman.* Dodd, 1975.

Leo Politi. *Mr. Fong's Shop.* Scribner's, 1979.

A. Ritchie. *The Treasure of Li-Po.* Harcourt Brace Jovanovich, 1949. Short stories.

*Suitable for primary grades.

C. Treffinger. *Li Lun, Lad of Courage.* Abingdon, 1947.

Jay Williams. *Everyone Knows What a Dragon Looks Like.* Four Winds, 1976.

Jade Snow Wong. *Fifth Chinese Daughter.* Harper, 1945.

Laurence Yep. *Dragonwings.* Harper, 1977.

————. *Child of the Owl.* Harper, 1977.

————. *Sea Glass.* Harper, 1979.

Jane Yolen. *The Seeing Stick.* Crowell, 1977.

Nonfiction

Gwenn Boardman. *Across the Bridge to China.* Nelson, 1979.

Jack Chen. *The Chinese of America.* New York: Harper and Row, 1980.

*Hou-tien Cheng. *The Chinese New Year.* Holt, 1976.

Frank Chin. *The Chicken Coop Chinaman: The Year of the Dragon: Two Plays.* University of Washington, 1981.

Laverne Mau Dicker. *The Chinese in San Francisco: A Pictoral History.* Dover, 1979.

Dorothy Dowdell. *The Chinese Helped Build America.* Messner, 1972.

Leonard Fisher. *The Great Wall of China.* Macmillan, 1986.

Jean Fritz. *Homesick: My Own Story.* Putnam, 1982.

————. *China Homecoming.* Putnam, 1985.

Clarence Glick. *Sojourners and Settlers.* University of Hawaii, 1980.

Noel Gray. *Looking at China.* Lippincott, 1975.

Corrine Hoexter. *From Canton to California.* Four Winds, 1976.

Ellen Hsiao. *A Chinese Year.* Evans, 1970.

Claire Jones. *The Chinese in America.* Lerner, 1972.

Stanford Lyman. *Chinese Americans.* Random, 1974.

Pat Mauser. *A Bundle of Sticks.* Atheneum, 1982.

Ruthanne Lum McCunn. *An Illustrated History of the Chinese in America.* Design Enterprises of San Francisco, 1979.

Milton Meltzer. *The Chinese Americans.* Crowell, 1980.

Joe Molnar. *A Chinese-American Child Tells His Story.* Watts, 1973.

Victor Nee and Brett D. Nee, eds. *Longtime Californians: A Documentary Study of an American Chinatown.* Pantheon, 1972.

Margaret Rau. *Our World: The People's Republic of China.* Messner, 1974.

————. *The People of New China.* Messner, 1978.

Seymour Reit. *Rice Cakes and Paper Dragons.* Dodd, 1973.

J. R. Roberson. *China from Manchu to Mao.* Atheneum, 1980.

*Suitable for primary grades.

M. Sasek. *This Is Hong Kong.* Macmillan, 1965.

Ruth Sidel. *Revolutionary China: People, Politics, and Ping-Pong.* Delacorte, 1974.

Cornelia Spencer. *The Yangtze, China's River Highway.* Garrard, 1963.

Stan Steiner. *Fusang: The Chinese Who Built America.* Harper, 1979.

Betty Lee Sung. *An Album of Chinese Americans.* Watts, 1977.

―――. *The Chinese in America.* Macmillan, 1972.

Kurt Wiese. *You Can Write Chinese.* Viking, 1945.

Ed Young. *High on a Hill: A Book of Chinese Riddles.* World, 1980.

Folklore

*Claire Bishop. *The Five Chinese Brothers.* Coward, 1938.

Frances Carpenter. *Tales of a Chinese Grandmother.* Doubleday, 1937.

Hou-tien Cheng. *Six Chinese Brothers.* Holt, 1979.

Dorothy Hoge. *The Black Heart of Indri.* Scribner's, 1966.

Lotta Hume. *Favorite Children's Stories from China and Tibet.* Tuttle, 1962.

Carol Kendall and Yao-wen Li. *Sweet and Sour: Tales from China.* Seabury, 1982.

Jeanne Lee. *Legend of the Li River.* Holt, 1983.

―――. *Legend of the Milky Way.* Holt, 1982.

―――. *Toad Is the Uncle of Heaven.* Holt, 1985.

Adet Lin. *The Milky Way and Other Chinese Folk Tales.* Harcourt, 1961.

Ai-Ling Louie. *Yeh-Shen: A Cinderella Story from China.* Philomel, 1982.

Arlene Mosel. *Tikki Tikki Tembo.* Holt, 1968. (Illustrated by Blair Lent; film from Weston Woods.)

Neil Philip, ed. *The Spring of Butterflies and Other Folktales of China's Minority Peoples.* Lothrop, 1986.

Catherine Sadler. *Treasure Mountain: Folktales from Southern China.* Atheneum, 1982.

Diane Wolkstein. *White Wave: A Chinese Tale.* Crowell, 1982.

*Jane Yolen. *The Emperor and the Kite.* World, 1957.

Ed Young. *The Terrible Nung Gwama: A Chinese Tale.* Philomel, 1978.

Nathan Zimelman. *I Will Tell You of Peach Stone.* Lothrop, 1976.

Feenie Ziner. *Cricket Boy: A Chinese Tale Retold.* Doubleday, 1977.

Exploring the Backgrounds of Japanese Americans

General Resources

Japan Chronicle. The Pacific and Asian Affairs Council, Pacific House, 2004 University Ave., Honolulu, HI 96822.

*Suitable for primary grades.

Japan External Trade Organization (JETRO). 360 Post St., Suite 501, San Francisco, CA 94108.

Japan Information Service. 1737 Post St., Suites 4–5, San Francisco, CA 94115.

Japanese American Citizenship League. 224 So. San Pedro St., Room 506, Los Angeles, CA 90012.

Japanese American Curriculum Project. Box 367, San Mateo, CA 94401.

Nichi Bei Times (daily). 2211 Bush St., San Francisco, CA 94119 (in Japanese and English).

Social Studies Development Center. Indiana University, 2805 E. 10th St., Bloomington, IN 47405.

Stanford Program on International and Cross-Cultural Education: The Japan Project. Stanford University, Stanford, CA 94305.

Books for Adults

Frank Gibney. *Japan: The Fragile Superpower.* New American Library, 1985.

Akemi Kikumura. *Through Harsh Winters: The Life of a Japanese Immigrant Woman.* Chandler, 1981.

Harry Kitano. *Japanese Americans: The Evolution of a Subculture.* Prentice-Hall, 1976.

Joy Kogawa. *Obasan: A Novel.* Godine, 1982.

Gene Levine and Robert Rhodes. *The Japanese American Community: A Three-Generation Study.* Praeger, 1981.

Edwin Reishauer. *The Japanese.* Harvard, 1977.

Thomas Rohlen. *Japan's High Schools.* University of California; 1983.

Jared Taylor. *Shadows of the Rising Sun.* Morrow, 1983.

United States Department of Education. *Japanese Education Today.* U.S. Government Printing Office, 1987.

Robert Wilson and Bill Hosokawa. *East to Africa: A History of the Japanese in the United States.* Morrow, 1980.

Books for Students

Fiction

P. Buck. *The Big Wave.* Day, 1948 (new edition 1973).

Miriam Chaikin. *Yossi Asks the Angels for Help.* Harper, 1985.

E. Coatsworth. *The Cat Who Went to Heaven.* Macmillan, 1958.

*L. Hawkinson. *Dance, Dance Amy-Chan!* Whitman, 1964.

Hadley Irwin. *Kim/Kimi.* Macmillan, 1987.

Tetsuko Kuroyanagi. *Totto-Chan.* Harper, 1982.

*Suitable for primary grades.

*B. J. Lifton. *The Cock and the Ghost Cat*. Atheneum, 1965.

*———. *The Dwarf Pin Tree*. Atheneum, 1963.

*M. Matsuno. *A Pair of Red Clogs*. Collins, 1963.

S. J. Myers. *The Enchanted Sticks*. Coward, 1979.

Katherine Paterson. *The Master Puppeteer*. Crowell, 1976.

———. *Of Nightingales That Weep*. Crowell, 1974.

*Leo Politi. *Mieko*. Golden Gates, 1969.

Allen Say. *The Inn-keeper's Apprentice*. Harper, 1982.

*Yoshiko Uchida. *The Birthday Visitor*. Scribner's, 1975.

———. *The Best Bad Thing*. Atheneum, 1983.

———. *The Forever Christmas Tree*. Scribner's, 1963.

———. *The Happiest Ending*. Atheneum, 1985.

———. *Journey Home*. Atheneum, 1978.

———. *Journey to Topaz*. Scribner's, 1971.

———. *The Promised Year*. Harcourt, 1959.

———. *The Rooster Who Understood Japanese*. Scribner's, 1976.

———. *Samurai of Gold Hill*. Scribner's, 1972.

———. *Sumi & the Goat & the Tokyo Express*. Scribner's, 1969.

———. *Sumi's Prize*. Scribner's, 1964.

Yoko Kawashima Watkins. *So Far from the Bamboo Grove*. Lothrop, 1986.

Taro Yashima. *Crow Boy*. Viking, 1955.

———. *The Golden Footprints*. World, 1960.

———. *A Jar of Dreams*. Atheneum, 1981.

———. *Seashore Story*. Viking, 1967.

———. *Umbrella*. Viking, 1958.

Nonfiction

Gwynneth Ashby. *Looking at Japan*. Lippincott, 1969.

*Edith Battles. *What Does the Rooster Say, Yoshio?* Whitman, 1978.

Gwenn Boardman. *Living in Tokyo*. Nelson, 1970.

Maisie Conrat and Richard Conrat. *Executive Order 9066: The Internment of 110,000 Japanese Americans*. California Historical Society, 1972.

Jane Dallinger. *Swallowtail Butterflies*. Lerner, 1983 (originally published in Japan).

Daniel Davis. *Behind Barbed Wire*. Dutton, 1982.

Dorothy Dowdell. *The Japanese Helped Build America*. Messner, 1970.

*Suitable for primary grades.

Sam Epstein. *A Year of Japanese Festivals.* Garrard, 1974.

Budd Fukei. *The Japanese American Story.* Dillon, 1976.

Jane Goodsell. *Daniel Inouye.* Crowell, 1977.

Jeanne Wakatsuki Houston and James Houston. *Farewell to Manzanar.* Houghton Mifflin,1973.

Estelle Ishigo. *Lone Heart Mountain.* Japanese American Curriculum Project.

Takeo Kaneshiro. *Internees War Relocation Center Memoirs and Diaries.* Vantage Press, 1976.

Noel Leathers. *The Japanese in America.* Lerner, 1967.

Toshi Maruki. *Hiroshima No Pika.* Lothrop, 1982.

Robert Masters. *Japan in Pictures.* Sterling, 1978.

Dennis Ogawa. *Jan Ken Po.* Japanese American Research Center, 1973.

Robert San Souci. *The Samurai's Daughter.* Dial, 1992.

Allen Say. *The Bicycle Man.* Parnassus, 1982.

Shizuye Takashima. *A Child in Prison Camp.* Tundra Brooks, 1971.

Tobi Tobias. *Isamu Noguchi: The Life of a Sculptor.* Crowell, 1974.

Josephine B. Vaughan. *The Land and People of Japan.* Lippincott, 1972.

*Taro Yashima. *The Village Tree.* Viking, 1953.

Folklore

Joanne Algarin. *Japanese Folk Literature: A Core Collection and Reference Guide.* Bowker, 1982.

Virginia Haviland. *Favorite Fairy Tales Told in Japan.* Little, 1967.

Margaret Hodges. *The Wave.* Houghton, 1964.

Jane Hori Ike. *The Japanese Fairy Tale.* Warne, 1982.

Nancy Luenn. *The Dragon Kite.* Harcourt, 1982.

Gerald McDermott. *The Stonecutter.* Viking, 1975.

Arlene Mosel. *The Funny Little Woman.* Dutton, 1972.

Patricia Newton. *The Five Sparrows.* Atheneum, 1982.

*Michelle Nikly. *The Emperor's Plum Tree.* Greenwillow, 1982.

Florence Sakade, ed. *Japanese Children's Favorite Stories.* Tuttle, 1958.

*Allen Say. *The Bicycle Man.* Houghton, 1982.

————. *Once under the Cherry Blossom Tree.* Harper, 1974.

Yoshiko Uchida. *The Magic Listening Cap.* Harcourt, 1955.

Elizabeth Winthrop. *Journey to the Bright Kingdom.* Holiday, 1979.

*Taro Yashima. *Seashore Story.* Viking, 1967.

*Suitable for primary grades.

Kaethe Zemach. *The Beautiful Rat.* Four Winds, 1979.

Poetry

Virginia Olsen Baron, ed. *The Seasons of Time; Tanka Poetry of Ancient Japan.* Dial, 1968.

Harry Behn, comp. *Cricket Songs; Japanese Haiku.* Harcourt Brace Jovanovich, 1964.

————. *More Cricket Songs; Japanese Haiku.* Harcourt Brace Jovanovich, 1971.

Sylvia Cassidy, comp. *Birds, Frogs, and Moonlight: Haiku.* Doubleday, 1967.

Richard Lewis, ed. *In a Spring Garden.* Dial, 1965. (Also on film; Weston Woods.)

————. *The Moment of Wonder; A Collection of Chinese and Japanese Poetry.* Dial, 1964.

Exploring the Backgrounds of Korean Americans

General Resources

Bong-youn Choy. *Koreans in America.* Nelson-Hall, 1979.

H. Brett Melendy. *Asians in America: Filipinos, Koreans, and East Indians.* Twayne, 1977.

Books for Students

Fiction

Elisabet McHugh. *Raising a Mother Isn't Easy.* Greenwillow, 1983.

Yoko Kawashima Watkins. *So Far from the Bamboo Grove.* Lothrop, 1986.

Nonfiction

Gene Gurney, *North & South Korea.* Watts, 1973.

Sylvia McNair. *Korea.* Children's Press, 1986.

Wayne Patterson. *The Koreans in America.* Lerner, 1977.

S. E. Solberg. *The Land and People of Korea.* Lippincott, 1973.

Folklore

So-un Kim. *The Story Bag: A Collection of Korean Folktales.* Tuttle, 1955.

Kathleen Seros. *Sun and Moon: Fairy Tales from Korea.* Holly, 1982.

Exploring the Backgrounds of Filipino Americans

This group is placed in the Asian American section because of the location of the Philippines and because varied languages (Spanish is only one) are spoken by Filipinos.

General Resources

Periodicals

Filipino American Herald (monthly). 508 Maynard Avenue, Seattle, WA 98108.

Philippines Mail. Filipino American Media of California, Box 1783, Salinas, CA 93901.

Books for Adults

Carlos Bulosan. *America Is in the Heart*. University of Washington, 1973.

Hyung-chan Kim and Cynthia Mejia, eds. *The Filipinos in America*. Oceana Publications, 1976.

Teresita Laygo, ed. *Well of Time: Eighteen Short Stories from Philippine Contemporary Literature*. American Bilingual Center, 1977.

Alfredo Muñoz. *The Filipinos in America*. Mountainview Press, 1971.

Luis Teodoro. *Out of This Struggle: The Filipinos in Hawaii, 1906–1981*. The University of Hawaii, 1981.

Books for Students

Fiction

*Janet Bartosiak. *A Dog for Ramón*. Dial, 1966.

Carlos Bulosan. *The Laughter of My Father*. Harcourt, 1942.

Al Robles. *Looking for Ifugao Mountain*. Children's Book Press, 1977.

Nonfiction

Manuel Buaken. *I Have Lived with the American People*. Caxton, 1948.

John Nance. *The Land and People of the Philippines*. Lippincott, 1977.

Luis Taruc. *Born of the People*. International Publishers, 1953.

Folklore

Jose Aruego. *A Crocodile's Tale: A Philippine Folk Story*. Scholastic, 1975.

Elizabeth Sechrist. *Once in the First Times: Folk Tales from the Philippines*. Macrae, 1969.

Exploring the Backgrounds of African Americans

General Resources

James Banks and Cherry Banks. *March toward Freedom: A History of Black Americans*. Fearon, 1978.

John H. Franklin. *From Slavery to Freedom: A History of Black Americans*. Vintage, 1980.

Alex Haley. *Roots: The Saga of an American Family*. Doubleday, 1976.

Vincent Harding. *There Is a River: The Black Struggle for Freedom in America*. Harcourt, 1981.

W. A. Low and Virgil Clift, eds. *Encyclopedia of Black America*. McGraw-Hill, 1981.

Nelson Mandela. *The Struggle Is My Life*. Pathfinder, 1986.

---

*Suitable for primary grades.

William Nelson and Charles Henry, eds. *Black Studies*. Ohio State, 1982.

Rudine Sims. Shadow and Substance. *Afro-American Experience in Contemporary Children's Fiction*. National Council of Teachers of Enigsh, 1982.

Geneva Smitherman. *Talkin and Testifyin: The Language of Black America*. Houghton Mifflin, 1977.

Dorothy Strickland. *Listen, Children: An Anthology of Black Literature*. Bantam, 1982.

Periodicals

Africana Library Journal: A Quarterly Bibliography and Resource Guide. 101 Fifth Ave., New York, NY 10003. Evaluations of books on Africa published throughout the world; current bibliographies, information on African writers and scholars; children's books and AV materials, adult books.

The Black Scholar, P.O. Box 908, Sausalito, CA 94965. Highly influential, Black-oriented publication; contains valuable book review section.

Crisis. Organization of the National Association for the Advancement of Colored People. The Crisis Publishing Co., 1790 Broadway, New York, NY 10019.

Ebony. Johnson Publishing Co., 1820 S. Michigan Ave., Chicago, IL 60616.

Freedomways. Quarterly Review of the Negro Freedom Movement. Freedomway Associates, 799 Broadway, New York, NY 10013.

Jet. Johnson Publishing Co., 1820 S. Michigan Ave., Chicago, IL 60616.

Journal of Black Studies. 275 S. Beverly Dr., Beverly Hills, CA 90210.

The Journal of Negro History. Published quarterly by the Association for the Study of Negro Life and History, 1538 Ninth Street, NW., Washington, D.C. Contains scholarly articles on Negro culture and history, book reviews, important documents.

Negro-American Literature Forum for School and University Teachers. Indiana State University, Terre Haute, IN 47809.

Negro Heritage. P.O. Box 1057, Washington, D.C. 20013.

Negro History Bulletin. The Association for the Study of Negro Life and History, Inc., 1538 Ninth Street, NW., Washington, D.C. 20001.

Sepia. Sepia Publishing Co., 1220 Harding St., Fort Worth, TX 76102.

Books for Young Readers

Read as many of these books as possible. You will learn as you read, and you can begin to plan lessons that are based on multicultural literature.

Fiction

C. S. Adler. *Always and Forever Friends*. Clarion, 1988.

Nana H. Agle. *Maple Street*. Seabury, 1970.

Martha Alexander. *Bobo's Dream*. Dial, 1970.

William H. Armstrong. *Sounder*. Harper, 1969.

Martha Bacon. *Sophia Scrooby Preserved*. Little, 1968.

Charlotte Baker. *Cockleburr Quarters*. Prentice-Hall, 1972.

Simi Bedford. *Yoruba Girl Dancing*. Viking, 1992.

Kathleen Benson. *Joseph on the Subway Trains*. Addison-Wesley, 1981.

Clayton Bess. *Story for a Black Night*. Houghton Mifflin, 1982.

Joan Blos. *A Gathering of Days*. Scribner's, 1979.

Barbara Brenner. *Wagon Wheels*. Harper, 1978.

Clyde Bulla. *Charlie's House*. Crowell, 1983.

Peter Burchard. *Bimby*. Coward, 1968.

*Jeannette Caines. *Abby*. Harper, 1973.

*————. *Just Us Women*. Harper, 1982.

Ann Cameron. *More Stories Julian Tells*. Knopf, 1986.

————. *The Stories Julian Tells*. Pantheon, 1981.

Natalie Carlson. *Ann Aurelia and Dorothy*. Harper, 1968.

Peter Carter. *The Sentinels*. Oxford, 1982.

Alice Childress. *A Hero Ain't Nothin' but a Sandwich*. Coward, 1973.

Bess Clayton. *Story for a Black Night*. Houghton, 1982.

*Lucille Clifton. *Amifica*. Dutton, 1977.

————. *The Boy Who Didn't Believe in Spring*. Dutton, 1973.

————. *The Lucky Stone*. Delacorte, 1979.

————. *My Friend Jacob*. Dutton, 1980.

————. *Three Wishes*. Viking, 1976.

Barbara Cohen. *Thank You, Jackie Robinson*. Lothrop, 1974.

James Collier. *Jump Ship to Freedom*. Delacorte, 1981.

Molly Cone. *The Other Side of the Fence*. Houghton, 1967.

Olivia Coolidge. *Come by Here*. Houghton, 1970.

*Pat Cummings. *Jimmy Lee Did It*. Lothrop, 1985.

Jane L. Curry. *The Daybreakers*. Harcourt, 1970.

Alexis Devereaux. *Na-Ni*. Harper, 1973.

Beth Engel. *Big Words*. Dutton, 1982.

*Tom Feelings and Eloise Greenfield. *Daydreams*. Dial, 1981.

Carol Fenner. *The Skates of Uncle Richard*. Random, 1978.

Dale Fife. *Who's in Charge of Lincoln?* Coward, 1965.

Louise Fitzhugh. *Nobody's Family Is Going to Change*. Farrar, 1974.

*Suitable for primary grades.

Paula Fox. *How Many Miles to Babylon?* White, 1967.

————. *The Slave Dancer.* Bradbury, 1973.

*D. Freeman. *Corduroy.* Viking, 1968.

Jean Fritz. *Brady.* Coward, 1960.

Lorenz Graham. *North Town (and other titles).* Crowell, 1965.

Bette Greene. *Get On out of Here, Philip Hall.* Dial, 1981.

————. *Philip Hall Likes Me, I Reckon Maybe.* Dial, 1974.

*Eloise Greenfield. *Grandmamma's Joy.* Collins, 1980.

————. *Me and Nessie.* Crowell, 1975.

————. *She Come Bringing Me That Little Baby Girl.* Lippincott, 1974.

————. *Sister.* Crowell, 1974.

————. *Talk about a Family.* Lippincott, 1978.

Virginia Hamilton. *Arilla Sun Down.* Greenwillow, 1976.

————. *House of Dies Drear.* Macmillan, 1968.

————. *M. C. Higgins the Great.* Macmillan, 1974.

————. *The Magical Adventures of Pretty Pearl.* Harper, 1983.

————. *The Mystery of Drear House.* Greenwillow, 1987.

————. *Time-Ago Lost: More Tales of Jahdu.* Macmillan, 1973. Short stories.

————. *The Time-Ago Tales of Jahdu.* Macmillan, 1969. Short stories.

————. *Zeely.* Macmillan. 1967.

Sarah Hayes. *Happy Christmas, Gemma.* Lothrop, 1986.

*Elizabeth Hill. *Evan's Corner.* Holt, 1967.

William Hooks. *Circle of Fire.* Atheneum, 1982.

Lila Hopkins. *Eating Crow.* Watts, 1988.

Kristin Hunter. *Soul Brothers and Sister Lou.* Scribner's, 1968.

Belinda Hurmence. *A Girl Called Boy.* Clarion, 1982.

Hadley Irwin. *I Be Somebody.* Atheneum. 1984.

June Jordan. *Kimakao's Story.* Houghton, 1982.

————. *New Life: New Room.* Crowell, 1975.

May Justus. *A New Home for Billy.* Hastings, 1966.

*Ezra Jack Keats. *The Snowy Day.* Viking, 1962. (Caldecott Award; see other books about Peter and his friends.)

Elaine Konigsburg. *Jennifer, Hecate, Macbeth, William McKinley, and Me, Elizabeth.* Atheneum, 1967.

Jill Krementz. *Sweet Pea: A Black Girl Growing up in the Rural South.* Harcourt, 1969.

*Suitable for primary grades.

Julius Lester. *This Strange New Feeling*. Dial, 1982.

*Joan Lexau. *Benjie*. Dial, 1964.

*————. *I Should Have Stayed in Bed*. Harper, 1965.

*————. *Me Day*. Dial, 1971.

*————. *The Rooftop Mystery*. Harper, 1968.

————. *Striped Ice Cream*. Lippincott, 1968.

*Lessie Little and Eloise Greenfield. *I Can Do It Myself*. Crowell, 1978.

Bette Bao Lord. *In the Year of the Boar and Jackie Robinson*. Harper, 1984.

*Patricia M. Martin. *The Little Brown Hen*. Crowell, 1960.

*Sharon Bell Mathis. *The Hundred Penny Box*. Viking, 1976.

————. *Teacup Full of Roses*. Viking, 1972.

Walter Myers. *Fast Sam, Cool Clyde and Stuff*. Viking, 1975.

————. *Mojo and the Russians*. Viking, 1977.

Ann Petry. *Tituba of Salem Village*. Crowell, 1964.

Harriette Robinet. *Ride the Red Cycle*. Houghton, 1980.

*Ann Scott. *Sam*. McGraw, 1967.

Ouida Sebestyen. *Words by Heart*. Little, 1979.

John Shearer. *I Wish I Had an Afro*. Cowles. 1970.

Louisa Shotwell. *Roosevelt Grady*. Collins, 1963.

Alfred Slote. *Jake*. Lippincott, 1971.

John Steptoe. *Marcia*. Viking, 1976.

————. *Train Ride*. Harper, 1971.

*————. *Stevie*. Harper, 1969.

————. *Uptown*. Harper, 1970.

Mary Stolz. *A Wonderful Terrible Time*. Harper, 1967.

Eleanor Tate. *Just an Overnight Guest*. Dial, 1980.

Mildred Taylor. *Let the Circle Be Unbroken*. Dial, 1981.

————. *Roll of Thunder, Hear My Cry*. Dial, 1976.

————. *Song of the Trees*. Dial, 1975.

Theodore Taylor. *The Cay*. Doubleday, 1969.

Ianthe Thomas. *Hi, Mrs. Mallory*. Harper, 1979.

*————. *Walk Home Tired, Billy Jenkins*. Harper, 1974.

*————. *Willie Blows a Mean Horn*. Harper, 1981.

Janice Udry. *What Mary Jo Shared*. Whitman, 1966.

*Suitable for primary grades.

Cynthia Voight. *Come a Stranger.* Atheneum, 1986.

Jane Wagner. *J. T.* Dell, 1971.

Mildred Walter. *The Girl on the Outside.* Lothrop, 1982.

Karen Whiteside. *Brother Mouky and the Falling Sun.* Harper, 1980.

Brenda Wilkinson. *Ludell.* Harper, 1975.

————. *Not Separate, Not Equal.* Harper, 1987.

Vera Williams. *Cherries and Cherry Pits.* Greenwillow, 1986.

Nonfiction

Ashley Bryan. *I'm Going to Sing: Black American Spirituals.* Vol. 2. Atheneum, 1982.

H. Buckmaster. *Flight to Freedom.* Crowell, 1958.

*Lucille Clifton. *The Black BCs.* Dutton, 1970.

Henry Commager. *The Great Proclamation.* Bobbs, 1960.

Burke Davis. *Black Heroes of the American Revolution.* Harcourt, 1976.

Eloise Greenfield. *Childtimes: A Three Generation Memoir.* Crowell, 1979.

J. H. Griffin. *A Time to Be Human.* Macmillan, 1977.

James Haskins. *Black Theater in America.* Crowell, 1982.

L. W. Ingraham. *Slavery in the United States.* Watts, 1968.

Florence Jackson. *The Black Man in America, 1932–1954.* Watts, 1979.

————. *Blacks in America, 1954–1979.* Watts, 1980.

Jesse Jackson. *Blacks in America.* Messner, 1973.

Julius Lester. *To Be a Slave.* Dial, 1968.

Don Lawson. *South Africa.* Watts, 1986.

Milton Meltzer. *All Times, All Peoples: A World History of Slavery.* Harper, 1980.

————. *In Their Own Words, 3 vols.* Crowell, 1964–67.

————. *The Truth about the Ku Klux Klan.* Watts, 1982.

Christine Price. *Dance on the Dusty Earth.* Scribner's, 1982.

Roger Rosen and Patra McSharry, eds. *Apartheid: Calibrations of Color.* Icarus World Issues Series. Rosen Publishing Group, 1991.

Conrad Stein. *Kenya.* Children's Press, 1985.

Dorothy Sterling. *Tear Down the Walls.* Doubleday, 1968.

————. *The Trouble They Seen: Black People Tell the Story of Reconstruction.* Doubleday, 1976.

Charles Sullivan, ed. *Children of Promise: African-American Literature and Art for Young People.* Harry Abrams, 1991.

Hildegarde Swift. *North Star Shining.* Morrow, 1947.

*Suitable for primary grades.

Biography

David Adler. *Martin Luther King: Free at Last*. Holiday, 1986.

Arnold Adoff. *All the Colors of the Race*. Lothrop, 1986.

———. *Black on Black*. Macmillan, 1968.

———. *Malcolm X*. Crowell, 1970.

Rae Alexander. *Young and Black in America*. Random, 1970.

*Aliki. *A Week Is a Flower: The Life of George Washington Carver*. Prentice-Hall, 1965.

Caroline Arnold. *Pelé: The King of Soccer*. Watts, 1992.

Jean H. Berg. *I Cry When the Sun Goes Down: The Story of Herman Wrice*. Westminster, 1975.

Jacqueline Bernard. *Journey Toward Freedom: The Story of Sojourner Truth*. Norton, 1967.

Roland Bertol. *Charles Drew*. Crowell, 1970.

C. Bishop. *Martin de Porres, Hero*. Houghton, 1954.

Arna Bontemps. *Fredrick Douglass: Slave—Fighter—Freeman*. Knopf, 1959.

Susan Brownmiller. *Shirley Chisholm*. Doubleday, 1970.

A' Lelia P. Bundles. *Madam C. J. Walker*. Chelsea, 1991.

Olive Burt. *Negroes in the Early West*. Messner, 1969.

Bradford Chambers. *Chronicles of Negro Protest*. Parents, 1968.

Elizabeth Chittenden. *Martin Luther King: Peaceful Warrior*. Prentice-Hall, 1968.

———. *Profiles in Black and White*. Scribner's, 1973.

James Collier. *Louis Armstrong: An American Success Story*. Macmillan, 1985.

Barbara Cohen. *Thank You, Jackie Robinson*. Lothrop, 1974.

Jean Cornell. *Louis Armstrong, Ambassador Satchmo*. Garrard, 1979.

Ossie Davis. *Langston: A Play*. Delacorte, 1982.

James De Kay. *Meet Martin Luther King, Jr.* Random, 1969.

Esther Douty. *Charlotte Forten: Free Black Teacher*. Garrard, 1971.

Ophelia Egypt. *James Weldon Johnson*. Crowell, 1974.

Mark Evans. *Scott Joplin and the Ragtime Years*. Dodd, 1976.

Doris Faber. *The Assassination of Martin Luther King, Jr.* Watts, 1978.

*Tom Feelings. *Black Pilgrimage*. Lothrop, 1972.

H. Felton. *Edward Rose: Negro Trail Blazer*. Dodd, 1967.

———. *Mumbet: The Story of Elizabeth Freeman*. Dodd, 1970.

Franklin Folsom. *The Life and Legends of George McJunkin, Black Cowboy*. Nelson, 1973.

*Suitable for primary grades.

Florence Freedman. *Two Tickets to Freedom: The True Story of Ellen and William Craft, Fugitive Slaves.* Simon and Schuster, 1971.

Miriam Fuller. *Phillis Wheatley: America's First Black Poet(ess).* Garrard, 1971.

Berry Gordy. *Movin' Up.* Harper, 1979.

Shirley Graham. *Booker T. Washington.* Messner, 1955.

Eloise Greenfield. *Mary McLeod Bethune.* Crowell, 1977.

———. *Paul Robeson.* Crowell, 1975.

———. *Rosa Parks.* Crowell, 1973.

——— and Lessie Jones Little. *Childtimes: A Three-Generation Memoir.* Crowell, 1982.

Virginia Hamilton. *Paul Robeson: The Life and Times of a Free Black Man.* Harper, 1974.

———. *W. E. B. Du Bois.* Crowell, 1972.

Richard Hardwick. *Charles Richard Drew.* Scribner's, 1967.

James Haskins. *From Lew Alcindor to Kareem Abdul Jabbar.* Lothrop, 1972.

———. *I'm Gonna Make You Love Me: The Story of Diana Ross.* Dial, 1980.

———. *Katherine Dunham.* Coward, 1982.

———. *The Life and Time of Martin Luther King, Jr.* Lothrop, 1977.

———. *One More River to Cross: The Stories of Twelve Black Americans.* Scholastic, 1992.

———. *A Piece of the Power: Four Black Mayors.* Dial, 1972.

———. *Shirley Chisholm.* Dial, 1975.

Robert Hayden. *Eight Black American Inventors.* Addison-Wesley, 1972.

———. ed. *Kaleidoscope: Poems by American Negro Poets.* Harcourt, 1967.

———. *Seven Black Scientists.* Addison-Wesley, 1970.

Dorothy Hoobler and Thomas Hoobler. *Nelson and Winnie Mandela.* Watts, 1987.

Genie Iverson. *Louis Armstrong.* Crowell, 1976.

Johanna Johnston. *A Special Bravery.* Dodd, 1967.

Hettie Jones. *Big Star Fallin' Mama: Five Women in Black Music.* Viking, 1974.

June Jordan. *Fannie Lou Hamer.* Crowell, 1972.

———. *Harriet and the Runaway Book: The Story of Harriet Beecher Stowe.* Harper, 1977.

Mervyn Kaufman. *Jessie Owens.* Crowell, 1973.

Jacob Lawrence. *Harriet and the Promised Land.* Windmill, 1968.

Bill Libby. *Joe Louis, The Brown Bomber.* Lothrop, 1980.

———. *The Reggie Jackson Story.* Lothrop, 1979.

Aletha Lindstrom. *Sojourner Truth.* Messner, 1980.

Robert Lipsyte. *Free to Be Muhammad Ali.* Harper, 1978.

Polly Longsworth. *Charlotte Forten: Black and Free*. Crowell, 1970.

Bette Bao Lord. *In the Year of the Boar and Jackie Robinson*. Harper, 1984.

Sharon Bell Mathis. *Ray Charles*. Crowell, 1973.

Ann McGovern. *Runaway Slave: The Story of Harriet Tubman*. Four Winds, 1965.

Patricia McKissack. *Mary McLeod Bethune: A Great American Educator*. Childrens, 1985.

Milton Meltzer. *Langston Hughes*. Crowell, 1968.

———. *Winnie Mandela: The Soul of South Africa*. Viking, 1986.

Howard Meyer. *Colonel of the Black Regiment: The Life of Thomas Wentworth Higginson*. Norton, 1967.

Elizabeth Montgomery. *Duke Ellington: King of Jazz*. Garrard, 1972.

———. *William C. Handy: Father of the Blues*. Garrard, 1968.

Carman Moore. *Somebody's Angel Child: The Story of Bessie Smith*. Crowell, 1970.

Elizabeth Myers. *Langston Hughes*. Garrard, 1970.

Corinne Naden. *Ronald McNair* (Black American of Achivement). Chelsea, 1991.

Shirlee Newman. *Marian Anderson*. Westminster, 1966.

Victoria Ortiz. *Sojourner Truth*. Lippincott, 1974.

Steve Otfinowski. *Marian Wright: Defender of Children's Rights*. Blackbirdy Rosen, 1991.

Rosa Parks. *Rosa Parks: My Story*. Dial, 1992.

Diane Patrick. *Coretta Scott King*. Franklin Watts, 1991.

Lillie Patterson. *Benjamin Banneker*. Abington, 1978.

———. *Sure Hands, Strong Heart: The Life of Daniel Hale Williams*. Abington, 1981.

Kathilyn S. Probosz. *Alvin Ailey*. Bantam, 1991.

*Jackie Robinson. *Breakthrough to the Big League*. Harper, 1965.

Charlemae Rollins. *Famous American Negro Poets*. Dodd, 1965.

———. *They Showed the Way: Forty American Negro Leaders*. Crowell, 1964.

Jeanne Rowe. *An Album of Martin Luther King, Jr.* Watts, 1970.

Robert Rubin. *Satchel Paige*. Putnam, 1974.

Kenneth Rudeen. *Jackie Robinson*. Crowell, 1971.

Pearle Schulz. *Paul Laurence Dunbar*. Garrard, 1974.

P. Sterling. *Four Took Freedom*. Doubleday, 1967.

———. *Freedom Train: The Story of Harriet Tubman*. Doubleday, 1954.

Emma Gelders Sterne. *Mary McLeod Bethune*. Knopf, 1957.

Katherine S. Talmadge. *The Life of Charles Drew*. Twenty-First Century Books (Holt), 1992.

*Suitable for primary grades.

Tobi Tobias. *Arthur Mitchell*. Crowell, 1975.

———. *Marian Anderson*. Crowell, 1972.

Midge Turk. *Gordon Parks*. Crowell, 1971.

Elizabeth Van Steenwyk. *Ida B. Wells-Barnett: Woman of Courage*. Franklin Watts, 1992.

Alice Walker. *Langston Hughes, American Poet*. Crowell, 1974.

John A. Williams. *The Most Native of Sons*. Doubleday, 1970.

Diane Wolkstein. *The Cool Ride in the Sky*. Knopf, 1973.

Elizabeth Yates. *Amos Fortune: Free Man*. Dutton, 1950.

Bernice E. Young. *Harlem: The Story of a Changing Community*. Messner, 1972.

Margaret E. Young. *Black American Leaders*. Watts, 1969.

*———. *The Picture Life of Ralph J. Bunche*. Watts, 1968.

Folk Literature

Verna Aardema. *Behind the Back of the Mountain*. Dial, 1973.

*———. Bimwili & the Zimibi; A Tale from Zanzibar. Dial, 1985.

———. *Black Folktales from Southern Africa*. Dial, 1973.

*———. *Bringing the Rain to Kapiti Plain*. Dial, 1981.

*———. *Half-a-Ball-of Kenki; An Ashanti Tale*. Warner, 1979.

———. *Oh, Kojo! How Could You?* Dutton, 1984.

———. *Tales from the Story Hat*. Coward, 1960.

———. *What's So Funny, Ketu?* Dial, 1982.

———. *Who's in Rabbit's House? A Masai Tail*. Dial, 1977.

———. *Why Mosquitoes Buzz in People's Ears*. Dial, 1975. (Caldecott Award winner)

Joyce Arkhurst. *The Adventure of Spider; West African Tales*. Little, 1964.

Kathleen Arnott. *African Myths and Legends*. Oxford, 1962.

Ellen Babitt. *Jataka Tales*. Prentice-Hall, 1940.

Terry Berger. *Black Fairy Tales*. Atheneum, 1969.

Ashley Bryan. *The Adventures of Aku*. Atheneum, 1976.

Harold Courlander. *Beat the Story Drum, Pum, Pum*. Atheneum, 1980.

———. *The Crest and the Hide and Other African Stories . . . .* Coward, 1982.

———. *The Hat-Shaking Dance and Other Tales. . . .* Harcourt, 1957.

———. *The King's Drum*. Harcourt, 1962.

———. *Olade the Hunter*. Harcourt, 1968.

Elphinstone Dayrell. *Why the Sun and the Moon Live in the Sky*. Houghton, 1968.

William Faulkner. *The Day the Animals Talked*. Follett, 1977.

*Suitable for primary grades.

Harold Felton. *John Henry and His Hammer.* Knopf, 1950.

Mary Joan Gerson. *Why the Sky Is Far Away.* Harcourt, 1974.

Linda Ghan. *Muhla, The Fair One.* Nu Age Editions, 1991.

Ann Grifalconi. *The Village of Round and Square Houses.* Little, 1986.

Gail Haley. *A Story, A Story.* Atheneum, 1970.

*Ezra Jack Keats. *John Henry.* Pantheon, 1965.

Julius Lester. *The Knee-High Man.* Dial, 1972.

Joan Lexau. *Crocodile and Hens.* Harper, 1969.

Gerald McDermott. *Anansi the Spider.* Holt, 1972.

Van Dyke Parks. *Jump! The Adventures of Brer Rabbit.* Harcourt, 1986.

Adjai Robinson. *Singing Tales of Africa.* Scribner's, 1974.

Peter Seeger. *Abiyoyo.* Macmillan, 1986.

Philip Sherlock. *Anansi, the Spider Man.* Crowell, 1954. (Also on film; Weston Woods.)

Poetry

Arnold Adoff. *All the Colors of the Races.* Lothrop, 1982.

———. *Big Sister Tells Me I'm Black.* Holt, 1976.

———. *Black Out Loud: An Anthology of Modern Poetry.* Macmillan, 1970.

———. *I Am the Darker Brother.* Macmillan, 1968.

———. *I Am the Running Girl.* Harper, 1979.

———, ed. *My Black Me: A Big Book of Poetry.* Dutton, 1974.

———. *Under the Early Morning Trees.* Dutton, 1978.

Ama Bontemps. *Golden Slippers. An Anthology. . . .* Harper, 1941.

Gwendolyn Brooks. *Bronzeville Boys and Girls.* Harper, 1956.

Lucille Clifton. *Everett Anderson's Friend.* Holt, 1976. (See other books about Everett Anderson.)

Paul Dunbar. *Greet the Dawn.* Atheneum, 1978.

*Nikki Giovanni. *Spin a Soft Black Song.* Hill and Wang, 1971.

Eloise Greenfield. *Daydreamers.* Dial, 1981.

———. *Honey, I Love, and Other Love Poems.* Crowell, 1978.

Nikki Grimes. *Something on My Mind.* Dial, 1978.

Langston Hughes. *Don't You Turn Back.* Knopf, 1970.

———. *The Dream Keeper and Other Poems.* Knopf, 1986.

June Jordan. *Who Look at Me?* Crowell, 1969.

Jacob Lawrence. *Harriet and the Promised Land.* Simon & Schuster, 1968.

*Suitable for primary grades.

Exploring the Backgrounds of Hispanics

The largest group in this category is Americans with Mexican backgrounds. However, we also need to be aware of such other groups as Filipino, Cuban, Puerto Rican, Latin American, and Spanish (from Spain) Americans.

General Resources

Patricia Beilke and Frank Sciara. *Selecting Materials for and about Hispanic and East Asian Children and Young People.* Shoestring, 1986.

Daniel Duran. *Latino Materials: A Multimedia Guide for Children and Young Adults.* American Bibliographic Center—CLIO Press, 1979.

A. J. Jaffee et al. *The Changing Demography of Spanish Americans.* Academic Press, 1980.

Milton Meltzer. *The Hispanic Americans.* Crowell, 1982. (For students also.) National Hispanic University. 225 East 14th Street, Oakland, CA 94606.

Febe Orozco. "A Bibliography of Hispanic Literature." *English Journal* (November 1982).

Isabel Schon. *Basic Collection of Children's Books in Spanish.* Scarecrow, 1986.

―――. *Books in Spanish for Children and Young Adults.* Scarecrow, 1985.

―――. *A Hispanic Heritage.* Scarecrow Press, 1980.

Shirley Wagoner. "Mexican-Americans in Children's Literature Since 1970." *The Reading Teacher* (December 1982).

Exploring the Backgrounds of Mexican Americans/Chicanos

Nearly six million Americans have Mexican backgrounds, and this number is growing. These Americans tend to be located in the large cities of California and the southwestern states that border Mexico.

General Resources

Rodolfo Acuña. *Occupied America: A History of Chicanos.* Harper, 1981.

Rudolfo Anaya. *Bless Me Última.* Tonatiuh, 1972.

Livie Duran and Bernard Russell, eds. *Introduction to Chicano Studies.* Macmillan, 1982.

Matt Meier and Feliciano Rivera, eds. *Dictionary of Mexican American History.* Greenwood Press, 1981.

Margarita Melville, ed. *Twice a Minority: Mexican American Women.* Mosby, 1980.

Isabel Schon. *A Bicultural Heritage: Themes for the Exploration of Mexican and Mexican-American Culture in Books for Children and Adolescents.* Scarecrow, 1978.

James Vigil. *From Indian to Chicanos: A Sociocultural History.* Mosby, 1980.

Periodicals

Aztlán: International Journal of Chicano Studies Research. Campbell Hall, Rm. 3122, University of California, Los Angeles, CA 90024.

Bronze. 1560 34th Avenue, Oakland, CA 94601.

Carta editorial. P.O. Box 54624, Terminal Annex, Los Angeles, CA 90054.

Chicano Student Movement. P.O. Box 31322, Los Angeles, CA 90031.

Compass. 1209 Egypt Street, Houston, TX 77009. (Free)

El gallo. 1265 Cherokee Street, Denver, CO 80204.

El grito del norte. Rt. 2, Box 5, Española, NM 87532.

El hispanoamericano. 630 Ninth Street, Sacramento, CA 95825.

Inside Eastside. P.O. Box 63273, Los Angeles, CA 90063.

Lado. 1306 N. Western Avenue, Chicago, IL 60622.

El malcriado. P.O. Box 130, Delano, CA 93215.

Mexican American Sun. 319 North Soto St., Los Angeles, CA 90033.

La opinión. 1426 S. Main Street, Los Angeles, CA 90015.

La prensa libre. 2973 Sacramento Street, Berkeley, CA 94702.

Proyecto Leer Bulletin, 1736 Columbia Road, NW., St. 107, Washington, D.C. 20009.

La raza. 2445 Gates Street, Los Angeles, CA 90031.

Times of the Americas. P.O. Box 1173, Coral Gables, FL 33134.

La verdad. P.O. Box 13156, San Diego, CA 92113.

Books for Students

Fiction

Ruth Adams. *Fidelia.* Lothrop, 1970.

Anne Alexander. *Trouble on the Treat Street.* Atheneum, 1974.

Lorraine Babbit. *Pink Like the Geranium.* Children's Press, 1974.

*Jan Balet. *The Fence.* Delacorte, 1969.

Laura Bannon. *Manuela's Birthday.* Whitman, 1972.

Patricia Beatty. *Lupita Mañana.* Morrow, 1982.

*Harry Behn. *The Two Uncles of Pablo.* Harcourt Brace Jovanovich, 1959.

Frank Bonham. *Viva Chicano.* Dutton, 1970.

Rose Blue. *We Are Chicanos.* Watts, 1974.

Clyde Robert Bulla. *The Poppy Seeds.* Crowell, 1955.

Hila Colman. *Chicano Girl.* Morrow, 1973.

Mary Dunne. *Reach Out, Ricardo.* Abelard, 1971.

*Marie Hall Ets. *Bad Boy, Good Boy.* Crowell, 1967.

*———. *Nine Days to Christmas.* Viking, 1959. (Easy)

*Suitable for primary grades.

Bob Fitch and Lynne Fitch. *Soy Chicano; I am Mexican-American*. Creative Education, 1971.

Marjorie Flack and Karl Larrson. *Pedro*. Macmillan, 1940.

Ayiesa Forsee. *Too Much Dog*. Lippincott, 1957.

Ed Foster. *Tejanos*. Hill and Wang, 1970.

Suzanne Fulle. *Lanterns for Fiesta*. Macrae, 1973.

Claire Galbraithe. *Victor*. Little, 1971.

Helen Garrett. *Angelo, the Naughty One*. Viking, 1944.

Marian Garthwaite. *Tomás and the Red-Haired Angel*. Messner, 1966.

Maurine Gee. *Chicano Amiga*. Morrow, 1972.

Loren Good. *Panchito*. Coward, 1955.

Dorothy Hamilton. *Anita's Choice*. Herald, 1971.

Kathryn Hitte and William B. Hayes. *Mexican Soup*. Parents', 1970.

Carl Kidwell. *Arrow in the Sun*. Viking, 1961.

Joseph Krumgold. *And Now Miguel*. Crowell, 1970.

Evelyn S. Lampman. *Go Up the Road Slowly*. Atheneum, 1972.

Marion Lay. *Wooden Saddles: The Adventures of a Mexican Boy in His Own Land*. Morrow, 1939.

*Thomas P. Lewis. *Hill of Fire*. Harper and Row, 1971.

Claudia Mills. *Luisa's American Dream*. Four Winds, 1981.

Joe Molnar, ed. *Graciela: A Mexican-American Child Tells Her Story*. Watts, 1972.

Grace Moon. *Tita of México*. Stokes, 1934.

Elizabeth Morrow. *The Painted Pig*. Knopf, 1930.

Iris Noble. *Tingambatu: Adventure in Archaeology*. Messner, 1983.

James Norman. *Charro: Mexican Horseman*. Putnam, 1970.

Scott O'Dell. *The Black Pearl*. Houghton Mifflin, 1967.

———. *Carlotta*. Houghton, 1977.

———. *The King's Fifth*. Houghton Mifflin, 1966.

Helen Rand Parish. *Estebánico*. Viking, 1974.

Paula Paul. *You Can Hear a Magpie Smile*. Nelson, 1980.

*Leo Politi. *Juanita*. Scribner's, 1948.

*———. *The Mission Bell*. Scribner's, 1953.

*———. *Pedro, the Angel of Olvera Street*. Scribner's, 1946.

*———. *Rosa*. Scribner's, 1963.

*Suitable for primary grades.

*———. *Three Stalks of Corn*. Scribner's, 1978.

Barbara Ritchie. *Ramón Makes a Trade: Los Cambios de Ramón*. Parnassus, 1959.

Jessie Ruiz. *El gran Cesar*. Education Consulting, 1973.

Ruth Sawyer. *The Least One*. Viking, 1941.

*Byrd Baylor Schweitzer. *Amigo*. Macmillan, 1963.

Nancy Smith. *Josie's Handful of Quietness*. Abingdon, 1975.

*Barbara Todd. *Juan Patricio*. Putnam, 1972.

Elizabeth Borton de Treviño. *Nacar, the White Deer*. Farrar, Straus, and Giroux, 1963.

Dorothy Witton. *Crossroads for Chela*. Messner, 1956.

Nonfiction

Rudy Acuña. *Cultures in Conflict*. Charter School Books, 1970.

Bernadine Bailey. *Famous Latin American Liberators*. Dodd, Mead, 1960.

———. *Picture Book of New Mexico*. Whitman, 1960.

Patricia Beatty. *Lupita Mañana*. Morrow, 1981.

Jacqueline Bernard. *Voices from the Southwest*. Scholastic, 1972.

Sonia Blecker. *The Aztec: Indians of Mexico*. Morrow, 1963.

———. *The Maya: Indians of Central America*. Morrow, 1961.

Rose Blue. *We Are Chicano*. Watts, 1973.

Susan Carver and Paula McGuire. *Coming to North America: From Mexico, Cuba, and Puerto Rico*. Delacorte, 1981.

Harold Coy. *Chicano Roots Go Deep*. Dodd, 1975.

Mark Day. *Forty Acres: César Chávez and the Farm Workers*. Praeger, 1971.

Patricia de Garza. *Chicanos: The Story of Mexican Americans*. Messner, 1973.

Discoverers of the New World, by the editors of American Heritage. American Heritage, 1960.

Arnold Dobrin. *The New Life—La Vida Nueva*. Dodd, 1971.

Sam Epstein. *The First Book of Mexico*. Watts, 1967.

Ruth Franchere. *César Chávez*. Crowell, 1970.

Shirley Glubok. *The Art of Ancient Mexico*. Harper and Row, 1968.

Delia Goetz. *Neighbors to the South*. Harcourt Brace Jovanovich.

Clara Louise Grant. *Mexico, Land of the Plumed Serpent*. Garrard, 1968.

Dorothy Childs Hogner. *Children of Mexico*. Heath, 1942.

Robert Jackson. *Supermax: The Lee Treviño Story*. Walck, 1973.

W. J. Jacobs. *Hernando Cortés*. Watts, 1974.

*Suitable for primary grades.

William Loren Katz. *Modern America, 1957 to the Present.* Watts, 1975.

———. *Years of Strife, 1929–1956.* Watts, 1975.

Rebecca B. Marcus and Judith Marcus. *Fiesta Time in Mexico.* Garrard, 1974.

Albert Marrin. *Aztecs and Spaniards: Cortés and the Conquest of Mexico.* Atheneum, 1986.

Patricia M. Martin. *Chicanos: Mexicans in the United States.* Parents, 1971.

May McNeer. *The Mexican Story.* Ariel, 1953.

Marie Neurath. *They Lived like This in Ancient Mexico.* Watts, 1971.

Clarke Newlon. *Famous Mexican-Americans.* Dodd, 1972.

Jane Pinchott. *The Mexicans in America.* Lever, 1973.

Patricia Rose. *Let's Read about Mexico.* Fideler, 1955.

Elizabeth Hough Sechrist. *Christmas Everywhere.* Macrae Smith, 1962.

———. *It's Time for Brotherhood.* Macrae Smith, 1973.

Ronald Syme. *Cortés of Mexico.* Morrow, 1951.

———. *Juárez: The Founder of Modern Mexico.* Morrow, 1972.

Sandra Weiner. *Small Hands, Big Hands.* Pantheon, 1970.

Florence White. *César Chávez: Man of Courage.* Garrard, 1973.

Barbara Kerr Wilson. *Fairy Tales of Mexico.* Casell, (London)-Dutton, 1960.

Bernard Wolf. *In This Proud Land: The Story of a Mexican American Family.* Lippincott, 1979.

Folklore

John Bierhorst, ed. *The Hungry Woman: Myths and Legends of the Aztecs.* Morrow, 1984.

Anita Brenner. *The Boy Who Could Do Anything & Other Mexican Folk Tales.* Young Scott, 1942.

Camilla Campbell. *Star Mountain, and Other Legends of Mexico.* McGraw-Hill, 1968.

Patricia F. Ross. *In Mexico They Say.* Knopf, 1942.

B. Traven. *The Creation of the Sun and the Moon.* Hill and Wang, 1968.

Poetry

Toni De Gerez. *2-Rabbit, 7-Wind.* Viking, 1971.

Richard Lewis, ed. *Still Waters of the Air: Poems by Three Modern Spanish Poets.* Dial, 1970.

Alastair Reid and Anthony Kerrigan. *Mother Goose in Spanish/Poesías de la Madre Oca.* Crowell, 1968.

David Santiago. *Anton Tiruliruliruler, Anton Tiruliruliruler: Valancicos y poemas de Navidad.* Author, 1989.

Gary Soto, *Neighborhood Odes.* Harcourt, 1992.

Exploring the Backgrounds of Puerto Ricans

General Resources

Kenneth Aran et al. *Puerto Rican History and Culture: A Study Guide and Curriculum Outline*. United Federation of Teachers.

A Handbook for Teaching Portuguese-Speaking Students. California State Dept. of Education, 1983.

Patricia Beilke and Frank Sciara. *Selecting Materials for and about Hispanic and East Asian Children and Young People*. Shoestring, 1986.

Diane Herrera, ed. *Puerto Ricans and Other Minority Groups in the Continental United States*. Blaine Ethridge, 1979.

Books for Adults

María Theresa Babin and Stan Steiner, eds. *Borinquen: An Anthology of Puerto Rican Literature*. Vintage, 1974.

Joseph Fitzpatrick. *Puerto Rican Americans: The Meaning of Migration to the Mainland*. Prentice-Hall, 1971.

Clifford Haubert. *Puerto Rico and Puerto Ricans: A Study of Puerto Rican History and Immigration in the United States*. Hippocrene Books, 1974.

Karl Wagenheim. *Cuentos: An Anthology of Short Stories from Puerto Rico*. Shocken Books, 1978.

———, ed. *Puerto Rico: A Profile*. Praeger, 1975.

Books for Students

Fiction

Robert Barry. *The Musical Palm Tree*. McGraw, 1968.

*Edna Barth. *The Day Luís Was Lost*. Little, 1971.

Pura Belpré. *Santiago*. Warne, 1969.

Rose Blue. *I Am Here; Yo Estoy Aquí*. Watts, 1971.

Lois Bouchard. *The Boy Who Wouldn't Talk*. Doubleday, 1969.

Nardi Campion. *Casa Means Home*. Holt, 1970.

Arthur Getz. *Tar Beach*. Dial, 1979.

Gloria Gonzalez. *Gaucho*. Knopf, 1977.

Lynn Hall. *Danza!* Scribner's, 1981.

Ezra Jack Keats and Pat Cherr. *My Dog Is Lost!* Crowell, 1960.

Myron Levoy. *A Shadow like a Leopard*. Harper, 1981.

*Suitable for primary grades.

Peggy Mann. *The Street of Flower Boxes*. Coward, 1966.

Nicholasa Mohr. *El Bronx Remembered*. Harper, 1975.

———. *Felita*. Dial, 1979.

———. *Nilda*. Harper, 1973.

Louisa Shotwell. *Magdalena*. Viking, 1971.

Ruth Sonneborn. *Friday Night Is Papa Night*. Viking, 1970.

Piri Thomas. *Stories from El Barrio*. Knopf, 1978.

Sandra Weiner. *They Call Me Jack: The Story of a Boy from Puerto Rico*. Pantheon, 1973.

Nonfiction

Stuart Brahs. *An Album of Puerto Ricans in the United States*. Watts, 1973

Peter Buckley. *I Am from Puerto Rico*. Simon, 1971.

*Antonio J. Colorado. *The First Book of Puerto Rico*. Watts, 1978.

Morton Golding. *A Short History of Puerto Rico*. Watts, 1978.

Wendy Kesselman. *Joey*. Hill, 1972.

Arlene Kurtis. *Puerto Ricans*. Messner, 1969.

Ronald Larsen. *The Puerto Ricans in America*. Lerner, 1973.

Barry Levine. *Benjy Lopez: A Picaresque Tale of Emigration and Return*. Basic Books, 1980.

Jack Manning. *Young Puerto Rico*. Dodd, 1962.

Cruz Martel. *Yagua Days*. Dial, 1976.

Robin McKown. *The Image of Puerto Rico: Its History and Its People: On the Island—On the Mainland*. McGraw, 1973.

Joe Molnar. *Elizabeth: A Puerto Rican-American Child Tells Her Story*. Watts, 1974.

Lila Perl. *Puerto Rico: Island between Two Worlds*. Morrow, 1979.

Geraldo Rivera. *Puerto Rico: Island of Contrasts*. Parents, 1973.

Warren Schloat, Jr. *María and Ramón: A Girl and Boy of Puerto Rico*. Knopf, 1966.

Elizabeth Sechrist. *It's Time for Brotherhood*. Macrae, 1973

Julia Singer. *We All Come from Puerto Rico Too*. Atheneum, 1977.

Philip Sterling and Maria Brau. *The Quiet Rebels*. Doubleday, 1968.

Morris Weeks, Jr. *Hello, Puerto Rico*. Grosset, 1972.

Biography

Paul Allyn. *The Picture Life of Herman Badilla*. Watts, 1972.

Alfredo Matilla and Ivan Silen, eds. *The Puerto Rican Poets: Los Poétas Puertorriqueños*. Bantam, 1972.

*Suitable for primary grades.

Clarke Newlon. *Famous Puerto Ricans*. Dodd, 1975.

Philip Sterling and Maria Brau. *The Quiet Rebels*. Doubleday, 1968.

Folklore

Ricardo Alegría. *The Three Wishes*. Harcourt, 1969.

Pura Belpré. *Dance of the Animals*. Warne, 1972.

————. *Once in Puerto Rico*. Warne, 1973.

————. *Oté*. Pantheon, 1969.

————. *Perez and Martina*. Warne, 1961.

————. *The Rainbow-Colored Horse*. Warne, 1978.

————. *The Tiger and the Rabbit*. Lippincott, 1965.

Exploring the Backgrounds of Cuban Americans

As you can see, the material is limited for this group. Check the *Reader's Guide* for articles in magazines.

General Resources

Esther Gonzales. *Annotated Bibliography on Cubans in the United States 1960–1976*. Florida International University, 1977.

Books for Adults

Richard Fagan et al. *Cubans in Exile*. Stanford University Press, 1968.

Geoffrey Fox. *Working-Class Emigrés from Cuba*. R. E. Research Associates, 1979.

Irving Horowitz. *Cuban Communism*. Transaction, 1984.

William Mackey and Von Beebe. *Bilingual Schools for a Bicultural Community*. Newburg House, 1977.

Rafael Probías and Lourdes Casal. *The Cuban Minority in the U.S.* Florida Atlantic University, 1973.

Eleanor M. Rogg. *The Assimilation of Cuban Exiles: The Role of Community and Class*. Aberdeen, 1974.

Hugh Thomas. *Cuba—The Pursuit of Freedom*. Harper, 1971.

————. *The Cuban Revolution*. Westview, 1984.

Books for Students

Margaretta Curtin. *Cubanita in a New Land: Cuban Children of Miami*. Miami Press, 1974.

Virginia Ortiz. *The Land and People of Cuba*. Lippincott, 1973.

Lorin Philipson and Rafael Llerena. *Freedom Flights*. Random, 1980.

Exploring the Backgrounds of Indochinese Americans (Vietnamese)

The number of persons coming from Indochina to the United States is increasing, but the literature is still scarce.

General Resources

Brent and Melissa Ashabranner. *Into a Strange Land: Unaccompanied Refugee Youth in America.* Dodd, Mead and Co., 1987.

Duong Thanh Binh. *A Handbook for Teachers of Vietnamese Students: Hints for Dealing with Cultural Differences in Schools.* Center for Applied Linguistics, 1975.

Paul Rutledge. *The Vietnamese in America.* Lerner Pub., 1987.

Tam Thi Dang Wei. *Vietnamese Refugee Students: A Handbook for School Personnel.* National Assessment and Dissemination Center for Bilingual/Bicultural Education, 1980.

Books for Adults

Charles Anderson. *Vietnam: The Other War.* Presidio Press, 1982.

Center for Applied Linguistics. *Vietnamese Refugee Education Series.* The Center, 1975.

Frances Fitzgerald. *Fire in the Lake: The Vietnamese and the Americans in Vietnam.* Vintage, 1972.

Bruce Grant, ed. *The Boat People.* Penguin, 1979.

Gail P. Kelly. *From Vietnam to America: A Chronicle of Vietnamese Immigration to the United States.* Westview, 1977.

Stephen Wright. *Meditations In Green.* Scribner's, 1983 (fiction).

Books for Students

Fiction

Tricia Brown. *Lee Ann: The Story of a Vietnamese Girl.* G. P. Putnam's Sons, 1991.

Ann Nolan Clark, *To Stand against the Wind.* Viking, 1978.

Helen Coutant. *First Snow.* Knopf, 1974.

Marylois Dunn. *The Absolutely Perfect Horse.* Harper, 1983.

Katherine Paterson. *Park's Quest.* Dutton, 1988.

Nonfiction

Janet Bode. *New Kids on the Block: Oral Histories of Immigrant Teens.* Franklin Watts, 1989.

Hal Buell. *Vietnam, Land of Many Dragons.* Dodd, 1968.

Joseph Buttinger. *A Defiant Dragon: A Short History of Vietnam.* Praeger, 1972.

John Caldwell. *Let's Visit Vietnam.* Day, 1966.

Edward F. Dolan. *America after Vietnam: Legacies of a Hated War.* Franklin Watts, 1989.

Mace Goldfarb. *Fighters, Refugees, Immigrants: A Story of the Hmong.* Carolrhoda, 1982.

Peter Goldman and Tony Fuller. *What Vietnam Did to Us.* Morrow, 1983.

James Haskins. *The New Americans: Vietnamese Boat People.* Enslow, 1980.

————. *The War and the Protest: Vietnam.* Doubleday, 1973.

Don Lawson. *An Album of the Vietnam War.* Watts, 1986.

Robert Mason. *Chickenhawk.* Viking, 1983.

Bernard Newman. *Let's Visit Vietnam.* Burke, 1983.

Huynh Quang Nhuong. *The Land I Lost: Adventures of a Boy in Vietnam.* Harper, 1982.

Jon Nielson. *Artist in South Vietnam.* Messner, 1969.

Tim Page. *Tim Page's Vietnam.* Knopf, 1983.

Marc Talbert. *The Purple Heart.* Harper, 1992.

Vuong Thuy. *Getting to Know the Vietnamese and Their Culture.* Ungar, 1976.

Lynda Van Devanter. *Home before Morning: The Story of an Army Nurse in Vietnam.* Beaufort, 1983.

Folklore

Ann Nolan Clark. *In the Land of Small Dragon: A Vietnamese Folktale.* Viking, 1979.

Mark Taylor. *The Fisherman and the Goblin.* Golden Gate, 1971.

L. D. Vuong. *The Brocaded Slipper and Other Vietnamese Tales.* Addison-Wesley, 1982.

Exploring the Backgrounds of Native Americans

Background Information for the Teacher

Howard M. Bahr, Bruce A. Chadwick, and Robert C. Day. *Native Americans Today: Sociological Perspectives.* Harper, 1972.

Russell Barsh and James Henderson. *The Road: Indian Tribes and Political Liberty.* University of California, 1980.

William M. Beauchamp. *A History of the New York Iroquois.* Friedman, 1968.

Dee Brown. *Bury My Heart at Wounded Knee.* Holt, 1970.

————. *Creek Mary's Blood.* Holt, 1971.

————. *Killdeer Mountain.* Holt, 1972.

Robert Burnette and John Koster. *The Road to Wounded Knee.* Bantam, 1974. Analysis of events leading up to Wounded Knee, 1973.

Mary Gloyne Byler. *American Indian Authors for Young Readers.* Association on American Indian Affairs, 432 Park Ave., South, New York, NY 10016. An annotated bibliography.

The Council on Interracial Books for Children. *Chronicles of American Indian Protest.* A collection of documents recounting the American Indian's struggle for survival. Offers supplemental reading assignments for classes.

John Lane Deer and Richard Erdoes. *Lame Deer, Seeker of Visions.* Washington Square, 1984.

Vine Deloria, Jr. *Custer Died for Your Sins.* Avon, 1970.

———. *God Is Red.* Laurel, 1979.

David Edmunds, ed. *American Indian Leaders: Studies in Diversity.* University of Nebraska Press, 1980.

William N. Fenton, ed. *Parker on the Iroquois.* Syracuse University Press, 1968.

Zane Grey. *The Vanishing American.* Washington Square, 1984.

Barbara Graymont. *The Iroquois in the American Revolution.* Syracuse U. Press, 1972.

William T. Hagan. *American Indians.* University of Chicago Press, 1961.

Jamake Highwater. *The Primal Mind.* Harper, 1981.

Alvin Josephy, Jr. *Now That the Buffalo's Gone.* Knopf, 1981.

Frank LaPointe. *The Sioux Today.* Macmillan, 1972. Stories of young Indians.

R. J. Lenarcic. *Pre-Columbian Indians: New Perspectives.* Community College Social Science Assoc., 1974.

Peter Navakov, ed. *Native American Testimony.* Crowell, 1978.

Wendell H. Oswalt. *This Land Was Theirs.* Wiley, 1966. Pre-Columbian cultural aspects.

Francis Paul Prucha. *American Indian Policy in the Formative Years.* University of Nebraska Press, 1962. Trade and Intercourse Acts, 1790–1834.

Anna Lee Strensland. *Literature by and about the American Indian: An Annotated Bibliography for Jr. and Sr. High School Students.* NCTE, 1978.

William Sturtevant, ed. *Handbook of North American Indians.* U.S. Government, 1981.

Dale Van Every. *Disinherited.* Morrow, 1966. Removal of the Cherokee.

Alan Velie. *American Indian Literature.* Harper, 1980.

Frank Waters. *The Man Who Killed the Deer.* Swallow, 1970.

Edmund Wilson. *Apologies to the Iroquois.* Vintage, 1959. Historical and contemporary problems.

Journals

AAIA. 432 Park Ave., New York, NY 10016. General and legislative information; newsletter.

Akwesasne Notes. Mohawk Nation via Roosevelt Town, NY 13683. Indian paper; current events and activities. Donation, publishes calendar.

American Indian Culture and Research Journal. 3220 Campbell Hall, University of California, Los Angeles CA 90004.

American Indian Media Directory. American Indian Press Association, Room, 206, 1346 Connecticut Ave., NW., Washington, D.C. 20036. Listing press, radio, TV/video, film, theater.

Warpath. United Native Americans, Inc. Box 26149, San Francisco, CA 94126.

Wassaja. American Indian Historical Society, 1451 Masonic Ave., San Francisco, CA 94117. Monthly newspaper; significant events.

Sources of Materials

Alaska Rural School Project. Univ. of Alaska, College, AK 99701.

American Indian Education Handbook. California State Dept. of Education, 1982.

Navajo Curriculum Center. Rough Rock Demonstration School, Rough Rock, AZ.

Navajo Social Studies Project. College of Education. The Univ. of New Mexico, Albuquerque, NM 87106.

Senate Committee on Labor and Public Welfare, Washington, D.C.

South Central Regional Ed. Lab. Corp., 408 National Old Line Bldg., Little Rock, AR 72201.

Nonprint Media

Bibliography of Nonprint Instructional Materials on the American Indian prepared by the Instructional Development Program for the Institute of Indian Services and Research, Brigham Young University. Brigham Young University Printing Service, Provo, Utah 84601, 1972. A 220-page publication including films of all types, slides, recordings, varied visual teaching aids, and multimedia kits. Entries are annotated and indexed with a reference to the grade level.

Books for Children

Fiction

Betty Baker. *And One Was a Wooden Indian.* Macmillan, 1970.

Olaf Baker. *Where the Buffaloes Begin.* Warne, 1981.

Carol Ann Bales. *Kevin Cloud; Chippewa Boy in the City.* Reilly and Lee, 1972.

Lynne Banks. *The Return of the Indian.* Doubleday, 1986.

Byrd Baylor. *When Clay Sings.* Scribner's, 1972.

Patricia Beatty. *The Bad Bell of San Salvador.* Morrow, 1973.

Denton Bedford. *Tsali.* Indian Historian Press, 1972.

*Nathaniel Benchley. *Small Wolf.* Harper and Row, 1972.

Clyde Bulla. *Conquista!* Crowell, 1978.

Patricia Calvert. *The Hour of the Wolf.* Scribner's, 1983.

Elizabeth Cleaver. *The Enchanted Caribou.* Atheneum, 1985.

Eth Clifford. *The Year of the Three-Legend Deer.* Houghton Mifflin, 1972.

*Suitable for primary grades.

Eleanor Clymer. *The Spider, the Cave and the Pottery Bowl.* Atheneum, 1971.

Belle Coate. *Mak.* Parnassus, 1982.

*Alice Dalgliesh. *The Courage of Sarah Noble.* Scribner's, 1954.

Ann Dixon. *How Raven Brought Light to People.* MacMillan, 1992.

T. A. Dyer. *A Way of His Own.* Houghton, 1981.

Dale Fife. *Ride the Crooked Wind.* Coward, 1973.

James Forman. *The Life and Death of Yellow Bird.* Farrar, Straus and Giroux, 1973.

Jean Craighead George. *The Talking Earth.* Harper, 1983.

Paul Goble and Dorothy Goble. *The Friendly Wolf.* Bradbury, 1975.

*————. *The Girl Who Loved Wild Horses.* Bradbury, 1978.

*————. *Lone Bull's Horse Raid.* Bradbury, 1973.

*————. *Red Hawk's Account of Custer's Last Battle.* Pantheon, 1970.

Arnold A. Griese. *At the Mouth of the Luckiest River.* Crowell, 1973.

Janet Hale. *The Owl's Song.* Avon, 1976.

Danita Haller. *Not Just Any Ring.* Knopf, 1982.

Virginia Hamilton. *Arilla Sun Down.* Greenwillow, 1976.

Christie Harris. *Raven's Cry.* Atheneum, 1966.

James Houston. *Eagle Mask.* Harcourt, 1966.

————. *Ghost Paddle.* Harcourt, 1966.

Weyman Jones. *Edge of Two Worlds.* Dial, 1968.

Ruth Karen. *Feathered Serpent: The Rise and Fall of the Aztecs.* Four Winds, 1982.

Evelyn Sibley Lampman. *Squaw Man's Son.* Atheneum, 1975.

————. *White Captives.* Atheneum, 1978.

————. *The Year of Small Shadow.* Harcourt, 1971.

*Gerald McDermott. *Arrows to the Sun: A Pueblo Indian Tale.* Viking, 1974.

D'Arcy McNickle. *The Surrounded.* University of New Mexico, 1978.

————. *Wind from an Enemy Sky.* Harper, 1978.

*F. N. Monjo. *Indian Summer.* Harper and Row, 1968.

Scott O'Dell. *The Amethyst Ring.* Houghton Mifflin, 1983.

————. *Island of the Blue Dolphins.* Houghton Mifflin, 1960.

————. *Sing Down the Moon.* Houghton Mifflin, 1970.

————. *Streams to the River, River to the Sea: A Novel of Sacagawea.* Harper, 1986.

Harry Paige. *Johnny Stands.* Warne, 1982.

Katy Peake. *The Indian Heart of Carrie Hodges.* Viking, 1972.

*Suitable for primary grades.

William Sleator. *The Angry Moon*. Little, Brown, 1970.

Virginia Driving Hawk Sneve. *Betrayed*. Holiday House, 1974. Fictional account of historical episode.

Elizabeth Speare. *The Sign of the Beaver*. Houghton Mifflin, 1983.

Hyemeyohsts Storm. *Seven Arrows*. Harper, 1972.

*Betty Waterton. *A Salmon for Simon*. Atheneum, 1981.

Barbara Williams. *The Secret Name*. Harcourt Brace Jovanovich, 1972.

Bernard Wolf. *Tinker and the Medicine Man: The Story of a Navajo Boy of Monument Valley*. Random House, 1973.

Nonfiction

Terry Allen, ed. *The Whispering Wind*. Doubleday, 1972. Poetry written by young Eskimo, Aleut, and American Indian students.

Aline Amon. *The Earth Is Sore; Native Americans on Nature*. Atheneum, 1981.

Virginia Irving Armstrong, ed. *I Have Spoken*. Sage Books, 1971.

Brent Ashabranner. *Morning Star, Black Sun: The Northern Cheyenne Indians and America's Energy Crisis*. Dodd, 1982.

————. *Children of the Maya; A Guatemalan Indian Odyssey*. Dodd, 1986.

White Deer Autumn. *Ceremony In the Circle of Life*. Carnival, 1982.

Paul D. Bailey. *Ghost Dance Messiah*. Westernlore, 1970.

Betty Baker. *At the Center of the World*. Macmillan, 1973. Based on Papago and Pima myths; includes six myths about the Arizona Indians.

————. *Settlers and Strangers*. Macmillan, 1977.

Gordon C. Baldwin. *The Apache Indians: Raiders of the Southwest*. Four Winds, 1978.

————. *How Indians Really Lived*. Putnam, 1967.

Byrd Baylor. *Before You Came This Way*. Dutton, 1969.

————. *They Put on Masks*. Scribner's, 1974.

————. *When Clay Sings*. Scribner's, 1972.

Alex W. Bealer. *Only the Names Remain: The Cherokee and the Trail of Tears*. Little, Brown, 1972.

William M. Beauchamp. *A History of the New York Iroquois*. Friedman, 1968.

Barbara L. Beck. *The First Book of the Aztecs*. Watts, 1966.

John Bierhorst, ed. *A Cry from the Earth: Music of the North American Indians*. Four Winds, 1978.

————. *In the Trail of the Wind; American Indian Poems and Ritual Orations*. Farrar, Straus and Giroux, 1971.

Sonia Bleeker. *The Cherokee: Indians of the Mountains*. Morrow, 1952.

*Suitable for primary grades.

————. *The Crow Indians: Hunters of the Northern Plains*. Morrow, 1951.

————. *The Delaware Indians: Eastern Fishermen and Farmers*. Morrow, 1953.

————. *Indians of the Longhouse: The Story of the Iroquois*. Morrow, 1950.

————. *The Maya*. Morrow, 1961.

————. *The Mission Indians of California*. Morrow, 1956.

————. *The Navajo: Herders, Weavers and Silversmiths*. Morrow, 1958.

————. *The Sioux Indians: Hunters and Warriors of the Plains*. Morrow, 1962.

Charles Blood. *The Goat in the Rug*. Parents, 1976.

Victor Boesen. *Edward S. Curtis, Photographer of the North American Indian*. Coward, 1977.

Mary Bringle. *Eskimos*. Watts, 1973.

Dee Brown. *Bury My Heart at Wounded Knee*. Holt, Rinehart and Winston, 1970.

Clyde Bulla. *Pocahontas and the Strangers*. Crowell, 1971.

Jesse Clifton Burt. *Indians of the Southeast: Then and Now*. Abingdon, 1973.

Ann Nolan Clark. *Circle of Seasons*. Farrar, Straus and Giroux, 1970. Describes ceremonies of the Pueblo Indians.

John Collier. *The Indians of the Americas*. Norton, 1947.

Peter Collier. *When Shall They Rest? The Cherokees' Long Struggle with America*. Holt, Rinehart and Winston, 1970.

Harold Coy. *Man Comes to America*. Little, Brown, 1973.

Margaret Crary. *Susette La Fiesche: Voice of the Omaha Indians*. Hawthorne, 1973.

Chief Eagle Dallas. *Winter Count*. Golden Bell, 1968.

Janet D'Amato. *Algonquian and Iroquois Crafts for You to Make*. Messner, 1979.

————. *American Indian Craft Inspirations*. Evans, 1972.

Walter M. Daniels, ed. *American Indians*. Wilson, 1957.

Russell David and Brent Ashabranner. *Chief Joseph, War Chief of the Nez Percé*. McGraw-Hill, 1962.

Vine Deloria. *Indians of the Pacific Northwest*. Doubleday, 1977.

Edith Dorian. *Hokahey! American Indians Then and Now*. McGraw-Hill, 1957.

Charles A. Eastman. *Indian Boyhood*. Dover, 1971.

Amy Ehrlich. *Wounded Knee: An Indian History of the American West*. Holt, Rinehart and Winston, 1974.

Paul Elliott. *Eskimos of the World*. Messner, 1976.

Mary Elting. *The Hopi Way*. Evans, 1969.

Richard Erdoes. *The Pueblo Indians*. Young Readers' Indian Library, 1967.

————. *The Native Americans: Navajos*. Sterling, 1978.

————. *The Rain Dance People: The Pueblo Indians*. Knopf, 1976.

————. *The Sun Dance People*. Knopf, 1972.

Norma Farber. *Mercy Short*. Dutton, 1982.

William N. Fenton, ed. *Parker on the Iroquois*. Syracuse University Press, 1968.

Franklin Folsom. *Red Power on the Rio Grande: The Nature of the American Revolution of 1680*. Follett, 1973.

Grant Foreman. *Indian Removal*. University of Oklahoma Press, 1932.

Russell Freedman. *An Indian Winter*. Paintings and Drawings by Karl Bodmer. Holiday, 1992.

George Fronval. *Indian Signs and Signals*. Sterling, 1978.

Frieda Gates. *North American Indian Masks: Craft and Legend*. Walker, 1982.

Shirley Glubok. *The Art of Ancient Mexico*. Harper and Row, 1964.

————. *The Art of the North American Indian*. Harper and Row, 1964.

————. *The Art of the Northwest Coast Indians*. Macmillan, 1975.

————. *The Art of the Southwest Indians*. Macmillan, 1971.

Bruce Grant. *American Indians Yesterday and Today*. Dutton, 1958.

Barbara Graymont. *The Iroquois in the American Revolution*. Syracuse University Press, 1972.

Marion E. Gridley. *American Indian Women*. Hawthorne, 1974. Describes the lives of 19 women ranging over a period of 300 years.

————. *Indian Tribes of America*. Hubbard, 1973.

Miriam Gurko. *Indian America: The Black Hawk War*. Crowell, 1970.

William T. Hagan. *American Indians*. University of Chicago Press, 1961.

Charles Hamilton. *Cry of the Thunderbird*. Macmillan, 1950.

Mary Sayre Haverstock. *Indian Gallery*. Four Winds, 1973. A bibliography of artist George Catlin who traveled among the Indian tribes painting Indian subjects and collecting materials for an Indian museum.

Wilma P. Hays. *Foods the Indians Gave Us*. Washburn, 1973.

S. Carl Hirsch. *Famous American Indians of the Plains*. Rand McNally, 1973.

Charles Hofmann. *American Indians Sing*. Day, 1967.

Robert Hofsinde. *Indian Arts*. Morrow, 1971.

————. *The Indian and His Horse*. Morrow, 1960.

————. *The Indian Medicine Man*. Morrow, 1966.

————. *Indian Music Makers*. Morrow, 1967.

————. *Indian Sign Language*. Morrow, 1956.

————. *Indian Warriors and Their Weapons*. Morrow, 1965.

————. *Indians at Home*. Morrow, 1964.

W. Ben Hunt. *The Complete Book of Indian Crafts and Lore*. Golden, 1976.

Indian Culture Series. Montana Reading Publications, Level 4, Stapleton Building, Billings, MT 59101. Series written and illustrated by Indian children for Indians.

Daniel Jacobson. *Great Indian Tribes*. Hammond, 1970.

Johanna Johnston. *The Indians and the Strangers*. Dodd, Mead, 1972.

Jayne Clark Jones. *The American Indian in America*. Lerner, 1973.

———. *The Patriot Chiefs*. Viking, 1958.

———. *Red Power: The American Indians' Fight for Freedom*. American Heritage Press, 1971.

Alvin Josephy. *The Nez Percé Indians and the Opening of the Northwest*. Yale University Press, 1965.

William Loren Katz. *Early America, 1492–1812*. Watts, 1974.

Ruth Kirk. *David, Young Chief of the Quileutes: An American Indian Today*. Harcourt Brace Jovanovich, 1967.

———. *Hunters of the Whale*. Morrow, 1974.

Theodora Kroeber. *Ishi: Last of His Tribe*. Parnassus, 1964.

Oliver La Farge. *The American Indian*. Golden, 1960.

———. *Pictorial History of the American Indian*. Crown, 1956.

Sigmund Lavine. *The Games the Indians Played*. Dodd, 1974.

———. *Indian Corn and Other Gifts*. Dodd, 1974.

R. J. Lenarcic. *Pre-Columbian Indians: New Perspectives*. Community College Social Science Assoc., 1974.

Grant Lyons. *The Creek Indians*. Messner, 1978.

Richard Lytle. *People of the Dawn*. Atheneum, 1980.

David Mangurian. *Children of the Incas*. Four Winds, 1979.

Rebecca Marcus. *The First Book of the Cliff Dwellers*. Watts, 1968.

Alice Marriott. *The First Comers*. Longman's, 1960.

———. *Indians on Horseback*. Crowell, 1968, © 1948.

May McNeer. *The American Indian Story*. Ariel, 1963.

J. Walker McSpadden. *Indian Heroes*. Crowell, 1950.

Patricia Miles Martin. *Indians, the First Americans*. Parents', 1970.

Sherry Mathers et al. *Our Mother Corn*. Daybreak, 1981.

Emerson N. Matson. *Legends of the Great Chiefs*. Nelson, 1972. Focuses on the Pacific Coastal tribes.

Julian May. *Before the Indians*. Holiday, 1969.

N. Scott Momaday. *The Way to Rainy Mountain*. Ballantine, 1970. A poetic mixture of retellings of Kiowa tales, stories for the history of the Kiowa, and the author's memories of his grandmother.

Dorothy Morrison. *Chief Sarah. Sarah Winnemullen's Fight for Indian Rights.* Atheneum, 1980.

Gerald Newman. *The Changing Eskimos.* Watts, 1979.

Ethel Nurge, ed. *The Modern Sioux.* University of Nebraska Press, 1970.

Peggy Parish. *Let's Be Indians.* Harper and Row, 1962.

Arthur C. Parker. *Skunny Wundy: Seneca Indian Tales.* Whitman, 1970. Useful for practicing creative storytelling for students of all ages.

Elizabeth Payne. *Meet the North American Indians.* Random House, 1965.

Tillie S. Pine. *The Indians Knew.* McGraw-Hill, 1957.

Peter Pitseolak. *Peter Pitseolak's Escape from Death.* Delacorte, 1978.

Hermina Poatgieter. *Indian Legacy.* Messner, 1981.

C. Fayne Porter. *Our Indian Heritage: Profiles of 12 Great Leaders.* Chilton, 1964.

William K. Powers. *Here Is Your Hobby: Indian Dancing and Costumes.* Putnam, 1966.

Seymour Reit. *Child of the Navajos.* Dodd, Mead, 1971.

Thomas L. Robertson. *The Yellow Cane.* Steck, 1956.

Maudie Robinson. *Children of the Sun: The Pueblos, Navajos, and Apaches of New Mexico.* Messner, 1973.

Glen Rounds. *Buffalo Harvest.* Holiday Harvest. Holiday House, 1952.

William E. Scheele. *The Mound Builders.* World, 1960.

Charles and Martha Shapp. *Let's Find Out about Indians.* Watts, 1962.

Sally Sheppard. *Indians of the Eastern Woodlands.* Watts, 1975.

Paul Showers. *Indian Festivals.* Crowell, 1969.

Beatrice Siegel. *Indians of the Woodland before and after the Pilgrims.* Walker, 1972.

Nancy Simon. *American Indian Habitats.* McKay, 1978.

William O. Steele. *Talking Bones.* Harper, 1978.

Stan Steiner. *The Tiguas: The Lost Tribe of Indians.* Collier, 1972.

Craig Kev Strete. *When Grandfather Journeys into Winter.* Greenwillow, 1979.

Alfred Tamarin. *Ancient Indians of the Southwest.* Doubleday, 1975.

————. *We Have Not Vanished.* Follet, 1974.

Helen H. Tanner. *The Ojibwa.* Chelsea House, 1992.

Tobi Tobias. *Maria Tallchief.* Crowell, 1970.

Edwin Tunis. *Indians.* Crowell, 1979.

Dale Van Every. *Disinherited.* Morrow, 1966.

Olivia Vlahos. *New World Beginnings, Indian Cultures in the Americas.* Viking, 1970.

Betsy Warren. *Indians Who Lived in Texas.* Steck, 1970.

Charles Morrow Wilson. *Gerónimo.* Dillon, 1973.

Edmund Wilson. *Apologies to the Iroquois*. Vantage, 1959.

Shirley Hill Witt. *The Tuscaroras*. Crowell-Collier, 1972.

Nancy Wood. *Hollering Sun*. Simon and Schuster, 1972.

————. *The World of the American Indian*. National Geographic Society, 1974.

Edgar Wyatt. *Cochise, Apache Warrior and Statesman*. McGraw-Hill, 1973.

Rosebud Yellow Robe. *An Album of the American Indian*. Watts, 1969.

Charlotte Yue. *The Pueblo*. Houghton Mifflin, 1986.

————. *The Tipi: A Center of Native American Life*. Knopf, 1984.

Folklore

Betty Baker. *And Me, Coyote!* Macmillan, 1982.

————. *Rat Is Dead and Ant Is Sad*. Harper, 1981.

John Bierhorst, ed. *Lightning Inside You and Other Native American Riddles*. Morrow, 1992.

Byrd Baylor. *A God on Every Mountain Top*. Scribner's, 1981.

————. *Moon Song*. Scribner's, 1982.

Natalia Belting. *Our Fathers Had Powerful Songs*. Dutton, 1974.

————. *Whirlwind Is a Ghost Dancing*. Dutton, 1974.

Margery Bernstein and Janet Kobrin. *The Summer Maker*. Scribner's, 1977.

Charles Blood. *The Goat in the Rug*. Parents', 1976.

Henry Chafetz. *Thunderbird and Other Stories*. Pantheon, 1964.

Elizabeth Cleaver. *The Enchanted Caribou*. Atheneum, 1985.

Jane Louise Curry. *Down from the Lonely Mountain*. Harcourt, 1964.

Edward Curtis. *The Girl Who Married a Ghost*. Four Winds, 1978.

Tomie DePaola. *The Legend of the Bluebonnet*. Putnam, 1983.

Dorothy DeWit, ed. *The Talking Stone: An Anthology of Native American Tales and Legends*. Greenwillow, 1979.

Anne B. Fisher. *Stories California Indians Told*. Parnassus, 1957.

Mirra Ginsburg. *The Proud Maiden, Tungak, and the Sun*. Macmillan, 1974.

*Paul Goble. *The Great Race of the Birds and Animals*. Bradbury, 1985.

————. *Star Boy*. Bradbury, 1983.

————and Dorothy Goble. *The Gift of the Sacred Dog*. Bradbury, 1980.

George Grinnell. *The Whistling Skeleton, American Indian Tales of the Supernatural*. Four Winds, 1982.

Christie Harris. *Mouse Woman and the Mischief-Makers*. Atheneum, 1977.

————. *Mouse Woman and the Muddleheads*. Atheneum, 1977.

*Suitable for primary grades.

————. *Mouse Woman and the Vanished Princesses.* Atheneum, 1976.

————. *Once More upon a Totem.* Atheneum, 1982.

————. *The Trouble with Adventurers.* Atheneum, 1982.

————. *The Trouble with Princesses.* Atheneum, 1980.

Virginia Haviland, ed. *North American Legends.* Collins, 1978.

Jamake Highwater. *Anpao: An American Indian Odyssey.* Lippincott, 1977.

Hilda M. Hooke. *Thunder in the Mountains: Legends of Canada.* Oxford, 1947.

Ken Kesey. *The Sea Lion: A Story of the Sea Cliff People.* Viking, 1991.

Alice Marriott and Carol Rachlin. *American Indian Mythology.* Crowell, 1968.

D'Arcy McNickle. *Runner in the Sun: A Story of Indian Maize.* Holt, 1954.

*Jane Mobley. *The Star Husband.* Doubleday, 1979.

Gail Robinson. *Raven the Trickster. Legends of the North American Indians.* Atheneum, 1982.

Ann Siberell. *Whale in the Sky.* Dutton, 1982.

William Toye. *The Fire Stealer.* Oxford, 1980.

Alex Whitney. *Stiff Ears: Animal Folktales of the North American Indian.* Walck, 1974.

Sheron Williams. *And in the Beginning* . . . Atheneum, 1992.

Rosebud Yellow Robe. *Tonweya and the Eagles and Other Lakota Indian Tales.* Dial, 1978.

Poetry

Terry Allen. *The Whispering Wind.* Doubleday, 1972. Poetry by young American Indians.

Aline Amon. *The Earth Is Sore: Native Americans on Nature.* Atheneum, 1981.

Natalia Belting. *Our Fathers Had Powerful Songs.* Dutton, 1974.

John Bierhorst. *In the Trail of the Wind.* Farrar, Straus and Giroux, 1971. American Indian poems and ritual orations.

*Jamake Highwater. *Moonsong Lullaby.* Lothrop, 1981.

James Houston. *Songs of the Dream People.* Atheneum, 1972. Chants and images from the Indians and Eskimos of North America.

Hettie Jones. *The Trees Stand Shining.* Dial, 1971. Poetry of the North American Indians.

Henry Wadsworth Longfellow. *The Song of Hiawatha.* Dutton, 1960.

Ramaho Navajo Students. *Reflections on Illusion—Reality.* Pine Hill Media Center, 1981.

Judith Ullom, comp. *Folklore of the North American Indians: An Annotated Bibliography.* Library of Congress, 1969.

Nancy Wood. *War Cry on a Prayer Feather.* Colorado Centennial Commission.

*Suitable for primary grades.

Biography

Ingri d'Aulaire and Edgar P. d'Aulaire. *Pocahontas*. Doubleday, 1946.

Russell Davis. *Chief Joseph: War Chief of the Nez Percé*. McGraw, 1962.

Mary Gardner. *Mary Jemison: Seneca Captive*. Harcourt, 1966.

Marion Gridley. *American Indian Women*. Hawthorn, 1974.

Johanna Johnston. *The Indians and the Strangers*. Dodd, 1972.

Lois Lenski. *Indian Captive: The Story of Mary Jemison*. Lippincott, 1941.

William Steele. *The Wilderness Tattoo: A Narrative of Juan Ortiz*. Harcourt, 1972.

Ronald Syme. *Osceola. Seminole Leader*. Morrow, 1976.

Exploring the Backgrounds of Jewish Americans

Crossing ethnic and national lines throughout the world, the Jews have probably suffered from more prejudice and stereotyping than any other group. Students will benefit from reading fiction and nonfiction about the history of the Jews and their contemporary life, a complex study that covers broad issues and concerns.

General Resources

Nathan Belth. *A Promise to Keep: A Narrative of the American Encounter with Anti-Semitism*. New York Times, 1979.

Max Dimont. *The Jews in America: The Roots, History and Destiny of American Jews*. Simon and Schuster, 1978.

Nathan Glazer. *American Judaism*. University of Chicago Press, 1972.

Sidney Goldstein and Calvin Goldschieder. *Jewish-Americans: Three Generations in a Jewish Community*. Prentice-Hall, 1968.

Irving Howe. *World of Our Fathers: The Journey of the East European Jews to America and the Life They Found and Made*. Simon and Schuster, 1976.

———— and Kenneth Libo. *How We Lived: A Documentary History of Immigrant Jews in America, 1880–1930*. Richard Marek, 1979.

Anita L. Lebeson. *Pilgrim People: A History of the Jews in America from 1492 to 1974*. Minerva Press, 1975.

Milton Meltzer. *Never to Forget: The Jews of the Holocaust*. Harper, 1976.

————. *Taking Root: Jewish Immigrants in America*. Farrar, 1976.

Chain Potok. *The Chosen*. Simon and Schuster. 1967.

————. *My Name Is Asher Lev*. Knopf, 1972.

————. *The Promise*. Knopf, 1976.

Jerome Rothenberg, ed. *A Big Jewish Book: Poems and Other Visions of the Jews from Tribal Times to the Present*. Doubleday, 1978.

Books for Students

Fiction

Lynne Reid Banks. *One More River.* Morrow, 1992.

Tamar Bergman. *The Boy from over There.* Houghton, 1988.

Marge Blaine. *Dvora's Journey.* Holt, 1979.

Miriam Chaiken. *Finders Weepers.* Harper, 1980.

———. *Getting Even.* Harper, 1982.

———. *I Should Worry, I Should Care.* Harper, 1979.

———. *Yossi Asks the Angels for Help.* Harper, 1985.

Eth Clifford. *The Remembering Box.* Houghton Mifflin, 1985.

Barbara Cohen. *Bitter Herbs and Honey.* Lothrop, 1976.

———. *The Carp in the Bathtub.* Lothrop, 1972.

Gloria Goldreich. *Lori.* Holt, 1976.

———. *Season of Discovery.* Nelson, 1976.

———. *A Treasury of Jewish Literature.* Holt, 1982.

Bette Greene. *Summer of My German Soldier.* Dial, 1973.

Anita Heyman. *Exit from Home,* Crown, 1977.

*Marilyn Hirsh. *Ben Goes into Business.* Holiday, 1973.

Anne Holm. *North to Freedom.* Harcourt, 1965.

Johanna Hurwitz. *Once I Was a Plum Tree.* Morrow, 1980.

Naomi Karp. *Turning Point.* Harcourt, 1976.

Phyllis Krasilovsky. *L. C. Is the Greatest.* Nelson, 1975.

Robert Lehrman. *The Store That Mama Built.* Macmillan, 1992.

Sonia Levitin. *Journey to America.* Atheneum, 1970.

———. *A Sound to Remember.* Harcourt, 1976.

Lois Lowry. *Number the Stars.* Houghton Mifflin, 1989.

Harry Mazer. *The Last Mission: A Novel.* Delacorte, 1979.

Marietta Moskin. *Waiting for Mama.* Coward, 1975.

Emily Neville. *Berries Goodman.* Harper, 1965.

I. L. Peretz. *The Case against the Wind and Other Stories.* Macmillan, 1975.

*Mildred Phillips. *The Sign on Mendel's Window.* Macmillan, 1985.

Shalom Rabinowitz. *Holiday Tales of Sholom Aleichem.* Scribner's, 1979.

Lois Ruby. *Two Truths in My Pocket.* Viking, 1982.

Marilyn Sachs. *Mary.* Doubleday, 1970.

*Suitable for primary grades.

Alezra Shevin. *Holiday Tales of Sholom Aleichem.* Scribner's, 1976.

Carol Snyder. *Ike and Mama and the Block Wedding.* Coward, 1979.

Fannie Steinberg. *Birthday in Kishenev.* Jewish Publication Society, 1976.

*Sadie Weilerstein. *The Best of K'onton.* Jewish Publication Society, 1960.

Nonfiction

Chana Abells. *The Children We Remember.* Kav-Ben Copies, 1983.

*David Adler. *A Picture Book of Hanukkah.* Holiday, 1982.

Mary Antin. *The Promised Land.* Houghton Mifflin, 1969.

Joanne E. Bernstein. *Dmitry: A Young Soviet Immigrant.* Ticknor and Fields, 1981.

Deborah Brodie. *Stories My Grandfather Should Have Told Me.* Hebrew Publishers, 1977.

Miriam Chaikin. *Ask Another Question; The Story and Meaning of Passover.* Clarion, 1985.

————. *Sound the Shofar; The Story and Meaning of Rosh Hashanah and Yom Kippur.* Clarion, 1986.

Hila Coleman. *Rachel's Legacy.* Morrow, 1978.

Michelle Edwards. *Alef-Bet: A Hebrew Alphabet Book.* Lothrop, 1992.

Norman Finkelstein. *Remember Not to Forget.* Watts, 1985.

Howard Greenfeld. *Rosh Hashanah and Yom Kippur.* Holt, 1979.

Arlene Kurtis. *The Jews Helped Build America.* Messner, 1970.

Milton Meltzer, ed. *The Jewish Americans: A History in Their Own Words 1650–1950.* Crowell, 1982.

Bert Merter. *Bar Mitzvah, Bat Mitzvah: How Jewish Boys & Girls Come of Age.* Houghton, 1984.

Shirley Milgrim. *Haym Salomon: Liberty's Son.* Jewish Publications Society, 1976. (Biography).

Susan Purdy. *Jewish Holiday Cookbook.* Watts, 1979.

Johanna Reiss. *The Upstairs Room.* Crowell, 1972.

Ellen N. Stern. *Embattled Justice: The Story of Louis Dembitz Brandeis.* Jewish Publication Society, 1971. (Biography)

Folklore

Barbara Cohen. *Yussel's Prayer.* Lothrop, 1981.

Florence Freedman. *Brothers; A Hebrew Legend.* Harper, 1985.

Marilyn Hirsh. *Could Anything Be Worse? A Yiddish Tale.* Holiday, 1974.

Jose Patterson. *Angels, Prophets, Rabbis and Kings from the Stories of the Jewish People.* Illustrated by Claire Bushe. Peter Bedrick, 1991.

*Suitable for primary grades.

Uri Shulevitz. *The Magician*. Macmillan, 1973.

Isaac B. Singer. *The Golem*. Farrar, 1982.

———. *Mazel and Shlimazel*. Farrar, 1967.

———. *When Shlemiel Went to Warsaw & Other Stories*. Farrar, 1968.

———. *Zlateh, the Goat, and Other Stories*. Harper, 1966.

Margot Zemach. *It Could Always Be Worse: A Yiddish Folk Tale Retold*. Farrar, 1976.

Exploring Additional National Origins

In addition to the more detailed lists of books for children for important minority groups presented in the preceding pages, here are recommended books about specific countries or areas of the world.

Australia, New Zealand, and Tasmania

*Pamela Allen. *Who Sank the Boat?* Coward, 1983.

Patricia Beatty. *Jonathan Down Under*. Morrow, 1982.

Godfrey Blunden. *The Land and People of Australia*. Lippincott, 1972.

Diane Hebley, comp. *Off the Shelf: Twenty-one Years of New Zealand Books for Children*. Associated Books Publishers, Ltd.

W. F. Henderson. *Looking at Australia*. Lippincott, 1977.

Edna M. Kaula. *The Land and People of New Zealand*. Lippincott, 1972.

National Geographic Society. *Amazing Animals of Australia*. The Society, 1984.

Ruth Park. *Playing Beatie Bow*. Atheneum, 1982.

Joyce Powzyk. *Tasmania, A Wildlife Journey*. Lothrop, 1987.

Marilyn Sachs. *Call Me Ruth*. Doubleday, 1982.

Austria and Lichtenstein

Carol Greene. *Austria*. Children's Press, 1986.

Egypt

Aliki. *Mummies Made in Egypt*. Crowell, 1977.

Norma Katan. *Hieroglyphs: The Writing of Ancient Egypt*. Atheneum, 1981.

*Lise Maniche. *The Prince Who Knew His Fate*. Philomel, 1982.

England

Joan Aiken. *The Shadow Guests*. Delacorte, 1980.

Rachel Anderson. *The Poacher's Son*. Oxford, 1983.

*Suitable for primary grades.

Mitsumasa Anno. *Anno's Britain*. Philomel, 1982.

Shirley Blumenthal. *Coming to America: Immigrants from the British Isles*. Delacorte, 1980.

Nancy Bond. *Country of Broken Stone*. Atheneum, 1980.

John Branfield. *The Fox in White*. Atheneum, 1982.

Alan Hamilton. *Queen Elizabeth II*. Hamilton Hamish, 1983.

Barbara Hill. *Cooking the English Way*. Lerner, 1982.

Gene Kemp. *The Turbulent Term of Tyke Tiler*. Faber, 1977.

Penelope Lively. *Fanny's Sister*. Dutton, 1980.

Richard Mabey. *Oak and Company*. Greenwillow, 1983.

Michelle Magorian. *Good Night, Mr. Tom*. Harper, 1982.

Alison Morgan. *Paul's Kite*. Atheneum, 1982.

Ann Schlee. *Ask Me No Questions*. Holt, 1982.

Rosemary Sutcliff. *Frontier Wolf*. Dutton, 1981.

————. *Song for a Dark Queen*. Crowell, 1982.

France

Lilian J. Bragdon. *The Land and People of France*. Lippincott, 1972.

Walter Buehr. *The French Explorers in America*. Putnam, 1961.

Vivian Grey. *The Chemist Who Lost His Head: The Story of Antoine Lavoisier*. Coward, 1983.

Virginia Haviland. *Favorite Fairy Tales Told in France*. Little, 1959.

Virginia Kunz. *The French in America*. Lerner, 1966.

Robert Lexalt. *Sweet Promised Land*. Harper, 1957.

Robert C. Sieur de Syme. *La Salle of the Mississippi*. Morrow, 1953.

Germany

Margot Benary-Isbert. *The Ark*. Harcourt, 1953.

Lee Cooper. *Fun with German*. Little, 1965.

T. Degens. *The Visit*. Viking, 1982.

John Dornberg. *The Two Germanys*. Dial, 1974.

Bathold Fles. *East Germany*. Watts, 1973.

Robert Goldston. *The Life and Death of Nazi Germany*. Bobbs, 1967.

Evert Hartman. *War without Friends*. Crown, 1982.

Mara Kay. *In Face of Danger*. Crown, 1977.

Ilse Koehn. *My Childhood in Nazi Germany,* Greenwillow, 1972.

Virginia Kunz. *The Germans in America*. Lerner, 1966.

Otfried Preussler. *The Satanic Mill*. Macmillan, 1973.

Hans Richter. *Friedrich*. Holt, 1970.

Julia Singer. *Impressions. A Trip to the German Democratic Republic*. Atheneum, 1979.

Ellen Switzer. *How Democracy Failed*. Atheneum, 1975.

Raymond Wohlrabe. *The Land and the People of Germany*. Lippincott, 1972.

Greece

A study of Greek American backgrounds fits well with mythology and the Olympics.

Isaac Asimov. *The Greeks: A Great Adventure*. Houghton, 1965.

Olivia Coolidge. *The Golden Days of Greece*. Crowell, 1968.

Julie Delton. *My Uncle Nikos*. Crowell, 1983.

Theodore Giankoulis. *The Land and People of Greece*. Lippincott, 1972.

Margaret Hodges. *The Avenger*. Scribner's, 1982.

Norma Johnston. *The Days of the Dragon's Seed*. Atheneum, 1983.

Winifred Madison. *The Party That Lasted All Summer*. Little Brown, 1976.

Charles Robinson. *The First Book of Ancient Greece*. Watts, 1960.

Jonathan Rutland. *See Inside an Ancient Greek Town*. Warwick, 1979.

Miroslav Sasek. *This Is Greece*. Macmillan, 1966.

Janet Van Duyn. *The Greeks: Their Legacy*. McGraw, 1972.

Jill P. Walsh. *Children of the Fox*. Farrar, 1978.

Ruth Warren. *Modern Greece*. Watts, 1979.

Jane Yolen. *The Boy Who Had Wings*. Crowell, 1974.

India and Pakistan (Sri Lanka)

Mulk Raj Arand. *Indian Fairy Tales*. Bombay: Bhatkal, 1966. Colorful tales; good illustrations.

*Ellen C. Babbitt. *The Jatakas, Tales of India*. Appleton, 1940. Animal stories from India.

Aaron Shepard. *Savitri: A Tale of Ancient India*. Illustrated by Vera Rosenberry. Whitman, 1992.

Leona Bagai. *The East Indians and the Pakistanis in America*. Lerner, 1967.

Astrid Bergman Sucksdorff. *Chendru*. Harcourt, 1960.

Jean Bothwell. *The First Book of India*. Watts, 1978.

Joseph Gaer. *Fables of India*. Little, 1955.

Madhur Jaffrey. *Seasons of Splendour: Tales, Myths, and Legends of India*. Atheneum, 1985.

*Suitable for primary grades.

Rudyard Kipling. *The Jungle Book and Just So Stories.* Varied editions.

Robert Lang. *The Land and People of Pakistan.* Lippincott, 1974.

Daulat Panday. *The Tales of India.* India: Ashram, 1963. Descriptive text; good illustrations.

Barbara Leonie Picard. *The Story of Rama and Sita.* London: Harrap, 1960. Exciting legend; good color illustrations.

F. W. Rawding. *Gandhi and the Struggle for India's Independence.* Lerner, 1982.

Madhu Bazaz Wangu. *Hinduism: World Religions.* Facts on File, 1991.

Ireland

Karen Bransom. *Streets of Gold.* Putnam, 1981.

Rhoda Fagen. *Ireland in Pictures.* Sterling, 1978.

Patricia Giff. *The Gift of the Pirate Queen.* Delacorte, 1982.

James Johnson. *The Irish in America.* Lerner, 1976.

Sondra Langford. *Red Bird of Ireland.* Atheneum, 1983.

Joan L. Nixon. *The Gift.* Macmillan, 1983.

Elinor O'Brien. *The Land and People of Ireland.* Lippincott, 1972.

Miroslav Sasek. *This Is Ireland.* Macmillan, 1965.

Catherine Sefton. *Island of the Strangers.* Harcourt, 1985.

Mary Tannen. *The Lost Legend of Finn.* Knopf, 1982.

Margaret Wetterer. *The Giant's Apprentice.* Atheneum, 1982.

Italy

Penrose Colyer. *I Can Read Italian: My First English-Italian Word Book.* Watts, 1983.

*Tomie De Paola. *Big Anthony and the Magic Ring.* Harcourt, 1979.

Sam Epstein. *The First Book of Italy.* Watts, 1972.

Ronald Grossman. *The Italians in America.* Lerner, 1966.

Erik Haugaard. *The Little Fishes.* Houghton, 1967.

Virginia Haviland. *Favorite Fairy Tales Told in Italy.* Little, 1965.

Frances Winwar. *The Land and People of Italy.* Lippincott, 1972.

Middle East

Aramco World Magazine. 1800 Augusta Dr., Suite 300, Houston, TX 77057. Wonderful photography and informative articles; request free subscription.

Barbara Cohen and Bahija Lovejoy. *Seven Daughters and Seven Sons.* Atheneum, 1982.

*Suitable for primary grades.

Russell Davis and Brent Ashabranner. *Ten Thousand Desert Swords*. Little, Brown, 1960. Good adventure story.

*Olga Economakis. *Oasis of the Stars*. Coward, McCann and Geoghegan, 1965. Text vague and derogatory, nonfactual; good illustrations.

L. E. Leipold. *Folktales of Arabia*. Denison, 1973. Six of the best-known Arabian tales are retold in a simplified form.

Arthur Scholey, comp. *The Discontented Dervishes and Other Persian Tales*. Deutsch, 1982.

William Spencer. *Islamic States in Conflict*. Watts, 1983.

*Virginia A. Tashjian. *Three Apples Fell from Heaven*. Little, Brown, 1971. Entertaining stories; excellent illustrations.

*Barbara K. Walker. *The Courage of Kazan*. Crowell, 1970. Well-written story; beautiful illustrations.

Persia

Arthur Scholey, comp. *The Discontented Dervishes and Other Persian Tales*. Deutsch, 1982.

Peru

Emilie Lepthien. *Peru*. Enchantment of the World Series. Children's Press, 1992.

Poland

Sollace Hotze, *Summer Endings*. Clarion, 1991.

Anne Pellowski. *Winding Valley Farm: Annie's Story*. Philomel, 1982.

Cass Sandak. *Poland*. Watts, 1986.

Christine Szambelan-Stravinsky. *Dark Hour of Noon*. Lippincott, 1983.

Portugal

Esther Cross. *Portugal*. Children's Press, 1986.

Russia and Other Former Soviet Socialist Republics

E. M. Almedingen. *Land of Muscovy: The History of Early Russia*. Farrar, 1972.

Bonnie Carey. *Baba Yaga's Geese and Other Russian Stories*. Indiana University Press, 1973.

Kornei Chukovsky. *The Silver Crest: My Russian Boyhood*. Holt, 1976.

Barbara Cohen. *Molly's Pilgrims*. Lothrop, 1983.

Guy Daniels. *Ivan the Fool and Other Tales of Leo Tolstory,* tr. by the author. Macmillan, 1966.

*Suitable for primary grades.

Nancy Eubank. *The Russians in America*. Lerner, 1973.

Virginia Haviland (retold by). *Favorite Fairy Tales Told in Russia*. Little, 1961.

Philip Hewitt. *Looking at Russia*. Lippincott, 1977.

Cynthia Jameson. *The Clay Pot Boy*. Coward-McCann, 1973.

Kathryn Lasky. *The Night Journey*. Warne, 1981.

Albert Likhanov, translated by Richard Lourie. *Shadows across the Sun*. Harper, 1983.

Miriam Morton. *Pleasures and Palaces: The After-School Activities of Russian Children*. Atheneum, 1972.

Claire R. Murphy. *Friendship across Arctic Waters: Alaskan Cub Scouts Visit Their Soviet Neighbors*. Photographs by Charles Mason. Dutton, 1991.

Alexander Nazaroff. *The Land and People of Russia*. Lippincott, 1972.

Tamara Talbot Rice. *Finding Out about the Early Russians*. Lothrop, 1964.

James Riordan. *Tales from Tartary*. Viking, 1977.

Uri Shulevitz. *Soldier and Tsar in the Forest*. Farrar, 1972.

Ernest Small. *Baba Yaga*. Houghton Mifflin, 1966.

Alke Zei. *The Sound of the Dragon's Feet*. Dutton, 1979.

Scandinavia

Ulla Andersen. *We Live in Denmark*. Watts, 1984.

Peter Asbjørnsen. *East of the Sun and West of the Moon*. Doubleday, 1977.

James Bowman. *Tales from A Finnish Tupa*. Whitman, 1936.

Patricia Coombs. *The Magic Pot*. Lothrop, 1977.

Mary Hatch. *13 Danish Tales*. Harcourt, 1947.

Virginia Haviland. *Favorite Fairy Tales Told in Denmark*. Little, 1971.

———. *Favorite Fairy Tales Told in Norway*. Little, 1961.

———. *Favorite Fairy Tales Told in Sweden*. Little, 1966.

Martin Hintz. *Sweden*. Children's Press, 1985.

Anita Lobel. *King Rooster, Queen Hen*. Greenwillow, 1975.

*———. *The Pancake*. Greenwillow, 1978.

Sylvia Munsen. *Cooking the Norwegian Way*. Lerner, 1982.

Elsa Olenius, comp. *Great Swedish Fairy Tales*. Delacorte, 1973.

Kari Olsson. *Sweden: A Good Life for All*. Dillon, 1983.

Joan Sandin. *The Long Way to a New Land*. Harper, 1981.

Otto Svend. *The Giant Fish and Other Stories*. Larousse, 1983.

*Suitable for primary grades.

Scotland

Susan Cooper. *The Selkie Girl*. McElderry, 1986.

Thailand

Fiction

Astrid Lindgren. *Noy Lives in Thailand*. Macmillan, 1967.

Judith Spiegelman. *Galong, River Boy of Thailand*. Messner, 1970.

Nonfiction

Frederick Poole. *Thailand*. Watts, 1973.

United States

In addition to the many books already listed under special categories, here are a few additional resources that will be helpful.

Kathryn Cusick and Faye Morrison. *Golden Poppies: An Annotated Bibliography of California Historical Fiction and Non-Fiction for Young Readers*. Shoestring, 1986.

Elva Harman and Anna Milligan. *Reading for Young People: The Southwest*. American Library Association, 1982.

Barbara Immroth. *Texas in Children's Books: An Annotated Bibliography*. Shoestring, 1986.

Appalachia

George Ella Lyon. *Borrowed Children*. Watts, 1988.

Katherine Paterson. *Come Sing, Jimmy Jo*. Dutton, 1985.

Doris B. Smith. *Return to Bitter Creek: A Novel*. Viking, 1986.

Ethel F. Smothers. *Down in the Piney Woods*. Knopf, 1992.

Cajun (Acadia and Louisiana)

Berthe Amoss. *The Loup Garou*. Pelican, 1979.

John Bergeron. *Cajun Folklore*. Bergeron, 1980.

Muriel Fontenot Blackwell. *The Secret Dream*. Broadman, 1981.

Marguerite Bougere. *Louisiana Stories for Boys and Girls*. Louisiana University Press, 1966.

Allan Carpenter. *Louisiana*. Children's Press, 1967.

Elaine C. Crump. *Chinaberry Beads*. Pelican, 1978. (poetry)

*Alice Durio. *Cajun Columbus*. Pelican, 1975.

Tim Edler. *The Adventures of Crawfish-Man*. Little Cajun Books, 1979.

*Suitable for primary grades.

————. *Dark Gator, Villain of the Atchafalaya*. Little Cajun Books, 1980.

————. *Maurice the Snake and Gaston the Near-Sighted Turtle*. Little Cajun Books, 1977.

————. *Santa's Cajun Christmas Adventure*. Little Cajun Books, 1981.

————. *T-Boy, The Little Cajun*. Little Cajun Books, 1978.

————. *T-Boy in Mossland*. Little Cajun Books, 1978.

————. *T-Boy and the Trial for Life*. Little Cajun Books, 1978.

Zelma Engelhardt. *Beyond the Bayous*. Clarios, 1962. (poetry)

*Mary Alice Fontenot. *Clovis and E. Escargot*. Acadiana, 1979.

————. *Clovis Crawfish and Curious Crapaud*. Acadiana, 1970.

————. *Clovis Crawfish and His Friends*. Acadiana, 1962.

————. *Clovis Crawfish and Michelle Mantis*. Acadiana, 1976.

————. *Clovis Crawfish and Spinning Spider*. Acadiana, 1968.

————. *Clovis Crawfish and the Big Betail*. Acadiana, 1963.

————. *Clovis Crawfish and the Singing Cigales*. Pelican, 1981.

————. *Ghost of Bayou Tigre*. Clairos, 1965.

Lois Lenski. *Bayou Suzette*. Lippincott, 1943.

*James Rice. *Cajun Alphabet*. Pelican, 1976.

————. *Gaston Goes to Mardi Gras*. Pelican, 1977.

————. *Gaston Lays an Off-Shore Pipeline*. Pelican, 1979.

Corrine L. Saucier. *Folktales from French Louisiana*. Clarios, 1962.

George Smith. *Bayou Boy and the Wolf Dog*. Quality Books, 1973

Isadore L. Sonnier. *Cajun Boy*. Exposition Press, 1980.

Robert Tallant. *Evangeline and the Acadians*. Random, 1957.

*Trosclair. *Cajun Night before Christmas*. Pelican. 1974.

Eskimos

Carolyn Meyer. *Eskimos: Growing Up in a Changing Culture*. Atheneum, 1977.

Peter Pitseolak. *Peter Pitseolak's Escape from Death*. Delacorte. 1978.

CHILDREN'S BOOKS IN OTHER LANGUAGES

As you conduct studies of other groups, children will be especially interested in books published in different languages. These books can be obtained in the original language, or they may be found in translation. There is a value in having both, but English translations are more easily obtained.

*Suitable for primary grades.

Translations

Notice that these translations have been published by American publishing companies.

Afrikaans

Sam Hobson and George Hobson. *The Lion of the Kalahari*. Greenwillow.

Danish

Ole Lund Kirkegaard. *Otto Is a Rhino*. Addison-Wesley.

Ib Spang Olsen. *The Little Locomotive*. Coward.

Thorsteinn Stefansson. *The Golden Future*. Nelson.

Dutch

Thea Beckman. *Crusade in Jeans*. Scribner's.

Margriet Heymans. *Cats and Dolls*. Addison-Wesley.

Flemish

Gommaar Timmermans. *The Great Balloon Race*. Addison-Wesley.

———. *The Little White Hen and the Emperor of France*. Addison-Wesley.

Willy Vandersteen. *The Circus Baron*. Hiddigeigei Books.

———. *An Island Called Hoboken*. Hiddigeigei Books.

———. *The Merry Musketeers*. Hiddigeigei Books.

———. *The Tender-Hearted Matador*. Hiddigeigei Books.

French

Paul Jacques Bonzon. *The Runaway Flying Horse*. Parents'.

Laurent de Brunhoff. *Babar's French Lessons*. Random.

Nancy Gurney. *The King, The Mice and the Cheese*. Beginner Books.

Hergé (4th series). *The Adventures of Tintin*. Atlantic—Little Brown.

Sesyle Joslin. *There Is a Dragon in My Bed. . .* Harcourt.

Tanobe Miyuki. *Québec: Je t'aime. . . .* Tundra.

Dr. Seuss. *The Cat in the Hat*. Random.

Edward Smith. *The Frogs Who Wanted a King*. Four Winds.

German

Hans Baumann. *The Hare's Race*. Morrow.

Max Bollinger. *The Giant's Feast*. Addison-Wesley.

Achim Broger. *Outrageous Kasimir*. Morrow.

Hans and Monique Dossenbach. *Animal Babies of East Africa*. Putnam.

Hans Isenbart and Hanns-Jorg Anders. *The Foal Is Born*. Putnam.

Luis Murschetz. *A Hamster's Journey*. Prentice-Hall.

———. *Mister Mole*. Prentice-Hall.

Hannelore Valencak. *When Half-Gods Go*. Morrow.

Japanese

Chiyoko Nakatani. *My Teddy Bear*. Crowell.

Hiroyuki Takahaski. *The Foxes of Chironupp Island*. Windmill/Dutton.

Polish

Jerzy Ficowski. *Sister of the Birds and Other Gypsy Tales*. Abingdon.

Russian

Kornei Chukovsky. *The Silver Crest: My Russian Boyhood*. Holt, Rinehart and Winston.

Mirra Ginsburg, ed. *The Air of Mars and Other Stories of Time and Place*. Macmillan.

———, ed. *Pamalche of the Silver Teeth*. Crown.

Spanish

John Bierhorst, ed. *Black Rainbow* (Inca Legends and Peruvian Myths). Farrar.

Thomas Blanco. *The Child's Gifts*. Westminster.

Doris Dana. *The Elephant and His Secret*. Atheneum.

P. D. Eastman. *Are You My Mother?* Beginner Books.

Asun Esteban. ¿Donde has estado, Aldo? Editorial Juventrud, 1986.

Antonio Frasconi. *The Snow and the Sun*. Harcourt.

Sesyle Joslin. *There Is a Bull on My Balcony* . . . Harcourt.

Nancy Guerney. *The King, The Mice and the Cheese*. Beginner Books.

Anne Rockwell. *El Toro Pinto, and Other Songs in Spanish*. Macmillan.

Isabel Schon. *Basic Collection of Children's Books in Spanish*. Scarecrow, 1986.

———. *Books in Spanish for Children and Young Adults*. Scarecrow, 1985.

Dr. Seuss. *The Cat in the Hat*. Random.

Swedish

Bo Carpelan. *Dolphins in the City*. Delacorte/Seymour Lawrence.

Stig Ericson. *Dan Henry in the Wild West*. Delacorte/Seymour Lawrence.

Maria Gripe. *Elvis and His Friends*. Delacorte/Seymour Lawrence.

———. *Elvis and His Secret*. Delacorte/Seymour Lawrence.

————. *In the Time of the Bells*. Delacorte/Seymour Lawrence.

Astrid Lindgren. *Pippi on the Run*. Viking.

EXPLORING SPECIAL IDENTITY GROUPS

Although many identity groups could be included, we have selected only three major groups: (1) the aged, (2) the disabled, and (3) women and girls.

Aging and the Aged

Anne E. Baldwin. *Sunflowers for Tina*. Four Winds, 1978.

Gunnel Beckman. *That Early Spring*. Viking, 1977.

Lenore Blegvard. *Moon-Watch Summer*. Harcourt, Brace & Jovanovich, 1972.

Rose Blue. *Grandma Didn't Wave Back*. Watts, 1972.

Pearl Buck. *The Beach Tree*. John Day, 1955.

Clyde Robert Bulla. *The Sugar Pear Tree*. Crowell, 1961.

Robert Burch. *Two That Were Tough*. Viking, 1976.

————. *The House of Wings*. Viking, 1972.

Betsy Byars. *Trouble River*. Viking, 1969.

Vera Cleaver. *Queen of Hearts*. Lippincott, 1978.

Eth Clifford. *The Rocking Chair Rebellion*. Houghton Mifflin, 1978.

Barbara Corcoran. *The Faraway Island*. Atheneum, 1977.

Tomie de Paola. *Nana Upstairs and Nana Downstairs*. Putnam and Sons, 1973.

————. *Now One Foot, Now the Other*. Putnam and Sons, 1981.

————. *Watch Out for the Chicken Feet in Your Soup*. Prentice Hall, 1974.

Norma Farber. *How Does It Feel to Be Old?* Dutton, 1979.

Patricia Lee Gauch. *Grandpa & Me*. McGann, 1972.

Rumer Goden. *The Fairy Doll*. Viking, 1956.

Susan Goldman. *Grandma Is Somebody Special*. Whitman, 1976.

Bob Graham. *Rose Meets Mr. Wintergarten*. Candlewick Press, 1992.

Phyllis Green. *Mildred Murphy, How Does Your Garden Grow?* Dell, 1977.

Constance Greene. *The Unmaking of Rabbit*. Dell, 1972.

Lucille Heins. *My Very Special Friend*. Judson, 1974.

Kevin Henkes. *Grandpa & Bo*. Greenwillow, 1986.

Charlotte Herman. *Our Snowman Had Olive Eyes*. Dutton, 1977.

Edith T. Hurd. *I Dance in My Red Pajamas*. Harper and Row, 1982.

Johanna Hurwitz. *Roz and Ozzie*. Morrow, 1992.

Mildred Kantrowitz. *Maxie*. Parents Magazine Press, 1970.

Dayal K. Khalsa. *Tales of a Gambling Grandma*. Potter, 1986.

Barbara Kirk. *Grandpa, Me, & Our House in the Tree*. MacMillan, 1976.

Kathryn Lasky. *I Have Four Names for My Grandfather*. Little, Brown, 1976.

———. *My Island Grandma*. Warne, 1979.

Gen LeRoy. *Emma's Dilemma*. Harper and Row, 1975.

Joan Lexau. *Benjie on His Own*. Dial, 1970.

Sharon Bell Mathis. *The Hundred Penny Box*. Viking, 1975.

Norma Fox Mazer. *A Figure of Speech*. Delacourt, 1973.

J. F. Mearian. *Someone Slightly Different*. Dial, 1980.

Miska Miles. *Annie and the Old One*. Little, Brown, 1971.

Elaine Moore. *Grandma's House*. Lothrop, Lee and Shepard, 1985.

Evaline Ness. *Josefina February*. Scribner's, 1963.

Melinda Pollowitz. *Cinnamon Cane*. Harper and Row, 1977.

Fran Pratt. *Understanding Aging*. Conant School, 1982.

Jean Robinson. *The Secret Life of T. K. Dearing*. Seabury, 1973.

Eleanor Schick. *Peter and Mr. Brandon*. Macmillan, 1973.

David M. Schwartz. *Supergrandpa*. Lothrop, 1991.

Leisel Skorpen. *Mandy's Grandmother*. Dial, 1975.

Ruth Sonneborn. *I Love Gram*. Viking, 1971.

Vera and Bill Cleaver. *The Whys and Wherefores of Litta Belle Lee*. Atheneum, 1974.

Susan Varley. *Badger's Parting Gifts*. Lothrop, Lee and Shepard, 1994.

Elizabeth Winthrop. *Walking Away*. Harper and Row, 1973.

Sally Wittman. *A Special Trade*. Harper and Row, 1978.

Charlotte Zolotow. *I Know a Lady*. Greenwillow, 1984.

———. *My Grandson Lew*. Harper & Row, 1974.

Positive Images of the Elderly

Primary Grades

Josephine Aldridge. *Fisherman's Luck*. Parnassus, 1966.

Martha Alexander. *The Story Grandmother Told*. Dial, 1969.

Edward Ardizzone. *Tim of the Lighthouse*. Walck, 1968.

Jeannie Baker. *Grandmother*. Deutsch, 1978.

Jennifer Bartoli. *Nona*. Harvey, 1975.

Barbara Borack. *Grandpa*. Harper, 1967.

Kay Chorao. *Lester's Overnight*. Dutton, 1977.

Helen Constant. *The Gift.* Knopf, 1983.

Tomie de Paola. *Nana Upstairs and Nana Downstairs.* Putnam 1973.

———. *Watch Out for Chicken Feet in Your Soup.* Prentice, 1974.

Arnold Dobrin. *Scat!* Four Winds, 1971.

James Flora. *Grandpa's Farm.* Harcourt, 1965.

Patricia Lee Gauch. *Grandpa and Me.* Coward, 1972.

M. B. Goffstein. *Fish for Supper.* Dial, 1976.

Susan Goldman. *Grandma Is Somebody Special.* Whitman, 1978.

———. *Grandpa and Me Together.* Whitman, 1979.

Lucille Heins. *My Very Special Friend.* Judson, 1974.

Russell Hoban. *How Tom Beat Captain Najork and His Hired Sportsman.* Atheneum, 1974.

Louise A. Jackson. *Grandpa Had a Windmill, Grandma Had a Churn.* Parent, 1977.

Mildren Kantrowitz. *Maxie.* Parent, 1970.

Eleanor J. Lapp. *The Mice Came in Early This Year.* Whitman, 1976.

Kathryn Lasky. *I Have Four Names for My Grandfather.* Little, Brown, 1976.

Joan M. Lexau. *Benjie and His Own.* Dial, 1970.

Jan Loof. *My Grandpa Is a Pirate.* Harper, 1968.

Max Lundgren. *Matt's Grandfather.* Putnam, 1972.

Miska Miles. *Annie and the Old One.* Little, Brown, 1971.

Evaline Ness. *Josefina February.* Scribner's, 1963.

Shirley P. Newman. *Tell Me, Grandpa; Tell Me, Grandma.* Houghton, 1979.

Steven Palay. *I Love My Grandma.* Raintree, 1977.

Dorka Raynor. *Grandparents around the World.* Whitman, 1977.

Eleanor Schick. *Peter and Mr. Brandon.* Macmillan, 1974.

Liesel Moak Skorpen. *Mandy's Grandmother.* Dial, 1975.

———. *Old Arthur.* Harper, 1972.

William Sleator. *The Angry Moon.* Little, Brown, 1970.

Ianthe Thomas. *Hi, Mrs. Mallory.* Harper, 1979.

Tobi Tobias. *Jane Wishing.* Viking, 1977.

Janice May Udry. *Mary Jo's Grandmother.* Whitman, 1970.

Barbara Williwns. *Kevin's Grandma.* Dutton, 1975.

Sally Wittman. *A Special Trade.* Harper, 1978.

Joyce Wood. *Grandmother Lucy Goes on a Picnic.* World, 1970.

Charlotte Zolotow. *My Grandson Lew.* Harper, 1974.

———. *William's Doll.* Harper, 1972.

Books for Older Students

Patricia Beatty. *The Coach That Never Came*. Morrow, 1985.

Mem Fox. *Wilfrid Gordon McDonald Partridge*. Miller, 1985.

Nancy Smiler Levinson. *The Ruthie Greene Show*. Lodestar, 1985.

The Disabled

General Resources

Barbara Adams. *Like It Is: Facts and feelings about Handicaps from Kids Who Know*. Walker, 1979. Photographs.

Gilda Berger. *Physical Disabilities*. Watts, 1979.

Joanne E. Bernstein and Bryna J. Fireside. *Special Parents, Special Children*. Whitman, 1991.

Tricia Brown. *Someone Special, Just like You*. Holt, 1984. Photographs.

Lorraine Henriod. *Special Olympics and Paralympics*. Watts, 1979.

Theodore Huebener. *Special Education Careers: Training the Handicapped Child*. Watts, 1977.

Richard Lyttle. *Challenged by Handicap: Adventures in Courage*. Reilly, 1971.

*Mary Ellen Powers. *Our Teacher's in a Wheelchair*. Whitman, 1986.

Margaret Pursell. *A Look at Physical Handicaps*. Lerner, 1976. Photographs.

Ron Roy. *Move Over, Wheelchairs Coming Through: Seven Young People in Wheelchairs Talk about Their Lives*. Clarion, 1985.

Autism

Ruth Arthur. *Portrait of Margarita*. Atheneum, 1968.

Phyllis Gold. *Please Don't Say Hello*. Human Science Press. 1975.

Blindness/Problems with Eyesight

James Garfield. *Follow My Leader*. Viking, 1957.

———. *Smith*. Pantheon, 1967.

Lynn Hall. *The Soul of the Silver Dog*. Harcourt, 1992.

Florence Heide. *Sound of Sunshine, Sound of Rain*. Parents', 1972.

Virginia Jensen and Dorca Haller. *What's That?* World, 1977. A book that blind children can read, too.

Madeleine L'Engle. *The Young Unicorns*. Farrar, Straus, 1968. The training of a mime who becomes expert.

Ramona Maher. *The Blind Boy and the Loon and Other Eskimo Myths*. Day, 1969.

Sharon Mathis. *Listen for the Fig Tree*. Viking, 1974.

*Suitable for primary grades.

*Ellen Raskin. *Spectacles*. Atheneum, 1978.

Glen Rounds. *The Blind Colt*. Holiday, 1969.

Aimee Sommerfelt. *The Road to Agra*. Criterion, 1961.

Theodore Taylor. *The Cay*. Doubleday, 1969.

William Thomas. *The New Boy Is Blind*. Thomas, 1980.

Malcolm Weiss. *Seeing through the Dark: Blind and Sighted—A Vision Shared*. Harcourt, 1976.

Bernard Wolf. *Connie's New Eyes*. Lippincott, 1976.

Brain Damage

Daniel Keyes. *Flowers for Algernon*. Harcourt, 1966.

Kim Platt. *Hey, Dummy*. Dell, 1971.

C. L. Rinaldo. *Dark Dreams*. Harper, 1974.

Cerebral Palsy

*Joan Fassler. *Howie Helps Himself*. Whitman, 1975.

Jean Little. *Mine for Keeps*. Little, 1962.

Jan Slepian. *The Alfred Summer*. Macmillan, 1980.

*Sara Stein. *About Handicaps: An Open Family Book for Parents and Children Together*. Walker, 1974.

Deaf/Blind

Margaret Davidson. *Helen Keller*. Hastings, 1969.

Francene Sabin. *The Courage of Helen Keller*. Troll Associates, 1982.

Deafness

Remy Charlip et al. *Handtalk: An ABC of Finger Spelling & Sign Language*. Parents', 1974.

Olivia Coolidge. *Come by Here*. Houghton, 1970.

Elaine Costello. *Signing: How to Speak with Your Hands*. Bantam, 1983.

Etta DeGering. *Gallaudet: Friend of the Deaf* McKay, 1964.

Meindert DeJong. *Journey from Peppermint Street*. Harper, 1968.

Judith Greenberg. *What Is the Sign for Friend?* Lothrop, 1985.

Ellen Howard. *The Cellar*. Atheneum, 1992.

Edna Levine. *Lisa and Her Soundless World*. Human Sciences Press, 1974.

Mary Riskind. *Apple Is My Sign*. Houghton, 1981.

Veronica Robinson. *David in Silence*. Philadelphia, 1966.

*Suitable for primary grades.

Eleanor Spence. *The Nothing Place*. Harper, 1972.

Lou Walker. *Amy: The Story of a Deaf Child*. Lodestar, 1985.

Maia Wojciechowska. *A Single Light*. Bantam, 1968.

Deformity

Frederich Drimmer. *The Elephant Man*. Putnam, 1985.

Down Syndrome

Elaine Ominsky. *Jon O: A Special Boy*. Prentice, 1977.

Dwarfism

M. E. Kerr. *Little Little*. Harper, 1981.

Susan Kuklin. *Thinking Big; The Story of a Young Dwarf*. Lothrop, 1986.

Dyslexia

Margot Marek. *Different, Not Dumb*. Watts, 1985.

Michele Murray. *Nellie Cameron*. Seabury, 1971.

Emotional Problems/Mental Illness

Virginia Axline. *Dibs in Search of Self: Personality Development in Play Therapy.* Houghton, 1964.

Eve Bunting. *One More Flight*. Warne, 1976.

Beverly Butler. *Feather in the Wind*. Dodd, 1965.

Carol Carrick. *Stay Away from Simon*. Clarion, 1985.

Joanne Greenberg. (Hannah Green). *I Never Promised You a Rose Garden*. Holt, 1964.

Virginia Hamilton. *The Planet of Junior Brown*. Macmillan, 1971.

Deborah Hautizig. *Second Star to the Right*. Greenwillow, 1981.

Florence Heide. *Secret Dreamer, Secret Dreams*. Lippincott, 1978.

M. E. Kerr. *Dinky Hocker Shoots Smack!* Dell, 1972.

Norma Klein. *It's Not What You Expect*. Pantheon, 1973.

John Langone. *Goodby to Bedlam: Understanding Mental Illness and Retardation.* Little, 1974.

Mary MacCracken. *A Circle of Children*. Lippincott, 1973.

Phyllis Naylor. *The Keeper*. Atheneum, 1986.

John Newfeld. *Lisa, Bright and Dark*. Phillips, 1969.

Zibby O'Neal. *The Language of Goldfish*. Viking, 1980.

Virginia Sorensen. *Miracles on Maple Hill*. Harcourt, 1956.

Patricia Windsor. *The Summer Before*. Harper, 1973.

Epilepsy

Ellen Howard. *Edith Herself*. Atheneum, 1987.

General Health Problems

Alice Bach. *Waiting for Johnny Miracle*. Harper, 1980. Cancer.

Virginia Lee. *The Magic Moth*. Seabury, 1972. Heart defect.

Elizabeth Winthrop. *A Little Demonstration of Affection*. Harper, 1975. Asthma.

Learning Disabled

*Joe Lasker. *He's My Brother*. Whitman, 1974.

Marilyn Levinson. *And Don't Bring Jeremy*. Holt, 1985.

*Muriel Stanek. *Left, Right; Left, Right!* Whitman, 1969.

Missing Limbs

Cynthia Voigt. *Izzy, Willy-Nilly*. Atheneum, 1986.

Bernard Wolf. *Don't Feel Sorry for Paul*. Lippincott, 1974. Photographs.

Orthopedic Impairment

James Aldridge. *A Sporting Proposition*. Little, 1973.

Harold Courlander. *The Son of the Leopard*. Crown, 1974.

Marguerite DeAngeli. *The Door in the Wall*. Doubleday, 1949.

Meindert DeJong. *The Wheel on the School*. Harper, 1954.

Ester Forbes. *Johnny Tremain*. Houghton, 1971.

Patricia Lee Gauch. *This Time, Tempe Wick?* Putnam, 1992.

Isabelle Holland. *Heads You Win, Tails I Lose*. Lippincott, 1973.

Irene Hunt. *No Promise in the Wind*. Follett, 1970.

Mollie Hunter. *The Stronghold*. Harper, 1974.

Sulamith Ish-Kishor. *Our Eddie*. Pantheon, 1969.

Katherine Paterson. *Of Nightingales That Weep*. Crowell, 1974.

Doris Smith. *Tough Chauncey*. Morrow, 1974.

Elizabeth Speare. *The Witch of Blackbird Pond*. Houghton, 1958.

Bonnie Turner. *The Haunted Igloo*. Houghton Mifflin, 1991.

Phillis Whitney. *Nobody Likes Trina*. New American Library, 1976.

*Suitable for primary grades.

Retardation

Frank Bonham. *Mystery of the Fat Cat*. Dutton, 1968.

Betsy Byars. *Summer of the Swans*. Viking, 1970.

Vera Cleaver and Bill Cleaver. *Me, Too*. Lippincott, 1973.

Lucille Clifton. *My Friend Jacob*. Dutton, 1980.

Barthe DeClements. *6th Grade Can Really Kill You*. Viking, 1985.

Robert Dunbar. *Mental Retardation*. Watts, 1978.

Maria Farrai. *A Look at Mental Retardation*. Lerner, 1976. Photographs.

*Joan Fassler. *One Little Girl*. Human Sciences, 1969.

Sharon Grollman. *More Time to Grow: Explaining Mental Retardation to Children, A Story*. Beacon, 1977.

Lynn Hall. *Sticks and Stones*. Follett, 1972.

Irene Hunt. *Up a Road Slowly*. Grosset, 1966.

Edwin Kaplan. *No Other Love*. Bantam, 1979.

Gerda Klein. *The Blue Rose*. Hill, 1974.

Earlene Luis and Barbara Millar. *Listen, Lissa: A Candy Striper Meets the Biggest Challenge*. Dodd, 1968.

Marlene Shyer. *Welcome Home, Jellybean*. Scribner's, 1978.

Gene Smith. *The Hayburners*. Delacorte, 1974.

Ivan Southall. *Hill's End*. Macmillan, 1962.

Susan Wexler. *The Story of Sandy*. Bobbs-Merrill, 1970.

Patricia Wrightson. *A Racecourse for Andy*. Harcourt, 1968.

Shyness

Muriel Blaustein. *Jim Chimp's Story*. Simon and Schuster, 1992.

Speech Impediments

Rebecca Caudill. *A Certain Small Shepherd*. Holt, 1965.

Julia Cunningham. *Burnish Me Bright*. Pantheon, 1970.

Joan Fassler. *Don't Worry, Dear*. Human Sciences, 1971.

Marguerite Henry. *King of the Wind*. Rand, 1948.

Breaking Down Stereotypes of Women

Readers of all ages need to read books that present positive images of women engaged in varied lifestyles and careers. From fantasy to nonfiction, books can support the self-esteem

*Suitable for primary grades.

of the girls who are reading, and they can provide an enlightened perspective on women for male readers. This potpourri is grouped by difficulty levels.

Primary Grades

Arlene Alda. *Sonya's Mommy Works.* Simon, 1982. A photographic essay of a contemporary family in which mother has a career.

Roshyn Banesh. *I Want to Tell You about My Baby.* Wingbow Press, 1982. Black and white photos tell story of preparation for new baby.

Jeanette Caines. *Daddy.* Harper, 1977. Story of child's special relationship with father who is separated from her Mother.

Norma Klein. *Girls Can Be Anything.* Dutton, 1973. Marina lets her kindergarten pal, Adam, know that "girls can be anything."

Mercer Mayer. *Liza Lou and the Yeller Belly Swamp.* Four Winds, 1976. How Liza Lou outwits the swamp devil.

Eve Merrian. *Mommies at Work.* Scholastic, 1973. Picture book showing all kinds of mommies at all kinds of jobs.

Harlow Rockell. *My Doctor.* Picture book of female doctor who removes child's fears of visiting the doctor.

Miriam Schlein. *The Girl Who Would Rather Climb Trees.* About a tomboy who receives a doll and what she does with it.

Amy Schwartz. *Bea and Mr. Jones.* Puffin, 1982. A kindergartner and her father change places.

John Steptoe. *Daddy Is a Monster . . . Sometimes.* Lippincott, 1980. Story of a single, loving parent and his two children.

———. *My Special Best Words.* Viking, 1974. A delightful picture book about Bweela, age three, Javaka, age one, and their father.

Middle Grades

Karen Ackerman, *When Mama Retires.* Knopf, 1992.

Sally Hobart Alexander. *Maggie's Whopper.* Macmillan, 1992.

Sue Alexander. *Nadia the Willful.* Pantheon, 1983. Nadia, daughter of Sheik Tarik, deals with her brother's death.

Caroline Bauer. *My Mom Travels a Lot.* Warne, 1982. Story about good and bad situations caused by mother's many absences from home.

Eve Bunting. *Summer Wheels.* Harcourt, 1992.

Vera and Bill Cleaver. *Hazel Rye.* Lippincott, 1983. The struggles between an eleven-year-old girl and her father.

Barbara Cohen and Bahija Lovejoy. *Seven Daughters and Seven Sons.* Atheneum, 1982. Buran, the daughter of Malik, is educated as though she were a son and later poses as a man. Set in ancient Baghdad.

B. Cole. *Princess Smartypants*. Putnam, 1986.

Walter de la Mare. *Molly Whuppie*. Farrar, 1983. An old tale retold; a girl outwits a giant.

Mary Jett-Simpson. "Girls Are Not Dodo Birds! Exploring Gender Equity Issues in the Language Arts Classroom." *Language Arts*. 70:104–108. Feb., 1992.

Madeline L'Engle. *A Wrinkle in Time*. Ariel, 1962.

Ruth Meyers and Beryle Banfield. *Embers: Stories for a Changing World*. Feminist Press, 1983. Includes fiction, biography, poetry, and oral history portraying people struggling to overcome barriers of sex, race, and disability.

Ogden Nash. *The Adventures of Isabel*. Illustrated by James Marshall. Little, Brown, 1991.

Tamora Pierce. *Alanna, The First Adventure*. Atheneum, 1983. Lord Alan's twin daughter, Alanna, and son, Thom, trade places. Alanna trains to be a knight, and Thom trains to be a sorcerer.

Robert Peck. *Trig*. Little, 1982. An independent girl chooses a name to fit her new gun.

Doreen Rappaport. *Living Dangerously: American Women Who Risk Their Lives*. Harper, 1991.

Barbara Robinson. *The Best Christmas Pageant Ever*. Harper, 1972. Story of family of six children who wreak havoc on the town's annual Christmas pageant.

Phyllis Root. *The Listening Silence*. Harper, 1992.

Cynthia Voight. *Homecoming*. Atheneum, 1981. Dicey, a thirteen-year-old girl, cares for her brothers and sisters after they are abandoned. See also *Dicey's Song, The Calandar Papers,* and *Solitary Blue* by the same author.

M. Waddell and P. Benson. *The Tough Princess*. Philomel, 1986.

Jay Williams. *Petronella*. Parents, 1973. Petronella, third child who turns out to be a girl, sets out with brothers to seek her fortune and find a prince.

———. *The Practical Princess*. Parents, 1978. Princess Bedelia fights dragons and rescues a prince.

Young Adults

Carol Brink. *Caddie Woodlawn*. Macmillan, 1970. Caddie, who lives in the Wisconsin frontier, is an adventurous tomboy who resists accepting her sex role.

Barbara Cohen. *Seven Daughters and Seven Sons*. Atheneum, 1982. Buran of Baghdad disguises herself as a boy to help her family.

Lois Duncan. *Daughters of Eve*. Little, 1979. Thriller about a club of teenage girls who decide to rebel against the dominating men in their lives.

Norma Klein. *Give and Take*. Viking, 1985. The summer before Spence enters college provides unexpected experiences with women. See also *Lovers, Angel Face, the Swap,* and *Beginners' Love* by the same author.

———. *Mom, the Wolf Man and Me*. Pantheon, 1972. Brett's unmarried mother decides to marry without asking her daughter's permission.

Norma Fox Mazer. *Dear Bill, Remember Me?* Delacorte, 1977. Collection of eight short stories in which young girls break away from conventional female role.

Robin McKinley. *The Blue Sword.* Greenwillow, 1983. Harry, a teenage girl, exhibits courage in this story of magic and fantasy.

Marilyn Sachs. *Call Me Ruth.* Doubleday, 1982. Rifka (Ruth) and her mother, Faigel, are Russian immigrants. Ruth is torn between the old and new ways.

Folktales with Active Heroines

"At the Controls." Carole Briggs. (Women in Aviation.) Lerner, 1991.

"Atlanta" in *Free to Be . . . You and Me.* Marlo Thomas, conceiver. McGraw, 1974.

"Baba Yaga" in *Old Peter's Russian Tales.* Arthur Ransome and Nelson, 1916. Out of print; Dover reprint.

"The Barber's Clever Wife' in *Tales from the Punjab.* Flora A. Steele. Macmillan, 1894. Out of print; *Fools and Funny Fellows.* Phyllis Fenner. Knopf, 1947.

"The Betrothal Gifts" in *Czechoslovak Fairy Tales.* Parker Fillmore. Harcourt, 1919.

"The Bigger Giant." Retold by Nancy Green. Follett, 1963.

"The Black Bull of Norroway" in *More English Folk and Fairy Tales.* Joseph Jacobs. Putnam, 1904.

"Boadicea . . . The Warrior Queen" in *The World's Great Stories: 55 Legends That Live Forever.* Louis Untermeyer. Lippincott, 1964.

"Cap O'Rushes" in *English Folk and Fairy Tales.* Joseph Jacobs. Putnam, 1904. Dover reprint as *English Fairy Tales; Womenfolk and Fairy Tales.* Rosemary Minard. Houghton, 1975.

"Chinese Red Riding Hoods" in *Chinese Fairy Tales.* Isabelle C. Chang. Barre, 1965.

"Clever Grethel" in *Tales Told Again.* Walter de la Mare. Knopf, 1927. Dover reprint as *English Fairy Tales; Womenfolk and Fairy Tales.* Rosemary Minard. Houghton, 1975.

"Clever Kadra" in *African Wonder Tales.* Frances Carpenter. Doubleday, 1963.

"Clever Manka" in *The Shepherd's Nosegay.* Parker Fillmore. Harcourt, 1920 out of print; *Fools and Funny Fellows.* Phyllis Fenner. Knopf, 1947. Dover reprint as *English Fairy Tales; Womenfolk and Fairy Tales.* Rosemary Minard. Houghton, 1975.

"Clever Ooagh' in *William Mayne's Book of Giants.* Dutton, 1969.

"The Dragon's Revenge" in *Magic Animals of Japan.* Davis Pratt. Parnassus, 1967.

East of the Sun and West of the Moon. P. C. Asbjounsen. Dover reprint as *English Fairy Tales; Womenfolk and Fairy Tales.* Rosemary Minard. Houghton, 1975.

"The Feather of Finist the Falcon" in *Russian Wonder Tales.* Post Wheeler. Thomas Yoseloff, 1957.

"Fin M'Coul and Cucullin" in *A Book of Giants.* Ruth Manning-Sanders. Dutton, 1963.

The Forest Princess. Harriet Herman. Rainbow Press, 1974.

"The Forty Thieves" in *The Blue Fairy Book*. Andrew Lang. Longmans, 1889. Dover reprint as *English Fairy Tales; Womenfolk and Fairy Tales*. Rosemary Minard. Houghton, 1975.

"A Fox Who Was Too Sly" in *Magic Animals of Japan*. Davis Pratt. Parnassus, 1967.

"The Gnome Maiden" in *Piskey Folk, a Book of Cornish Legends*. Elizabeth Yates. John Day, 1940.

"Gyda's Saucy Message" in *Viking Tales*. Jennie Hall. McNally, 1902.

The Handsome Prince. Nancy Schimmel. Franciscan Films, 1975.

"The Husband Who Was to Mind the House" in *East of the Sun and West of the Moon*. P.C. Asbjornsen. Dover reprint as *English Fairy Tales; Womenfolk and Fairy Tales*. Rosemary Minard. Houghton, 1975.

"Kate Crackernuts" in *English Folk & Fairy Tales*. Joseph Jacobs. Putnam, 1904. Dover reprint as *English Fairy Tales; Womenfolk and Fairy Tales*. Rosemary Minard. Houghton, 1975.

"The Lass Who Went Out at the Cry of Dawn" in *Thistle and Thyme*. Sorche Nic Leodhas. Holt, 1962. Dover reprint as *English Fairy Tales; Womenfolk and Fairy Tales*. Rosemary Minard. Houghton, 1975.

The Little Red Hen. Janina Domanska, adapt. and illus. Macmillan, 1973. Paul Galdone, Seabury, 1973.

"Luck and Wit" in *Rumanian Folk Tales*. Jean Ure. Watts, 1960.

"Mr. Fox" in *More English Folk and Fairy Tales*. Dover reprint as *English Fairy Tales; Womenfolk and Fairy Tales*. Rosemary Minard. Houghton, 1975.

"Mollie Whuppie" in *English Folk & Fairy Tales*. Joseph Jacobs. Putnam, 1904. *Tales Told Again*. Walter de la Mare. Knopf, 1927. Dover reprint as *English Fairy Tales; Womenfolk and Fairy Tales*. Rosemary Minard. Houghton, 1975.

Molly and the Giant. Retold by Kurt Werth and Mabel Watts. Parents, 1973.

"Mutsmag" in *Grandfather Tales*. Richard Chase. Houghton, 1948.

"The Old Woman and Her Dumpling" in *Japanese Fairy Tales*. Lafcadio Hearn. Pauper, 1948. Dover reprint as *English Fairy Tales; Womenfolk and Fairy Tales*. Rosemary Minard. Houghton, 1975.

Petronellia. Jay Williams. Parents, 1973.

The Practical Princess. Jay Williams. Parents, 1969.

"Rabbit and Hedgehog" in *American Negro Folktales*. Richard M. Dorson. Fawcett, 1967.

"The Salt at Dinner" in *Rumanian Folk Tales*. Jean Ure. Watts, 1960.

The Silver Whistle. Jay Williams. Parents, 1971.

"The Skull" in *The Book of Ghosts and Goblins*. Ruth Manning Sanders. Dutton, 1973.

"The Squire's Bride" in *True and Untrue, and Other Norse Tales*. Sigrid Undset. Knopf, 1945.

"The Stolen Bairn and the Sidh" in *Thistle and Thyme*. Sorche Nic Leodhas. Holt, 1962.

"Tamlane" in *More English Folk and Fairy Tales.*

This Time, Tempe Wick? Patricia Gauch. Coward, 1974.

"Three Sisters Who Were Entrapped into a Mountain" in *English Fairy Tales; Womenfolk and Fairy Tales.* Rosemary Minard. Houghton, 1975.

Three Strong Women: A Tall Tale from Japan. Claus Stamm. Viking, 1962. Dover reprint as *English Fairy Tales; Womenfolk and Fairy Tales.* Rosemary Minard. Houghton, 1975.

Turnabout; A Norwegian Tale. William Wiesner. Seabury, 1972.

"Twelve Brothers" in *Household Stories from the Collection of the Brothers Grimm.* Lucy Crane, trans. Dover reprint as *English Fairy Tales; Womenfolk and Fairy Tales.* Rosemary Minard. Houghton, 1975.

"The Two Old Women's Bet" in *Grandfather Tales.* Richard Chase. Houghton, 1948.

"Umai" in *The Inland Whale.* Theodore Kroeber. Indiana University Press; University of California Press, 1959.

"Unanana and the Elephant" in *African Myths and Legends.* Kathleen Arnott. Walck, 1962.

"The Wise Wife" in *Eurasian Folk and Fairy Tales.* I. F. Balatkin. Abelard, 1965.

The Wolf and the Seven Little Kids. Brothers Grimm. Harcourt out of print; in the *Arbuthnot Anthology of Children's Literature.*

The Wolf Who Had a Wonderful Dream: A French Tale. Anne Rockwell, ret. Crowell, 1973.

Index